LEGAL CAPACITY, DISABILITY AND HUMAN RIGHTS

The publication of this book was supported by

Suprema Corte
de Justicia de la Nación

**Unidad General de
Conocimiento Científico
y Derechos Humanos**

LEGAL CAPACITY, DISABILITY AND HUMAN RIGHTS

Edited by
Michael Bach
Nicolás Espejo-Yaksic

Cambridge – Antwerp – Chicago

Intersentia Ltd
8 Wellington Mews
Wellington Street | Cambridge
CB1 1HW | United Kingdom
Tel: +44 1223 736 170
Email: contact@larcier-intersentia.com
www.larcier-intersentia.com

Distribution for the UK and
Rest of the World (incl. Eastern Europe)
NBN International
1 Deltic Avenue, Rooksley
Milton Keynes MK13 8LD
United Kingdom
Tel: +44 1752 202 301 | Fax: +44 1752 202 331
Email: orders@nbninternational.com

Distribution for Europe
Lefebvre Sarrut Belgium NV
Hoogstraat 139/6
1000 Brussels
Belgium
Tel: +32 (0)2 548 07 13
Email: contact@larcier-intersentia.com

Distribution for the USA and Canada
Independent Publishers Group
Order Department
814 North Franklin Street
Chicago, IL 60610
USA
Tel: +1 800 888 4741 (toll free) | Fax: +1 312 337 5985
Email: orders@ipgbook.com

Legal Capacity, Disability and Human Rights
© The editors and contributors severally 2023

The editors and contributors have asserted the right under the Copyright, Designs and Patents Act 1988, to be identified as authors of this work.

No part of this book may be reproduced, stored in a retrieval system, or transmitted, in any form, or by any means, without prior written permission from Intersentia, or as expressly permitted by law or under the terms agreed with the appropriate reprographic rights organisation. Enquiries concerning reproduction which may not be covered by the above should be addressed to Intersentia at the address above.

Artwork on cover: © Danny Juchtmans

ISBN 978-1-83970-334-8
D/2023/7849/113
NUR 820

British Library Cataloguing in Publication Data. A catalogue record for this book is available from the British Library.

FOREWORD

For more than a decade, Mexico has undergone a substantive constitutional transformation. The 2011 constitutional reform on human rights empowers judges to strengthen the protection of all fundamental rights recognised both by the Political Constitution and the human rights norms recognised in international treaties ratified by Mexico. This transformation has included the effective protection of the constitutional rights of persons with disabilities.

The Supreme Court of Justice of Mexico has undertaken several actions to fully adopt the social model of disability, whose main tenet is the elimination of all barriers that prevent the full exercising of rights under equality of opportunities. On the one hand, this Court has consistently affirmed in its judicial precedents, the equal right of all people to exercise their legal capacity, to be assisted to this end and to be safeguarded against abuses. To fully achieve this goal, the Court has exhorted legislative authorities to adopt concrete measures to align domestic laws with Article 12 of the UN Convention on the Rights of Persons with Disabilities. On the other hand, the Court has adopted specific protocols to facilitate access to justice for people with disabilities and has designed and promoted training programmes and activities to consolidate a deeper legal awareness about this matter.

This book represents a valuable contribution to deepening our understanding of what is required to protect the equal right to legal capacity and to avoid any discrimination based on the intellectual, cognitive, and psychosocial disabilities of a person. By looking at the theoretical, historical, comparative and critical dimensions of new legal regimes for legal capacity in Latin America and the world, the Supreme Court of Mexico expects to contribute towards the global goal of making all human rights effective to all.

Supreme Court of Justice of Mexico

ACKNOWLEDGEMENTS

We express our sincere thanks and gratitude to all the people and institutions that have supported this project and trusted in the work of its editors. In particular, we thank the authors of this work, whose contributions have been a source of inspiration for a series of debates, reforms and struggles in different jurisdictions. Likewise, we would like to thank the support of those who, from the Supreme Court of Justice of Mexico, seek to carry out a radical transformation in the understanding of the right to legal capacity, and make advances towards the full recognition of the dignity and the rights of persons with disabilities.

A Spanish edition of this book was published in 2022 by the Supreme Court of Justice of Mexico, Human Rights and Scientific Knowledge Division. We are grateful for their financial and editorial support for both the Spanish and English editions of this work. Our gratitude to Intersentia Ltd. for taking on the English translation of the book and to the stellar team there, led by Senior Editor Rebecca Moffat who has been a pleasure to work with. Thank you for your guidance and deep appreciation for what we were hoping to accomplish with this collection.

The project has been supported through research support of Pavel Koval, Researcher at IRIS – Institute for Research and Development on Inclusion and Society based in Canada.

Michael Bach would like also to extend thanks to Open Society Foundations for their financial support to him through an Open Society Fellowship, which enabled both his research and collaborations with many of the authors who have contributed to make this collection possible. Additionally, support for the research and development of this collection through the Wellcome 'Mental Health and Justice' award 203376/Z/16/Z is gratefully acknowledged.

Nicolás Espejo-Yaksic would like to thank many colleagues and friends that were key in the development of this project and in providing ideas and inspiration for this book. In particular, Ann-Christin Maak-Scherpe, Ahmed Hegazi, Fabiana Estrada, Ana María Ibarra, Gabriela Gutiérrez, Andrea Santos, Regina Castro, Alejandra Rabasa and Vinka Jackson.

CONTENTS

Foreword v
Acknowledgements vii
List of Cases xv
List of Contributors xxi

Legal Capacity, Disability and Human Rights: Introduction
    Michael Bach and Nicolás Espejo-Yaksic 1

1. Historical Perspective and Theoretical Frames 2
2. Law Reform: National and Regional Perspectives 5
3. Legal Issues and Persistent Challenges 9

PART I. HISTORICAL PERSPECTIVES AND THEORETICAL FRAMES

A Historical Review of Legal Capacity
    Javier Barrientos Grandon 15

1. *Status* as a Key to the Culture of Ius Commune: Without *Status*, there
   is No Person 15
2. *Capax*: A Particular Aptitude in the Culture of Ius Commune 25
3. *Capacitas* and its Generalisation Linked to the Construction of the
   Category of Subject of Law 28

Respect for the Will of the Person
    Wayne Martin 31

1. An Ancient Law Reform and its Ontology 32
2. A Legally Primitive Notion 35
3. *Furiosi voluntas nulla est* 39
4. Will and Law Reform 43

Disability and Intersectionality: The Construction of Vulnerability in Sexual and Reproductive Matters
    Constanza López Radrigán 49

1. Introduction 49
2. Intersectional Violence and Discrimination 52

Intersentia   ix

Contents

3. Legal Capacity and Construction of Vulnerability. 56
4. Conclusions 61

Losing Legal Capacity and Power Over Personal Life: The "Decision-Making Capability" Alternative
Michael BACH 65

1. Introduction 65
2. Legal Capacity: Mainstream Approaches and Critique. 66
3. Reformulating the Principle of "Respect for Autonomy" for an Inclusive Approach to Legal Capacity 70
4. The "Decision-Making Capability" Alternative: Key Concepts 74
5. Implications for Further Research and Development 83
6. Summary and Conclusion. 86

Legal Capacity, Vulnerability and the Idea of "Person"
Nicolás ESPEJO-YAKSIC 89

1. Introduction 89
2. Capability for Decision-Making: Article 12 of the UNCRPD 90
3. Justice and Legal Capacity. 92
4. Vulnerability, Relational Autonomy and Legal Capacity. 97
5. Conclusions 105

PART II. LAW REFORM: COUNTRY AND REGIONAL PERSPECTIVES

Emerging Judicial Precedents Related to Legal Capacity in Latin American High Courts
Agustina PALACIOS. 109

1. Introduction 110
2. Legal Capacity in Court Precedents: Making the Path as We Walk. 110
3. Conclusions 127

Legal Capacity Regime Reforms in Costa Rica, Peru and Colombia: A Comparative and Critical Analysis
Alberto VÁSQUEZ, Federico ISAZA and Andrea PARRA 131

1. Introduction 132
2. Article 12 of the CRPD and its Impact in Latin America 132
3. Challenges of Reform on Legal Capacity in Latin America 149

A Critical Review of Legal Capacity Reform in the U.S.
Kristin Booth GLEN 153

x
Intersentia

1. Introduction 154
2. Context.. 155
3. The Rise of Supported Decision-Making............................. 158
4. Critiques of Existing Statutes 170
5. Supported Decision-Making New York (SDMNY): A Successful
   Empirical Model Advancing the Right of Legal Capacity.............. 173
6. Challenges and Barriers to Advancing Legal Capacity through SDM 174
7. The Future of an Equal Right to Exercise Legal Capacity in the U.S. 175

A Critical Review of Legal Capacity Reforms in the African Region
Dianah MSIPA 177

1. Introduction 177
2. Legal Capacity and the Role of Support............................... 179
3. The Right to Legal Capacity in Kenya, Zambia, and South Africa........ 181
4. Reviewing the Reforms in Kenya, Zambia, and South Africa 185
5. Conclusion.. 197

Changing the Paradigm of Substituted Decision-Making in Bulgaria:
The Tipping Point
Nadia SHABANI and Marieta DIMITROVA 199

1. The Bulgarian Concept of Supported Decision-Making................ 200
2. Changes in Jurisprudence and the Practice of the Courts 207
3. Changes in the "Social Laws" which Introduce Supported
   Decision-Making 210
4. Lessons Learnt and Main Conclusions for the Way Forward........... 215
5. Conclusion.. 218

Evaluating the Induction of Article 12 Jurisprudence in Indian Law:
Is Half a Loaf Better?
Amita DHANDA... 221

1. Introduction 221
2. Indian Laws and Legal Capacity....................................... 222
3. Reforming Legal Capacity... 225
4. Legal Capacity and the Courts: *Suchita Srivastav v Chandigarh
   Administration*... 233
5. So what is the Verdict?... 235

Legal Capacity in China's Mainland
Huang YI and Chen BO 237

Contents

1. Introduction 237
2. Status of the Convention at Domestic Level in China's Mainland 238
3. Legal Capacity and Adult Guardianship 239
4. Legal Capacity and Mental Health Law 247
5. Conclusion 252

Lessons from a Reformist Path to Supported Decision-Making in Australia
Piers GOODING and Terry CARNEY 255

1. Background: Australia and Human Rights 257
2. Legal Developments 263
3. Discussion 270
4. Conclusion 274

Mental Capacity in Hong Kong: Inconsistencies, Uncertainties, and the Need for Reform
Urania CHIU and Pok Yin S. CHOW 277

1. Introduction 277
2. The Development of Mental Capacity Law in Hong Kong 278
3. The Definitions of Mental (In)Capacity in Hong Kong Law 281
4. Consent to Medical Treatment (Other than for Mental Disorder) 285
5. Guardianship and Management of Property by the Court 288
6. Decision-Making in Cases of Future Incapacity 293
7. Conclusion 297

PART III. LEGAL QUESTIONS, PERSISTENT CHALLENGES

Informed Consent and Support for Decision-Making: A Critical Review of Legal Reforms in Latin America
Pablo MARSHALL 301

1. Introduction 301
2. Capacity in Informed Consent 304
3. Supports for Informed Consent 307
4. Informed Consent and Reforms to Legal Capacity in Latin America 312
5. Conclusions 317

Contractual Capacity of Persons with a Disability in the Spanish Civil Code
Maria Paz GARCIA RUBIO 319

1. Contractual Capacity in the Spanish Civil Code 319
2. Contractual Capacity of Persons with Disability under the "LAPD" 322

Contents

3.	The Annulment Action	330
4.	Limitations to the Power to Annul and Restitution	330

**Safeguards for the Exercise of Legal Capacity by Persons with Disabilities:
A Form of Justified Paternalism**
Renato Antonio Constantino Caycho and
Renata Anahí Bregaglio Lazarte 333

1.	Introduction	334
2.	Starting Point: Disability as a Vulnerability	335
3.	Safeguards in Conjunction with the Vulnerability of a Person with a Disability	341
4.	Conclusion: Safeguards, a Form of Justified Paternalism	351

**Legal Capacity in Canada: An Equality Rights Analysis in Light of the
Canadian Charter of Rights and Freedoms and the Convention
on the Rights of Persons with Disabilities**
Lana Kerzner 353

1.	Introduction	354
2.	The Prevailing Test of Capacity in Canada's Laws: The Cognitive "Understand and Appreciate" Test	356
3.	An Inclusive Approach to Legal Capacity: Decision-Making Capability	357
4.	Implementation of Article 12 in Canada: Relevance of the Canadian Charter of Rights and Freedoms	358
5.	An Examination of the Cognitive Test of Capacity against the Equality Right in the Canadian Charter of Rights and Freedoms	359
6.	The CRPD's Approach to Equality in the Exercise of Legal Capacity: Putting the s. 15 Analysis in Perspective	366
7.	Limitation of Rights: Can Discriminatory Legal Capacity Tests be Saved as a Justifiable Violation of Charter Rights under s. 1 of the Charter?	368
8.	Conclusion	372

Index 375

LIST OF CASES

AFRICAN COMMISSION ON HUMAN AND PEOPLES' RIGHTS

Purohit and another v. The Gambia 2003 AHRLR 96 (ACHPR 2003) 182

ARGENTINA

STJ Rio Negro, Civil Court Clerk No.1, G-3BA-1525-F2017 L. H., M. A. C/
    F., A. E. S/ PERSONAL CARE(f) (S / CASACION), 21/10/2020 37 P 5/9 117–118
Supreme Court of Justice of Argentina (CSJN), B., J.M. s/insania, 12/06/2012, p.7 115

AUSTRALIA

Dietrich v. The Queen (1992) 177 CLR 292, 305. 258
Minister for Immigration and Ethnic Affairs v. Teoh (1995) 183 CLR 273. 257

BRAZIL

Court of Justice of Rio Grande do Sul, TJRS, Civil Appeal No.
    0431052-80.2016.8.21.7000, 09/03/2017. 124
São Paulo Court of Justice, TJSP, Primeira Câmara de Direito Privado,
    Apelação Cível núm. 0006336-97.2012.8.26.0099, 06/02/2018. 124
São Paulo Court of Justice, TJSP, Apelação Cível núm.
    1006852-85.2017.8.26.0597, 28/01/2020. 124

BULGARIA

Interpretative Decree No. 5/1979 of 13 February 1980 of the Plenum
    of the Supreme Court on certain issues of the proceedings for placing
    people under guardianship. 204
Judgment No 226 of 31.10.2016 in civil case 4922/2015 of Sofia County
    Court, 4th panel of judges, civil division 202, 204
Judgment of the Supreme Court of Cassation No 596 of 28.08.2006, civil
    case No 1342/2005. 200

Intersentia   XV

List of Cases

Judgment of the Sofia Regional Court, 158th panel of judges, civil case
No 516916/2018 209
Judgment of the Sofia Regional Court, 158th panel of judges, civil case
No 524739/2018 209

CANADA

Alberta v. Hutterian Brethren of Wilson Colony, [2009] 2 S.C.R. 567,
2009 SCC 37 371
Andrews v. Law Society of British Columbia, [1989] 1 S.C.R. 143 361
Edmonton Journal v. Alberta (Attorney General), [1989] 2 S.C.R. 1326,
[1989] S.C.J. No. 124 371
Fraser v. Canada (Attorney General), 2020 SCC 28 . . . . .360, 362–365
Gray v. Ontario [2006] OJ No 266 (Div Ct) 73
Health Services and Support – Facilities Subsector Bargaining Assn. v.
British Columbia, [2007] 2 S.C.R. 391, 2007 SCC 27 359
Leung v. Chang, 2013 BCSC 976 78
Nova Scotia (Workers' Compensation Board) v. Martin; Nova Scotia (Workers'
Compensation Board) v. Laseur, 2003 SCC 54 364
Ontario (Attorney General) v. G, 2020 SCC 38 365–366
Park and Park, 2010 ONSC 2627 (S.C.J.) 369–370
Quebec (Attorney General) v. A, [2013] S.C.R. 61, 2013 SCC 5 360
Quebec (Attorney General) v. Alliance du personnel professionnel et technique
de la sante et des services sociaux, [2018] S.C.R. 464, 2018 SCC 17 360
Quebec (Commission des droits de la personne et des droits de la Jeunesse) v.
Bombardier Inc. (Bombardier Aerospace Training Center), [2015]
2 S.C.R. 789, 2015 SCC 39 363
Reference Re Public Service Employee Relations Act (Alberta), [1987]
1 S.C.R. 313, [1987] S.C.J. No. 10 359
R. v. Big M Drug Mart Ltd., [1985] 1 S.C.R. 295 369
R v. Kapp, [2008] 2 S.C.R. 483, 2008 SCC 41 . . . . .361, 366
R. v. Oakes, [1986] 1 S.C.R. 103, [1986] S.C.J. No. 7 369
Withler v. Canada (Attorney General), [2011] 1 S.C.R. 396, 2011 SCC 12 365

COLOMBIA

Colombian Constitutional Court, Judgment C-131 of 2014 122
Colombian Constitutional Court, Judgment T-741/2015 126
Colombian Constitutional Court, Judgment C-182 of 2016 . . . . .111, 116
Colombian Constitutional Court, Judgment T-573 of 2016 123
Colombian Constitutional Court, Judgment T-655 of 2017 123
Colombian Constitutional Court, Judgment T-665 of 2017 123
Colombian Constitutional Court, Judgment T-525 of 2019 128
Colombian Constitutional Court, Judgment T-231/2020 116
Colombian Constitutional Court, Judgment C-025 of 2021 .111–112

xvi

Intersentia

List of Cases

Colombian Constitutional Court, Sentences C-022 of 2021, M.P: Cristina Pardo
  Schlesinger and C-118 of 2021, M.P: Gloria Stella Ortiz Delgado 150
D-13525, D-13575, D-13585, D-13658, D-13738, D-13743, D-14076 and
  D-14077.. 152

COSTA RICA

Constitutional Court of Costa Rica, Judgment No. 2019009287, 24/05/2019.......... 111

ENGLAND AND WALES

Airedale NHS Trust v. Bland [1993] 1 All ER 821 ....281, 295
CC v. KK and STCC [2012] EWHC 2136 (COP)................................... 282
Re C (Adult: Refusal of Treatment) [1994] 1 All ER 819 (QBD).............281–282, 286
Re F (Mental Patient: Sterilisation) [1990] 2 AC 1...........................282, 286
Re MB [1997] EWCA Civ 3093 ....281, 283, 287
Re SB (A Patient; Capacity to Consent to Termination) [2013]
  EWHC 1417 (COP)... 282
Re T (Adult: Refusal of Treatment) [1992] 4 All ER 649 (CA) 281–282, 289
WBC (Local Authority) v. Z, X, Y [2016] EWCOP 4 282

EUROPEAN COURT OF HUMAN RIGHTS

D.D. v. Lithuania, Application No. 13469/06, judgment of 14 February 2012.......... 97
Salontaji-Drobnjak v. Serbia, Application No. 36500/06, judgment of
  13 October 2009... 97
Stanev v. Bulgaria, Application No. 36760/06, judgment of 17 January 2012 202
Stefan Stankov v. Bulgaria, Application No. 25820/07, judgment of 17 March 2015 202
X & Y v. Croatia, Application No. 5193/09, judgment of 3 November 2011 97

HONG KONG

China Field Ltd v. Appeal Tribunal (Buildings) (No 2) (2009) 12 HKCFAR............ 279

INDIA

Suchita Srivastava & Anr v. Chandigarh Administration (2009) 14 SCR 989,
  (2009) 9 SCC..233–235

List of Cases

KENYA

Cradle – Children Foundation (suing through the Trustee Geoffrey Maganya) v.
 Nation Media Group Limited ex parte Cradle – Children Foundation
 (suing through Geoffrey Maganya) [2012] eKLR 187
Satrose Ayuma & 11 others v. Registered Trustees of the Kenya Railways Staff
 Retirement Benefits Scheme & 2 others [2011] eKLR........................... 187
Wilson Morara Siringi v. Republic, Criminal Appeal No. 17 of 2014.............186–187

MEXICO

SCJN, First Chamber, Amparo en Revisión 159/2013, October 16, 2013 118
SCJN, First Chamber, Amparo Directo en Revisión 2805/2014,
 January 14, 2015...97, 113–114
SCJN, First Chamber, Amparo Directo en Revisión, 5904/2015,
 September 28, 2016 125
SCJN, First Chamber, Amparo en Revisión 1043/2015, March 29, 2017..........115–116
SCJN, First Chamber, Amparo en Revision 1368/2015, March 13, 2019...........97, 112
SCJN, First Chamber, Amparo en Revisión 702/2018, September 11, 2019 ....113, 115
SCJN, Plenary, Acción de Inconstitucionalidad 38/2014 and its accumulated
 case 91/2014, 92/2014 and 93/2014, October 2, 2014........................... 113

PERU

Constitutional Court of Peru, Guillén Domínguez, STC Exp.
 No. 00194-2014-PHC/TC, 2019... 120
Constitutional Court of Peru, Judgment C-025/2021............................. 121
Constitutional Court of Peru, STC, File. No. 00194-2014-PHC/TC
 AREQUIPA, 2014 111

SPAIN

Supreme Tribunal of Spain, Civil Chamber, ECLI:ES:TS:2021:3276 325

UNITED STATES

Matter of Dameris L., 956 N.Y.S. 2d 848 (Surr. Ct. N.Y. Co. 2012) 159
Olmstead v. L.C., 527 U.S. 581, 595 (1999) 157
Re Guardianship of A.E., 552 S.W.3d at 879, 880 (Texas S. Ct., 2018)................ 171

xviii

ZAMBIA

Attorney-General v. Roy Clarke (2008) 1 ZR 38 192
Gordon Maddox Mwewa & Others v. Attorney-General & Another
    2017/HP/204 (unreported)...188–189
Sarah Longwe v. Intercontinental Hotel 1992/HP/765 (HC)........................ 192
Wilson Morara Siringi v. Republic, Criminal Appeal No. 17 of 2014..............186–188
Zambia Sugar PLC v. Fellow Nanzaluka Supreme Court of Zambia Appeal
    No. 82/2001.. 192

LIST OF CONTRIBUTORS

Michael Bach
Managing Director, Institute for Research and Development on Inclusion and Society (IRIS), Canada

Javier Barrientos Grandon
Full Member, Chilean Academy of History and Professor of History of Law and Institutions, Faculty of Law, Autonomous University of Madrid, Spain

Chen Bo
Assistant Professor, Faculty of Law, Macau University of Science and Technology, Macao SAR, China

Renata Anahí Bregaglio Lazarte
Associate Professor, Law Academic Department, Pontifical Catholic University of Peru (PUCP); Coordinator, Interdisciplinary Research Group on Disability of the PUCP (GRIDIS), Peru

Terry Carney AO
Emeritus Professor, University of Sydney Law School, Australia

Urania Chiu
DPhil Candidate, Centre for Socio-Legal Studies, Faculty of Law, University of Oxford, United Kingdom

Pok Yin S. Chow
Senior Lecturer, Newcastle Law School, New South Wales, Australia

Renato Antonio Constantino Caycho
Full-Time Professor, Law Academic Department, Pontifical Catholic University of Peru (PUCP); Member of the Interdisciplinary Research Group on Disability of the PUCP (GRIDIS), Peru

Amita Dhanda
Professor Emerita, NALSAR University of Law, Hyderabad, India

Marieta Dimitrova
Lawyer specialising in human rights and disability rights; Legal consultant, Bulgarian Center for Not-for-Profit Law, Bulgaria

List of Contributors

Nicolás Espejo-Yaksic
Researcher, Centre for Constitutional Studies (CEC), Supreme Court of Justice of Mexico; Visiting Fellow, Exeter College, University of Oxford, United Kingdom; Guest Lecturer in Law, Leiden University, the Netherlands; Adjunct Professor, School of Law, University College Cork, Ireland

Maria Paz Garcia Rubio
Professor of Civil Law, Universidad de Santiago de Compostela, Spain; Permanent Member, First Section, General Coding Commission of Spain

Kristin Booth Glen
University Professor and Dean Emerita, City University of New York School of Law; Justice of the New York Supreme Court and the Appellate Term, First Judicial Department; Surrogate Judge, New York County, (ret.); Director, Supported Decision-Making New York, United States of America

Piers Gooding
Senior Research Fellow, Melbourne Law School, University of Melbourne, Australia

Federico Isaza
Human Rights Activist and Lawyer with Specialisation in Justice, Victims and Peacebuilding; Legal Advisor, Action Program for Equality and Social Inclusion-PAIIS, Universidad de Los Andes, Bogotá, Colombia

Lana Kerzner
Barrister and Solicitor specialising in disability law, Toronto, Canada

Constanza López Radrigán
Doctoral Candidate in Interdisciplinary Studies on Thought, Culture and Society, Universidad Valparaíso, Chile; Fellow, National Agency for Research and Development of Chile; Postgraduate Student, MICARE Institute for Care Research, ANID Millennium Scientific Initiative Program, Chile

Pablo Marshall
Professor, Institute of Public Law, Austral University of Chile; Co-Director Millennium Nucleus Studies on Disability and Citizenship (DISCA), Chile; Associate Researcher Millennium Institute for Care Research (MICARE), Santiago, Chile

Wayne Martin
Professor of Philosophy, University of Essex, United Kingdom

Dianah Msipa
Manager, Disability Rights Unit, Centre for Human Rights, University of Pretoria, South Africa; Doctoral Candidate, Centre for Human Rights, University of Pretoria, South Africa

xxii

Intersentia

Agustina Palacios
Adjunct Researcher, National Board of Scientific and Technical Research of Argentina (CONICET)

Andrea Parra
Lawyer, Colombia; Co-Coordinator, Latin American Network Art. 12; Co-Director, ALCE initiative (Abolition of Logics of Punishment and Confinement), Colombia; Director of Talleristas por la Justicia (Workshop Leaders for Justice)

Nadia Shabani
Lawyer specialising in human rights; Director, Bulgarian Center for Not-for-Profit Law, Bulgaria

Alberto Vásquez
Co-Director, Center for Inclusive Policy (CIP), United States of America; President, Society and Disability (SODIS), Peru

Huang Yi
Director of Shenzhen Autism Society, China

LEGAL CAPACITY, DISABILITY AND HUMAN RIGHTS

Introduction

Michael Bach and Nicolás Espejo-Yaksic

1. Historical Perspective and Theoretical Frames. 2
2. Law Reform: National and Regional Perspectives 5
3. Legal Issues and Persistent Challenges 9

The United Nations Convention on the Rights of Persons with Disabilities (hereinafter CRPD) recognises in its Article 12 the equal right to exercise legal capacity without discrimination based on disability. In addition, the CRPD establishes the obligation of the States parties to ensure access to the supports a person may require for decision-making. Since its adoption, there has been a growing effort by the United Nations Committee on the Rights of Persons with Disabilities, domestic human rights courts, legal and policy researchers, and activists to critically examine the laws that restrict or nullify the exercise of legal capacity based on disability. Traditionally, this effort has focused on reforming those constitutional or legal standards regulating the exercise of legal capacity: laws on interdiction and guardianship or substitution of decision-making and mental health laws.

However, a fuller examination of legal capacity reforms or transformations reveals a wide range of laws, jurisprudence and administrative regulations. Analysed jointly, these sources constitute a patchwork of provisions that regulate legal capacity in many different directions: from a particular individual decision – medical care, inheritance, matrimonial or cohabitation arrangements – to how an entire population is labelled and treated by laws and policies, for example, people with intellectual disabilities or people diagnosed with a "mental disorder." Together, this multiplicity of norms, provisions and rules regulate the exercise of legal capacity in a wide range of settings – for example, in making health care decisions or exercising personal care decisions in a long-term care facility, in financial decisions, in contracting goods and services, in transacting in labour and housing markets, in pursuing justice – for instance, appearing before a tribunal to appeal a decision, meeting capacity requirements to be a witness or stand trial or file a complaint about the violation of one's rights, and in political participation such as exercising the right to vote. Accordingly, the processes of legal capacity reform require a comprehensive view, with attention not only to historical, social and legal contexts, but also to the vast regulatory regime in any particular jurisdiction and the array of institutional arrangements which permeate it.

This volume includes contributions of scholars and practitioners in the field of legal capacity, disability studies and human rights, who critically examine fundamental aspects of these regimes. Specifically, this book aims to achieve three main goals. First, to undertake a comparative exploration of the historical evolution, theoretical constructs and the institutional features of legal regimes and to determine the legal and social contours of current legislative reforms. In doing so, contributions help reveal the multiple dimensions and institutional arrangements that constitute contemporary "regimes" of legal capacity. Second, contributions examine the specific ways in which principles, rights and standards derived from disability law and human rights are evolving and how they impact and transform both the right to exercise legal capacity on an equal basis and the practice of supporting people to exercise it in jurisdictions around the world. Third, this book examines the issues and challenges, both emerging and persistent, in conceiving of, designing and implementing more comprehensive reform of legal capacity regimes, consistent with the obligations and aims of Article 12 of the CRPD.

The book is divided into three main parts, each corresponding to one of the three guiding objectives. Each part has a selection of chapters which explore these themes in detail and point to unresolved questions for further research.

1. HISTORICAL PERSPECTIVE AND THEORETICAL FRAMES

In the first part, authors explore key concepts – through a historical, theoretical, sociological and normative lens – that structure and define the parameters of legal capacity and its legal and social organisation. Concepts of "*status*", the "person", "capacity", "will and preferences", "autonomy", "vulnerability", "dependence" and "intersectionality" are examined throughout five chapters in this part of the book.

In the first chapter, Javier Barrientos Grandon traces the "long and complex historical course" of the concepts of "*status*", "person" and "capacity". Tracing the contributions of key thinkers, including Pufendorf, Leibniz, Savigny and others, he demarcates critical junctures in the construction of legal personhood. Barrientos Grandon examines how the scope of a person's legal and political recognition historically depended on their *status naturalis* and *status civilis*.

His analysis shows that, by the eighteenth century, the legal principle was already clearly established that "without *status*, there is no person". This author points out the range of *statuses*, and therefore of the persons recognised under law, and the shaping of what a person could or could not do in law by the *status* they were accorded. Legal persons are configured on this foundation. The concepts of "capacity" and "legal capacity" emerge to define the scope of legal action in specific circumstances and are essential in coming to see persons as "subjects of law" with aptitudes and abilities to act. The deeply rooted historical foundations of the conceptual and legal architecture Barrientos Grandon lays out helps to understand the hold that concepts such as "capacity" still have in contemporary regimes regulating legal capacity, in addition to the challenges in reforming them and the resistance encountered in doing so. He also points to new foundations for conceiving of capacity in the equation between personhood and dignity on which later human rights instruments are grounded. As enticing as that horizon is, he tells us "this is a story for another time."

In the second chapter, Wayne Martin complements the conceptual architecture of the notion of *status* with a genealogy of the concept of "will", a concept which figures prominently in Article 12 of the CRPD. Article 12.4 requires respect for the "rights, will and preferences" of the person. Martin traces the concept's pivotal role in legal regimes, going back to the Athenian lawmaker Solon, 26 centuries ago. The author goes on to critically examine the evolution and current use of this term in contemporary law, both in Europe and Latin America, to examine its exclusions from the vantage point of people with more significant cognitive and psychosocial disabilities. He also examines how the legal doctrine of the will constructs these exclusions through what he refers to as practices of "will-attribution", "will-attestation" and "will-nullification." With this theoretical framework in mind, Martin explores its implications for contemporary movements seeking universal recognition of legal capacity and asks: can the link between legal capacity and the will, as currently formulated in law, be made more fully inclusive of those still excluded? Or do we need to review how we practice will-ascription and will-attestation?

Constanza López Radrigán argues in the next chapter that we must guard against an abstracted formulation of key concepts associated with Article 12 of the CRPD. She urges that the analysis of such concepts be underscored with an intersectional approach. This approach must be such that it materialises the realities of disability, gender and vulnerability to reveal the complex and gendered ways in which capacity is constructed, regulated and lived. Examining the exercise of capacity – in the context of property, sexual and reproductive rights –, Lopez reveals the "epistemic and material violence" that adolescent girls and women with disabilities experience when they are medicalised and objectified, organised as "irrational" and subject to guardianship and removal of legal rights on that basis. For the author, this socio-legal incapacitation, bred through social control and institutionalised violence, is not inevitable.

By bringing a feminist perspective to the question of how capacity is both formed and regulated, the relational autonomy of subjects can be demonstrated. This can open us to other questions about how to organise supports in specific contexts and local communities. The author suggests confronting the complex dynamics of inequality, supporting resistance to systemic marginalisation and considering more substantive reforms that account for the intersectional realities of violence, disadvantage and discrimination.

In the fourth chapter, Michael Bach tackles the conceptual architecture of legal capacity regimes from the vantage point of their organising principle of respect for autonomy. In Bach's assessment, the usual formulation of the principle of autonomy is unnecessarily attached to cognitive capacities and decision-making skills. As such, this requirement systematically excludes people with significant intellectual, cognitive and psychosocial disabilities from the enjoyment of respect for autonomy and, thus, from exercising legal capacity. He proposes a reformulation of the principle which is first and foremost grounded on a respect for another person's true intentions, will and preferences. Guided by this *non-cognitive* or *more-than-cognitive* approach he argues for an alternative to the mainstream approaches to defining the requirements for legal capacity, all of which are firmly reliant on cognitive capacities in their foundations. The "decision making capability" approach he elaborates is based on three main concepts: the non-cognitive capability to manifest intentions, will and preferences; a "planning theory" of agency which recognises that others always assist in making and executing the plans to realise our intentions, will and preferences; and the "interpretive supports" that some people require to interpret their intentions and translate them into plans and decisions. He suggests that the decision-making capability alternative is the basis of recent law reform replacing guardianship systems with supported decision-making regimes; and he points to areas for further research needed to elaborate the approach and develop guidance for related law, policy and practice reforms.

The first part of this volume closes with the work of Nicolás Espejo-Yaksic. In this text, Espejo-Yaksic suggests that the model of equal recognition of legal capacity established in Article 12 of the CRPD constitutes a "hard case", which challenges the assumptions of theories of justice and contemporary law. In particular, the author suggests that to recognise the equal right to recognition of legal capacity for all people is to accept the intrinsic value of all human life and the equal capacity to flourish, regardless of the limitations generated by the vulnerabilities associated with disability. In a capability-based approach, "support for the exercise of legal capacity" is aimed at facilitating a better understanding of the role played by people other than the individual agent of a given decision in the decision process itself. Through such supports, a person transforms an abstract good – as the equal right to legal capacity – into a specific operation – decision-making chapter. In other words, in a relational conception of autonomy, the development and sustained exercise of this capacity requires

Introduction

extensive and continuous institutional, social and interpersonal scaffolding. This scaffolding serves as a counterweight to the specific vulnerabilities that arise in the context of disability. Espejo-Yaksic suggests that, considered cumulatively, these supports provide people having some intellectual, cognitive or psychosocial disability with the necessary resilience to face the barriers of their environment and to protect their personal autonomy.

2. LAW REFORM: NATIONAL AND REGIONAL PERSPECTIVES

The second part examines how the concepts discussed in the first part of this book are being applied concretely in various legal reforms and development of jurisprudence taking place in recent years. These include experiences developed in Latin America, the United States, Bulgaria, some countries in the African region, India, mainland China, Hong Kong and Australia. Despite the diversity of these jurisdictions and the legal systems that operate within them, notable similarities in the trajectories of legal transformation are identified in these chapters. In particular, reform efforts in these jurisdictions confront multiple levels of resistance to the promise of change and transformation envisioned by Article 12 of the CRPD. In most cases, the reforms fall far short of the promise of structural transformation. Nonetheless, these chapters recount numerous lessons for driving more comprehensive transformation efforts and outcomes.

In the sixth chapter, Agustina Palacios reviews the past decade of precedents of high courts in Latin America to identify key themes in the evolving jurisprudence on legal capacity. This progress includes recognition, without discrimination, of legal capacity, support for decision-making, access to justice, informed consent, sexual and reproductive rights and family life, among other matters. Her analysis points to jurisdictional developments in the highest courts of Mexico, Peru, Argentina, Costa Rica and Colombia, providing an insightful guide to evolving standards for respecting and guaranteeing rights recognised in the CRPD. Despite these jurisprudential advances, Palacio identifies crucial inconsistencies and gaps in some areas of judicial reasoning, such as reproductive rights and the right to family life. These shortcomings include, for example, adolescent girls' and women's sexual and reproductive rights, often restricted based on pathologising stereotypes. Looking at trends across the region, Palacios finds that, despite some progress in the jurisprudential domain, there remains endemic colonisation of people's lives and life projects, with many people with disabilities continuing to face immense restrictions on liberty and legal capacity in their daily lives.

In the next chapter, Alberto Vásquez, Federico Isaza and Andrea Parra focus their analysis on the legal reforms recently adopted in Costa Rica, Peru and Colombia. In these three jurisdictions, interdiction/guardianship has been

Intersentia

5

invalidated, and new support systems for decision-making have been recognised. For each country, the authors track the legal context, the reform processes and the results obtained so far, considered by many as an international benchmark. The authors critically examine these reforms and their implementation, pointing out the various challenges to be faced when viewed from the perspective of the standard established by Article 12 of the CRPD: the recognition of universal legal capacity. The authors identify the abundance of administrative and public policy challenges, including the need for notaries' training in recognising decision-making support. In addition, the authors point to the broad social context of systemic marginalisation of persons with disabilities, the lack of supportive policies and public awareness of the reforms, and the presence of proactive resistance to the reforms by some justice system actors, medical personnel and the legal profession. The authors conclude that, despite their importance, legal reforms alone are not enough to address the deeply entrenched social determinants that result in a *de facto* denial of legal capacity within families and communities, and social and economic structures.

In the next chapter, Judge Kristin Booth Glen examines the legal reforms adopted in the U.S. that recognise and establish provisions for "supported decision-making". While there are inconsistent approaches to conceptualising and implementing supported decision-making – or providing decision-making supports to individuals to enable them to exercise legal capacity –, Booth Glen finds two general approaches in legislative reform in that country. First, limiting – but not repealing – guardianship laws by recognising supported decision-making as a "less restrictive alternative." Second, the enactment of laws that recognise supported decision-making agreements and require that decisions made and executed through such agreements be legally recognised. The author surveys legislative developments in 15 U.S. states. In her assessment, these statutes provide greater recognition of the right to legal capacity but also embed exclusions about who can make such agreements. As with other authors in this collective work, Booth Glen argues that legislation is not sufficient, at least not in its current form, to realise the rights recognised in Article 12. A deeper understanding is needed of supported decision-making in practice. Her chapter highlights some innovative community initiatives, in particular in New York. Booth Glen concludes that to address the limitations of current legal reforms, there is a need to heighten public awareness about this issue and build stronger alliances with other marginalised communities who have also faced systemic exclusion and denial of self-determination.

Dianah Msipa then discusses developments in the African region in the next chapter. The author focuses in particular on Kenya, Zambia and South Africa. Msipa explains how, with the possible exception of South Africa, efforts in the region have failed to meet the standard set in Article 12 of the CRPD. The reforms that have been achieved are often more rhetorical than substantial, thus re-entrenching the provisions that restrict the exercise of legal capacity based on "mental" capacity. In both Kenya and Zambia, efforts by civil society organisations and disability communities to overhaul the legal regime were successful in general recognition of equal rights. However, these regimes continue to institutionalise exceptions in mental health and other laws, thus denying recognition of universal legal capacity and failing to shift from substituted to supported decision-making. The legislative reform proposals being debated in South Africa at the time of writing could, however, be a glimmer of hope in the normative transformations required in light of Article 12. It is a transformation, she argues, that should be accompanied in a more concerted manner by the courts and congresses of the African region.

Nadia Shabani and Marieta Dimitrova in the next chapter examine a decade of efforts in Bulgaria to transition from a model of substitute decision-making to a support model. They review the entrenched legal doctrine and provisions which justify and deeply institutionalise resort to guardianship. They trace multiple efforts and strategies since Bulgaria ratified and domesticated the CRPD to crack the foundations of the old regime. These include: strategic litigation challenging guardianship; pilot initiatives to demonstrate supported decision-making in practice; a new draft law based on an alternative legal doctrine and introducing a new legal regime based on support for decision-making; the adoption of legally recognised decision-making support measures introduced into the social services, though not yet, the legal domain; sustained public awareness campaigning; and knowledge dissemination and delivery of training to a wide range of actors in the justice system, legal profession, health and social sectors. This comprehensive approach, which the authors themselves have been instrumental in designing, supporting and delivering, has not yet fully realised its aims. The authors suggest that the lessons learnt to date – collaboration across sectors, committed leadership by self-advocates and parents, dedicated public awareness campaigning, and commitment to ongoing action research and reflection to adjust strategies as needed – will continue to serve the change process. The processes activated they suggest are now irreversible. Overturning the old guardianship paradigm, they suggest, is no longer a matter of if, but when.

In her critical appraisal of the law reform process and its results in India, developed in the next chapter, Amita Dhanda examines the dilemmas that arise between legal capacity reform ideals and the final legislative compromises of a complex negotiation process. Should advocates uncompromisingly protect the principles of universal legal capacity provided by multiple interpretations of Article 12 and demand nothing less than radical change, or "is it okay to make concessions and carry everyone along?" The author assesses what has been achieved in the reform process in India, reviewing reform proposals and processes related to The Rights of Persons with Disabilities Act and the Mental Health Care Act. Dhanda examines the reform processes with each piece of legislation. The former was designed to enable broader civil society participation and public education, which led to more robust challenge and even protests because of the failure to deliver on promised fundamental reform. The more limited engagement and top-down direction of the process with the Mental Health Act resulted in more limited change, restitution of the medical paradigm of disability and, along with it, exclusions from recognising legal capacity. In both cases, Dhanda turns the reader to assessing the design of the related public consultations and questions whether the compromises can be justified. Dhanda urges a careful and contextual approach for making that evaluation in the specific circumstances of legislative reform.

In the next chapter, based on their field social research, Huang Yi and Chen Bo review the practice of legal capacity and guardianship in mainland China, outlining the current legal framework and the broader cultural and social context in which the practice is implemented. A starting point for understanding guardianship in mainland China is the social and cultural expectation that families will play a central role. The legal regime reinforces a pre-existing "moral authority" of family members for this role, which comprises a cluster of expectations based on the idea that they are the ones who can act on behalf of the best interests of their family members with disabilities. Nonetheless, the authors identify that there is a growing awareness of supported decision-making arrangements as an alternative to guardianship, reflective of a broader and growing social recognition of the right to personal autonomy. Even if legal reforms could be secured, Huang Yi and Chen Bo wonder to what extent cultural expectations and dominant practices regarding substitute decision-making and the central role of families in managing it might be transformed. Resolving these tensions will require, they argue, public education and a cultural redefinition of the current role of family members as decision-makers, which will need to keep pace with any legal reform efforts.

Urania Chiu and Pok Yin S. Chow in the following chapter expose the inconsistencies of the provisions of the Hong Kong legal regime – which regulate the exercise of legal capacity – with international human rights norms and standards. The authors find that the medical model of mental incapacity still dominates both law and public policy in Hong Kong, and that legal reforms in this field have lagged far behind international law. There is no uniform approach to setting out the legal requirements, and the equation between a mental or psychosocial disability and legal incapacity persists. Substitute decision-making and a compulsory psychiatric regime remains the default approach, even when it is clear that what a person needs is support. The regime provides little or no room for persons with intellectual, cognitive or psychosocial disabilities to participate in decisions about their lives, much less direct them. Combined with a rapid increase in the prevalence of cognitive impairment – given the rapidly aging population of Hong Kong –, and the increase in the demand for guardianship, the current political moment seems resistant to substantial change. There are, however, hopes for some more specific legal reforms and efforts to introduce supported decision-making in practice.

In the final chapter in this part, Piers Gooding and Terry Carney analyse the multi-dimensional law, policy and practice reforms put into place in Australia since the coming into force of the CRPD in that country. These changes encompass both statutory and non-statutory supported decision-making options and are informed by probably the most comprehensive conceptual and empirical research programme globally. For Gooding and Carney, legislative reform in Australia has focused on guardianship and mental health provisions; but it has also begun to cover areas where legal capacity remains restricted, including criminal law, matrimonial, property and contract law. The authors characterise Australia's path to reform as "incremental" in nature, though "broad by global standards". Key factors, affecting the incremental scope of the reform are the federal structure of the Australian state, resulting in uneven development between states, and the fact that Australia lodged an interpretive declaration on Article 12 of the CRPD, which limits its recognition of the universal right to legal capacity. The authors point to the lessons that Australia's trajectory and its resulting "patchwork" of reforms provide to civil society organisations and other State parties, globally seeking to undertake necessary reforms in public law, private law, public policy and practice.

3. LEGAL ISSUES AND PERSISTENT CHALLENGES

Each of the chapters in the third part of this volume grapple with fundamental questions and core challenges in designing legal regimes consistent with Article 12 of the CRPD. A particular challenge, which all the chapters in this part deal with, is whether safeguards to address vulnerability – faced by many people with intellectual, cognitive or psychosocial disabilities – may, in some way, justifiably restrict the exercise of capacity. There is no simple answer. The authors expose what is at stake and seek to articulate guidance for proportional and justified responses in respecting autonomy, while protecting people from harm.

In the next chapter, Pablo Marshall delves into the question of how to conceptualise supports needed for informed consent, considering the bioethical discourses that shape the practice of health care decision-making and the risks of harm in this context. Marshall seeks to square the interpretation of Article 12 by the UN Committee on the Rights of Persons with Disabilities in its General Comment No. 1 which rejects a functional approach to capacity assessment as discriminatory based on cognitive disability, with functional requirements which play a constitutive role in securing informed consent. In biomedical ethics, such requirements are justified to guard against harm, particularly vulnerable people with disabilities, among other groups. The author critically examines the extent to which decision-making supports can avoid the need to resort to substitution of will in health care decisions. In examining this question, in theoretical and ethical terms, Marshall also considers its implications for legal capacity reform processes. The author notes that such processes are not adequately attending to decision-making supports specifically for health care consent. This leaves conflicting approaches to supports for decision-making within the same jurisdiction. For example, recognising supports for decision-making in some contexts, but keeping in place the conventional capacity requirements for informed consent. The author suggests research is needed about the specific requirements for legally valid decisions in health care decision-making and in other spheres, including mental health care in particular, criminal law and reproductive rights, among others. Marshall argues for a more contextual approach that recognises that legal capacity requirements, regulation, and the nature of decision-making supports may vary across these spheres.

In the next chapter, Maria Paz Garcia Rubio traces the provisions of the Spanish Civil Code concerning disability and legal capacity with respect to contract law. While focused on the Spanish legal regime, her in-depth critical examination brings the lens of Article 12 of the CRPD to the study of contract law more generally. She grapples with a series of challenges that emerge over the course of recent reforms to the Code which recognise supports for contracting and provide for voidability of contracts under certain circumstances where one of the parties has a disability and may be incapacitated as a result. In her analysis, she points to how the Civil Code's provisions for judicial recognition of support measures to contract provides the basis for removing requirements for interdiction, without imposing that the person must necessarily use the supports for the contracts they enter to be considered valid. Garcia Rubio is insistent that while the CRPD recognises that supports may be required to exercise legal capacity, the interpretation by the UN Committee on the Rights of Persons with Disabilities that supports cannot be imposed, must guide both the interpretation and the administration of supports measures in the contracting context. She examines the challenges in doing so and concludes that this interpretation strikes the right balance between protecting autonomy and protecting a person's interests. The same cannot be said, she suggests, for provisions which limit the liability of persons with disabilities whose obligations to provide restitution when contracts are nullified is limited by the fact of their disability. She argues that the CRPD called for equal recognition of autonomy and also responsibility. By limiting liability in this respect, she fears that such provisions will lead to further excluding people with disabilities from markets for goods and services, because other parties will see disincentives to contracting with them. Her chapter provides guidance for crafting provisions for contract law to better strike a balance between recognising supports, respecting autonomy and imposing contractual obligations on an equal basis with others.

Renato Antonio Constantino Caycho and Renata Anahí Bregaglio Lazarte examine, in the following chapter, the tricky territory of designing CRPD-compliant safeguards. Constantino Caycho and Bregaglio Lazarte suggest that dispensing with the functional requirements for legal capacity in light of interpretations of Article 12 of the CRPD, as urged by many advocates, is not so easily done if we take seriously the realities of vulnerability. The authors see a need for some level of functional assessment, not to determine who has legal capacity in general terms, but to determine the validity of a person's will in specific circumstances of a legal transaction. They argue that, to ensure safeguards that protect people from the undue influence of people who play a supportive role or are parties to a legal transaction, the concept of a person's "true will" is essential. In this vein, they suggest that not all manifestations of will or preference can be considered true or authentic enough to create, modify or terminate legal relationships. The law must set the terms of what counts as valid expressions of the will, for the purpose of determining the legal consequences of decisions. The authors inquire into the rules the State should adopt for balancing respect for autonomy and paternalistic interventions to protect a person from harm or abuse.

In the final chapter of this volume, Lana Kerzner critically assesses common cognitive capacity requirements for decision-making. The author contrasts the cognitive/functional approach of legal capacity predominant in law, with the decision-making capability approach – previously described in the chapter by Michael Bach. Such an approach recognises that the cognitive capacities, presumed necessary for a legally valid decision in specific circumstances, can be contributed by supporters who are guided by a person's authentic will. The question for Kerzner is whether the limitation in rights that comes from a situation of cognitive disability can be justified in any circumstance. To address this question, she looks to the justification for limiting rights as articulated in section 1 of the Charter of Rights and Freedoms, Canada's highest law on guaranteeing rights. It provides for "reasonable limits prescribed by law as can be demonstrably justified in a free and democratic society." In this context she examines the extent to which individual autonomy rights, and rights to equal recognition must be balanced against the societal interest to protect from harm vulnerable persons who are unable to meet the cognitive test of capacity. She considers whether that protection necessarily involves substitute decision-making. The assumption that such protection is justified is pervasive in law in Canada and internationally as she notes. Ultimately, she concludes that because support options are available and can be designed for people in extremely vulnerable situations, the discrimination that comes part and parcel with the cognitive test of capacity cannot be justified in a free and democratic society.

PART I

HISTORICAL PERSPECTIVES AND THEORETICAL FRAMES

A HISTORICAL REVIEW OF LEGAL CAPACITY

Javier Barrientos Grandon[*]

1. *Status* as a Key to the Culture of Ius Commune: Without *Status*,
   there is No Person. 15
2. *Capax*: A Particular Aptitude in the Culture of Ius Commune 25
3. *Capacitas* and its Generalisation Linked to the Construction of the
   Category of Subject of Law 28

1. *STATUS* AS A KEY TO THE CULTURE OF IUS COMMUNE: WITHOUT *STATUS*, THERE IS NO PERSON

The legal culture of ius commune – medieval Roman law developed into a system of rules that formed a universal common law for Western Europe – built and deployed its categories and discourses on the reading and re-reading of various passages of the *Corpus Iuris Civilis*, which included the *Digest*, the Code and the Institutions. Jurists from the 12th century onwards found in the *Corpus* that the words *"status"*, *"persona"*, and *"homo"* were used in very varied contexts, especially in Title I of the *Digest*[1] and two titles of the *Institutions*.[2]

In Title I of Book I of the *Digest* and the first of the *Institutions*, specific passages from the *Institutions* of Gaius were, to a greater or lesser extent, reproduced; these may be regarded as a decisive point of reference for the construction of a discipline of the person, before codifications in law were developed. A triple division of personal law – *de jure personarum* – resulted from these texts, i.e., the *summa divisio: liberi aut servi*, followed by a second division, *sui iuris* or *alieni iuris*, and finally *quae in tutela, quae in curatela* or *ceteras personas, quae neutro iure tenentur*. In the culture of ius commune, these

---

[*] Full Member of the Chilean Academy of History, Professor of History of Law and Institutions at the Faculty of Law of the Autonomous University of Madrid.

[1] See *CIC, Digest*, l.1, 5.

[2] See *CIC, Institutions*, l. I, 3 and l. I, 16.

passages were read, in general, with a tendency to highlight the divisions they consecrated between the people, rather than a division of the law of the people.[3] This interpretation consolidated a central idea in that culture: the "division" of people so that a perspective was imposed that highlighted plurality.

The second title of the *Institutions* refers to the *capitis deminutio*, conceived as *prioris status commutatio*, a change that could happen in three different ways – *tribus modis accidit*. These ways enabled jurists to establish, from very early on, the basic idea according to which there were three *statuses* of persons: *civitatis, libertatis, familiae*. This was not a trilogy typical of Roman jurisprudence, but it was articulated by ius commune jurists, and enjoyed singular fortune; so much so that the exposition of the right of persons conformed to this trilogy.[4] Thus, a second guiding idea would be consolidated in terms of persons, that of *status* as a factor determining their divisions.

Based on such ideas, the 16th and 17th centuries saw an extensive and sustained discussion about the notions of *status, caput* and *capitis deminutio*, with particular concern for determining what was to be understood by the *status* of individuals. With the natural nuances that could be observed from one jurist to another, the idea was established that, in this context, the word *status* meant the "condition" of individuals in terms of freedom, citizenship, or family.[5]

One of the most important and influential aspects in the attempt to specify the notion of *status* was the reading of *status* in light of notions that came from the field of philosophy – in the context of humanism and the *usus modernus Pandectarum*. In particular, the notions of "quality", "cause", and "effect" extended the operative field of *status* to a series of realities of its time (i.e. the different types of people recognised at the time) and to which, naturally, the Roman texts did not refer.

---

[3] In the *ordinary Glossa*, this reading was already established, and it was assumed by the commentators of the 14th and 15th centuries. See Accursius, *Institutiones Iuris Civilis, D. Iustiniani Magni Imperio per Triumviros Tribonianum, Dorotheum, ac Theophilum conscriptae: & Fran. Accursii glossis illustratae*, Apud Antonium Vincentium, Lugduni, 1555, gl. "*Summa*", fol. 30; A. Gambiglioni de Aretio, *In quatuor Institutionum Iustiniani Libros Commentaria*, Ad Candentis Salamandrae Insignae, Venetiis, 1574, fol. 20v; B. Ubaldi, *Commentaria ad quatuor Institutionum libros*, Apud haeredes Nicolai Bevilaquae, Augustae Taurinorum, 1586, fol. 8; B. Saxoferrato, *Commentaria in primam ff. Veteris partem*, Vincentium de Portonariis, Lugduni, 1538, fol. 41v.

[4] In the *ordinary Glossa* a reading could be found that established that the idea of the existence of three "states of persons" was already assumed. See Accursius, *Institutions* (n. 3), gl. "*Status*", fol. 101; cf. J. Linck, *De statu libertatis, civitatis, et familiae, ut et de sponsalibus et nuptiis*, Argentorati, 1737.

[5] See, among others, F. Hotman, *In quatuor libros Institutionum Iuris Civilis*, ex officina Hervagiana, Basileae, 1569, fol. 66, *ad Inst.* 1, 16, 1; J. Harprecht, *In quatuor Institutionum Divi Imp. Justiniani Books, Commentarii privati, breves ac perspicui*, Sumptibus Johannis Beyeri. Typis Aegidii Vogelii, Francofurti, 1562, *ad Inst.* 1, 16, 1, fol. 107; A. Pichardo de Vinuesa, *In quatuor Institutionum Imperatoris Iustiniani libros*, Ex officina viduae Francisci Fernandez de Cordova, Valladolid, 1630, *ad Inst.* 1, 16, n. 2, fol. 83; A. Pérez, *Institutiones Imperiales erotematibus distinctae et explicatae. Rationibus ex principiis Iuris passim depromptis*, Apud Everardum, Witte & Ioannem Vryenborch, Lovanii, 1639, *ad Inst.* 1, 3, fol. 11.

A Historical Review of Legal Capacity

One of the first jurists who read *status* in light of philosophy was Ulric Zasius (1461–1536), who qualified *status* as a "habitual quality" – *habitualis qualitas*. Because of this, Zasius did not define it by the textual trilogy *libertas, civitas, familia*, but by a certain quality "to be" – *ut esse* –, specifically, free, slave, noble, legitimate, etc.[6] His disciples followed him, including the highly influential Joachim Mysinger von Frundeck (1514–1588), for whom *status* was nothing more than a quality and condition – *qualitas et conditio* – of the person to be – *ut esse* – free, ingenuous, noble, or slave.[7] In a similar perspective, Hugo Donellus (1527–1591) focused on clarifying the relationship between *status* and *ius*, explaining it from the categories of *causa* and *effectus*. Thus, *status* was the condition of each person, and *ius* the ability to live and do what the person pleased, and therefore *ius* was attributed to *status*. Thus, it turned out that the *status* was the *cause*, and the person's right was the *effect* of that state and condition.[8] This same conception was upheld by Arnoldo Vinnius (1588–1657), for whom the person's right was that which followed the state and condition of the person. For *status* itself was nothing more than the condition or quality of the person that made him or her use this or that right, such as being free, servant, ingenuous, freedman, *alieni iuris, sui iuris; status* operated as a cause, and the right as an effect.[9]

Among the jurists who extended the space in which the notion of *status* operated, Hermann Vulteius (1555–1634) occupies a prominent place with his *Commentarius* on the Justinian *Institutions*. In this work, he justified a distinction between the *status publicus* and the *status privatus* of a person. His starting point resided in the relationship that existed between *homo* and *persona*. The first was a word of nature, and the second of civil law, since a person was nothing more than one with a *caput civile*.[10] Among the original aspects of this reading is that it was shown to be especially linked to the reality of the time, which allowed it to move with greater freedom in relation to Roman texts and their categories. Hence, he affirmed that in German law, the consideration of person was threefold; one for reasons of sex, another for reasons of dignity, and another for reasons of *status*.[11] Thus, it surpassed the established trilogy *libertas, civitas, familia*, and established a new one: *ex sexu, ex dignitate, ex statu*.

---

[6]   U. Zasius, *In Primam Digestorum Partem paratitla*, Apud Mich. Ising, Basileae, 1539, *ad Dig.* 5, 1, 5, fol. 10.

[7]   J. Mynsiger a Frundeck, *Apotelesma, corpus perfectum scholiorum ad Institutiones Iustinianeas pertinentium*, ex Officina Iacobi Lucii, Helmaestadii, 1595, *ad Inst*. 1, 3, 1, n. 7, fol. 24.

[8]   H. Donnellus, *Commentariorum de jure civili*, I, ad Signum Clius, Florentia, 1840, lib II, c. IX, II, col. 241.

[9]   A. Vinnius, *In quatuor libros Institutionum Imperialium Commentarius Academicus & Forensis*, Apud Danielem Elzevirium, Amstelodami, 1665, *ad Inst*. 1, 3, fol. 23.

[10] H. Vulteius, *In Institutiones Juris Civilis a Justiniano compositas Commentarius*, Apud Paulum Egenolphum, Marpurgi, 1613, *ad Inst*. 1, 3, fol. 40.

[11] Ibid., fol. 41.

Two important consequences would derive from this new trilogy; it shifted the distinction between *cives* and *peregrinus*, from *status* to *dignitas*, and narrowed the operative field of the *status* category. For the first consequence, *ex dignitate*, humans could be "public" or "private". "Public" humans were those who were endowed with *imperium*, like a prince and magistrates, or charges or trades, such as the ministers of princes and magistrates. As for "private" humans, some were categorised as such for reasons of order – *ratione ordinis* – and others for their way of life – *ex vitae instituto*. Of those categorised by order, some were pilgrims and others were citizens. Citizens were either nobles or commoners. For those categorised by their way of life, each had chosen their life condition. As for the second consequence, the notion of *status* was limited only to the distinctions between free and enslaved people – *sui iuris* and *alieni iuris* – and were subject to guardianship or curatorship, or not subject to either.[12]

Of greater interest so far as this discussion is concerned, was the novel introduction of the distinction between *status naturalis* and *status civilis*. In general terms, this distinction was established in two different methodological spaces; first, in the *usus modernus Pandectarum*, where it could already be read extensively in the works of Georg Adam Struve (1619–1692), in particular in his *Syntagma jurisprudentiae* (1658); and secondly, linked to the tradition of humanism, the most representative expression of which was found in the works of Jean Domat (1625–1696), especially in his *Les lois civiles* of 1689.

For Struve, *person* was a word that meant someone who lived in civil society, since every human being had some state or condition attributed to him or her, either by nature itself, or by law.[13] He called the first distinction *status naturalis*, and according to him, humans were first distinguished by reason of sex – *ratione sexus*;[14] and then by reason of birth – *ratione nativitatis* –, so that one was either yet to be born – *nasciturus* – or already born – *natus*.[15] He called the second distinction *status civilis*, on the grounds that it clarified that the right, by virtue of which the person was constituted in a specific condition, was called *jus Personarum*, and so *Status hominum*.[16] *Status* here was, therefore, the condition of the person, political or civil, which made them use one right or another in civil society.[17] Such condition or *status* was either *absolute*, according to which

---

[12]   Ibid.

[13]   G. A. STRUVE, *Syntagma Jurisprudentiae secundum ordinem Pandectarum concinnatum quo solida juris fundamenta traduntur Digestorum, et affine Codicis, Novellarum ac Juris Canonici tituli methodice explicantur, controversiae nervose resolvuntur et quid in foro usum habeat, monetur. Editio post varias hactenus adornatas concinnior et ab innumeris mendis typographicis solicite purgata, Editio post varias hactenus adornatas concinnior*, Sumtibus [sic] Matthaei Birckneri, Bibliopolae, Jenae, 1692, "Exercitatio tertia Ad libr. I, Tit. 5, 6, 7, 8, Tit. V, De Statu Hominum", n. II, fol. 51.

[14]   Ibid.

[15]   Ibid., n. III, fol. 52.

[16]   Ibid., n. V, fol. 53.

[17]   Ibid., n. VI, fol. 53.

humans were differentiated into free and enslaved people, or *relative*, and this could be in relation to the *family* – according to which they were distinguished in *sui iuris* and *alieni iuris* –, or in relation to a specific *city* – according to which persons were differentiated into pilgrims and citizens.[18]

The distinction between *status naturalis* and *status civilis* dates back to a reading by Matthaeus Wesenbeck (1531–1586). He read Title III of the Justinian *Institutions* – *De jure personarum* – from the following premise: the *summa divisio personarum* with which this title opened – *liberi aut servi* – was a division of law *iuris divisio* – assumed from the law of peoples, and not a division of nature – *ex natura* – because, according to the latter, the *prima* and *summa divisio* was what differentiated males and females.[19] The same premise was at the basis of his reading of the title *De statu hominum* of the *Digest*,[20] allowing him to establish a triple division of persons, one natural, another by the law of peoples, and another by civil law.[21] Heinrich Hahn, of whom Struve was a disciple, assumed and developed this way of understanding the texts (1605–1668). Hahn, in his observations on the *Commentaries* on the Wesenbeck *Digest*, wrote that one of the two meanings in which the jurists admitted the word *status* was that of some condition or quality and that it could be applied:

- *broadly and generally*, as when speaking of the state of the republic or the public and private state or;
- referring to the human being.

In this last sense, it admitted a triple use:

1. It generally denoted any natural condition of the human being, that is, natural characteristics, such as those that exist, by reason of sex, between men and women, and those that exist between the already born the those that are still in the maternal womb (the unborn);
2. In a strict and particular use, it referred to "the civil status of men" – *ad statum hominum civilem* – or political;
3. In rigorous use, it referred to *pro part status*, as when it was taken for "freedom" or "citizenship".[22]

---

[18]   Ibid., n. VII, fol. 53–54.

[19]   M. WESENBECK, *Institutionum D. Iustiniani, Sacratiss. Principis P. P. A. Libri IIII*, Per Eusebium Episcopium & Nicolai fr. Haeredes, Basileae, 1585, *ad Inst.* 1, 3, 1, n. 1, fol. 12.

[20]   See *Digesto* (n. 1).

[21]   M. WESENBECK, *In Pandectas Iuris Civilis, & Codicis Iustinianei, Lib. iix. Commentarii*, In offic. Q. Philip. Tinghi, Apud Simphorianum Beraud, Lugduni, 1585, *ad Dig.* 1, 5, fol. 19.

[22]   H. HAHN, *Observata theoretico practica, Ad Matthaei Wesenbecii in L. libros Digestorum Commentarios*, I, Typis & sumtibus Henningi Mulleri, Helmaestadii, 1668, *ad Dig.* 1, 5, n. 1, fol. 83.

A similar distinction was established in the tradition of French jurists linked to rationalism, and had one of its most influential exponents in Jean Domat (1625–1696). Domat pointed out that although civil laws recognised the equality that natural law had constituted among all people, certain qualities were distinguished, which referred peculiarly to matters of natural law and constituted what was called *status personarum*.[23] Since some were natural and others established by themselves, the distinctions that constituted qualities that addressed the state of a person were of two kinds: *statum secundum naturae* and *secundum legum ordinem*.[24] Domat devoted the first section of the title *De personis* to discussing *De statu personarum circa naturam*. This *status* admitted three distinctions; *Distinctio, personarum ex sexu*,[25] *Distinctio ex nativitate & patria potestate*,[26] and *Distinctio ex aetate*.[27] The second section was devoted to the scrutiny of the *statu personarum juxta leges civiles*, whose distinctions were established at the discretion of the laws, so that they had no basis in nature, such as the distinction between free and enslaved people or those that derived from some natural quality, such as that established between adults and children.[28]

This was, in general terms, the state of the readings on *status* that could be observed in the culture of ius commune during the second half of the 17th century. It is interesting here to highlight that he had established a key idea, the right – conceived as faculties – incumbent upon a person, depended on their *status*, and this was not unique but numerous; that is, there were as many different rights as recognised *statuses*.

During the 18th century, that tradition was maintained, but a new way of conceiving it was affirmed, which, in principle, became the most common until the time of the codifications. It was formulated in the last decades of the 17th century by Samuel Pufendorf (1632–1694), who, in his *De iure naturae et gentium* of 1672, from a clear philosophical perspective, made a novel reading of the traditional categories of *person* and *status*.

Pufendorf considered persons as moral entities (*entia moralia*), and he understood these *entia moralia* in an analogous way to "substances". Physical substances presupposed the *spatium* in which they placed their natural existence and exercised their physical movements. By analogy, persons, and mainly moral persons, would be understood as "*esse in Statu*". This *status*, likewise, was assumed or extended "under them" so that they exercise their actions and effects on it. Thus, certain states were instituted, not by themselves, but so that

---

[23]   J. Domat, *Leges civiles juxta naturalem earum ordinem; Jus publicum & legum delectus*, vol. I, Sumptibus Francisci ex Nicolao Pezzana, Venetiis, 1785, tit. II, pr., fol. 15.

[24]   Ibid., fol. 16.

[25]   Ibid., tit. II, sect. I, n. 1, fol. 17.

[26]   Ibid., tit. II, sect. I, n. 2–15, fol. 17–19.

[27]   Ibid., tit. II, sect. I, n. 16, fol. 19.

[28]   Ibid., tit. II, sect. II, pr., fol. 19.

the existence of persons as moral entities could be understood in them.[29] *Status,* by analogy with *spatium,* was presented as the space in which people acted. It was understood as an ability to act, that is an "active quality", just as freedom was said to be a *status* and not a characteristic of state. Characteristics of state were thought of as "passive qualities".[30] The characterisation of *status* as a *qualitas* had the consequence that Pufendorf completely abandoned the use of the word "*conditio*", which had been usual among the jurists who had defined *status,* and which was still preserved in the *usus modernus Pandectarum.*

People could exist in many states, and inasmuch as conceived as singular but united by a moral bond in a system, they were considered in their *status* or *munus,* and admitted a series of distinctions. In dealing with such distinctions, Pufendorf continued the concern that Vulteius had shown regarding the situation of his time, using these differences to explain the composition of his society.

So, the state in which the persons existed founded the distinctions between them. Thus, moral persons either were simple – *simplices* – or compound – *compositae.*[31] By reason of their *status* or *munus,* simple persons could be public – *publicae* – or private – *privatae.* As for private persons, it could only be said that there was a great variety of them, and that their main differences derived from the following criteria:

1. *Ex negotio, quaestu aut artificio,* that is, the shop, trade, or art in which they were engaged;
2. *Ex conditione seu situ quasi morali, quo quis utitur in civitate,* that is, the position held in the city, from which some were *cives,* with full or less than full rights, others *inquilinus,* and others *peregrinus*;
3. *Ex conditione in familia,* in which some were *paterfamilias,* others *uxor,* others *filius,* and others *servus,* and were, essentially, members of the ordinary family, and to which the *hospes* was sometimes exceptionally added;
4. *Ex stirpe,* in which some were *nobles,* although their grades could vary in different cities, and others *plebeji*;
5. *Ex sexu & aetate,* from which it followed that some were men and others women, and that they were: *puer, juvenis, vir* or *senex.*[32]

Pufendorf's reading of *status* does not seem to have immediately influenced German jurists at the end of the 17th century and the first decades of the 18th.

---

[29] S. Pufendorf, *De Jure naturae et gentium. Libri octo,* Sumptibus Friderici Knochii, Francofurti ad Moenum, 1684 *De Jure naturae et gentium. Libri octo,* Sumptibus Friderici Knochii, Francofurti ad Moenum, 1684, fol. 5, lib. I, cap. I, 6.

[30] Ibid., lib. I, cap. I, 11, fol. 9.

[31] Ibid., lib. I, cap. I, 12, fol. 10.

[32] Ibid., lib. I, cap. I, 12, fol. 11–12.

In general, in the works of the jurists of that time, the distinction of *status*, in *naturalis* and *civilis*, which was the characteristic of the *usus modernus Pandectarum*, was consolidated.[33] However, it should be noted that some authors referred to Pufendorf's opinions but made it clear that they did not follow his understanding of certain species of *status*.[34] For Johann Gottlieb Heineccius (1681–1741), Pufendorf's reading of *status*, and all his work, would exert a singular influence. Heineccius dealt particularly with those questions in his *Elementa juris naturae et gentium* of 1737. However, his fundamental ideas could already be found in his explanation of the *Institutions* contained in his *Elementa Iuris Civilis secundum ordinem Institutionum* of 1725. They were also contained in his *Recitationes in Elementa Iuris Civilis secundum ordinem Institutionum* of 1765.

Heineccius assumed that, in general, *status* was a quality by which everything was limited and that those qualities by which the person himself was properly limited were called *status hominis*. Those qualities which, by God himself as creator of humans, limited their soul or body constituted the *statum physicum*. And those others that, by law, limited their free actions, constituted the so-called *statum moralem*,[35] which in turn could be *naturalis* or *adventitius*.[36] In his *Elementa*, Heineccius had taken care to specify that the jurisconsults called *status naturalis* what he designated as *status physicum*, and that they called *status civilis* what he referred to as *status moralis*.[37] This was the terminology that he had assumed in his *Elementa Iuris Civilis secundum ordinem Institutionum* and that was read in his *Recitationes*. With this warning, Heineccius did no more than affirm that he read that distinction of *status*, characteristic of the *usus modernus Pandectaurm*, from his conception of *status*, – *physicum* and *moralis* – which was the reading that depended on his interpretation of Pufendorf, based on which was the analogy with material substances and *spatium*.

Heineccius – from the usual distinction that existed in law between *homo* and *person*[38] – emphasised that *homo* was any mind endowed with reason that corresponded to the human body, and that *person* was "the man when he was

---

[33] J. Ch. Herold, *Tractatus novus de jure ratificationis sive ratihabitionis*, Sumptibus Haeredum Friderici Lanckisii, Lipsiae, 1737, cap. III, sect. I, n. 1, fol. 56. With some novelty in N. H. Gundling, *Digesta in quibus rationis principia Jus Romanum et Teutonicum et genuinis fontibus simul ac pragmatica connexa ratione expenduntur confusaque nova et accurata methodo separantur*, vol. I, Prostat in Officina Libraria Rengeriana, Halae Magdeburgicae, 1723, *ad Inst.* 1, 5, fol. 58.

[34] J. Ch. Von Wolzogen, *Dissertatio academica de Quaestione status*, typis Christophori Zeitleri, Francofurti ad Viadrum, 1688, cap. I, n. 35–36, fol. 8.

[35] J. G. Heineccius, *Elementa Juris Naturae, et Gentium, commoda Auditoribus Methodo adornata*, Ex Typographia Balleoniana, Venetiis, 1746, lib. II, cap. I, 2, fol. 367.

[36] Ibid., lib. II, cap. I, 3, fol. 368.

[37] Ibid., lib. II, cap. I, 2, nota *, fol. 368.

[38] J. G. Heineccius, *Elementa Juris Civilis secundum ordinem Institutionum*, Apud Io. Philipp. Kriegerum, Giessae, 1730, n. 75, fol. 43.

A Historical Review of Legal Capacity

considered in a certain *status*" or "considered in his *status*";[39] from the foregoing, the conclusion followed, in his *Recitationes*, that he who had no *status* was not a person.[40]

In the path of Pufendorf, he characterised *status* as a "quality", and with this the abandonment of the description of *status* as a specific "condition" was affirmed in this tradition. Quality was that by which human beings used a different right; for example, one was the right used by the free man, another by the enslaved person, another by the citizen, another by the pilgrim, and from this it followed that *libertas* and *civitas* were called *status*.[41]

The *status* was either *naturalis* or *civilis*.[42] *Status naturalis* was the *status* that came from nature itself that, for example, made some male and others female, or some already born and others yet to be born.[43] *Status civilis* was, instead, the *status* derived from civil law, which differentiated between free and enslaved people, citizens and pilgrims, fathers of families and sons of families, so this *status civilis* was *threefold: libertatis, civitatis, familiae*.[44]

The simplicity of these *status* distinctions, which were in the tradition of the *usus modernus Pandectarum*, rested on a conception of person that Pufendorf had initiated and which implied a clear break from the previous tradition. The analogy of *status* with *spatium* was what allowed it to be characterised as a quality and, therefore, made it a "space of freedom". According to Pufendorf, it was thought of as a space of freedom as certain people, who were essentially free, acted within it. Or, as Heineccius said, it was a space that set the limits for people to act freely.

That simplicity was one of the decisive factors that explain the diffusion that the reading of Heineccius had in various European and non-European spaces and, especially, in the kingdoms of Spain and the Indies. In these kingdoms (Spain and the Indies), it was received, among others, in the widely used *Royal Law Institutions of Castile* – Madrid, 1771 – by the Aragonese Ignacio Jordán de Asso y del Río (1742–1814) and by Miguel de Manuel Rodríguez (17?–1797); in the *Illustration of Royal Law of Spain* – Valencia, 1803 – the aforementioned Juan Sala Bañuls (1731–1806); and in the *Royal Law Institutions of Castile and*

---

[39]   Ibid., n. 75, fol. 43–44; J. G. HEINECCIUS, *Recitationes in Elementa Iuris Civilis secundum ordinem Institutionum*, Impensis Io. Friederici Kornii, Vratislaviae, 1773, n. 75, fol. 51. He insisted on this characterisation in his notes to Vinnius's *Commentarius*, J. G. HEINECCIUS, *Ad Arnoldi Vinnii Commentarium in quatuor libros Institutionum Imperialium. Additiones & Notae*, s/l, 1747, fol. 6, *ad Inst.* 1, 3: "Ast *persona* est homo, statu quodam veluti indutus".

[40]   J. G. HEINECCIUS, *Recitationes* (n. 39), n. 75, fol. 51: "Qui itaque statum non habet, is nec est persona".

[41]   J. G. HEINECCIUS, *Elementa* (n. 38), n. 76, fol. 44; J. G. HEINECCIUS, *Recitationes* (n. 39).

[42]   J. G. HEINECCIUS, *Elementa* (n. 38), n. 76, fol. 44; J. G. HEINECCIUS, *Recitationes* (n. 39), n. 76, fol. 52; J. G. HEINECCIUS, *Ad Arnoldi Vinnii* (n. 39), *ad Inst.* 1, 3, fol.

[43]   J. G. HEINECCIUS, *Recitationes* (n. 39), n. 76, fol. 52.

[44]   Ibid.

Intersentia

23

the Indies – Guatemala, 1818 – by José María Álvarez (1777–1820), which is the version closest to Heineccius's *Recitationes*.

The characterisation that Heineccius had made of the person as a man considered in his *status*, was definitively established in these works. Thus, Asso and Manuel began their explanation with a definition of person that was literally taken from Heineccius: "The *Person* is man considered in his state; whereby it is said that there cannot be a person unless considered in one state or another [sic]";[45] and Álvarez practically limited himself to translating the corresponding passage from the *Recitationes*:

> These words, *man* and *person* are grammatically synonyms, but legally they are very different. The word man is more extensive than the word person: because every person is a man, but not every man is a person. Man is everyone who has a rational soul attached to the human body; and person is the man considered in some state. Under this assumption: he who has no status, is not a person [sic].[46]

In summary:

- the adoption of the reading of Heineccius, in these works of the late 18th and early 19th centuries, established, in the legal culture of the kingdoms of Spain and the Indies, a particular conception of the "status of persons", which could be "natural" or "civil";
- this primary distinction allowed inclusion in its different distinctions the diverse species of persons that inhabited the kingdoms;
- "time" became, along with sex, one of the basic criteria to define the "natural state" of a person through two of its distinctions, i.e., already born and unborn, and adults and minors;
- "space" was established as one of the criteria that founded certain distinctions of "civil status", in which "domicile" played a central role;
- from a "systematic" perspective, the *sedes materiae* of the person's status had been extended to operational fields to which it had not been linked in the Justinian texts, with its consequent attraction of a series of questions that had had their place in other settings.[47]

---

[45] IJ Asso and del Rio and M. Manuel Rodriguez, *Instituciones del Derecho Real de Castilla* [Institutions of Royal Law of Castile] *[...] The differences in this Law observed in Aragon by provision of its Charters are added at the end of each Title*, Francisco Xavier García's printing house, Madrid, 1771, lib. I, tít. I, p. I.

[46] J. M. Alvarez, *Instituciones de Derecho Real de Castilla y de Indias* [Institutions of Royal Law of Castile and the Indies], In the printing house of D. Ignacio Beteta, Guatemala, 1818, tit. III, p. 87.

[47] See J. Barrientos Grandon, "Sobre el 'Espacio' y el 'Tiempo' y el 'Estado de las personas'. Una mirada desde la Historia del Derecho" in M. Meccarelli and J. Plaice Tailor (eds), *Spatial and Temporal Dimensions for Legal History Research Experiences and Itineraries*, Max Planck Institute for European Legal History, Frankfurt am Main, 2016, pp. 63–99.

The detailed description of the preceding paragraphs allows us to verify that, in the culture of common law, the key category to structure the "law of persons" was that of *status*. Its weight and radicalism were such that, during the 18th century, the principle according to which "without *status* there is no person" was established. Two important consequences followed from this; first, that the legal culture was structured on a conception in which a plurality of persons coexisted, founded precisely on the plurality of states, and second, that the *status* determined the right a person could dispose of, or, in other words, *status* determined what a person could or could not legally do.

This conception and its consequences foresaw a break with tradition that would take place from the end of the 18th century. The new culture established since the time of the codifications did not continue the old tradition of *status*, but, rather, broke with it.

2. *CAPAX*: A PARTICULAR APTITUDE IN THE CULTURE OF IUS COMMUNE

In ius commune culture, *status* was the central notion that determined a person's existence and, consequently, the right they had – conceived as a faculty to act, *facultas agendi* in the Pufendorf expression. But the jurists resorted to the word "*capax*" to refer to certain capacity to act in very specific operational fields.

The word *capax* could also be read in some passages of the *Corpus Iuris Civilis* and was not strange to the jurists because it was in use in the Latin of their time, with a common meaning that did not deviate from the one it had had in Roman culture. There, *capax* was a word that, due to its connection with the verb *capio*, implied the ideas of capturing and receiving something; both were part of the nucleus that remained in the culture of the ius commune era. If, for example, the pages of the most famous *general dictionary* of the entire Old Regime, the work of Ambrosio Calepino (1440–1510), are reviewed, it is noted that the word *capax* is defined as the following: "That which takes or contains, or can contain (*quod capit, seu continet, aut continere possit*)".[48]

In this precise sense, the term *capax* was particularly appropriate to the field of operation in which ius commune jurists treated *status* as a certain "active quality." Along these lines, they referred to it in relation to the precise and singular spaces in which they found it in the texts of the *Corpus Iuris Civilis*. It was also the orientation by which some references were extended when it did not appear in the Roman texts.

In the *Corpus Iuris Civilis*, the word *capax* had a very rare and limited use, always conditioned by a context of patrimonial connotation. The references in

---

[48] A. CALEPINO, *Dictionarium linguae latinae*, Basilaeae, 1566, unfoliated.

which it was found were those of private crimes, those of certain obligations, and those of the institution of heir. In all of them, the jurists accepted its usage, and although they were not primarily concerned with it as a technical category, they contributed to establishing its use in legal language, in some very specific fields and in which, directly or indirectly, it was linked to the notion of *status*.

One of the fields in which the use of the word *capax* was established was crime. This use was based on those Roman texts that used it specifically to refer to wilful misconduct, through the expression "*doli capax*", as seen in a text included in the title *De furtis* of the *Digest*,[49] in another title *De vi bonorum raptorum*,[50] and in another entitled *De iniuriis et de famosis libellis*.[51] Due to its operating range, this expression was linked to *status* when one of its characteristics was that the person was capable of wilful misconduct and, consequently, of crimes. Thus, its interest was, above all, in the distinctions of *status* based on age – *infans/maior* –, but also generically in all those persons who experienced a particular physical or mental change due to illness, which did not change their *status* but did condition them. For example, *fury* or madness could operate irrespective of *status*; or with muteness, in relation to which there was a continuous discussion about the assumptions that mutes could be considered *doli capaces*.

In principle, the link between *status* and the expression "*doli capax*" is considered in terms of time – *tempus* –. For example, Pufendorf proposes as a second division of *status* – based in time – one that distinguishes between adults and minors: "In *majority*, when a person, by his or her age, is judged suitable to manage his or her own assets; and *minority*, when there is a need for a curator or tutor".[52] After pointing out that these states of greater and lesser age differed with different peoples, who established them in different terms, he warned that: "Minority differs from the age to be capable of wilful misconduct (*aetas doli capax*), whose term could not be assigned in a general way."[53] The use of this expression in relation to the *furiosus* was common among jurists. The fact declared about them not being capable of wilful misconduct was the circumstance that brought them closer to those minors who were not capable of wilful misconduct either[54] and, by equal proximity this also encompassed mutes.[55]

The interest of the issue regarding the discussion about *status*, and who were *capable doli*, did not lie only in the possibility of incurring the penalty assigned to the crime, but especially, in deciding if the obligation arose for them to redress

---

[49]   See *De furtis*, in *Digesto* (n. 1), l. 47, 2, fol. 23.
[50]   See *De vi bonorum raptorum*, ibid., l. 47, 8, 2, fol. 19.
[51]   See *De iniuriis et de famosis libellis*, ibid., l. 47, 10, fol. 3, 1.
[52]   S. PUFENDORF, *De Jure naturae* (n. 29), lib. I, cap. I, §10, fol. 9.
[53]   Ibid.
[54]   See for all, D. COVARRUBIAS, *Clementinae, Si furiosus. De homicidio, relectio*, Excudebat Andreas a Portonariis, Salmanticae, 1554, Pars III, n. 1–5, fol. 64r–67t.
[55]   See P. ZACHIAE, *Quaestionum medico-legalium*, vol. III, Sumtibus Johannis Melchioris Bencard, Francofurti ad Moenum, 1688, *consilium* L, fol. 93–97.

A Historical Review of Legal Capacity

the damage caused by the crime committed. In other words, the term *capax* thus showed its operability limited to a typical civil and patrimonial field.

Another of the fields in which the use of the word *capax* was established in the ius commune culture was that of certain obligations. This was a consequence of the presence of this word in some of the Roman texts with which the jurists of the time worked. In the title *De obligatione servorum* of the *Digest*, there was a passage that contained the expression "*obligationis capax*",[56] in the context of the issues concerned with whether an enslaved person could enter into an agreement. In the title *De solutionibus et liberationibus*, one could read "*solutionis capax*",[57] to deal with those who could make the payment of an obligation. This was also the case in reference to successions, based on a passage of the title *De heredibus instituendis*, when the heir specified in the will was *nullius* capax and, consequently had to be "substituted" by another.[58]

This use of the word *capax* in very precise areas contributed to jurists resorting to the more generic term "*capacitas*", which had also been commonly used since Roman times. From the word *capax* – referring to those who were able to capture or receive something – i.e., an agent – the term "*capacitas*" was derived. Although not widely used in Roman times, it was also used in the culture of ius commune as a predicate quality of a thing or object. In the aforementioned *Dictionarium* of Calepino, this word was spoken of in such terms, "Place that can capture or contain" *locus qui capere et continere potest*.[59]

Among jurists, the use of the word *capacitas* was more restricted. In principle, they referred to it primarily in succession matters, by way of dealing with the *capacitas testamenti*, that is, the making a will. This tendency was much more marked among those who followed the Germanic tradition represented by Pufendorf and his way of conceiving the person.

Among others, Alberto Bruno referred early on to the expression "*capacitas testamenti factionis*", in the context of the ability or power to make a will that he considered should be understood as a rule.[60]

In short, the *capax* and *capacitas* categories were established in the culture of ius commune, specifically with regard to inheritance; this resulted from considering them as expressions of a certain quality of people, or of their ability to act. It was the relationship between capacity and aptitude to act that justified the connection with the notions of *status* and *person*. It was this same relationship that explained the tendency to generalise the categories of *capacity* and *person* in a dogmatic line linked to the construction of the idea of "subject of law."

---

[56]   See *De obligatione servorum, Digesto* (n. 1), 45, 3, 12.

[57]   See *De solutionibus et liberationibus*, ibid., 46, 3, 98, 7.

[58]   See *De heredibus instituendis*, ibid., 28,5,81.

[59]   A. CALEPINO, *Dictionarium* (n. 48), unfoliated.

[60]   A. BRUNI, *De rebus seus dispositionibus dubiis*, § *Habilitas*, n. 26, in *Tractatus illustrium in utraque tum Pontificii, tum caesarei iuris facultate Iurisconsultorum. De variis verbis Iuris*, vol. XVIII, Venetiis, 1584, fol. 360r.

Intersentia

3. *CAPACITAS* AND ITS GENERALISATION LINKED TO THE CONSTRUCTION OF THE CATEGORY OF SUBJECT OF LAW

The dogmatic line represented by Pufendorf begins with one of the critical moments in the history of the construction of the category of legal subject, whose projection can be followed through the works of Leibniz and Wolf.[61] In this history, the notion of capacity played a very prominent role, which contributed to its generalisation in the legal culture of common law, especially in its later stages.

For Leibniz, the treatment of moral quality led him to maintain that the subject – *subiectum* – was only "the rational person or substance" *persona seu substantia rationalis*, and he conceived the "moral person or quality" as "capable of right and obligation" – *person seu qualitas moralis, id est juris obligationis capax*.[62] From this moment on the link between person and capacity was a constant in the legal discussion about the very notion of person, and also about the more generic notion of "subject".

The development of the notion of capacity linked to the new category of "subject" posed a series of problems in relation to the traditional and prevailing conception of the person defined by their *status*. This question was discussed by Friedrich Karl von Savigny (1779–1861), in a way that was decisive in conceiving capacity as a certain nucleus around which the notion of person revolves; a nucleus that, without departing from the preceding patrimonial tradition, had an impact on the notion of person assuming the idea of a centre of patrimonial interest.

For Savigny, the notion of *status*, as a dogmatically admissible concept, had to be linked to that of "capacity". Along these lines, he argued that: "The doctrine of *status* is logically untenable, unless, stripping the word *status* of its ordinary meaning, that *of legal capacity* is imposed on it."[63]

"Legal capacity" was, for Savigny, the basic category on which the person's right was explained:

> Every legal relationship consists of a person-to-person relationship. The first element *of this relationship* that we will study is the nature of the persons whose reciprocal relationships are likely to create this relationship. Here, then, the question arises: Who can be the subject of a legal relationship? This issue concerns the possible possession of rights or *legal capacity*, not their possible acquisition or *ability to act*.[64]

---

[61] See A. Guzman Brito, "Los orígenes de la noción de sujeto de derecho" (2010) *Journal of Historical-Legal Studies* XXIV, 151–250.

[62] G. Leibniz, *Elementa juris civilis*, en *Sämtliche Schriften und Briefe*, Deutschen Akademie der Wissenschaften, Berlin, 1971, VI, 2, p. 50.

[63] F. K. Savigny, *Traité de Droit Romain*, vol. II, París, 1855, "*Appendice* VI. *Status et capitis deminutio*", p. 418.

[64] Ibid., II, cap. II, § LX.

A Historical Review of Legal Capacity

In this system, Savigny states, "Every right is the sanction of the moral freedom inherent in each man. Thus, the primitive idea of person or subject of law is confused with the idea of man, and the primitive identity of these two ideas can be formulated in these terms: each individual, and the individual only, has the legal capacity." But in truth, he continued,

> positive law, and this is implicit in the preceding formula, can doubly modify the primitive idea of person, restricting or extending it. It can, indeed, totally or partially ignore certain individuals' legal capacity; it can, in addition, transfer the legal capacity outside the individual and artificially create a legal person.[65]

The person was identified, thus, as a "capable subject", that is, capable of becoming the holder of a legal relationship, as capable of "acquiring" rights, and such capacity stood out as different from the "capacity to act". But, in addition, in this vision of Savigny, the attribution of legal capacity was a matter of law and, for this reason, he could attribute it to entities that were not identified with humans.

Savigny's vision was readily accepted in the legal culture of his time and quickly crossed the borders of the Germanic authors, projecting its influence on the reading of the *Code Civil* doctrine. This fact favoured its diffusion as a manifestation of the general appreciation it received in Europe and America in the 19th century. A singular example of the influence exerted by the reading of the *Code Civil*, in the light of Savigny's conception of the person and legal capacity, can be found in the work of Charles Aubry (1803–1883) and Charles-Frédéric Rau (1803–1877); through this work, it spread at a particularly fast pace in America.

In 1839 Aubry and Rau published a French version of the *Handbuch des Französischen Civilrechts* by Karl Salomon Zachariae (1769–1843), under the title of *Cours de Droit Civil Français par C.-Z. Zachariae*. In it one can appreciate the transition between the old notions of *status* and the more recent ones of *person* and *ability*. Its first part, under the simple rubric *De l'état civil*, opened with a definition of the person, centred on an already accepted vision of assets, linked to capacity in the field of obligations: "A person is a subject capable of binding others with respect to oneself, and of binding oneself with respect to others";[66] and as a sign of a moment of breaks and continuities, it dealt in §54 "On the status of men, civil status, political status"; and although he identified

---

[65] Ibid.

[66] K. S. ZACHARIAE, *Cours de Droit Civil Français par C.-S. Zachariae, Professeur à l'université de Heildelberg. Traduit de l'allemand sur la cinquième édition, et revu et augmenté avec l'agrément de l'auteur par Aubry et Rau*, vol. I, Société Belge de Librairie, Bruselles, 1842, §52, p. 53: "Une personne est une sujet capable d'obliger les autres envers lui, et de s'obliger envers les autres".

Intersentia

29

the old *status* with legal capacity, he did not fail to recall that, in a more restricted sense, it was used to designate family relations.[67]

In its fourth edition, reworked with evident autonomy from Zachariae's work, Savigny's influence on Aubry's and Rau's exposition of the person is notorious. They abandoned the identification of *status* with legal capacity and treated them as two different categories, as indicated by the new heading of the first part, renamed from the previous *De l'état civil*, to: *De l'état et de la capacité juridique*. *Status* was now simply defined as "the position of an individual, considered as a member of the political society or of the family to which he belongs",[68] and legal capacity acquired all the burden of its connection with the notion of subject of law, since it was understood as "the ability to become a subject of rights and obligations."[69] According to the rights it was concerned with, this capacity could be political and civil, so the latter was referring to the enjoyment and exercise of civil rights. It was susceptible to various restrictions, either in terms of the enjoyment or exercise of some civil rights or the power to contract and bind.[70] Discounting the restrictions derived from certain criminal convictions, "The other restrictions are related to physical or moral differences between men. They are established in the interest of those who, due to their age, intellectual infirmity, or excessive prodigality, are more or less absolutely unable to govern their persons or to manage their property properly."[71] This resulted in a patrimonial notion of capacity and its identification with the category of personality itself, "Legal capacity is confused with personality (*caput*). Every being capable of possessing rights and being subject to obligations is a person".[72]

The long and complex historical course of the "status", the "person", and "capacity" led to a situation in which, clearly during the second half of the 19th century, the "person" was conceived as a holder of patrimonial interest, in that it was defined by its "legal capacity", understood as the possibility of acquiring rights and contracting obligations. This was the view that prevailed, with no other to oppose it, until a new notion began to be articulated, rooted in dignity, but this is a story for another time.

---

[67] Ibid., §52, pp. 54–55. "L'etat (status) est la capacité juridique, en vertu de laquelle un individu peut obliger les autres envers lui, et s'obliger envers les autres. Cependant le mot état est encore pris, en droit civil, dans, un sens plus restreint, pour désigner l'ensemble des rapports qui existent entre un individu et une famille".

[68] Ch. AUBRY and Ch. F. RAU, *Cours de Droit Civil Français d'après la méthode de Zachariae*, vol. I, Imprimerie et Librairie Générale de Jurisprudence, Paris, 1869, §52, p. 177.

[69] Ibid., §52, p. 178.

[70] Ibid.

[71] Ibid., §52, pp. 178–179.

[72] Ibid., §52, p. 179.

RESPECT FOR THE WILL OF THE PERSON

Wayne Martin*

1. An Ancient Law Reform and its Ontology 32
2. A Legally Primitive Notion 35
3. *Furiosi voluntas nulla est* 39
4. Will and Law Reform 43

The concept of will plays a role in CRPD Article 12[1] in two different ways: one explicit and one implicit. The concept makes its explicit appearance in the provisions of Article 12 that address the need for *safeguards*. Specifically, CPRD Article 12(4) requires states parties to ensure that "measures relating to the exercise of legal capacity respect the rights, *will* and preferences of the person" (emphasis added). But already in this formulation we can detect the second, implicit reliance on the concept of the will. For this call to respect the will of persons with disabilities pertains specifically to measures concerning the *exercise of legal capacity*. As we shall find in detail below, the very idea of legal capacity itself implicates the concept of the will, as well as a broader *legal doctrine of the will* and *practices of ascription and attestation* in which that concept is embedded. In contemplating the next steps in the ongoing struggle for disability rights (and in understanding some recent setbacks in that struggle), we therefore need to come to terms with the concept of the will – not least because the legal doctrine of the will has long functioned to exclude persons with disabilities from full participation in society and full enjoyment of their rights.

My plan is as follows. I begin in Section 1 with some ancient history, examining one of the oldest recorded law reforms in Europe, together with an episode from the history of its interpretation in early modern times. In these episodes from the history of law reform we can trace the social and legal architecture of an ancient regime of legal capacity in which the concept of the will came to

---

*   PhD in Philosophy, University of California, Berkeley. Professor of Philosophy at the University of Essex.

[1]   UN General Assembly, Convention on the Rights of Persons with Disabilities (CRPD), A/RES/61/106. The CRPD was adopted by the General Assembly on 13 December 2006 and came into force on 3 May 2008.

Intersentia

occupy a crucial place. I then turn in Section 2 to contemporary law in Europe and Latin America, analysing modern civil codes in order to show that and how the concept of will plays a role as a legally primitive notion. In Section 3, I consider ways in which the legal doctrine of the will structures and constrains practices of will-ascription, will-attestation and will-nullification in ways that exclude persons with significant cognitive and psychosocial disabilities from full enjoyment of legal capacity. I conclude in Section 4 by considering the implications of these findings for reform initiatives intended to achieve more inclusive recognition of legal capacity for persons with disabilities, as required under CRPD Article 12.

Before turning to the work at hand, a preliminary terminological observation is in order. In the matters that concern us in what follows, the English language is unusual in using the one word where other languages typically use two. In one familiar sense, to speak of a person's will is to refer narrowly and specifically to a formal legal document (duly signed and witnessed) that relates to the distribution of a person's assets after death. Lawyers sometimes use the phrase "last will and testament" to refer to this distinctive legal instrument. A will in this narrow sense is known as a *testamentum* in Latin, *el testamento* in Spanish, *le testament* in French. But of course we also use the same English word, "will," in a broader and more fundamental sense, corresponding to the term *voluntas* in Latin, *la voluntad* in Spanish, *la volonté* in French. As these translations indicate, this second sense of the word "will" is closely related to the notion of an action being *voluntary*. Indeed as a first approximation we might say that a voluntary action is one that reflects the agent's will (*voluntas*). Both of these two concepts of will figure in the discussion below, but it is important not to confuse them. I shall also be concerned with the relation between these two concepts. In Section 1 we will see how the concept of will (*testamentum*) came to be elaborated in terms of the concept of will (*voluntas*). In Section 2 we will see that the concept of will (*voluntas*) has a distinctive status in modern civil law.

1. AN ANCIENT LAW REFORM AND ITS ONTOLOGY

In the early 6th century BCE, Solon organised a celebrated reform of the laws of Athens. Included among his reforms was a new law concerning inheritance. Writing nearly eight centuries later, Plutarch described Solon's legal innovation, crediting him with the invention of the legal instrument that we now refer to as a person's "last will and testament" (in Latin: *testamentum*; in Spanish: *el testamento*; in French: *le testament*). Here is the key passage from Plutarch's *Life of Solon*:

> He was also famous for his law on wills. Before Solon, you couldn't make a will; the money and the house had to remain in the family of the deceased. By allowing someone, if he does not have children, to give his possessions to whomever he wishes,

Solon gave more value to friendship than to ties of blood, and to favour than to obligation, and transformed wealth into the property of its owners.[2]

Plutarch's *Lives of the Noble Greeks and Romans* was hugely successful and influential, and nowhere more so than in the Spanish-speaking world.[3] The first translation of *Lives* into a western vernacular came already in the 14th century, when Juan Fernandez de Heredia, the Grand Master of the Knights Hospitaller, arranged for a translation into Aragonese. The first translation directly from the original Greek into Castilian Spanish followed in 1551, undertaken by Francisco de Enzinas.[4] Enzinas' translation is expansive and free. The last clause of the passage about wills had occupied just eight words in Plutarch's Greek: *kaì tà chrémata ktémata tõn èchónton époíesen*. Enzinas elaborated this thought as follows:

> In this way, it seemed necessary to establish and confirm the dominion and possession of things, judging that the estate and possessions were the property of the one who possesses them, and that he, as a lord, could do with his things at his will [*à su voluntad*].

My focus in this chapter is not primarily inheritance law and its history – although it is worth remembering that the rights to own and to inherit property figure among the enumerated rights in Article 12. What matters for our purposes here is rather the network of concepts, categories and relationships in terms of which Solon's innovation is articulated and understood, as well as the ontology of legal capacity that it both presupposes and projects.

We can map that structure in three stages. The most prominent concept in these reports on Solon's law reform is certainly that of the will (*testamentum*); the Greek word is *diathéke*, deriving from *diatíthemi*: to place separately, to distribute. The will is of course the now-familiar legal instrument whereby a person provides for the disposition of their property after death. On Plutarch's telling, this concept, and the practices associated with it, emerged with Solon's constitutional innovations in Athens.[5] Legally recognised inheritance itself

---

[2]   PLUTARCH, "Life of Solon," *Lives of the Noble Greeks and Romans*, 21.2.

[3]   A. PÉREZ-JIMÉNEZ, "Plutarch's Fortune in Spain" in S. Xenophontos and K. Oikonomopoulou (eds), *Brill's Companion to the Reception of Plutarch*, Brill, Leiden 2019, pp. 606–21.

[4]   PLUTARCO (1551), *Las Vidas de Illustres y excellentes varones Griegos y Romanos*, transl. Francisco d' Enzinas, Argentina [i.e., Strasbourg], Augustin Frisio. Enzinas was a significant figure in the Protestant Reformation and lived most of his life in exile. He studied Greek with Melanchthon at Wittenberg (where he prepared a Spanish translation of the New Testament) and briefly taught Greek at Cambridge University.

[5]   I set aside here the disputed question as to the reliability of Plutarch's reports. For discussion, see: R. LANE-FOX, "Aspects of Inheritance in the Greek World" (1985) 6 *History of Political Thought*, 208 and D. LEÃO, "Consistency and Criticism in Plutarch's Writings Concerning the Laws of Solon" in J. OPSOMER et al. (eds), *A Versatile Gentleman: Consistency in Plutarch's Writings*, Leuven University Press, Leuven 2016, pp. 243–54.

certainly pre-dates Solon; there are many surviving speeches in which Athenian lawyers quarrel about who should inherit an estate. But the adjudication of those disputes focused on the laws and customs of primogeniture (which varied in their particulars from city to city and over time) and the available evidence (which was often disputed and sometimes forged) about parentage, order of births and marriages. The innovation credited to Solon concerned the novelty of choosing one's heir.

Notice the way in which these explications of Solon's novel concept of the will implicates the further concept of *choice according to one's preferences*. Enzinas describes the new authority to give one's possessions "to whomever one wants" (*aquien quisiesse*). In this we find what we can aptly describe as *the primary essence of the will* (*testamentum*), which is a mechanism for *giving legal force to one's own preferences* in the disposition of one's wealth and possessions after death.

But there is more to the ontology of the will than just this connection between the psychological state of the testator and the legal fate of his estate. Here we come to the second stage of our ontological mapping. Both Plutarch and Enzinas claim that Solon's legal innovation inaugurates a new order, in the form of a new set of relationships between persons and objects, and a new understanding of the status and standing (the mode of being) of those persons and objects. As we have seen, Plutarch reports that the new law on wills (*testamenta*) "transforms wealth into the property of its owners." Enzinas goes further, emphasising the import of this change for the owner of this property, who now, "as a lord [*como señor*] could do with his things at his will." Plutarch's thought seems to be that, prior to the institution of the will (*testamentum*), a person could not properly be said to *own* his estate, since he could not dispose of it as he deemed fit. So what had been simply "useful things" or "wealth," (the Greek is *ktémata*; originally: things that were useful in the household, later money, or a generic term for wealth) now for the first time becomes *chrémata*: property. According to Enzinas, this transformation in the status of objects itself transforms the status of persons as well, bringing with it the new status of lordship. The lord, on Enzinas' 16th century accounting, is defined as someone who is recognised as having the authority to act according to his will (*à su voluntad*).

This new status, however, was not available to all. Here we come to the third and final stage of our mapping. Already inscribed in these early European regimes of legal capacity we find *principles of exclusion*. Some of these exclusionary principles pertain to socio-economic status. Obviously, the new law concerning wills (*testamenta*) could only be used by those who had something to bequeath. This served to exclude not only the unpropertied poor, but also slaves and most women, who lacked ownership rights. Moreover, under Solon's law, only someone who "has no children" (or, as Enzinas has it: "who lacked a legitimate heir") was recognised as having the legal authority to choose who would inherit their estate.[6] For other estate-holders, the principles of male primogeniture continued to apply.

But there is also a second set of exclusions woven into the new regime, and these pertain more to the *psychosocial* than to the socio-economic condition of the testator. For having enunciated this new authority to choose, Solon immediately goes on to curtail it. As Plutarch reports, Solon "did not permit all manner of gifts without restriction or restraint." In particular, no bequests were valid under Solon's law if the will was made under the influence of sickness, or under the influence of drugs, or while imprisoned or under compulsion, or consequent upon "yielding to the persuasions of his wife." And what is the principle that informs this list of exclusions? Plutarch explains that Solon saw these as forces with the power "to pervert a man's reason." Enzinas' ampliative translation goes on to explain that a valid bequest can only be made at a time when the testator is possessed of "healthy judgment" (*sano juicio*). The import is clear: the new testamentary authority to act on one's preferences was to be recognised only in those whose power of reasoning (*logismòn*) was deemed to be intact.

2. A LEGALLY PRIMITIVE NOTION

Let us turn our attention from the ancient to the modern world, and from ancient to modern regimes of legal capacity. Although it has been more than 26 centuries since Solon's law reforms, we find an underlying architecture of legal recognition which exhibits clear continuities with the ancients. In this section I focus on the place of the concept of will (*voluntas*) in the foundations of modern civil law. In the section that follows I consider the modern echoes of Solon's exclusion principles and their bearing on the rights of persons with disabilities.

As our point of re-entry into the modern world, let us come back to CRPD Article 12. As we have seen, the central focus of Article 12 is the concept of legal capacity. Its central normative principle is that persons with disabilities should "enjoy legal capacity on an equal basis with others in all aspects of life" (CRPD Article 12(2)). Despite its centrality to Article 12 and to the Convention as a whole, the concept of legal capacity is not itself defined in the CRPD. However, the UN Committee on the Rights of Persons with Disabilities (hereinafter: the Committee), has aptly emphasised that "[l]egal capacity includes the capacity to

---

[6]   "Has no children," in the Athenian context, effectively means *has no sons*. The application of the principle of male primogeniture to estates where the deceased had only daughters was a chronic source of debate and social instability in the ancient world. Solon's law of wills seems to have been devised in no small part as a legal strategy to resolve this social problem. For a discussion, see R. LANE-FOX, "Aspects of Inheritance in the Greek World" (1985) 6 *History of Political Thought*, 208.

be both a holder of rights and *an actor under the law*."[7] The Committee goes on to elaborate this second, active aspect of legal capacity as follows: "Legal capacity to act under the law recognizes that person as an agent with the power to engage in transactions and create, modify or end legal relationships." In what follows I shall refer to this power as *juridical agency*; I refer to particular exercises of juridical agency as *juridical acts*.[8]

Because juridical agency is so fundamental to legal capacity, and because legal capacity is so central to Article 12, it is worth considering carefully how the notion of juridical agency is constructed in modern law. Although the concept is highly abstract, it plays a fundamental role in structuring modern law and legal practice. Informally, we can think of the concept as the genus whose species include such actions as marrying, divorcing, concluding a contract, instructing a solicitor, and indeed making a will (*testamentum*). In each of these cases we find an instance of "creating, modifying or ending" legal relationships; and in each case we find the essential structure that we found articulated in Solon's law of wills (*testamenta*): a person's choice in accordance with their own preferences takes on legal standing and force.

So how is this overarching concept formally treated in modern law? One good way to find out is to look to modern civil codes. While such codes are by no means homogenous, a common conceptual structure recurs. As a first example, consider the Dutch Civil Code. The Dutch term for juridical act is *rechtshandeling*. It is defined in Article 3.3:

> A juridical act [*rechtshandeling*] requires the will [*wil*] of the acting person to establish a specific legal effect, which will must be expressed through a statement [*verklaring*] of the acting person.

The first thing to notice here is the use of the word "will" (*wil*) in the *definiens*. Under the Dutch Civil Code, every juridical act requires the will of the legal actor to establish a specific legal effect; moreover, it requires that this will be expressed through a statement (*verklaring*) by the person who is acting. The key point here is that the overarching and legally fundamental concept of a juridical act *is itself defined* in terms of the concepts of "will" and "expression of will." We shall soon see that this can already have significant exclusionary consequences. But what matters for present purposes is a second feature of the Dutch approach. For while the concept of will is *used in the definition* of this fundamental legal term, it is *never itself defined* in the Code. On this basis we can aptly describe

---

[7]   UN Committee on the Rights of Persons with Disabilities. General Comment No. 1: Article 12 (Equal recognition before the law), eleventh session, April 11th, 2014, CRPD/C/GC/1, para. 12; (emphasis added).

[8]   For a history of the term "juridical act," see N. DAVRADOS, "A Louisiana Theory of Juridical Acts" (2020) 80:4 *Louisiana Law Review*, 1119.

the concept of will as a *legal primitive* in Dutch law: it is used to define a legally fundamental concept but it is never itself given a legal definition. Will is legal bedrock.

Let us consider a second variation. The first Book of the German *Bürgerliches Gesetzbuch* (hereinafter: BGB) constitutes its "General Part."[9] Unlike the Dutch code, the BGB does not provide general positive definitions of the terms that concern us here. And while it does on occasion use the term *"Rechtshandlung"* (this would be the direct German correlate of the Dutch, *rechtshandeling*), this term does not play a significant role in the BGB. Despite these differences, however, we find a variation on the same commitments that we found in the Dutch code.

The initial Divisions (*Abschnitte*) of the BGB effectively lay out an ontology for German civil law. What are the kinds of entities with which the law concerns itself? It deals with persons (both natural and artificial); this is the focus of the First Division. It also deals with things (*Sache*) and animals – the focus of the Second Division. But every bit as fundamental to the ontology of the law is a third category of legally recognised entities: *Rechtsgeschäfte* or "legal transactions." This is the focus of the Third Division of BGB Book 1. The paradigmatic example of a legal transaction is signing a contract, but the term encompasses a range of other broadly financial or commercial actions such as taking out a mortgage, transferring ownership, forgiving a debt or even disclaiming an inheritance. (See BGB §§1822 and 1825 for lists of legal actions that are included under this heading.) So once again we have here a generic term. Moreover, the treatment of legal transactions in the BGB has broader implications for other areas of civil law, since the conditions associated with legal transactions are also used to restrict other exercises of legal capacity. (See for example, BGB §1304.) So the concept has far-reaching significance for articulating a regime of legal capacity.

Unlike the Dutch Civil Code, however, the BGB offers no explicit positive definition of this generic term. Instead, its meaning is effectively constructed contextually – and negatively. Let us attend to how this works in detail. The first Title of the Third Division of BGB Book 1 carries the title *Geschäftsfähigkeit*. This term is sometimes translated as "capacity to contract," but this is misleading. The term for "contract" in the BGB is *Vertrag*, which becomes the focus only in Title 3 et seq. *Geschäftsfähigkeit* is a broader legal concept, perhaps best rendered as "capacity to transact" – i.e., *the capacity to engage in legal transactions*. Here again, however, the BGB offers no positive definition.[10] What we find instead is a series of axioms that govern its use. The very first such axiom appears in §104,

---

[9]   *Bürgerliches Gesetzbuch* (BGB), in the version promulgated on January 2nd, 2002, *Bundesgesetzblatt* I, p. 42, 2909; 2003 I p. 738 (last amended by Article 3 of the Act of July 16th, 2021, *Bundesgezetsblatt* I p. 2947).

[10] On the absence of a definition of *"Rechsgeschäft"* from the BGB, see N. DAVRADOS, "A Louisiana Theory of Juridical Acts" (2020) 80:4 *Louisiana Law Review*, 1119, 1137.

and is formulated negatively. That is, what is defined is not the positive concept of *capacity to transact*, but instead its negative correlate: *incapacity to transact*.

> §104 Incapacity to transact. A person is incapable of transacting if: (1) he is not yet seven years old, (2) he is in a state of pathological mental disturbance that precludes the free exercise of will [*die freie Willensbestimmung*], unless the state by its nature is a temporary one.

The following section goes on to introduce the concept of a *Willenserklärung* – literally a "making clear of [one's] will," or more colloquially: a "statement or declaration of intent." Notice the three layers of conceptual structure here: legal (trans)actions are fundamental to the ontology of German law; legal (trans) actions themselves require agents who are capable of such transactions; in order to engage in a legal transaction, an agent must exercise their will. Although the legal details vary between the Dutch and German codes, the dependence on the concept of will recurs. And what is an "exercise of will"? The term is not defined in the BGB; once again we have reached legal bedrock.

This is not the place to undertake an exhaustive survey of civil codes, but it is perhaps worth mentioning a few other examples, particularly from the Latin American context. Article 49 of the Cuban Civil Code defines a juridical act as "an express or implied lawful manifestation of will, which produces the effects provided by law, consisting of the creation, modification or termination of a juridical relation."[11] The Peruvian Civil Code (Article 140) defines a juridical act as a "manifestation of will destined to create, regulate, modify or extinguish legal relations."[12] So in both of these cases we find variants of the direct conceptual dependence on the concept of the will, just as we found in the Dutch code.

Before turning to our next topic, it will be worth pausing over one instructive variation from the pattern that we have considered so far. The codes that we have examined to this point have one thing in common: they all rely on, but do not define, the concept of will. The Argentinian Civil Code varies from this pattern in two respects.[13] The first is incidental: rather than defining a juridical act with reference to the agent's *will*, the Argentinian code relies in its definition on the concept of a *voluntary act*:

> Art 259: Juridical act. A juridical act is a lawful voluntary act whose immediate purpose is the acquisition, modification or termination of legal relationships or situations.

---

[11] Cuban Civil Code (Código Civil de Cuba). Ley 59, de 17 de julio de 1987. Gaceta Oficial de la República de Cuba, 15 de octubre de 1987, Republic of Cuba.

[12] Peruvian Civil Code (Código Civil peruano). Decreto Legislativo N° 295, el 24 de julio de 1984, November 14th, 1984, Republic of Peru (la última modificación el 24 de julio 2021, que incorporó el artículo 2017-A).

[13] Argentinian Civil Code (Código Civil y Comercial de la Nación). Ley 26.994, de 7 de octubre de 2014. Boletín Oficia Republica Argentinal, 8 de octubre de 2014, núm. 32985, Argentina, p. 1.

The second difference is more substantial: the Argentinian Code then proceeds to provide a definition of this term.

> Art 260: Voluntary act. A voluntary act is an act executed with discernment, intent and freedom, which is manifested by an external fact.

We will have reason to return to this Argentinian provision in the next section. For now, the key point to note is that in order to be legally recognised in Argentina as acting voluntarily in a matter, a person's act must be characterised by "discernment, intent and freedom." The Argentinian code goes on to specify that an act is "involuntary on the grounds of lack of discernment" when, at the time of acting, the person is either (i) a child; or (ii) an adult who is "deprived of reason" (Article 261).

3. *FURIOSI VOLUNTAS NULLA EST*

Let us pause to take stock. We started by tracing to the ancient world a regime of legal capacity which makes it possible for the preferences of an ordinary individual (i.e., not a king or a designated legislator) to take on legal force and standing. We then saw how that ancient regime of legal capacity was articulated in early modern times in terms of the concept of a person's will (*voluntas*), and that the concept of will itself now occupies a prominent place at the foundation of all civil law. In this section, our task is to elicit and document a consequence that is already implicit in these initial findings. To hazard a first formulation: *the outer boundaries of a modern regime of legal capacity are set in part by its practices of will-ascription.*

Before considering this point in detail, we should note first that the absence of a legal definition of the concept of will in most modern civil codes certainly does not mean that the term lacks meaning in those jurisdictions. Formal definitions are, after all, only one (and an essentially derivative) method for fixing meaning. But the absence of a formal definition does show that the meaning of this foundational legal notion must somehow be determined outside those civil codes themselves. Where does this happen? Some might be inclined to look to philosophy or psychology or even theology for the answer; each of these discourses has its own ways of engaging the concept of the will – and its own controversies surrounding it. But if we want to know the meaning of the term will *in law*, then we need to look to the legal practices of will-ascription, will-attestation and (as we shall see shortly) *will-nullification* that prevail in a particular jurisdiction.[14] For it is ultimately by being embedded in these distinctive

---

[14] These practices are undoubtedly shaped, often profoundly, by debates and developments in philosophy, psychology and theology – and vice versa. The history of these intertwinements has yet to receive the attention that it merits. But the legal practices nonetheless also operate according to their own canon, as will become clear presently.

practices that the legal concept of will sustains its distinctive meaning. These practices are themselves governed both by explicit legal principles and by what I shall refer to here as *legal ethics*, by which I mean the habits, customs and mores that serve to define responsible legal practice.

The basic unit of analysis in this domain is what I shall call *will-ascription*: the act of ascribing a particular will in a particular matter to a particular person at a particular time. Example: if I answer "I do" in the appropriate context at a wedding ceremony, the presiding official ascribes to me the will to marry the person with whom I am exchanging vows. In so doing, the official assembles one of the elements of the juridical act of marrying. Will-ascription is often accompanied in legal practice by one or another form of *will-attestation*. In our example, the official's signature on the marriage certificate attests to the fact that the bride and groom manifested the will to marry one another.

At this juncture there are two points which, while perhaps obvious, nonetheless need to be emphasised. First, it is important to recognise that a will, in the sense relevant in law, is something distinct from a mere wish or a want, and that the ascription of a will to a person must go beyond a determination that the person *desires* a particular object or outcome. We can appreciate this point by thinking of the mundane act of consumer shopping. From a legal perspective, the act of purchasing a consumer product is a juridical act; the sale itself takes the legal form of a contract in which the purchaser agrees to pay a particular price in exchange for a particular object. In order for such a sale to proceed, both parties must *manifest the will* to effect the exchange. But of course *willing* to purchase a particular consumer object is not the same as simply *desiring* the object, or *wishing* that one owned it – as anyone shopping with limited funds can attest! On any particular shopping trip, I might *desire to purchase* a whole host of things, but I might *manifest the will to purchase* only one of them – or none at all. In the particular context of shopping, one manifests one's will not by expressing a desire or wish but by *making or accepting an offer*.

This in turn relates to a second point that is in its own way obvious, but perhaps also easy to miss: every act of will-ascription or will-attestation involves an act of *interpretation*. In the context of shopping, an offer might be made orally, or in writing, or in the gesture of handing over money, by clicking on a website or by touching one's ear at an auction. These actions are interpreted as manifestations of will in light of the prevailing local customs and norms of exchange, the meaning of words in the relevant natural language, the conventions regarding the meaning of symbols on a page or screen, etc. And of course the same point holds more generally: a particular will or intention is ascribed and recognised through an act of interpreting the behaviour (including, but not limited to, the linguistic behaviour) of the person to whom the will is ascribed.

To say that will-ascription involves interpretation certainly does not mean that anything goes. On the contrary, the practice of ascribing a will to a person is governed by a number of principles which we can think of collectively as the legal doctrine of the will. The major headings of this doctrine exhibit considerable consistency across jurisdictions, despite a number of significant variations in the details.[15] Interestingly, its central principles are formulated negatively, with the most striking example being the legal doctrines concerning the *vices of the will*, themselves closely related to the *vices of consent*. These so-called "vices" are factors which, when present, compromise or degrade (vitiate) the quality and legal status of an act of willing; in the limiting case they preclude the ascription of a will altogether.

The core list of these vices has remained largely the same across historical time and jurisdictional boundaries, comprising error, fraud, threat and coercion. If the presiding official at the wedding discovers that I have been coerced into agreeing to marriage, or that my intended bride has been secretly replaced with another woman, then he can no longer attest to my will to marry the person who stands at the altar. Depending on the jurisdiction, a purported juridical act of marriage under such conditions is either void or voidable. The Cuban civil code expresses the point concisely, describing juridical acts as voidable when "the manifestation of the will is vitiated by error, fraud or threat." In its catalogue of specific vices, the Argentinian code stipulates that an essential error of fact "vitiates the will and causes the nullity of the act." That is, where an act of willing is sufficiently compromised by vice, the juridical act of which it forms an essential part is nullified. Notice the logic at work here. Civil codes may not typically offer a *definition* of the concept of will, but in systematically elaborating the distinctive vices associated with the will, they both determine the concept and constrain the practices of will-attestation.

These negative legal principles regarding the vices of the will themselves have positive correlates in legal ethics. Consider the circumstance of a notary who is engaged by her client to certify a deed of gift of some property. A responsible legal professional acting in such circumstances will be alert for signs that her client is acting under coercion or duress, in the grip of an error, or as a victim of threat or fraud.[16] She will take positive steps designed to elicit such signs if she suspects that any of these factors may be present. Confronted with indicators that one or another vice of the will is at work, the ethical notary will adjust her practice appropriately. She may have a legal obligation to report or investigate such matters. But over and above any such obligations, the responsible notary will exercise particular care before attesting to her client's will in the matter. For example, if she suspects that her client is being coercively controlled by a

---

[15] For discussion, see the essays and case studies collected in R. SEFTON-GREEN (ed), *Mistake, Fraud and Duties to Inform in European Contract Law*, Cambridge University Press, Cambridge 2005.

[16] R. A. CONSTANTINO CAYCHO, "The Flag of Imagination: Peru's New Reform on Legal Capacity for Persons with Intellectual and Psychosocial Disabilities and the Need for New Understandings in Private Law" (2020) 14 *The Age of Human Rights Journal*, 155.

family member, she may take steps to meet with the client apart from that family member, or in the presence of a trusted supporter, seeking to ensure that the manifestation of will is indeed freely given and genuinely expresses the client's intention in the matter. Such steps are partly constitutive of ethical conduct in the practices of the responsible notary. The same point applies, *mutatis mutandis*, in the many other professions (solicitor, estate-planner, real estate agent, stockbroker, hospice admissions officer, etc.) which involve attesting to the will of a client in a matter.[17]

But the catalogue of vices by no means exhausts the legal doctrine of the will, nor does it provide a complete accounting of the practices and boundary conditions of will-attestation. A further set of principles are built into the very foundations of civil law that we examined above. Here we must recall the ancient principles of exclusion that we found at work already in Solon's laws, exclusions which restricted recognition of legal capacity to those whose reason was not "perverted," and who were acting at a time when they were possessed of "healthy judgment." In the ancient world, principles of exclusion were incorporated explicitly into the legal doctrine of the will in the Justinian Code (529–534 CE) at *Digest* 29.2.47: *Furiosi voluntas nulla est*. This Justinian axiom is difficult to translate with deference to modern sensibilities. Black's classic legal dictionary is undoubtedly dated, but captures something of its raw force: *The madman has no will*.[18]

The Justinian axiom reverberates through subsequent centuries of law reform and codification. We hear one modern echo in the Argentinian Civil code, which (as we have seen) recognises an act of will only where discernment is present, and recognises discernment only in those who are not "deprived of reason." It is important to appreciate the cascade of legal consequences that immediately follow. Where there is no discernment, there is no voluntary act; where there is no voluntary act there is no juridical act; where there is no juridical act there can be *no exercise of legal capacity*. In this way, the doctrine of the will, together with the practices of will-attestation that it regulates, serves to restrict recognition of full legal capacity, leaving some – particularly those with significant cognitive or psychosocial disabilities – outside its ambit altogether.

The details of the legal doctrine of the will vary by jurisdiction, and practices of will-attestation vary both across and within jurisdictions. As a result, the boundary conditions for recognition of full legal capacity can be more or less

---

[17] See R. A. CONSTANTINO CAYCHO and R. A. BREGAGLIO LAZARTE, "Safeguards for the Exercise of Legal Capacity by Persons with Disabilities: A Form of Justified Paternalism" in this volume.

[18] H. C. BLACK, *A Law Dictionary: Containing Definitions of the Terms and Phrases of American and English Jurisprudence, Ancient and Modern*, 2nd ed, West Publishing, St Paul, Minnesota, USA 1910, p. 530. A more literal rendering of the Latin might be: "The will of the furiously mad person is null [i.e., nothing, void]."

expansive, and more or less well defined. The Argentinian boundary is marked with the broad and rather ill-defined concept of being deprived of reason. But in other jurisdictions the boundary is marked differently. Consider again the Dutch code, which recognises a juridical act only where the acting person *wills to establish a specific legal effect.* This principle shapes and constrains the practices of will-ascription and will-attestation in the Netherlands. If a Dutch official is called upon to attest to a person's will in a matter, part of his role must be to determine whether the person wills to establish the specific legal effect in question – i.e., whether it is that person's intention to create, modify or terminate a particular binding legal relationship. In attesting to the presence of such a will, the official attests to the fact that the person in question *understands* the legal effect in question, and indeed has some understanding of what it means to be party to a binding legal relationship. In the absence of such an understanding, the person cannot be said to have the requisite will, so no juridical act can be recognised. The upshot: there is a *cognitive load* associated with legally attestable willing in the Netherlands. Only those with the capacity to carry that load are recognised as juridical agents. For persons with sufficiently severe cognitive or psychosocial disabilities, these legal principles, laid deep in the foundations of civil law and its history, can create an insurmountable bar to entry into the domain of full legal capacity.

4. WILL AND LAW REFORM

The adoption of the CRPD by the UN General Assembly in 2006 helped to create a legal and political environment that spawned law reform movements all over the world. The aims of these movements are diverse, but one common theme and challenge has been to devise more inclusive regimes of legal capacity in order to foster greater respect for the human rights of persons with disabilities. In its most ambitious form, the aim has been to eliminate all barriers to the recognition of full legal capacity for all persons, regardless of disability.[19] One important strategy in these movements has been to use strategic litigation and legislation to overturn or dismantle systems of plenary guardianship. But this negative moment goes hand-in-hand with a variety of positive initiatives, particularly those which have sought to establish systems of support for persons

---

[19] For an example of the most ambitious aim, see para. 14 of UN Committee on the Rights of Persons with Disabilities. General Comment No. 1: Article 12 (Equal recognition before the law), eleventh session, April 11th, 2014, CRPD/C/GC/1: "Legal capacity is an inherent right accorded to all people, including persons with disabilities. ... Legal capacity means that all people, including persons with disabilities, have legal standing and legal agency simply by virtue of being human."

with disabilities in their exercise of legal capacity, as required under CRPD Article 12(3). So what lessons does the foregoing analysis hold for this reform agenda? And what strategies does it suggest for those seeking to advance it?

In addressing these questions, we can take our bearings from our two principal findings: that the concept of will has long played a fundamental role in defining regimes of legal capacity, and that the boundary conditions for modern regimes of legal capacity are determined in part by practices of will-ascription, will-attestation and will-nullification that exclude persons with significant cognitive or psychosocial disabilities from full participation in those regimes. It is important to appreciate the extent to which these two findings constrain the strategic options for reform. Under prevailing regimes of legal capacity, juridical agency is recognised only where a particular will in a particular matter can be ascribed to the juridical actor. If the goal of law reform is to remove all barriers to the recognition of universal legal capacity, then either (a) this link between legal capacity and the will must be broken; or (b) we must revise our practices of will-ascription and will-attestation, along with the legal doctrine of the will and the principles of legal ethics that govern them. The two strategies are not necessarily exclusive, but they do point in rather different directions, and present different challenges and opportunities. By way of conclusion, it will be useful to consider the choice between these two strategic options as it pertains to a notable episode in the recent reform movement.

In Bulgaria, the *Natural Persons and Support Measures Bill* was introduced in the National Assembly in the Summer of 2016, following a series of national consultations about how to bring Bulgarian law into compliance with the CRPD.[20] The aim of the proposed legislation (which to date has not been adopted) was to abolish the existing system of guardianship in Bulgaria, replacing it with an innovative system of supported decision-making.[21] The original draft bill was notable, in part, for its explicit inclusion of language drawn directly from the CRPD, which Bulgaria had ratified in 2012. In particular, the bill enumerated a set of principles that were to regulate all supported decision-making measures in Bulgaria. In the initial draft of this list of principles, the second principle was formulated as follows: зачитане на волята и предпочитанията на подкрепения – *respect for the will and preferences of the supported person*. The term for "will" here is волята (pronounced "volyata") which is a direct etymological variant of the Latin, *voluntas*.

---

[20]   Natural Persons And Support Measures Bill. Introduced August 4th, 2016. Available in Bulgarian at: https://parliament.bg/bills/43/602-01-48.pdf.

[21]   N. SHABANI and M. DIMITROVA, "Changing the Paradigm of Substituted Decision-Making in Bulgaria: The Tipping Point" in this volume.

The incorporation of this principle into the legal architecture of the Bulgarian bill would seem to be natural and fitting. Systems of decision-making support are a prime example of "measures that relate to the exercise of legal capacity." And as we have seen, CRPD Article 12(4) requires safeguards to ensure that such measures respect the rights, will and preferences of the person. Moreover, the Bulgarian Assembly had at this stage already ratified the CRPD, which under Bulgarian law meant that it already had pre-emptive priority over any domestic legislation with which it conflicted. So the proposed language in effect served to reaffirm a principle to which Bulgaria was already legally committed. Despite all this, the inclusion of the draft second principle engendered resistance in Sofia, and in the end a compromise was sought. In the bill that was finally submitted in the Bulgarian Assembly in August 2016, the word "волята" was replaced with 'желанията' (zhelaniyata) – meaning "wishes" or "desires." As a result, the revised principle intended to govern the provision of supported decision-making in Bulgaria was ultimately formulated as follows: "зачитане на желанията и предпочитанията на подкрепения" – *respect for the wishes and preferences of the supported person.* Although the *Natural Persons and Support Measures Bill* has not itself become law, this revised principle was ultimately adopted by the Bulgarian Assembly as Article 66.5 of the *Persons with Disabilities Act* (2018).[22]

In thinking about this episode in the history of CRPD-inspired law reform, it is worth reflecting first on the resistance to the original drafting of this principle in the bill. The resistance is noteworthy in part because it falls outside the familiar controversies that so often characterise this area of law and public policy. Debates about reform in this area typically run in familiar grooves of "*respect v protect.*" One side argues for greater respect for the autonomy of persons with disabilities while the other side argues for protective measures that may compromise autonomy. The proponents of greater autonomy reply that the protective measures are unacceptably paternalistic, and the debate unfolds.[23] In this instance, however, it is clear that we are outside of these grooves. After all, if one's concern was that the original principle of "respect for will and preferences" might preclude appropriate protective measures when necessary, then one would hardly agree to the principle of respect for *wishes and preferences* as an acceptable compromise. So what motivated the resistance to the original framing?

---

[22]   Persons With Disabilities Act (Закон за хората с увреждания). December 11th, 2018. State Gazette no. 105, December 12th, 2018, Bulgaria, pp. 3–26.

[23]   See for example, P. Appelbaum, "Saving the UN Convention on the Rights of Persons with Disabilities – From Itself" (2019) 18:I *World Psychiatry*, 1, together with the response by G. Newton-Howes and S. Gordon, "Who Controls your Future?" (2020) 54:II *Australian and New Zealand Journal of Psychiatry*, 134.

If nothing else, the analysis undertaken above helps to make sense of this. From the perspective of the legal establishment, the original language of the Bulgarian bill challenged a long-standing, deeply entrenched, but often unstated assumption. Within the context of the prevailing regime of legal capacity, it was simply assumed that the people who were subject to guardianship orders were not capable of having a will of their own. As Shabani and Dimitrova explain in their contribution to this volume, "According to conservative legal doctrine, will is mainly inherent to a rational person".[24] In a potent illustration of the continuing afterlife of the Justianian axiom, one Bulgarian legal professional expressed the point bluntly in private conversation, saying simply: "*Those people don't have a will.*" In seeking to establish a principle of respect for the will of persons with cognitive and psychosocial disabilities, the reform movement was working against the grain of principles and practices of exclusion that are deeply embedded in civil law and its history. Moreover, these exclusionary practices themselves have an established legal rationale: if willing has cognitive prerequisites, then there will inevitably be forms of impairment that preclude ascription of will.

If our analysis in this way helps to make sense of the resistance to the original drafting of the Bulgarian principle, what can it teach us about the emancipatory potential of the compromise language? And more importantly: what can it tell us about the steps that need to be taken to realise that potential? In considering these questions, much comes to depend on which of the two reform strategies are adopted in seeking to achieve an inclusive regime of legal capacity. Is the strategy to dismantle the longstanding nexus of legal capacity, juridical agency and will? Or is the strategy to leave that entrenched interdependency in place while developing more inclusive practices of will-ascription and will-attestation?

In principle, the Bulgarian compromise might be put to work in the service of either of these strategies. On the first approach, the strategy must be to delink legal capacity from the requirement of a manifestation of will, making it possible to recognise juridical agency on the basis of a person's manifest wishes and preferences. In order for such a strategy to realise its potential, however, this delinking strategy will require far-reaching revisions elsewhere in civil law. The concept of will may have been excised from the principles governing Bulgarian supported decision-making, but it retains a prominent place elsewhere in Bulgarian law. Consider two notable examples: Article 20 of the Bulgarian *Obligations and Contracts Act* stipulates that "the actual common

---

[24] N. Shabani and M. Dimitrova, "Changing the Paradigm of Substituted Decision-Making in Bulgaria: The Tipping Point" in this volume.

Respect for the Will of the Person

will of the parties shall be sought in interpreting a contract."[25] Article 31 of the same Act establishes that a contract shall be subject to invalidation if "upon conclusion of the contract the person was not able to understand it or was not able to guide his acts." (It is noteworthy that even in the revisions to contract law that were proposed under the *Natural Persons and Support Measures Bill*, these provisions of the *Obligations and Contracts Act* were retained.) We can recognise in these provisions the entrenched *status quo ante*: the law as we have it recognises a contract (or any other juridical act) only where it attributes a will; and the law provides for nullification of juridical acts in circumstances where understanding is absent. As long as such provisions remain unchanged, the first strategy of reform remains incomplete. In order for all such provisions to be changed, civil law as we know it would require a thoroughgoing transformation.

The alternative strategy is to leave in place the traditional dependence of legal capacity on the concept of will, and to focus reform efforts instead on changes to the practices that sustain the ascription and attestation of will in cases where it has, in the past, been pre-emptively denied. There is more than one way in which this alternative strategy might be pursued. One possibility is to exploit the distinctive status of the concept of will as a largely undefined legal primitive. Precisely because the concept lacks an agreed legal definition, its meaning is open to ongoing legal development. Under prevailing conceptions of the will in legal practice and legal ethics, the will is understood to have cognitive prerequisites: only someone with the right *logismòn* is understood to be capable of willing. The good news here is that the history of philosophy, psychology and theology is filled with examples of *non-cognitive* conceptions of the will: Martin Luther, Thomas Hobbes and Arthur Schopenhauer each offer leads that are worth exploring.

Alternatively, the prevailing cognitive understanding of the will might be retained along with its entrenched place in the foundations in civil law, with the strategy for achieving greater inclusivity shifting to strategies for *cognitive load-sharing*. On this approach, the Bulgarian principle of respect for wishes and preferences would need to become the starting point and touchstone for an interpretative process that culminates in recognising an actionable will of the person who is being supported.[26] Exploiting this lead requires the development of practices whereby the cognitive load intrinsic to willing is carried jointly

---

[25]   Obligations And Contracts Act (Закон за задълженията и договорите), November 22nd, 1950, State Gazette (Държавен Вестник) no. 2, December 5th, 1950, Bulgaria (last amended on April 27th, 2021, State Gazette n. 35).

[26]   For a discussion, see W. Martin, "Recognition of the Will," in M. Congdon and T. Khurana (eds), *The Philosophy of Recognition: Expanded Perspectives on a Fundamental Concept*, Routledge, New York, forthcoming 2024.

between the supporting and supported person. Here the good news is that cognitive load-sharing does not need to be invented from scratch. It is a process that happens every day in the many professions (solicitor, estate planner, real estate agent, stockbroker, hospice admissions officer, etc.) in which the more-or-less inchoate wishes and preferences of a client are given a form that provides the basis for juridical action that is carried out for and in the name of the client. It is also a process that in recent years has been investigated intensively by philosophers, sociologists and cognitive scientists, so once again there are research foundations upon which to build. But much remains to be done in seeking to draw on these research findings in devising novel legal instruments which, like Solon's wills (*testamenta*), serve the function of giving legal force to a person's preferences.[27]

---

[27] An earlier version of this chapter was presented as an invited lecture at the University of Cork, Republic of Ireland. I am grateful to the organisers and participants of that event, and to the many friends and colleagues who have helped me along the way in exploring the materials discussed herein. Among them I would like to thank Joel Anderson, Matthew Burch, Sándor Gurbai, Beatrice Han-Pile, Sabine Michalowski, Alex Ruck Keene, Violin Radev, Nadya Shabani, Daniel Shipsides, Dahlia Torres, Adrian Ward and Daniel Watts. Emily Fitton and Margot Kuylen assisted in preparation of the manuscript. Particular thanks go to Michael Bach and Renato Antonio Constantino Caycho, who have both been extraordinarily generous in sharing their time and insight and expertise, and without whom the paper would never have been written at all.

DISABILITY AND INTERSECTIONALITY

The Construction of Vulnerability in Sexual and Reproductive Matters

Constanza López Radrigán[*]

1. Introduction 49
2. Intersectional Violence and Discrimination............................ 52
3. Legal Capacity and Construction of Vulnerability..................... 56
   3.1. Sexual Choices 56
   3.2. Reproductive Choices 58
   3.3. Institutionalised Settings..................................... 60
4. Conclusions... 61

1. INTRODUCTION

This chapter aims to analyse the construction of vulnerability in sexual and reproductive matters within the framework of the intersections between gender and disability. To this end, research with a feminist perspective and instruments of the international human rights system will be reviewed. At first, the concepts of violence, discrimination and intersectionality in the context of the specific situations experienced by women and girls in relation to their disability and legal capacity will be discussed. Subsequently, the dynamics of constructing vulnerability will be described in three areas: sexual choices, reproductive choices and institutionalised environments. Finally, an intersectional perspective is proposed as a roadmap for helping to advance realisation of Article 12 of the Convention on the Rights of Persons with Disabilities (hereinafter UNCRPD). An intersectional perspective deepens the understanding of legal capacity and the exercise of relational autonomy in consideration with diverse socio-historically produced categories.

---

[*] Doctoral candidate in Interdisciplinary Studies on Thought, Culture and Society at Universidad Valparaíso, Chile. Fellow of the National Agency for Research and Development of Chile (2019-21191264) and postgraduate student at the MICARE Institute for Care Research, ANID Millennium Scientific Initiative Program (ICS2019_024).

Intersentia

Since the 1960s, Anglo-Saxon activists have politically challenged the dominant bio-medical definitions of disability. They demanded independent and inclusive life in the community,[1] along with the freedom of choice and the ability to exercise control over the decisions that affected their lives, with the maximum degree of self-determination and interdependence with society. They promoted the creation of forms of support that would promote the full exercise of their rights and the construction of facilities that would conform to universal design principles.

Thus, they coined and shaped what is now known as *the comprehensive social model of disability*, through which the problems commonly associated with disability come to be seen as the result of social barriers.[2] In this way, disability emerged as a social category of a life worth living. Also, a socio-political field of study emerged which problematised intersecting axes of oppression. Consequently, progress was made during the 1980s in academic studies that conceived disability as a product of a particular type of social organisation, namely industrial capitalism,[3] and which drew from socio-critical and historical interpretations linked to political economy.

Along with the aforementioned developments, critical disability studies have considered the political, ontological and theoretical complexity of the category of disability and its links to other identifications, interrogating its psychic, cultural and social production.[4] In this regard, the social model distinction between "impairment" – as a value-neutral embodied characteristic – and "disability" – as socially constructed discriminatory norms – has been criticised. It has been stated that in this binary formulation the social model risks ignoring the material-semiotic complexity of the multiple interactions between the body and culture, nature and society, sex and gender, impairment and disability.[5] Likewise, critical feminist perspectives within disability social movements made visible during the 1990s the androcentric discourse that had silenced the experiences born of inequality, violence and medicalisation of disability specifically in association with gender. As a result, feminist disability studies emerged in the Anglo-Saxon context, which later gave rise to "functional diversity" feminism.[6] This is based on the Spanish model of functional diversity, which eliminates the

---

[1] Committee on the Rights of Persons with Disabilities (CRPD Committee), *General Comment No. 5. General comment No.5 on Article 19 – the right to live independently and be included in the community*, CRPD/C/GC/5, 27 October 2017.

[2] M. Montenegro, "La esterilización de menores de edad en situación de discapacidad intelectual" (2019) 37 *Revista De Derecho Privado*, pp. 85–117.

[3] M. Lopez, "Modelos teóricos e investigación en el ámbito de la discapacidad. Hacia la incorporación de la experiencia personal" (2006) 16 *Revista Docencia e investigación*, pp. 215–40.

[4] D. Goodley, *Disability Studies. Theorizing disablism and ableism*, Routledge, New York 2014.

[5] C. Kong, "Constructing female sexual and reproductive agency in mental capacity law" (2019) 66 *International Journal of Law and Psychiatry*, pp. 1–10.

[6] M. S. Arnau, "Políticas eugenésicas y derechos reproductivos. Una mirada desde la bioética (feminista) de/desde la diversidad funcional" (2017) 2 *Filanderas: Revista Interdisciplinar de Estudios Feministas*, pp. 29–51.

negative associations with disability and criticises the functional standard that has characterised some of the social model's derivations. Instead, it emphasises the intrinsic and extrinsic dignity of the life of every human being, as an imperfect and unique being who is recognised as a human singularity regardless of functional, physical or psychosocial differences.[7]

Girls and women with disabilities constitute a heterogeneous group that includes those of indigenous, ethnic, religious or racial origin; refugees, asylum seekers or displaced persons; those who are deprived of liberty in hospitals, residential institutions, juvenile or correctional centres and prisons; those in a situation of poverty or with multiple disabilities who require high levels of support; those who self-identify as lesbian, bisexual, and transgender, as well as intersex persons.[8] These groups have not achieved social, economic, cultural and political equality but have faced multiple forms of discrimination and barriers to their full inclusion in society and development, and in general find themselves in a worse position than women and men without disabilities. Girls and women with disabilities are twice as likely to live in poverty or lack sufficient and nutritious food; three times more likely to have unmet health care needs or not be able to read or write; and two times less likely to be employed, to use the Internet or – in case of being employed – to hold positions of power.[9] It has also been documented that to achieve an adequate standard of living comparable to that of others, individuals with disabilities must incur additional expenses, representing a particular disadvantage for children and older women with disabilities who live in extreme poverty or destitution.[10] In addition to environmental and attitudinal barriers against disability, in access to employment and justice as in cases related to sexual violence, the specific influence of gender is an added marker for disadvantage faced by people with disabilities. For example, sexual violence against women with disabilities is greater than against other women and is exacerbated by socio-economic conditions, sexual and gender orientation, identity and expression; race, and/or ethnicity.[11] Specifically, sexual abuse by male professionals in charge of providing support is often sustained over time, as well as domestic violence, given the economic, physical or emotional dependence on caregivers.[12]

---

[7] See M. Montenegro (n. 2).

[8] CRPD Committee, *General Comment No. 3 on women and girls with disabilities*, CRPD/C/GC/3, 2 September 2016.

[9] UN, Department of Economic and Social Affairs, "Disability and Development Report. Realizing the Sustainable Development Goals by, for and with persons with disabilities 2018", 2019. Available at <https://social.un.org/publications/UN-Flagship-Report-Disability-Final.pdf> accessed 26.03.2023.

[10] CRPD Committee, *General Comment No. 6 on equality and non-discrimination*, CRPD/C/GC/6, 26 April 2018.

[11] M. P. Cruz, "Mujeres con discapacidad y su derecho a la sexualidad" (2004) 22 *Revista Política y Cultura*, pp. 147–60.

[12] CRPD Committee, General Comment No. 5 (n. 1).

Women and girls with disabilities face multiple processes where they are categorised as "disabled", based on the interaction between the social construction and production of disability.[13] Among these processes is the lack of recognition of legal capacity to guarantee fundamental rights and freedoms through laws and official or *de facto* practices that substitute decision making over personal life decisions. These processes affect girls and women with intellectual and psychosocial disabilities more severely; and are aggravated by communicational, attitudinal and legal barriers, together with the absence or lack of staff training, resources, and support, especially in the field of access to justice. More generally, socio-legal incapacitation, configured from medical-legal hybrids of medical social control, constitutes a violation of human rights and institutional violence that is the key to other forms of abuse in the context of property and sexual and reproductive rights. It is, therefore, a specific form of epistemic violence that is later accompanied by material violence, based on what Steele and Dowse refer to as a legal ordering of violence as lawful or unlawful, in reference to a medical approach to mental capacity.[14]

2. INTERSECTIONAL VIOLENCE AND DISCRIMINATION

Steele and Dowse have denounced the ableism of certain feminist trends, which fail to address the intersectional violence faced by girls and women with disabilities as objects of medical interventions, reconstituted as therapeutic and benevolent, but carried out without duly informed consent; processes that therefore violate their physical and mental integrity.[15] These forms of violence are today outside the focus of campaigns against gender violence and outside the forms of criminally prohibited violence against women because they become legally and socially permissible when they occur in the circumstances structured around the "lack of mental capacity". In this vein, Steele and Dowse refer to the paradoxical accusation from feminist thought about the medicalisation and pathologisation of women's bodies and minds, from which influential lines of development were configured that connected these processes with erroneous attributions of irrationality. In the author's opinion, this would have been achieved by distancing the gendered political category of women from these characteristics, rather than politicising disability to displace it as an individualised and medicalised notion of identity.

---

[13] C. JAMPEL, "Intersections of disability justice, racial justice and environmental justice" (2018) 4 *Environmental Sociology*, pp. 122–35.

[14] L. STEELE and L. DOWSE, "Gender, disability, rights and violence against medical bodies" (2016) 31 *Australian Feminist Studies*, pp. 187–202.

[15] L. STEELE and L. DOWSE (n. 14). For a definition of ableism see C. JAMPEL (n. 13).

In other words, some traditional feminist arguments have depended on the exclusion and abjection of disability to support their claims for equality, affirming the rationality and capacity of women with educational, financial and legal capacity privilege, without exploring in depth the violence that occurs particularly against those categorised as "disabled". Within the social movement, as in some feminist schools of thought, the experiences of women with psychosocial or intellectual disabilities continue to be thought of as "subaltern" and are placed below those identified with physical or sensory disabilities.[16] Faced with this problem, feminist disability studies have aimed to resist and rewrite the notions of weakness, lack and impairment, commonly associated with gender and disability, and from which the production of their intersection as otherness is intensified.[17]

Feminist disability studies takes three threads from intersectional feminisms. First, they reveal the possibility of socio-historically situating the discursive construction of identification categories such as disability and gender. Second, they account for the conflict that emerges from it at the ontological level when considering them as defining conditions. And third, they analyse matrices of domination and resistance of the mechanisms of inequality that act in an interrelated way to construct and configure simultaneous and interdependent experiences of oppression. Also, they have proposed representation, the body, identity and activism as domains where disability generates critical research and addresses topics such as the unity of the category of "woman", the privilege of normality, the medicalisation of the body, sexuality and the social construction of identity.[18]

The social and political changes brought about by the UNCRPD resulted in the possibility of recognising and naming the previously mentioned examples of violence. Concepts already developed, such as violence against women and gender-based violence – together with the impact of these experiences on access to justice – were taken by the CRPD Committee to describe the global situation of girls and women with disabilities. In this way, it has been emphasised how, through guardianship and mental health laws, justified by virtue of their purpose of protecting and ensuring the best interests of the person, the most brutal forms of discrimination to which they continue to be subjected have occurred.[19] In fact, there is a direct relationship between these forms of discrimination and the persistence of harmful gender and disability stereotypes. These elements combine and promote attitudes, policies and practices that prevent the exercise of the right

---

[16]   R. MORAS, "Feminism, Rape Culture, and intellectual disability. Incorporating sexual self-advocacy and sexual consent capacity", in M. WAPPETT and K. ARNDT (eds), *Emerging Perspectives on Disability Studies*, Palgrave Macmillan, New York 2013, pp. 189–206.

[17]   L. STEELE and L. DOWSE (n. 14).

[18]   R. GARLAND THOMSON, "Integrating Disability, Transforming Feminist Theory" (2002) 14 *NWSA Journal*, pp. 1–32.

[19]   CRPD Committee, General Comments Nos. 3 and 6 (nn. 8, 10).

to protection against exploitation, abuse and violence, thereby contributing to the construction of vulnerability of girls and women with disabilities.[20] The foregoing, within patriarchal social models, affect this group's segregation, isolation and infantilisation, questioning their decisions and thereby increasing the risk of sexual violence. As such, in its institutional or structural form, the situations of violence to which they are subjected keep them in a subordinate physical and ideological position compared to others in their home or community.

The previous considerations are not merely academic. In addition to distinguishing between multiple discrimination and intersectional discrimination, where the grounds interact simultaneously and are inseparable,[21] various forms of discrimination have been identified:[22]

- Direct discrimination when the testimonies of women with intellectual or psychosocial disabilities are dismissed in legal proceedings on the grounds of legal capacity, thus denying them access to justice and effective remedies as victims of violence;
- Indirect discrimination, for example, in care facilities that may seem neutral but do not include accessible appliances;
- Discrimination by association frequently experienced by women who act as caregivers for people with disabilities;
- Discrimination by denial of reasonable accommodation, for example, towards women who cannot undergo procedures due to physically inaccessible health care and other facilities;
- Harassment discrimination especially common in segregated settings where it is more likely and invisible, as there is less chance of being punished;
- Structural or systemic discrimination manifested in hidden or covert patterns of institutional behaviour, cultural traditions, social norms and/or rules.

Discrimination is not only a negative dimension that directly affects girls and women with disabilities. With regard to what has been labelled as *discrimination by association*, it is worth noting the positive obligation for States parties to guarantee equal and effective legal protection, both for persons with disabilities and for their environment;[23] and to provide family caregivers with support

---

[20]   Ibid., General Comment Nos. 3, 5 and 6 (nn. 1, 8, 10).

[21]   These reasons include age, ethnic, indigenous, national or social origin, gender identity, race, gender or sexual orientation. CRPD Committee, General Comment No. 3 (n. 8). To combat multiple discrimination, the role of the States parties is highlighted through legislative measures such as the classification of sexual violence as a crime and the prohibition of sterilisation, forced abortion, all types of non-consensual birth control and all forms of medical intervention without consent. CRPD Committee, *General Comment No. 1 – Article 12: Equal recognition before the law (Adopted 11 April 2014) – Plain English version*, CRPD/C/GC/1 Plain English version, 19 May 2014.

[22]   CRPD Committee, General Comments Nos. 5 and 6 (nn. 1, 10).

[23]   CRPD Committee, General Comment No. 6 (n. 10).

services so they can facilitate the independent and community life of persons with disabilities. This is particularly relevant for persons with disabilities living in extreme poverty and unable to access the labour market. In this regard, the importance of personal assistance support services has also been stressed as a tool to eliminate this form of discrimination and guarantee protection.[24] At the same time, regarding systemic discrimination, the recognition, at the International Conference on Population and Development in Cairo and the World Conference on Women in Beijing,[25] of the multiple barriers that girls and women with disabilities face for the full equality, advancement and enjoyment of their sexual and reproductive rights, is relevant. For example, the rights of personal autonomy and self-determination are fundamental to achieving independent living and substantive equality. However, their inapplicability has been revealed for groups such as girls and women with disabilities, exposed to greater vulnerability and situations of risk and intersectional discrimination in areas such as abortion, harmful practices, gender-based violence, contraception and family planning, adolescence, and HIV transmission.[26]

In this regard, it is worth highlighting what Agustina Palacios points out in her chapter in this book, on the right to exercise sexual and reproductive rights as one of the thematic axes in the content and scope of standards of international law on legal capacity. Palacios gives an account of the persistent barriers to consent and the experience of sexuality for persons with disabilities in the Latin American region. She observes that, despite certain advances on the prohibition of forced sterilisations, there are worrying judicial precedents, which establish the impossibility of adult women with disabilities consenting to sexual relations. Likewise, with regard to the right to family life and the exercise of parental responsibility, she appreciates judicial precedents that recognise the severe violation that results in the loss of guardianship of daughters and sons and the division of family ties due to disability, together with the understanding of the requirement of systems that accompany the exercise of said right. However, she warns about rulings where medical diagnoses are used to justify restrictions of the right to legal capacity in situations deemed to be of imminent danger.

---

[24]   CRPD Committee, General Comment No. 3 (n. 8). On the elements that allow establishing this right, see CRPD Committee, General Observation No. 5 (n. 1).

[25]   UN, Population and Development Fund, "Action Programme of the International Conference on Population and Development in Cairo", 1994/2014 and UN Women, "Declaration and Action Platform" Beijing, Political declaration and results documents, Beijing+5, 1995/2014.

[26]   On sexual and reproductive rights and their codification in the international order see also: J. González Moreno, "Los derechos sexuales y reproductivos como categoría jurídico internacional revisable" (2017) 38 *Revista de Derecho Público*, pp. 1–29; J. Garcia and S. Hoyos, "La esterilización de las personas con discapacidad cognitiva y psicosocial: una perspectiva crítica a la jurisprudencia constitucional" (2017) 38 *Revista de Derecho Público*, pp. 1–38; OHCHR, "Information Series. Sexual and Reproductive Health and Rights", 2020, <https://www.ohchr.org/en/women/information-series-sexual-and-reproductive-health-and-rights> accessed 26.03.2023.

The absence of an intersectional perspective in these analyses leaves, in the background, the support needs of women who are mothering, and makes their poverty invisible.

3. LEGAL CAPACITY AND CONSTRUCTION OF VULNERABILITY

Pursuant to all of the above, it is possible to maintain that, at a global level, the vulnerability of women and girls with disabilities is created by the imposition of guardianship and material and attitudinal barriers, which deny them support for the exercise of their autonomy and legal capacity, particularly with regard to sexual and reproductive matters.[27] Also, in jurisdictions with higher rates of imposing surrogate decision-makers on women than on men,[28] those with psychosocial, intellectual, or developmental disabilities face additional layers of oppression given the assumption that they lack agency, which in turn justifies more restrictive clinical and social care, control and surveillance regimens.[29] In addition, in the case of institutionalised girls or women or users of the psychiatric system, there are unique experiences of forced treatment.[30] Consequently, reassessing how vulnerability is created could help reduce its effects and guarantee equal access to sexual and reproductive health services. Accordingly, the following analysis presents three areas where the dynamics of producing vulnerability result in the restriction or denial of legal capacity, and examines the forms of support necessary to enable the exercise of autonomy in these domains, namely sexual choices, reproductive choices and institutionalised settings.

3.1. SEXUAL CHOICES

Regarding the first area, adolescents and women with disabilities are considered incapable of making sexual choices or acts of consent, or prevailing patriarchal structures prevent them from doing so.[31] For those with psychosocial, intellectual,

---

[27] A. ARSTEIN-KERSLAKE, "Gendered denials: Vulnerability created by barriers to legal capacity for women and disabled women" (2019) 66 *International Journal of Law and Psychiatry*, pp. 1–9.

[28] CRPD Committee, General Comment No. 1 (n. 21).

[29] C. KONG (n. 5).

[30] CRPD Committee, General Comment No. 3 (n. 8).

[31] CRPD Committee, General Comment No. 3 and General Comment No. 1 (nn. 8, 21) Persons with intellectual and developmental disabilities are generally questioned about their ability to give consent, but various justifications for contemporary and historical practices of limitation in the sexual realm turn out to be false. A. ONSTOT, "Capacity to Consent: Policies and

or developmental disabilities, informal arrangements or policies that hinder their sexual and romantic relationships and access to sex education and information tend to be a stronger impediment.[32] The contingent vulnerability created leaves them without the tools to develop the skills necessary for this type of choice. It also leads to the belief that others will make better decisions about their sexuality.

A pattern of paternalism towards sexual freedom and the lack of resources to participate in their own safety and security[33] prevent practices that would make them less vulnerable to sexual violence in institutional, family and community settings.[34] This is the case for the population with disabilities in general,[35] as well as for adolescents and women with intellectual and developmental disabilities who (compared to their male peers[36]) are less likely to know how to identify abuse and as a result face a significant risk in these situations.[37] The increased inaccessibility and lack of information experienced by girls and women with visual and hearing impairments, those who are institutionalised and/or who live with psychosocial or intellectual disabilities further increases the risk of being subjected to sexual violence.[38] At the same time, restrictive court decisions – concerning maternity, reproduction and sexual partners of persons with intellectual and developmental disabilities, based on the consideration of their mental capacity and "best interest" – reinforce disabling and patriarchal norms that question their ability to express agency without the interference of third parties.[39]

People who diverge from and are invalidated by the hegemonic sex/gender system are subject to even greater regulation and surveillance of their sexual behaviour.[40] Furthermore, in the case of intellectual and developmental disabilities, this results in the suppression or concealment of their sexual identities. Although women generally are also the object of harmful stereotypes of asexuality or sexual hyperactivity which constitute internalised perceptions and lead to the desire for a normalised identity, the biases to which dissidents of the hegemonic sex/gender system are subjected are even more damaging.[41]

Practices that Limit Sexual Consent for People with Intellectual/Developmental Disabilities" (2019) 37 *Sexuality and Disability*, pp. 633–44 and; R. Moras (n. 16).

32   A. Onstot (n. 31).
33   CRPD Committee, General Comment No. 3 (n. 8).
34   CRPD Committee, General Comment No. 5 (n. 1).
35   A. Onstot (n. 31).
36   Committee on Economic, Social and Cultural Rights (ESCR Committee) *General comment No. 22 (2016) on the right to sexual and reproductive health (article 12 of the International Covenant on Economic, Social and Cultural Rights)*, E/C.12/GC/22, 2 May 2016.
37   A. Arstein-Kerslake (n. 27); and A. Onstot (n. 31).
38   CRPD Committee, General Comment No. 3 (n. 8).
39   C. Kong (n. 5).
40   See A. Onstot (n. 31).
41   CRPD Committee, General Comment No. 3 (n. 8). The definition used here for dissidences and the hegemonic sex/gender system is based on: L. Martínez, "Disidencias sexuales y

3.2. REPRODUCTIVE CHOICES

Three problems emerge in the dynamics of vulnerability construction, in relation to reproductive choices of women and adolescents/girls with disabilities: (a) forced sterilisation; (b) abortion and; (c) motherhood. Forced sterilisation has been classified as a severe crime of sexual violence that tends to occur above all in cases of total socio-legal incapacitation through laws and policies that prescribe or indirectly perpetuate it.[42] It has been classified as cruel, inhuman and degrading treatment or punishment where the decision is made against a person's will by a "legal guardian".[43] Forced sterilisation has also been considered a war crime and a crime against humanity[44] and it has been confirmed that the adolescent population is affected by this type of procedure in percentages up to three times higher than the rest of the population. Likewise, it is a practice marked by a medical model that facilitates, on the one hand, a discriminatory evaluation of mental capacity and denial of legal capacity when justified by the assessment; and, on the other hand, the application of the procedure under the (false) justification of the "higher good of women".[45] Forced sterilisation is carried out, for example, to avoid unwanted pregnancies. However, in the case of sexual abuse, which frequently occurs within the home and is perpetrated by members of the nuclear family who have been given formal or informal power over the sterilisation decision, forced sterilisation allows the perpetuation of the abuse without any punitive consequences.

Forced sterilisation is prevalent for women with psychosocial and intellectual disabilities, especially those who are institutionalised,[46] a group which has

---

corporales: Articulaciones, rupturas y mutaciones" (2018) 17 *Psicoperspectivas. Individuo y sociedad*, pp. 1–12; and A. OLIVA, "Debates sobre el género", in *Teoría Feminista. De los debates sobre el género al multiculturalismo*, Biblioteca Nueva, Madrid 2005/2019, pp. 15–60.

[42]   A. YUPANQUI CONCHA and V. F. FERRER PÉREZ, "Análisis de la producción científica mundial sobre esterilización forzada de mujeres con discapacidad entre 1997 y 2016" (2019) 33 *Gaceta Sanitaria*, pp. 381–88; A. M. CAVALCANTE CARVALHO, "Intersectional discrimination: concept and consequences in the incidence of sexual violence against women with disabilities" (2018) 7 *Journal of Feminist, Gender and Women Studies*, pp. 15–25; and V. MURTULA, "Los derechos reproductivos de las mujeres con discapacidad" (2019) 5 *Revista de Derecho Privado*, pp. 3–46. See also, UN Committee on the Elimination of Discrimination Against Women (CEDAW), General Recommendation 19 of CEDAW on Violence Against Women (llth session, 1992), U.N. Doc. A/47/38 at 1 (1993); CEDAW General Recommendation No. 19: Violence against women, A/47/38, 1992; UN Committee on the Elimination of Discrimination Against Women (CEDAW), CEDAW General Recommendation No. 24: Article 12 of the Convention (Women and Health), 1999, A/54/38/Rev.1 and; CEDAW, General recommendation No. 35 (2017) on gender-based violence against women, updating general recommendation No. 19 (1992), CEDAW/C/GC/35, 26 July 2017.

[43]   CRPD Committee, General Comment No. 3 (n. 8).

[44]   UN Women, "Declaration and Action Platform" (n. 25).

[45]   CRPD Committee, General Comment No. 5 and No. 1 (nn. 1, 21).

[46]   Report of the Special Rapporteur on the rights of persons with disabilities, *Sexual and reproductive health and rights of girls and young women with disabilities*, A/72/133, 14 July 2017.

historically been a focus of eugenic initiatives aimed at eradicating social problems by preventing the reproduction of persons categorised as having undesirable traits. Whether for menstrual hygiene or pregnancy prevention, the underlying objectives in these practices continues to be the prevention of the reproduction of defective traits that, in other times, were constituted based on race, ethnicity or social class.[47] This goal is also manifested in the coercive abortions currently practised as a means of population control in residential institutions, a practice based on negative stereotypes about the parenting capacity of women with disabilities and the concern that their children will have disabilities.[48]

The right to abortion has been recognised as a strategic measure to guarantee the enjoyment of sexuality and reproduction for women with disabilities. It is essential to women's right to health, therefore allowing them to be free from cruel, inhuman and degrading treatment.[49] Thus, the need to decriminalise and legalise abortion has been emphasised. The lack of access to abortion constitutes a public health failure due to its disproportionate effect on adolescents and women with disabilities living in poverty and located in non-urban areas.[50] Based on these realities, both the CRPD Committee and the CEDAW Committee have made statements to guarantee the sexual and reproductive health and rights of all women, particularly those with disabilities, recommending that access to safe and legal abortion services be assured through the implementation of measures to protect against discrimination based on disability.[51] These UN committees have urged access to unbiased and evidence-based information to strengthen respect for the rights and dignity of persons with disabilities and challenge stereotypes, attitudes, and behaviours that undermine women's autonomy and reproductive choice. In normative terms, the UNCRPD obliges a State that allows or prohibits abortion to do so "in the same way" without regard to whether the foetus, unborn child or unborn person has a disabling condition.[52] Protection

---

[47] L. JAFFEE and K. JOHN, "Disabling Bodies of/and Land: Reframing Disability Justice in Conversation with Indigenous Theory and Activism" (2018) 5 *Disability and the Global South*, pp. 1407–29.

[48] UN, Report of the Special Rapporteur on the rights of persons with disabilities (n. 46).

[49] Ibid.

[50] CEDAW Committee, General Recommendation No. 3. 4; on the rights of rural women, 2016. <https://digitallibrary.un.org/record/835897> accessed 26.03.2023.

[51] Office of the UN High Commissioner on Human Rights (OHCHR), Joint statement by the Committee on the Rights of Persons with Disabilities and the Committee on the Elimination of All Forms of Discrimination against Women, "Guaranteeing sexual and reproductive health and rights for all women, in particular women with disabilities", 29 August 2018, <https://www.ohchr.org/en/treaty-bodies/crpd/statements-declarations-and-observations> accessed 26.03.2023.

[52] A. PALACIOS, "¿Por qué el aborto eugenésico basado en discapacidad es contrario a la Convención Internacional sobre los Derechos de las Personas con Discapacidad" (2010) 105 *Revista Síndrome de Down*, pp. 50–58.

under the UNCRPD against discriminating in access to abortion will depend on each State's definition of when the protection of the right to life begins.

Finally, with regard to motherhood, various violations restrict the exercise of this right.[53] Women with disabilities are mistakenly perceived as dependent and incapable of mothering.[54] In particular, those categorised as intellectually and developmentally disabled are often denied this choice until it is proven – through a standardised assessment of the ability to provide care – that they are biologically and socially capable of fulfilling the normative function of motherhood.[55] This is in violation of States parties' obligations to guarantee the recognition of legal capacity and the capacity to exercise autonomous reproductive choices with assured access to the individualised support services that are required and desired.[56] However, given that parenting support can only be paid for by those with sufficient financial resources, and that domestic work and child care are not recognised as a public issue, the materialisation of the right to motherhood for women with disabilities results in a chimaera.[57] Stereotypes and structural barriers to financial support discourage or prevent women from deciding to have children naturally or by adoption, from providing care and from enjoying and exercising the rights to found a family, to health, and to independent living.[58] In line with the above, it is also relevant to mention the legal discrimination under procedures for the protection of children that causes especially women with intellectual or psychosocial disabilities to lose contact and custody of their children who are placed in institutions or adoption processes.[59]

3.3. INSTITUTIONALISED SETTINGS

Girls and women with disabilities face a higher risk of being institutionalised and being subject to guardianship proceedings for the formal removal of their legal capacity. Guardianship proceedings might justify forms of violence that significantly affect those with psychosocial and intellectual disabilities, who are often considered incapable of living outside these environments.[60] Although

---

[53]   On maternity, care and disability cf. C. FROHMADER and H. MEEKOSHA, "Recognition, Respect and Rights: Women with Disabilities in a Globalized World", in D. GOODLEY, B. HUGHES and L. DAVIS (eds), *Disability and Social Theory. New Developments and Directions*, Palgrave Macmillan, London 2012, pp. 287–307; and C. VALEGA, "Barreras que enfrentan las personas en situación de discapacidad en el ejercicio de su sexualidad y autodeterminación reproductive" (2016) 11 *Revista La manzana de la Discordia*, pp. 7–20.
[54]   CRPD Committee, General Comment No. 6 (n. 10).
[55]   See C. KONG (n. 5).
[56]   CRPD Committee, General Comment No. 3 (n. 8).
[57]   C. VALEGA (n. 53).
[58]   CRPD Committee, General Comment No. 5 (n. 1).
[59]   CRPD Committee, General Comment Nos. 3 and 5 (nn. 1 and 8).
[60]   Ibid and, also, CRPD Committee, General Comment No. 1 (n. 21).

they vary in size or organisation, institutionalised environments have common elements where the authoritarian imposition of activities, paternalism and the daily transgression of personal will and preferences are standard practices. In institutions, the denial of legal capacity without consent or a substitute's consent is usual. Moreover, the legal capacity of residents is usually conferred on the management of the institutions, leaving all the power and control over the person in their hands.[61] In these scenarios, girls, adolescents and women with disabilities experience internalised and systemic oppression. There is a historical association in the hegemonic sex-gender system between the feminine and hysteria, manifested in the significant gendered differences in diagnoses, treatments and forced interventions.[62] Thus, girls, women and non-binary persons are subjected to high levels of violence and cruel, inhuman and degrading treatment or punishment, which increases their vulnerability to physical and sexual assault, such as forced sterilisation, sexual abuse, physical and emotional abuse, and increased isolation. These violations go unpunished because access to judicial recourse is restricted, and isolation increases the obstacles to finding support and filing complaints.

4. CONCLUSIONS

This chapter has analysed the intersections between gender and disability, particularly in sexual and reproductive matters, based on a review of literature and international human rights instruments. The latter, together with research on the intersections between feminism and disability, gives an account of the theoretical and political trajectories that sediment the definitions of violence, harmful stereotypes, eugenic practices and discrimination experienced by women and girls with disabilities in various parts of the world. Erroneous ideas about what girls and women with disabilities can and should or should not do result in the annulment of their desires and contribute to the dehumanising operation of the series of paradoxes that cross their lives and expose them to instances of violation under the justification of protection. Gender-based social norms about mental capacity and sexuality construct their vulnerability, pathologise their conducts and life circumstances, facilitate their medicalisation and thereby shape the processes of degendering and dehumanisation that enable the highest rates of violence, incapacitation and denial of autonomy to which they are subjected. From the heterogeneity and fragmentation of their experiences and positions, these girls and women experience daily the denial of rights in the face of choices that involve their bodies, sexualities and caregiving

---

[61]   CRPD Committee, General Comment No. 1 (n. 21).
[62]   A. Arstein-Kerslake (n. 27) and; L. Steele and L. Dowse (n. 14).

abilities. At the same time, their representation as genderless and asexual beings generates responses of indifference to the gendered and disabling nature of the interventions to which they are subjected.[63]

In this vein, the study of legal capacity implies a study of vulnerability, violence and the protection of sexual and reproductive rights within the dynamics articulated by normative conceptualisations of mental capacity and the series of patriarchal barriers that stem from it. These dynamics are co-constituted within the legal system itself to justify discriminatory practices. Indeed, the denial of autonomy is evidence of the confluence of law with a normatively masculinised personality. This confluence has created the paradigmatic legal subject as an able-bodied, white and heterosexual man endowed with material anonymity.[64] It sets the standard of evaluation, regulation and materialisation allowed for subjects, providing their exteriority with a suspended, non-operational or diminished personality and autonomy, contingent on particular embodied experiences. This exteriority is partly constituted by persons with disabilities, women and dissidents of the hegemonic sex/gender system who, by not being able to obtain a complete legal personality, provide the starting point for identifying the problem of the mismatch to an unquestioned norm. Historically, they have been marked as legally and culturally visible. At the same time, their autonomy has been denied based on assumptions and expectations that, in the case of disability, are constituted by a norm of integrity that makes living in a state of physical or mental limitation (as defined by dominant norms) irrational. Along these lines, the categories "disability" and "woman" can been highlighted as being generated from repeated and ritualised acts and constrained by specific socio-historical conventions.[65] "Disability" and "woman" constitute differential marks and distributions of privileges, disadvantages and violence, modelled in relation to broader structures and contexts. These structures and contexts include the social and political organisations that contain, make, and undo all subjects. These subjects are always dependent on this infrastructure and are vulnerable to its dismantling or disappearance.[66]

Pursuant to all of the above, it is worth asking how the supremacy of a masculinised normativity and socialisation within the hegemonic sex/gender system of the West built the medical assessment of mental capacity and, consequently, constructed the vulnerability of subjects classified as girls, women and dissidents with disabilities, and how this process has justified their incapacitation and the denial of autonomy. Although vulnerability is inherent to

---

[63] L. STEELE and L. DOWSE (n. 14).

[64] M. TRAVIS, "Non-normative bodies, rationality, and legal personhood" (2014) 22 *Medical Law Review*, pp. 526–47.

[65] A. CANSECO, "Un diálogo entre las críticas butlerianas al sujeto liberal y los estudios de discapacidad" (2019) 51 *Politics and Culture*, pp. 145–67.

[66] J. BUTLER, "Rethinking vulnerability and resistance", *Vulnerability in resistance*, Duke University Press, Durham and London 2016, pp. 12–27.

existence and human bodies, always precarious and in need of material support that enables their agency, these supports are part of the political and public sphere where they are differentially distributed according to a normative and gendered horizon of normative abilities.[67]

The reading of Article 12 of the UNCRPD accounts for the duty to recognise the legal capacity of women and dissidents with disabilities, on equal terms with other people and in all aspects of life. This, together with the duty of States to adopt measures to ensure their access to the support they may require in exercising it. States parties are therefore obliged to identify areas or subgroups, such as women, girls and adolescents with disabilities, older persons and indigenous persons with disabilities, where intersectional discrimination is experienced and adopt specific measures to accelerate or achieve inclusive equality.[68] At the same time, States parties must guarantee access to all the support that is required and desired through affirmative egalitarian norms and the promotion of social practices that enable environments where personal will and preferences are respected. Personal will and preferences are expressions of individuals as well as of a context that conditions its emergence in indissoluble networks of interdependence. In this vein, the need to advance guarantees of the right to an independent sex-affective and community life has been emphasised, through individualised, acceptable, accessible and responsive decision-making support services and personal assistance, and adequate budgetary allocations and legal frameworks for their provision. Also, the importance of providing support services to individuals with intellectual and developmental disabilities has been emphasised, including children, adolescents, women, dissidents and racialised minorities.

Finally, throughout the analysis, an intersectional perspective has been highlighted as essential to ending the sexual division of labour. on which the feminisation of care and support, and the daily exercise of autonomy is structured. In consideration of this, care and support for people with disabilities and their community networks must be reconfigured as a public and political issue, rather than its usual relegation to the private sphere. This struggle constitutes a companion in the fight for the materialisation of Article 12 of the CRPD, as it leads to the questioning of and putting an end to medical-legal hybrids such as incapacitation and to better understanding the recognition of legal capacity and the exercise of autonomy in supported decision-making processes. In this way, intersectionality aims to inform what Article 12 of the CRPD generates in practice, thus contributing to the realisation and implementation of legal reforms and social policies.

---

[67]   A. CANSECO (n. 65).

[68]   CRPD Committee, General Comment No. 6 (n. 10).

Intersentia

LOSING LEGAL CAPACITY AND POWER OVER PERSONAL LIFE

The "Decision-Making Capability" Alternative

Michael Bach

1. Introduction 65
2. Legal Capacity: Mainstream Approaches and Critique.................. 66
   2.1. Mainstream Approaches to Legal Capacity 66
   2.2. Critique of Mainstream Approaches by the UN Committee on the
        Rights of Persons with Disabilities............................ 68
   2.3. The Principle of Respect for Autonomy Underlying the
        Mainstream Approaches 69
3. Reformulating the Principle of "Respect for Autonomy" for an Inclusive
   Approach to Legal Capacity 70
   3.1. Critique of the Standard Account of Autonomy 70
   3.2. The "Planning Theory" of what it Means to Respect Autonomy..... 71
4. The "Decision-Making Capability" Alternative: Key Concepts 74
   4.1. Capabilities 74
   4.2. Acting with "True" Intentions: The Basis of Legal Power.......... 77
   4.3. Interpretive Support and the Best Interpretation of Will and
        Preferences 79
   4.4. Formulating the Decision-Making Capability Approach.......... 81
5. Implications for Further Research and Development 83
6. Summary and Conclusion.. 86

1. INTRODUCTION

People with intellectual, cognitive, and psychosocial disabilities systematically and routinely lose their legal capacity – or their right to decide – when legal authority is vested in others to make decisions for them through guardianship or substitute decision-making. They also lose power over their lives more informally through everyday paternalism and the structural violence, constraints, institutionalisation, and abuse they experience at hugely disproportionate rates.

The assumption that because of their disability some people simply do not have the cognitive abilities to exercise choice and control over their lives, and as a result must be restricted in the name of protection, is at the root of the ableism that pervasively shapes their lives. People with disabilities have been subject to, violated, and harmed by these ableist assumptions for centuries, and they underlie the legal and social justification for restricting or obstructing their right to legal capacity and liberty.

This reality of structural exclusion of so many people with disabilities is in direct conflict with the equal right to exercise legal capacity recognised in Article 12 of the UN Convention on the Rights of Persons with Disabilities (CRPD), on "equal recognition before the law."[1] Article 12 recognises the right to enjoy and exercise legal capacity on an equal basis with others, without discrimination based on disability. It also recognises that States parties have an obligation to ensure that people have access to the supports they may require to exercise their legal capacity, based on their rights, will, and preferences.

To develop effective law, policy, and practice responses to recognising and promoting the right to equality in exercise of legal capacity, it is necessary to develop an alternative to the mainstream approaches to legal capacity which justify restrictive and exclusionary legal capacity regimes. This chapter explores a "decision-making capability" approach on which an alternative, more inclusive and universal legal capacity regimes can be built.

2. LEGAL CAPACITY: MAINSTREAM APPROACHES AND CRITIQUE

2.1. MAINSTREAM APPROACHES TO LEGAL CAPACITY

The assumptions and provisions structuring the recognition of legal capacity in most jurisdictions around the world reflect what have been referred to as "mainstream" approaches to defining the requirements for exercising and enjoying legal capacity. In its General Comment No.1 on Article 12 of the CRPD, the UN Committee on the Rights of Persons with Disabilities (UN Committee) identifies three mainstream approaches.[2] The "status approach" restricts the

---

[1] UN General Assembly. "Convention on the Rights of Persons with Disabilities, A/RES/61/106" (13 December, 2006). <https://www.un.org/development/desa/disabilities/convention-on-the-rights-of-persons-with-disabilities/convention-on-the-rights-of-persons-with-disabilities-2.html> accessed 10.11.2022.

[2] United Nations Committee on the Rights of Persons with Disabilities, "General comment No 1 (2014) Article 12: Equal recognition before the law," at para. 15. <https://tbinternet.ohchr.org/_layouts/treatybodyexternal/Download.aspx?symbolno=CRPD/C/GC/1&Lang=en> accessed 10.11.2022.

exercise of legal capacity based on having a disability-related diagnosis, condition, or identity. The "outcome approach" restricts legal capacity based on an assessment that a person with a disability status is acting, or will act, in ways that bring harm to themselves or others. The "cognitive/functional approach" restricts a person from exercising legal capacity on an assessment that they lack needed cognitive and functional abilities to make decisions independently.

Legal capacity regimes – the laws, policies, and practices regulating exercising of legal capacity – often embed some mix of these approaches. However, the cognitive/functional approach is predominant, and growing more so. The Ontario *Guidelines for Conducting Assessments of Capacity*, for example, make clear that the threshold for legal capacity is, "at its core, a cognitive function."[3] The guidelines go on to define this cognitive approach in a "two-part definition" of having the ability to "understand" and to "appreciate," including "cognitive abilities to factually grasp and retain information"; the "ability to express oneself"; "have a working knowledge of his or her financial, health or personal care status and be aware of any pressing issues that call for decision-making"; and "sufficient intellectual and cognitive ability to process and assimilate information about the available options for responding to the particular demands they face."[4] The "appreciate" standard is defined as "the evaluative nature of capable decision-making, and [it] reflects the attachment of personal meaning to the facts of a given situation."[5] The requirement is that "individuals not only possess the intellectual and cognitive capability to factually understand information; they must also be able to rationally manipulate this information and appraise it in a reality grounded fashion."[6] Assessing appreciation focuses on "the reasoning process behind the individual's decisions," and the "particular personal weights that the person attaches to one outcome or another."[7]

In a comprehensive review of capacity assessment tools[8] Deborah O'Connor notes that the cognitive approach, with its emphasis on understanding, appreciation, and ability to think "rationally," "underpins the development of many, if not all, of the assessment tools …".[9] The review confirms the trend towards a more functional approach, in which capacity is assessed in particular

---

3   Ontario Ministry of the Attorney General, "Guidelines for Conducting Assessments of Capacity" (Toronto: 2005), section 1. <https://www.attorneygeneral.jus.gov.on.ca/english/family/pgt/capacity/2005-06/guide-0505.pdf> accessed 10.11.2022.

4   Ontario Ministry of the Attorney General (n. 3), section II.3.

5   Ontario Ministry of the Attorney General (n. 3), section, II.4.

6   Ontario Ministry of the Attorney General (n. 3), section II.4.

7   Ontario Ministry of the Attorney General (n. 3), section II.4.

8   D. O'Connor, "Incapability Assessments: A Review of Assessment and Screening Tools: Final Report" (2009), 6 Prepared for the Public Guardian and Trustee of British Columbia <https://www.trustee.bc.ca/documents/STA/Incapability_Assessments_Review_Assessment_Screening_Tools.pdf> accessed 10.11.2022.

9   O'Connor (n. 8), p. 6.

domains (health care, finance, driving, participation in research, etc.), and where the "focus is on observable behaviour, and attention is paid to measurable and adaptive behaviours that the adult shows in everyday life." While observable behaviours rather than strictly cognitive measures characterise this approach, it still entails, and amounts to, assessing whether a "person is capable of making the decision ... [and] if the person is able to implement and adapt those decisions."[10]

2.2. CRITIQUE OF MAINSTREAM APPROACHES BY THE UN COMMITTEE ON THE RIGHTS OF PERSONS WITH DISABILITIES

In one manner or another, all these approaches use disability-specific characteristics to systematically restrict certain people with disabilities from exercising legal capacity. In its General Comment, the UN Committee finds the denial of legal capacity which these mainstream approaches justify, discriminatory:

> In all of those approaches, a person's disability and/or decision making skills are taken as legitimate grounds for denying his or her legal capacity and lowering his or her status as a person before the law. Article 12 does not permit such discriminatory denial of legal capacity, but, rather, requires that support be provided in the exercise of legal capacity.[11]

The Committee makes clear that using cognitive ability as the overriding condition for enjoying legal capacity violates the rights and obligations recognised in Article 12.

However, the General Comment does not articulate an alternative approach to defining the conditions of legal capacity, other than reiterating that State parties must recognise supports for decision-making and ensure access to supports where required, as per Article 12.3. But what does it mean to say supports are "required" in some circumstances, and how can "supports" for decision-making address situations where a person, even with every available communication and other assistance, is still unable to meet legally established cognitive requirements for exercising legal capacity? The General Comment states that any such requirements are a violation of the CRPD but provides no coherent alternative.

---

[10]   O'Connor (n. 8), p 6.
[11]   United Nations Committee on the Rights of Persons with Disabilities (n. 2), para. 15.

In the absence of an alternative, the General Comment is unable to provide guidance in addressing the apparent contradictions in the CRPD – where meeting cognitive requirements is clearly implied as a condition for exercising other rights. For example, Article 25 requires that health professionals provide care "on the basis of free and informed consent"[12] and the UN Committee reiterates this requirement and obligation on State parties "to require all health and medical professionals (including psychiatric professionals) to obtain the free and informed consent of persons with disabilities prior to any treatment."[13] But the theory of autonomy which underlies the principle of informed consent requires that a person meet the cognitive tests of capacity as a condition for their autonomy to be respected in this context. The General Comment provides no way out of contradictory requirements. Resolving the contradictions requires a critical examination of what I refer to as the "standard account" of autonomy, on which the right to exercise legal capacity and the principle of informed consent rest. Let us begin with what the standard account demands.

2.3. THE PRINCIPLE OF RESPECT FOR AUTONOMY UNDERLYING THE MAINSTREAM APPROACHES

Tom Beauchamp and James Childress's often-quoted version defines autonomy as "self-rule that is free from both controlling interference by others and from limitations, such as inadequate understanding, that prevent meaningful choice."[14] Autonomous action, they argue, takes place when a person acts: "(1) intentionally, (2) with understanding, and (3) without controlling influences that determine their action."[15] Cognitive abilities are elemental to each stage of this formulation.

This standard account is found in one form or another in various statements and guidelines on respecting autonomy and legal capacity and is reflected, for example, in the Ontario guidelines. It requires that a person be able to meet the understanding and appreciation test, as defined, by themselves, even with some supports and accommodations that enable them to meet that test. Eliminating the cognitive test of legal capacity would appear to give up on this formulation of autonomy. Where does it leave us in advancing the autonomy of people with more significant disabilities if they are not able to meet the most basic tenets of its formulation?

---

[12]   UN Convention (n. 1), para. 25.
[13]   United Nations Committee on the Rights of Persons with Disabilities (n. 2), para. 41.
[14]   T. BEAUCHAMP and J.F. CHILDRESS, *Principles of Biomedical Ethics*, 6th ed., New York: Oxford University Press 2009, p. 99.
[15]   BEAUCHAMP and CHILDRESS (n. 14), p. 101.

3. REFORMULATING THE PRINCIPLE OF "RESPECT FOR AUTONOMY" FOR AN INCLUSIVE APPROACH TO LEGAL CAPACITY

If the General Comment provides that recognising legal capacity is no longer about respecting autonomy in the conventional sense, on what foundations would it rest? An Article 12-compliant approach to legal capacity would appear to become untethered from its ethical foundations unless a more inclusive understanding of autonomy can be formulated, one that is shed of its strict cognitive requirements.

An outline of that reformulation is the purpose of this section.

3.1. CRITIQUE OF THE STANDARD ACCOUNT OF AUTONOMY

Despite its pervasive application in biomedical ethics and its implications for the regulation of legal capacity, there is a growing critique of the standard account of autonomy. The perspective from "relational autonomy" points to the legal, social, and economic structures and relationships that directly affect capacities for autonomy.[16] Who makes decisions entirely on their own, this perspective asks? We make our decisions intersubjectively, in relation to others. Other accounts show how pathological social relationships can affect a person's autonomy and "mental capacity,"[17] and how social conditions of disadvantage, disrespect, exclusion, and lack of needed supports may operate to influence the decision-making of persons with disabilities – for example in requesting medical assistance in dying in jurisdictions like Canada that now provide this service based on having a disability, for people who do not have a terminal illness nor who are at the end of their lives.[18] The standard account is also critiqued on the basis that no one actually meets the requirements of the "rational" self the account seems to rest upon; instead, we are embodied subjects, shaped by gender identity, cultural, and other factors, and motivated by often unconscious drives and desires.[19]

---

[16] J. NEDELSKY, *Law's Relations: A Relational Theory of Self, Autonomy and Law*, New York: Oxford University Press 2011.

[17] M. I. HALL, "Mental Capacity in the (Civil) Law: Capacity, Autonomy and Vulnerability" (2012) 58:1 *McGill LJ* 61, p. 63.

[18] J. S. BEADRY, "The Way Forward for Medical Aid in Dying: Protecting Deliberative Autonomy is Not Enough" (2018) 85 *SCLR* (2d), p. 331.

[19] For example, see D. T. MEYERS, "Decentralizing Autonomy: Five Faces of Selfhood" in J. CHRISTMAN and J. ANDERSON (eds), *Autonomy and the Challenges to Liberalism: New Essays*, Cambridge, Mass.: Cambridge University Press 2009, pp. 27–55.

3.2. THE "PLANNING THEORY" OF WHAT IT MEANS TO RESPECT AUTONOMY

A helpful place to start in this reconstruction is with the "planning theory" of autonomy, formulated by Michael Bratman. Through a series of studies over the past three decades, he has developed what he refers to as a "modest theory" of the autonomous will of a person to address the limitations of the standard account of the principle of respect for autonomy, suggesting instead that we aim for what he refers to as a "planning theory" of autonomy and agency.[20] His planning theory accords agency to the person whose will and preferences are prioritised to guide the making of a decision and who has plans for its achievement. It is based on the understanding that in an increasingly complex world, no single person can process the volumes of information that are potentially relevant in understanding and appreciating their options and making decisions. Implications of Bratman's planning theory of agency for law and legal regulation have been explored by scholars in philosophy of law and I draw on these insights below.[21]

Bratman's approach to autonomy and agency, on the one hand, would reject that a communicated desire or intention grounds legal agency simply because it is expressed. On the other, he also rejects the idea that having a certain quantity of cognitive capacity can be the sole criteria for recognising and respecting agency, because the test of agency is really whether someone can make, or get made, the "plans" to achieve one's "intentional states." The planning theory accords agency to the person in the context of their own ordering of their will and preferences – one who can express what matters to them most in the circumstances, and then has a plan to achieve it.

Plans are the means through which a person transforms their intentions into decisions with legal consequences. They are stepping-stones from intending to make something happen, to making it happen. For plans to do this, they must meet three criteria:

- The overall intention and plans to achieve it are internally consistent with one's expressed desires and preferences and their prioritisation or ordering.

---

[20] See, for example, M. BRATMAN, *Intention, Plans and Practical Reason*, Harvard, Mass.: Harvard University Press 1987; *Faces of Intention Selected Essays on Intention and Agency*, Cambridge: Cambridge University Press 1999; *Structures of Agency*, Oxford: Oxford University Press 2007; *Shared Agency: A Planning Theory of Acting Together*, Oxford: Oxford University Press 2014.

[21] The implications of Bratman's theory of planning agency for philosophy of law have been elaborated. See S. SHAPIRO, *Legality*, Cambridge, Mass.: The Belknap Press of Harvard University Press 2011.

- There is a means – end coherence between the overall intention and plans to achieve it. This means the plans will practically achieve the intended outcome.
- There is some relative stability of the intention and plans over time. This means that both a person's intention and the plans they have to achieve it must matter enough to forego other possibilities, some of which might also matter to a person. This is why prioritisation of preferences is so important in the planning theory of agency.

Bratman suggests that planning agency involves establishing second – or "higher-order" plans, within which various plans for their achievement can be "nested." The higher-order plan sets the direction over time and reflects the person's ordering of their intentions and preferences. The various nested plans for implementing the overall plan, or vision, may be open to all kinds of preferences and orientations, provided that together they help achieve the plan. When there is a choice to be made because of conflicts about which nested plan is better to help achieve the overall intention, this larger plan provides the vantage point from which to decide which nested plans, and related intentional states, are better to act upon than others.

Based on the planning theory of agency, an alternative account of autonomy can be formulated that helps fill the gap for those who do not meet the cognitive requirements of the standard account. This is a group who, nonetheless, express their intentions and have plans to achieve them, even if with the help of others. Indeed, this is one of Bratman's main points in his extensive body of work in this area.[22] We make plans together; no person is an island. We all rely on others to assist in making and executing plans to give effect to our intentions.

Informed by the planning theory of agency, this more *inclusive* account of autonomy still delivers on the basic requirements of the standard account: (i) acting intentionally; (ii) with corresponding decisions that reflect understanding and appreciation; and (iii) voluntariness. It recognises that all persons have intentionality that can be interpreted over time, including those with significant intellectual, cognitive, psychosocial, or communication disabilities, and that can guide the making of plans to give effect to these intentions.

However, this alternative would not demand that individuals meet requirements (ii) and (iii) all by themselves, as in the standard account, and in the mainstream approaches to legal capacity. Rather, it recognises that plans and decisions can be made with the input and support of others, who can interpret a person's manifest intentional behaviour as the basis for making plans and executing needed decisions.

---

[22] BRATMAN (n. 20).

What grounds a person's legal agency in the planning approach is their manifest intentions over time. With the support of others, people engage in making plans to give effect to those intentions, including the carrying out of various aspects of financial or other planning on their behalf. They might also engage others to execute the plans to give their intentions effect. In renting or buying an apartment, undergoing surgery, or arranging for air travel or a vacation, people engage many other agents to deliver on their intentions. The planning theory recognises that if all those nested or instrumental plans give effect to the person's intentions, then the plans, their implementation, and their consequences belong to the person. They reflect and constitute that person's legal agency and capacity. In this context, the role of the law in protecting people's autonomy and legal agency is to establish the rules and procedures by which (i) their plans will be given authority as reflections of their intentions; (ii) their representatives who are empowered to act on their behalf will be appointed for this purpose and regulated; and (iii) their autonomy will be safeguarded in the process.

The planning approach to legal agency already operates in personal, health care, and financial decision-making and in many community services. People can appoint powers of attorney to act for them under certain conditions. Increasingly, "advance directives" for health care, including mental health care, are recognised. Jurisprudence is also evolving in this area, as practices of person-centred and individualised planning and support arrangements become more recognised as valid alternatives to imposing substitute decision-making. These arrangements legally recognise that people can maintain their legal capacity and exercise power over their decisions even when they require extensive supports to do so.

For example, an Ontario Superior Court decision recognised supported decision-making in a case concerned in part with how to obtain consent and make community placement decisions for people with developmental disabilities moving from large residential institutions to the community. The judge found that under the alternative course of action provisions of the Ontario *Substitute Decisions Act*, supported decision-making arrangements could be recognised insofar as the Ontario Ministry of Community and Social Services had established person-centred planning principles and processes for making the decisions, which did not require persons involved to be assessed for capacity, declared incapable, or to have substitute decision-makers appointed on their behalf.[23]

However, this was an exceptional circumstance. While the decision provides a model for legal recognition, recognising planning agency rather than cognitive

---

[23] See *Gray v. Ontario* [2006] *OJ No 266* (Div Ct) at para. 47.

capacity in most jurisdictions is the exception, far from being the rule. This is especially the case for people with more significant intellectual, cognitive, and psychosocial disabilities. Even where people with psychosocial disabilities have made advance plans to deal with mental health crises, the authority of these plans or directives are often overridden in health care and other contexts.

4. THE "DECISION-MAKING CAPABILITY" ALTERNATIVE: KEY CONCEPTS

The planning theory of agency and autonomy provides an alternative to the mainstream approaches for defining the conditions for exercising legal capacity that is more inclusive of people who may not have the cognitive abilities the standard account of autonomy requires. Lana Kerzner and I have referred to this approach elsewhere as the "decision-making capability approach" to legal capacity.[24]

Here I work through a formulation for how the planning theory of agency can serve this function. That is, for how it can provide a justifiable account of autonomy that provides a foundation in ethics for an approach to legal capacity that truly is universal in scope. This is what the UN Committee calls for, even if it does not articulate its parameters. Such an approach would fully include people with significant intellectual, developmental, cognitive, and psychosocial disabilities.

To do so, I explore three main conceptual building blocks:

- "capabilities";
- "acting with true intentions";
- "interpretive support and the best interpretation of a person's will and preferences".

4.1. CAPABILITIES

Amartya Sen developed the "capabilities approach" to equality because he found that social and economic development strategies were not being measured

---

[24] M. Bach and L. Kerzner, "A New Paradigm for Protecting Autonomy and the Right to Self-Determination" (2010) *Toronto: Law Commission of Ontario*, 14–15, <https://www.lco-cdo.org/wp-content/uploads/2010/11/disabilities-commissioned-paper-bach-kerzner.pdf> accessed 11.11.2022.

for their impact on people's capabilities to function in their communities and societies in ways that are valuable to them. Their impact on a person's freedom to act in the world was being left out of the picture.[25] To address this limitation, he proposed the "capabilities approach" to conceptualising and measuring human capacity and opportunity. It has four basic components:

- What people want to do or be, which Sen refers to as the ways they want to "function" in society;
- The means, or "capabilities," to achieving these valued functionings;
- The "commodities," or goods and services, which enable a person to develop and exercise their capabilities; and
- The "conversion factors" – i.e., the personal, social, and environmental factors that enable a person to transform available goods and services into capabilities they need to accomplish what's valuable to them.

Sen's capabilities approach informs the framework of the UN Human Development Index, which places capability development at its core. The UN annual *Human Development Report* continues to use the capabilities approach as its organising and measuring framework. As its most recent report makes clear, the core capabilities that need to be developed are not just to secure well being, but to secure human agency as well.[26]

Applied to the issue of people who are denied the exercise of legal capacity and agency, the approach can be formulated to deliver on the basic elements of the standard version of autonomy: (i) acting intentionally; (ii) with corresponding decisions that reflect understanding and appreciation; and (iii) voluntariness. An inclusive approach to conceptualising decision-making capability would ground recognition of a person's autonomy in the first dimension of the account: acting intentionally. However, the capabilities approach would not require that individuals carry out steps (ii) and (iii) by themselves, as in the standard account. Rather, it recognises that plans and decisions can be made with the input and support of others, who can interpret a person's manifest intentional behaviour as the basis for their "planning agency" and for executing decisions. Implementation would require safeguards to ensure that these plans and

---

[25]   The concept of capabilities and its relationship to substantive equality is developed in several published works by Amartya Sen, including A. Sen, "Equality of what?" in S. McMurrin (ed) *The Tanner Lectures on Human Values*, Salt Lake City: University of Utah Press 1980; A. Sen, "Rights and Capabilities" in *Resources, Values and Development*, Cambridge, Mass.: Harvard University Press 1985; and *Commodities and Capabilities* Amsterdam: North Holland 1985.

[26]   For example, see United Nations Development Programme, *Human Development Report 2021/22*, New York, 2022, pp. 101–103.

decisions reflect the person's "true intentions." In this way, decisions executed under such arrangements could meet the test of voluntariness.

How does the capabilities approach apply to enabling persons with significant disabilities to meet requirements for exercising autonomy as outlined above? Applicability lies in how we formulate the decision-making supports, or goods and services, they may require so that their manifest intentions can be interpreted and translated into planning agency and decisions. Sen's capabilities framework includes "conversion factors" that operate at the personal, social, and environmental level to convert these goods and services into *actual* capabilities to exercise agency over one's life. In the case of decision-making capability, as formulated here, these conversion factors could be framed as follows:

- *Personal characteristics*: include a person's ability to act intentionally toward personal goals, things, qualities, and relationships that matter to them. Neuroscience as well as qualitative research evidence point to people with even the most significant cognitive disabilities acting intentionally and wilfully in consistent ways.
- *Social context:* includes the social norms, relationships, and power dynamics that operate in a person's life, community, and broader society and that shape the capacity for their intentions and will to be effective in the world. To the extent that a person has a social context and valuing relationships that respect their intentional and wilful expressions as the basis of decision-making, and that facilitate the decision-making goods and services they require, they will have the social possibilities for exercising power over their lives.
- *Environmental context:* includes the laws, policies, practices, and infrastructure that enable a person to transform their unique characteristics and social context into valuable outcomes or "functionings;" in this case, the function of exercising legal capacity in one's life, or of making or guiding decisions with legal consequences. We know that structural barriers conspire to restrict or deny certain people from exercising legal power over their lives through legal mechanisms, restrictive health and community service practices, social exclusion, inadequate paid and informal personal care, and the failure of adult protection and emergency services to effectively respond in ways that enhance and strengthen decision-making power. Accommodations across a range of decision-making processes in health care, community services, contracting, and financial decision-making are needed to enable people to more fully exercise their legal rights to make decisions in these settings.

How might the capabilities approach re-formulate the first condition of acting autonomously – with intention?

4.2. ACTING WITH "TRUE" INTENTIONS: THE BASIS OF LEGAL POWER

The concept of intentionality is foundational in the planning theory of agency and the more inclusive account of autonomy on which it rests. In their summary of theories of what count as "acts-in-law" or what they define as "legal power," Lars Lindahl and David Reidhav emphasise that common among them is the idea that what grounds a person's legal position and power are specified behaviours recognised to "manifest intention" to achieve certain results.[27] Their formulation raises two key questions: what behaviours count as manifestations of intention in a particular regime; and, relatedly, who is authorised to recognise them as such?

In their analysis of legal regimes, the authors point to three types of manifest intention:

- Explicit declarations through linguistic behaviour (e.g., "I wish to purchase this or that good or service"), in terms a third party understands;
- Non-linguistic behaviour that is an implicit declaration through some form of gesture (e.g., a handshake or paying a fee for a good or service); and
- What the authors refer to as mere manifestation of intention, where there is intentional behaviour and action but no clear message, and so it may be difficult to interpret what legal position of power the manifestation of intention creates in the circumstances.

In their theory of legal power, Lindahl and Reidhav assume a cognitive requirement to turn manifestations of will into legal results. Is there any scope in the authors' theoretical framework for people who are considered by others as unable to make declarations "explicit" enough to constitute a position of legal power, but who with some supports and accommodation could be assisted to do so? And what about those who can only make what appear to be "mere manifestations," something less than even "implicit messages," to ground a position of legal power? In theory, they too could have a position of legal power if one of the conditions for turning their manifestations of intention and wilful action into legal results was a legally recognised role for representatives who are in a relationship of personal knowledge and a trusting relationship with them.

There is ample evidence about persons with significant cognitive disabilities having supporters who can interpret for others what their manifestation of intention means in a given situation. Those with significant disabilities, who may

---

[27] L. LINDAHL and D. REIDHAV, "Legal Power: The Basic Definition" (2017) 30:2 *Ratio Juris,* pp. 158, 168.

Michael Bach

not be able to communicate in ways that most others understand, can still come to be seen as agents if the accounts of their expressions as intentional action, as witnessed and interpreted by their supporters, are given validity. Indeed, many qualitative research studies point to examples of support persons and networks interpreting the behaviour of individuals with significant cognitive or intellectual disabilities as intentional and as the basis for guiding decision-making.[28] For example, Beamer and Brookes suggest that:

> The starting point is not a test of capacity, but the presumption that every human being is communicating all the time and that this communication will include preferences. Preferences can be built up into expressions of choice and these into formal decisions. From this perspective, where someone lands on a continuum of capacity is not half as important as the amount and type of support they get to build preferences into choices.[29]

In these situations, supporters use their understanding to develop needed plans and arrange the making of decisions consistent with, and guided by, valid interpretations of the person's manifestations of intention.

If a person's manifest intentions are to be an alternative ground for exercising legal capacity to that of cognitive ability, how do we know what a person's true intentions are, when their manifest intentions appear to change or conflict, or when there is extreme difficulty in interpreting them as a basis for making plans to give them effect? Undue influence and coercion are significant concerns in a context where a person requires significant supports to exercise their legal capacity.

The idea that a person's true intentions can be validly interpreted to determine if a person is acting voluntarily or under coercion or the undue influence of others is well established in testamentary law. The British Columbia Supreme Court laid out its legal understanding of undue influence and coercion in the context of testamentary capacity in *Leung v. Chang* in 2013:[30]

> In order to invalidate a will on the grounds of undue influence, the asserting party must prove that the influence exerted against the will-maker amounted to coercion, such that the will did not reflect the true intentions of a free will-maker and was not the product of the will-maker's own act.

---

[28] For an overview of some of these studies, see H. Johnson, J. Douglas, C. Bigby and T. Iacono, "The Pearl in the Middle. A Case Study of Social Relationships with an Individual with a Severe Intellectual Disability" (2010) 35:3 *Journal of Intellectual and Developmental Disability*, pp. 175–186.

[29] S. Beamer and M. Brookes, *Making Decisions: Best Practice and New Ideas for Supporting People with High Support Needs to Make Decisions*, London: Values into Action 2001.

[30] *Leung v. Chang*, 2013 BCSC 976 at para. 35.

The undue influence must constitute coercion which could not be resisted by the will-maker and which destroyed his or her free agency. It is well-established on the authorities that if the will-maker remains able to act freely, the exercise of significant advice or persuasion on the will-maker or an attempt to appeal to the will-maker or the mere desire of the will-maker to gratify the wishes of another, will not amount to undue influence.

This legal standard from testamentary law could be adapted for interpreting a person's "true intentions" in the decision-making context more generally.

In summary, an alternative account of respect for autonomy can be formulated, one that does not rest on the test of cognitive decision-making. It still grounds autonomy in the exercise of intentionality. However, it recognises that intentions are not exclusively cognitive behaviours. They can be "manifest" in any number of ways, and when a person does not have the cognitive abilities to give their intentions full effect, the understanding and appreciation to do so could be provided by supporters who assist them in making and executing plans designed to do just that. The "voluntariness" requirement of the standard account of autonomy could be fulfilled in these situations, to the extent that (i) interpretations of a person's manifest intentions in the circumstances are as "true" and "valid" as possible; and (ii) the plans and decision-making based upon them do not in any manner reflect undue influence, coercion, or conflicts of interest on the part of those assisting a person to interpret and translate their intentions as the basis of their planning agency.

4.3. INTERPRETIVE SUPPORT AND THE BEST INTERPRETATION OF WILL AND PREFERENCES

Central to the alternative account of autonomy is that persons who have significant disabilities would have supporters who can interpret what might appear to others, at best, as "mere manifestations" of their intentions, will and preferences. I refer to this kind of decision-making support as "interpretive support." It includes interpreting a person's intentions, will and preferences when a person expresses these through actions and behaviour that often only supporters who know a person well can understand. Interpretive support also includes translating an understanding of the person's intentions into needed plans and decisions and taking the actions necessary for a person to achieve their intentions.

However, providing interpretive support comes with its challenges.

First, it may be difficult to interpret a person's behaviour as intentional action, if the person is socially and institutionally isolated, without anyone who knows them well enough to discern their manifest intentions.

Second, a person's manifest intentions do not always provide specific directions or actions for supporters to take. A person with a significant intellectual disability may not be able to give informed consent to treatment, but they can express a desire to be free of pain or discomfort they experience. Interpretive support in this context requires connecting a general intention – to be free of pain – with what could be many plans and decisions to give it effect.

Third, supporters have huge discretion to interpret the person's wishes in ways that may put them in a conflict of interest with the person and to unduly influence any plans and decisions that get made through such an arrangement.

Fourth, there may be situations in which it is challenging to interpret a person's current expression of intention if it conflicts with what decision-making supporters have observed as much longer-term and consistent manifestations of their intentions.

Fifth, where there is more than one decision-making supporter, they may have among them seriously conflicting interpretations about a person's intentional behaviour and what plans and decisions are required to fulfil them.

Sixth, where decision-making supporters develop plans and execute decisions guided by a person's manifest intention but which risk placing the person in a situation of harm, additional considerations must be raised about balancing the person's dignity of risk with safeguarding them from harm.

The principle of "best interpretation of will and preferences" identified in the UN Committee's General Comment on Article 12 could be used to guide decision-making supporters in these types of situations. The Committee introduces this principle as a replacement for the "best interests" test, which it finds "is not a safeguard which complies with article 12 in relation to adults."[31]

The "best interpretation of a person's will and preferences" recognises that there may be interpretive challenges when a person's manifest intentions are not explicit declarations or even implicit directions. At the same time, as noted in a submission to the UN Committee by the Canadian Association for Community Living (now Inclusion Canada), which formulated and recommended inclusion of the principle in the General Comment, there are always some interpretations that are better than others:

> [T]here are and will always be situations where a person's will and preference cannot be interpreted with any degree of certainty – either because of absence of prior planning documents/indications, or because a person has been so isolated and excluded s/he has no one whom they trust and who can learn their form of communication, at least in the short term. Substitute decision-making systems are in place to deal with this type of situation, and State parties will likely defend their provision given their obligations to protect vulnerable persons.

---

[31] UN Committee on the Rights of Persons with Disabilities (n. 2), para. 21.

> In recognizing the reality of such situations, we recommend that the GC [General Comment] advance the notion of "best interpretation of will and preference" to replace the best interest test for application in these situations. Such a test would recognize that will and preference cannot always be interpreted with certainty, but that there are always better interpretations than others.[32]

This principle is another building block in enabling a person's manifest intentions to ground their legal power and exercise of legal capacity. Applying the principle in the types of situations described above would require guidance and safeguards: to ensure that an interpretation is justifiable (there is clear evidence that it corresponds to a person's expressed intentions); that it is the "best" interpretation of the person's will and preferences in the circumstances; that decisions made under the interpretation would not violate a person's rights; and, that it does not constitute any form of undue influence, coercion, or conflict of interest on the part of supporters.

4.4. FORMULATING THE DECISION-MAKING CAPABILITY APPROACH

The components of a capabilities approach discussed above can be integrated into an inclusive framework for decision-making capability, which recognises that a person has decision-making capability to exercise legal capacity when:

1. They manifest true intentions that reflect their will and preferences as they should be understood to apply in the circumstances.
2. Understanding of the information relevant to making a decision and appreciation of the reasonably foreseeable consequences of a decision or lack of decision to act on the person's manifest true intentions, rights, will and preferences is accomplished either by:
   a. The person themselves with decision-making support as required; or
   b. Through the decision-making support provided by others who provide the interpretive and other supports required to make the plans and execute the decisions that give the person's manifest true intention legal effect in the circumstances; and
3. Where needed in a particular case to ensure the exercise of legal capacity on an equal basis with others, reasonable accommodation is provided for the

---

[32] See Canadian Association for Community Living, "Response to Draft General Comment No. 1 on Article 12, UN Committee on the Rights of Persons with Disabilities" (Toronto: 2014) <https://www.ohchr.org/EN/HRBodies/CRPD/Pages/DGCArticles12And9.aspx> accessed 11.11.2022.

ways a person manifests true intention and makes legal decisions, including the supports and adaptations to decision-making processes that may be required for this purpose.

Drawing on the planning theory of agency and the revised account of the principle of respect for autonomy as outlined above, the logic of the decision-making capability alternative to the mainstream approaches to legal capacity could be stated as follows:

- A person (P) is able to exercise legal capacity in a particular matter (M) when:
  o P has directly manifest, or can reasonably be ascribed through interpretive support, a true intention that can serve as the basis for the reasoning and planning necessary to execute that intention in M;
  o Where required, P has access to forms of decision-making support sufficient to translate that intention into an executable plan of action regarding M; and
  o Where needed, P has access to those forms of reasonable accommodations that are required to execute the plan of action that has its basis in P's manifest intention.[33]

Using decision-making capability as the basis for enjoying the right to exercise legal capacity is consistent with a universal and inclusive approach to legal capacity. Formulated within the social and human rights model of disability on which the CRPD is based, this approach recognises that the barriers a person faces to social and economic participation, including their exercise of legal capacity, does not rest in their genetic, physical, or mental make-up. Rather, social, legal, attitudinal, physical, and other barriers undermine their equal status, human dignity, and human rights.[34]

---

[33] Professor Wayne Martin, University of Essex, provided helpful critical feedback and suggestions in arriving at this summary formulation of a capabilities approach to defining the conditions for recognising and enjoying legal capacity as an alternative to the predominant account of "mental capacity" as its necessary and sufficient condition.

[34] Theresia Degener, current chair of the UN Committee on the Rights of Persons with Disabilities, distinguishes between a "social" and a "human rights" model, but acknowledges that the initial formulation of the CRPD was based on a social model. A human rights approach, she suggests, moves beyond the limitations of a social model approach, which is often focused on showing how a biomedical account of disability misses critical social factors that organise disadvantage of persons with disabilities. A human rights approach to disability starts with foundational assumptions that persons are fundamentally equal in human dignity and deserving of respect, and that an "impairment," biomedically defined, must be seen as that "which belongs to humanity and thus must be valued as part of human variation." See T. DEGENER, "Disability in a Human Rights Context" (2016) 5:3 Laws.

5. IMPLICATIONS FOR FURTHER RESEARCH AND DEVELOPMENT

What implications for further research and development are raised by formulating the grounds of legal agency on the universal capacity for intentional action, as a "more-than-cognitive" capacity of natural persons?

The analysis in this chapter points to four primary areas for further research and development:

1. *Examine the discriminatory assumptions in ethics and law about what it requires to respect a person's autonomy, and fully elaborate a revised principle for purposes of decision-making in personal life, financial, and health care decision-making*

More work is needed to fully elaborate the implications of reformulating the standard account of autonomy to fully recognise manifest true intentions and interpretive supports of others (including their capacity to translate a person's manifest intentions into plans and decisions), as a valid way of respecting and exercising autonomy.

It is not an insignificant shift to ground legal capacity on the universal capacity to intend, rather than the much less universal capacity to demonstrate certain cognitive capacities of rationality, reasoning, and understanding. Most bioethical and legal accounts of autonomy fully rely on, and are defined by, these capacities. We are beginning to see law reform to replace guardianship systems with provisions for supported decision-making, in which courts and public notaries are authorised to recognise a wide range of measures, which may include interpretive supports.[35] However, we are still at initial stages both conceptually and legally. The case for this major reformulation needs fuller elaboration in both bioethics and legal analysis.

In addition, consideration is needed of ethical limits to interdependent decision-making, where a person is fully reliant on interpretive supports. Decisions that fundamentally affect a person's physical and mental integrity may

---

[35] In 2019, for example, the Republic of Colombia adopted "Law 1996" (in Spanish Ley 1996 de 2019, https://www.funcionpublica.gov.co/eva/gestornormativo/norma.php?i=99712), which terminated provisions for guardianship, replacing it with measures for recognising supported decision-making, including provision of interpretive supports, and guidance with the principle of best interpretation of will and preferences for those who require more extensive supports (i.e., those with significant intellectual or cognitive disabilities). For a review of some reforms, see A. Vásquez, F. Isaza and A. Parra, "Legal Capacity Regime Reforms in Costa Rica, Peru and Colombia: A Comparative and Critical Analysis" in this volume.

need to be "off limits" to this approach. For example, should it be possible for supporters to make decisions for medical assistance in dying, or non-therapeutic sterilisation, or highly risky medical experimentation, based solely on their interpretation of a person's will and preferences? The risks of a new eugenics for this group loom on the horizon of "interdependent" decision-making. These risks should not undermine the justifications and utility for this approach. Safeguards can be built into the formulation to recognise limits to this approach where fundamental integrity is at stake, and a person is not able to comprehend, on their own, the nature and consequences of a decision.

2. *Articulate "interpretive supports" and their criteria of validity within standards for communication accessibility*

The nature of "interpretive supports" to assist in decision-making also requires further elaboration if the practice is to be better recognised in communications standards in accessibility or other legislation. For example, regulations under Ontario's *Accessibility for Ontarians with Disabilities Act*,[36] state in s. 12(1) "Except as otherwise provided, every obligated organization shall upon request provide or arrange for the provision of accessible formats and communication supports for persons with disabilities." Guidance on implementation of the regulation lists communication supports including sign language, speechreading, captions and text transcripts, assistive listening devices, and telephones. It also includes a general category of "communication supports for people who are non-verbal" and point to assistive and augmentative communication.[37] None of these kinds of provisions address the unique nature and role of interpretive supports in enabling a person to communicate their will and preferences as a basis for decision-making. This silence in accessibility and communications standards leaves unacknowledged the barriers to communication and the exercise of legal capacity faced by a growing population with significant disabilities, which could be addressed through provision and regulation of interpretive supports.

Concerns about the validity of interpretive support provided by informal supporters – such as family or friends – has also been raised[38] and needs to be considered in any guidance developed. There are legitimate concerns that the interpretations by family members and people close to a person reflect more

---

[36] Ontario, Accessibility for Ontarians with Disabilities Act, 2005, SO 2005, c 11.

[37] See G. THOMPSON, "What are communication supports?" (2018) *Accessibility for Ontarians with Disabilities Act* <https://www.aoda.ca/what-are-communication-supports/> accessed 11.11.2022.

[38] See, for example, S. DONALDSON and W. KYMICKA, "Rethinking Membership and Participation in an Inclusive Democracy: Cognitive Disability, Children, Animals" in B. ARNEIL and N. HIRSCHMANN (eds), *Disability and Political Theory*, Cambridge: Cambridge University Press 2016.

their preferences than a person's true intentions; and could thus constitute undue influence over the decisions that flow from those interpretations.

How can we best address these concerns so that interpretive support can be recognised as a valid way to enable a person to exercise legal capacity? Should those providing interpretive support have to attest to the nature of their relationship with a person, how well they understand their behaviour and expressions? Should a third party have to attest to this relationship and capacity of interpretive supporters? Should an interpretive supporter have to provide an account of how they arrive at their conclusions such that "expression A means intention B" showing others how they "'connect the dots" over time between a person's expressions and outcomes they are seeking.

Working through the legal, ethical, and practical questions is essential if this primary source of communication and decision-making support is to be recognised and respected in decision-making processes.

3. *Develop guidance on the duty to accommodate interpretive supports to enable a person to exercise legal capacity interdependently*

While there is some limited guidance on the duty to accommodate a person with a disability in the exercise of legal capacity,[39] it usually refers to accommodating a person in meeting the standard criteria of autonomy. That is, it references ways to accommodate a person so they can *independently* understand and appreciate the nature and consequences of a decision. As the law evolves to recognise more interdependent ways of exercising legal capacity through the provision of interpretive supports there is both scope and a critical need for expanding our understanding of the duty in this context. Guidance is needed for both interpretive support providers and third parties about what counts as valid interpretation and ways it should be accommodated so that a person does not face discriminatory barriers to exercising legal capacity. Guidance tools to assist individuals and their supporters in pushing the parameters of decision-making processes with third parties may help to expand adoption of this approach. Making requests and claims for reasonable accommodation for interdependent decision-making, even where it is subsequently denied as "unreasonable" or an "undue hardship" for the third party, may nonetheless provide the basis for successful litigation challenging this discrimination.

---

[39] See, for example, Ontario Human Rights Commission, *Policy on Preventing Discrimination Based on Mental Health Disabilities and Addictions*, Chapter 16 (Toronto: 2014). This chapter, titled "Consent and Capacity" references the duty to accommodate in the exercise of legal capacity in the Ontario human rights context. <http://www.ohrc.on.ca/en/policy-preventing-discrimination-based-mental-health-disabilities-and-addictions/16-consent-and-capacity> accessed 11.11.2022.

4. *Gather data on need for, and access to, decision-making assistance and accommodations in decision-making*

There is limited publicly available data on need for and access to decision-making assistance to enable people with disabilities to exercise choice, power, and control in their lives. This poses a serious data gap in developing needed public policy and law reform in this area. In the Canadian context, Statistics Canada, the national statistics agency, last collected this data through its 2006 Participation and Activity Limitation Survey. With demographic trends signalling an increasing prevalence of developmental, intellectual, and cognitive disability, and people living with significant mental health issues, the magnitude of the policy concern is growing. It is essential to close the data gap if we are to better regulate and deliver supports for decision-making and to provide needed guidance on the duty to accommodate in the exercise of legal capacity.

6. SUMMARY AND CONCLUSION

This chapter critically examined the assumptions underlying the account of autonomy on which mainstream approaches to legal capacity are based. The account states that an autonomous agent is one who acts "(1) intentionally, (2) with understanding, and (3) without controlling influences that determine their action."[40] If interpreted, as is usually the case, that a person must meet all three tests on their own to be considered an autonomous agent, this account systematically disadvantages persons with intellectual, cognitive, and psychosocial disabilities. Its corollary is that their legal capacity can be restricted on this basis.

Drawing on Amartya Sen's capabilities approach to equality, I have argued that the capacity to "intend," as the basis of legal power, is universally shared even if interpreting others' intentions can be a challenge when they communicate in ways most others are not able to understand. The capabilities approach can be formulated to recognise that the other two steps in being an autonomous agent can be accomplished either by oneself or with the support of others. In this sense, decision-making capability can be constituted universally, to the extent that people have access to decision-making supports they need.

One of the main challenges in constituting decision-making capability for people with more significant disabilities is securing needed access to the right "interpretive support." This is especially needed when a person may have challenges in communication or is in situations where others do not have the

---

[40] BEAUCHAMP and CHILDRESS (n. 14), p. 59.

personal knowledge or are not in a trusting relationship with the person to understand and translate their manifest intentions to other parties, or where the person's expressed will and preferences seem to fluctuate or be contradictory.

The principle of "best interpretation of will and preferences in the circumstances" acknowledges that some interpretations of decision-making supporters can be better than others. This chapter also suggests that the principle of "acting with true intentions," articulated in testamentary law is a useful normative guide in arriving at the best interpretation of will and preferences. It assumes that "true" or "truest" intentions do exist. While they may not be able to be determined with absolute certainty, asking the question about what a person's true intentions are in the circumstance requires an examination of any conditions or undue influence or coercion that may be influencing their expression.

Translating a person's intention into actual decision-making capability requires that a person's "plans," which are developed with the support of others, be given status in the making, changing, and ending of legal relationships. A planning theory of legal agency suggests that without legal recognition of a person's plans, and of the supported decision-making and other processes that go into the making of those plans, many persons will not enjoy legal capacity. While the planning agency of people with intellectual, cognitive, and psychosocial disabilities is increasingly recognised through policies and programs that encourage person-centred planning approaches, these are not yet, for the most part, considered as a basis for recognising the person's legal agency.

Finally, for decision-making capability to be a foundation for people to exercise legal capacity and to achieve legal power over their lives, other parties to legal relationships must accommodate their decision-making support needs. Translating this approach into law, policy and practice requires further research and development to detail its concepts, standards, and guidance and to consider its application in different legal regimes and jurisdictions.

The CRPD's recognition of the universal right to legal capacity holds immense promise for establishing conditions for inclusion, participation, and full citizenship of persons with disabilities, including those with the most significant intellectual, cognitive, and psychosocial disabilities. There *is* a pathway to universal legal capacity; however, it will take sustained leadership to reconstruct law, policy, and practice frameworks to lay the stepping-stones for its realisation. Until then, a growing proportion of people will not be able to count on having equal status as citizens and be assured equal power over their own lives.

LEGAL CAPACITY, VULNERABILITY AND THE IDEA OF "PERSON"

Nicolás Espejo-Yaksic[*]

To love, to derive joy from life, to learn the wonder of being: these are, I offer, the apotheosis of a good life, one that everyone can achieve – and that, perhaps, even a philosopher can appreciate.[1]

1.	Introduction	89
2.	Capability for Decision-Making: Article 12 of the UNCRPD	90
3.	Justice and Legal Capacity	92
	3.1. "Person"	93
	3.2. Capabilities	95
	3.3. Severe Disabilities and Care	96
4.	Vulnerability, Relational Autonomy and Legal Capacity	97
	4.1. Universal Vulnerability	99
	4.2. Situated Vulnerabilities	100
	4.3. Support Decision-Making and Relational Autonomy	102
	4.4. Safeguards and Vulnerability	103
5.	Conclusions	105

1. INTRODUCTION

The equal recognition of the legal capacity of persons with intellectual, cognitive and psychosocial disabilities is a matter whose normative relevance in the field of political and moral philosophy, as well as in that of legal doctrine, is not especially relevant. Perhaps this is due, in part, to the fact that deep-seated liberal political or moral philosophy, and the law built around it, have tended

---

[*] Researcher of the Centre for Constitutional Studies (CEC) of the Supreme Court of Justice of Mexico; Visiting Fellow, Exeter College, Oxford University and Guest Lecturer in Law, Leiden University; Adjunct Professor, School of Law, University College Cork.

[1] E. F. Kittay, *Learning from My Daughter. The Value and Care of Disabled Minds*, Oxford University Press, New York 2019, p. 54.

Intersentia

to do without the uncomfortable presence of vulnerability and dependency and without the capital function of interpersonal relationships in exercising individual autonomy. Thus, while these categories seem to be "relegated" to specific fields – and relatively marginal or secondary in the great scenario of legal doctrines, such as family law or labour law – private law inhabits a space of, at least, tension with them. Thus, while dogmatic debates are opened, and new regulatory frameworks are created that invigorate the relationship between private law and fundamental rights – for example, in terms of non-discrimination, privacy or access to information – other legal institutions remain alive and unquestioned. Such is the case of legal capacity.

My impression, however, is that the study of legal capacity – especially its specific conception as developed in the United Nation Convention on the Rights of Persons with Disabilities (UNCRPD) – is not a marginal nor a "niche" legal matter. The model of equal recognition of the legal capacity of all individuals and the establishment of a support system for decision-making, including the necessary safeguards for its exercise – is not an "irrelevant case" for theories of justice or the law. It is, instead, a *hard case*: a case that challenges its normative and legal dogmas. As such, studying the legal capacity of persons with intellectual, cognitive or psychosocial disabilities can allow us to improve philosophy and law. Not least significantly, a better understanding of the idea of legal capacity can help us reconstruct our conception of justice and the legal institutions derived from it in a way that is relevant, also, to specific people whose human lives deserve equal respect and consideration.

This work is an exploratory and general attempt to locate the right to equal recognition of legal capacity and support systems for decision-making based on certain specific assumptions about the human person, capabilities and vulnerability. Such assumptions – or approaches – allow us to conceive the idea of personal autonomy in "relational" terms. And from there, understand the central role played by the elimination of legal barriers for respecting the rights, will and preferences of persons with intellectual, cognitive, or psychosocial disability, on the one hand, as well as the design and implementation of a decision support system, with safeguards to protect against abuse, on the other.

2. CAPABILITY FOR DECISION-MAKING: ARTICLE 12 OF THE UNCRPD

Article 12, paragraph 2, of the UNCRPD, recognises that persons with disabilities "have legal capacity on an equal basis with others in all aspects of life". Legal capacity includes the capacity to be the holder of rights and to act legally; it grants the person the complete protection of the rights offered by the legal system. Understood this way, legal capacity and mental capacity emerge as two different concepts. *Legal capacity* is the capacity to be the holder of rights and obligations – legal capacity – and to exercise those rights and obligations – legitimacy to act. It is the key to gaining access to true participation in society. *Mental capacity*, on the other hand, refers to a person's ability to make decisions, which naturally varies from person to person and may be different for a given person depending on many factors, including environmental and social. Therefore, and as the Committee on the Rights of Persons with Disabilities (hereinafter CRPD) has pointed out, under Article 12 of the UNCRPD, deficits in mental capacity, whether alleged or real, should not be used as a justification for denying legal capacity.[2]

Why is this distinction between legal capacity and mental capacity significant? In a cognitive-functional conception, capacity appears as an objective, permanent fact that arises primarily from internal biological causes: one is capable, or one is not capable. However, the way we make decisions varies at different times in our lives. For example, making decisions may be more difficult due to stress, tiredness, a health condition, etc. When we learn new skills and have new experiences, our decision-making capability also improves. Something similar happens when we have resources and support that allow us to transform opportunities or general rights into specific functions or freedoms. In other words, a capabilities-based approach – as we have seen in the first section of this chapter – helps us realise the role that the various *conversion factors* play when exercising our autonomy. Therefore, instead of "mental capacity", it is preferable to speak of *decision-making skills* or *decision-making ability*.[3]

The UNCRPD thus goes beyond the model of "mental disability" as the basis for "legal incapacity", placing persons with disabilities at the centre of all decisions that concern them. Based on this, States are obliged to recognise, without discrimination, the right to legal capacity, together with providing access to people with an intellectual disability to the individualised support they may need to exercise that specific capacity. States are also obliged to establish adequate and effective safeguards to prevent abuses in the exercise of those supports. In other words, the UNCRPD model seeks compliance with two types of obligations: (i) a negative content, which requires the non-intervention or invasion of the State and third parties in the sphere of power

---

[2] Committee on the Rights of Persons with Disabilities (CRPD) (2013), *General Comment No. 1, on article 12: equal recognition as a person before the law*, CRPD/C/11/4, paras. 11–12. See, in a similar sense, Colombian Constitutional Court, *Judgment C-182* of 2016; Supreme Court of Justice of Mexico (SCJN), First Chamber, *Amparo in Revisión 702/2018*, September 11, 2019.

[3] World Health Organization, *Protecting the right to legal capacity in mental health and related services*, Geneva, 2017, p. 16; and M. BACH and L. KERZNER, "A New Paradigm for Protecting Autonomy and the Right to Self-Determination" [2010] *Law Commission of Ontario*, Toronto 2010. <https://www.lco-cdo.org/wp-content/uploads/2010/11/disabilities-commissioned-paper-bach-kerzner.pdf> accessed 19.01.2023.

the person's autonomous choice and that corresponds to the classical view of autonomy; and (ii) a positive content, which would demand the intervention of the State and society to promote and favour the power of autonomous choice of the person.[4] In more concrete terms, the positive dimension that the UNCRPD promotes consists of the creation of a *support system for the exercise of legal capacity*, that is, a set of relations, practices, measures and agreements of more or less formality and intensity, designed to assist a person with intellectual disability in the communication, understanding and consequences of legal acts, as well as in the manifestation and interpretation of their volition and preferences.[5]

With different complexities, comparative legislation has been consolidating a series of reforms that aim, precisely, at approaching the model proposed by the Convention. In cases such as Ireland, Costa Rica, Peru and, more recently, Colombia, these are processes of stricter adaptation to the mandates derived from the UNCRPD. Thus, in these legislations, the legal capacity of all people under equal conditions before the law is presumed, and support systems for decision-making – assisted and/or co-decision – and safeguards for protection against possible abuses are created.[6] In other cases, various laws have modified the regulations associated with guardianship to avoid declarations of absolute incapacity. This is the case, for example, of German legislation, in which interdiction (guardianship) cannot be total but must be strictly adjusted to those specific steps that the judging person determines and for as long as necessary, without ever exceeding seven years.[7] The same happens with Czech legislation, according to which declarations of absolute incapacity are not accepted. Such measure must be of "*ultima ratio*", only plausible under strict conditions of applicability.[8]

3. JUSTICE AND LEGAL CAPACITY

For a theory of justice and rights to be relevant for persons with intellectual, cognitive and psychosocial disabilities, it must guarantee two fundamental

---

[4]   R. De Asis Roig and M. D. C. Barranco, *El derecho de la autonomía personal y atención a las personas en situación de dependencia*, Dykinson, Madrid 2004, pp. 110–111.

[5]   CRPD (n. 2) paras. 13 and 29.

[6]   See, Assisted Decision-Making (Capacity) Act 2015, Ireland, ss. 10–30; Law No. 9379, for the Promotion of the Autonomy of Persons with Disabilities, of 2016, Costa Rica, arts. 6–15; Civil Code of Peru, arts. 659-A et seq.; *Law No. 1966*, Colombia, arts. 5 and 8–50.

[7]   German Civil Code –BGB–, version of January 2, 2002 –Bundesgesetzblatt–, I p. 42, 2909; 2003, I p. 738. Quoted in National University of Ireland –NUI–, Galway, Center for Disability Law and Policy, *A study on the Equal Recognition before the law*, Council of Europe, Strasbourg, France 2017, pp. 38–39.

[8]   Act N. 89/2012 Coll., Civil Code of the Czech Republic, cited in National University of Ireland –NUI–, Galway, Center for Disability Law and Policy (n. 7) pp. 41–42.

and concurrent principles: (i) equal treatment – respect –, which recognises their inalienable capacity to exercise their rights and have access to the same opportunities that enable the design of a life that can be called "their own"; and (ii) access to a network of permanent support – and care, in those cases in which it is necessary – that allow them to achieve the standard of living they desire and serve as support for making their personal decisions. While the idea and role of support – and care – for the exercise of personal autonomy will be specified later in this chapter, I am interested here in dwelling on the first of these two principles: equal respect for the development of one's own life, regardless of whether a person is in a situation of intellectual, cognitive or psychosocial disability.

3.1. "PERSON"

The recognition and promotion of every human being's ability to "flourish", that is, live a complete life, whatever their social, cultural, economic, environmental, physical, intellectual, cognitive or psychosocial circumstances, is an end in itself. However, an exclusive conception of the person as an ontological assumption in constructing a theory of justice and rights affects the possibility of having an effectively "universal" theory of justice.[9] In a classical liberal model, the idea of person that is assumed by theories of justice – at least concerning adults – seems to be based on specific essential moral and mental characteristics: our independence, capacity to formulate complete rational judgments, and moral autonomy.[10] This fundamental assumption of the theory of rights, strongly present in classical and modern contractual political theory, presupposes a high degree of rationality on the part of those who negotiate the fundamental terms of political justice. The dominant idea of contractarianism is that the principles of justice are self-chosen by rational, independent, physically and mentally capable actors. These subjects, who contract among themselves for social cooperation, do so from a perspective of mutual self-interest[11] or the respect of said contracting parties as ends.[12]

Thus, for example, *justice as fairness* presupposes a particular conception of the person according to which moral agents are independent of their particular interests, attributes and preferences, capable of distancing themselves from them to review, assess and modify them.[13] But this political conception of

---

[9] N. Espejo Yaksic, "Introducción: Persona, Autonomía y Capacidad", in N. Espejo Yaksic and F. Lathrop Gómez (coords and eds), *Discapacidad Intelectual y Derecho*, Thomson Reuters, Santiago de Chile 2019, pp. 1–21.

[10] S. Sevenhuijsen, "Too Good to be True?" (1999) 34 *Focaal* 207.

[11] D. Gauthier, *Morals by Agreement*, Oxford University Press, Oxford 1986.

[12] J. Rawls, *A Theory of Justice*, Harvard University Press, Cambridge 1971.

[13] Cf. ibid., p. 561.

justice exhibits two important limitations. The first is to assume that the individuals who are part of the definitions of justice – and the fundamental rights that derive from it – are more or less equal in powers and capabilities. The second is that the idea of mutual benefit in opting for cooperation presupposes that people define the terms of justice to the extent that they expect to get something out of it.

This image of cooperation is linked to a basic assumption: human beings have "normal" productive capabilities. As Rawls asks: "What is the most appropriate conception of justice to specify the terms of social cooperation between citizens regarded as free and equal, and as *normal* and *fully cooperating* members throughout a complete life?"[14]

As it is easy to see, this way of posing the problem of justice turns this normative enterprise into a pertinent question for *certain types* of people: rational and reasonable people who have the capacity to revise and alter their own conception of the good life, if they so wish. Indeed, as Rawls himself points out, while citizens do not have the same (equal) capacities: "They do have, at least to a minimal essential degree, the moral, *intellectual*, and physical capabilities that enable them to *cooperate fully* as members of society throughout their lives."[15]

The result of this theoretical operation is that those who do not conform to this conception of the person are not counted among the people for whom – and in reciprocity with whom – the primary institutions of society are structured. Conceiving the person in this way simply omits, from the discussion of basic political choices, those needs and dependencies that human beings may experience, both physically and mentally, temporarily or permanently.[16]

In other words, the exclusion of persons with physical or intellectual disabilities from the contractual theory results from a *homogeneity requirement*: only certain people, who share more or less the same capabilities, are competent to enter into the social contract.[17] In this way, the moral properties necessary to be part of the negotiation process of the social contract that will determine the rules that govern social agreements are, in turn, influenced by the dominant social group. In other words, these demands for homogeneity question the legitimacy of certain people as "legitimate participants", diverting attention from the ideas and experiences of these subjects and diminishing the value of reaching mutual agreements with them.[18]

---

[14] J. Rawls, *Political Liberalism*, Columbia University Press, New York 1996, p. 20 (emphasis added).

[15] Ibid., pp. 20, 21 and 183 (emphasis added).

[16] M. C. Nussbaum, *Frontiers of Justice. Disability, Nationality, Species Membership*, The Belknap Press of Harvard University Press, Cambridge, Mass./London, England 2006.

[17] L. Francis and A. Silvers, "Justice through Trust: Disability and the 'Outlier Problem' in Social Contract Theory" (2005) 116(1) *Ethics* p. 46.

[18] Cf. ibid., p. 41.

3.2. CAPABILITIES

A better way to find a solution to this problem may be to understand the idea of the person in relation to human dignity, and the latter, in correspondence with *capabilities*: the propitious circumstances in which specific abilities predispose us to what we want, which depend not only on the steps taken by the individual as an agent of his destiny but also on the relationships in which he develops his life.[19]

The capabilities approach argues that questions of justice should not be resolved by considering the goods or resources that people possess but rather "what people are, as matter of fact, capable of doing and being".[20] In other words, justice requires more than giving people an equal amount of goods or resources. It requires giving people the same capabilities to *function* in certain key human ways and asking what they need to live a life that is "worthy of the dignity of the human person".[21] In this order of ideas, the fact that someone has the capability to achieve certain doings or beings depends on the so-called "conversion factors": the degree to which a person can transform a resource into a functioning.[22] Therefore, to the extent that governments or societies do not guarantee their members a minimum level of *capability to function* in certain basic areas, such governments and societies are unjust. So conceived, justice becomes a central concern for people who are not provided with the institutional conditions to be able to function on an equal base with others.

This focus on justice and capabilities has direct – and profound – consequences for people with intellectual, cognitive or psychosocial disabilities. As Michael Bach suggests in his chapter in this book, to the extent that a person has a valued social context and relationships that respect a person's intentional and deliberate expressions as the basis for making their decisions – and that facilitate the goods and services necessary for making those decisions – that person will have the social possibilities to exercise power over their own life. The very idea of "support for the exercise of legal capacity" aims at facilitating a better understanding of the role played by people other than the individual agent of a given decision in the decision process itself. Through such supports, a person transforms an abstract good – as the equal right to legal capacity – into a specific operation, i.e., decision making.

---

[19] M. C. Nussbaum, 'Aristotle on Human Nature and the Foundations of Ethics', in J. E. G. Alham and R. Harrison (eds), *World Mind, and Ethics: Essays on the Philosophy of Bernard Williams*, Cambridge University Press, Cambridge 1995, pp. 86–131.

[20] M. C. Nussbaum (n. 16), p. 70.

[21] Ibid.

[22] A. Sen, *Inequality Re-examined*, Clarendon Press, Oxford 1992, pp. 19–21, 26–30, 37–38.

3.3. SEVERE DISABILITIES AND CARE

While a capabilities-based approach seems to connect quite clearly with the idea of "decision support", it is also true that such an approach has specific challenges when dealing with people with some type of severe intellectual, cognitive or psychosocial disability.[23] Despite the existence of both support for decision-making and care in their favour, a person with a severe intellectual, cognitive or psychosocial disability will never achieve *the same level* of "human flourishing" or "functioning" – actual capability – as that of the majority of the population. Unlike most of us, a person with a severe disability will not participate fully in political life, will not form and maintain a family of their own, will not read or write, and will not be able to dedicate their lives to the cultivation of the arts. However, and despite these restrictions, the life of these people is also a *human life;* their life can also be "richly human and full of dignity".[24] In other words, from the fact that a person is not able to exercise – on his/her own – one or several capacities, it does not follow that said person cannot also "flourish" or live a genuinely human life.[25]

In particular, the care exercised in relation to a person with a severe intellectual, cognitive or psychosocial disability can be understood as a tool that not only facilitates satisfying basic needs, such as feeding, dressing or receiving medical treatment. In a total normative sense, care is oriented towards promoting the individual's ability to flourish as a human being. And it is this conception of the human person that guides the caregiver, who, in a dialectic between dignity and care, makes care confer and recognise, at the same time, the dignity of the other.[26] In other words, there is no care without *respect*, which implies accepting that what the majority might want in a given case is not necessarily what a subject considered in his particularity will want for himself.[27] Therefore, if the caregiver of a person with high levels of dependency adopt autonomy as a relational construction – through an open, active and reflective attitude – and have more access to knowledge about communication and how to identify care needs, this will lead to better identification of the expectations for the autonomy of the person cared for.[28]

---

[23]   On severe disabilities and theories of justice, see, in particular, the interesting work of J. S. BEAUDRY, *The Disabled Contract. Severe Intellectual Disability, Justice and Morality*, Cambridge University Press, Cambridge 2021.

[24]   E. F. KITTAY, "Equality, Dignity and Disability", in M. LYONS and F. WALDRON (eds), *Perspectives on Equality*, Liffey Press, Dublin 2005, p. 95.

[25]   On the accuracy of this question in the context of Nussbaum's objective theory of human capabilities, cf., M. NUSSBAUM, "Human Dignity and Political Entitlements", in *The President's Council on Bioethics*, Washington, DC, 2008. <https://bioethicsarchive.georgetown.edu/pcbe/reports/human_dignity/chapter14.html> accessed 27.03.2023.

[26]   E. F. KITTAY (n. 1), p. 23.

[27]   J. HERRING, *Caring and the Law*, Hart Publishing, Oxford and Portland, Oregon 2013, p. 18.

[28]   G. STEFANSDOTTIR et al., "Autonomy and People with Intellectual Disabilities Who Require More Intensive Support" (2018) 20(1) *Scandinavian Journal of Disability Research* 162–171;

The previous points have a clear correlation in terms of legal capacity. When the will of a person with a severe intellectual, cognitive or psychosocial disability is externalised through another person – who acts "on their behalf"– externalisation can operate in two ways. On the one hand, it can be carried out in a "protective" way, acting according to what is considered to work in favour of the well-being of the person substituted in his/her will. This is what generally happens in the traditional system of civil interdiction or guardianship (*interdicción civil*) where a person is fully substituted in his/her decision-making.[29] On the other hand, however, such support can be carried out in such a way that the dignity of a person substituted in his/her will is respected. This is the case of when a guardian acts based on the "best interpretation of the will and preferences"[30] of the person with a severe intellectual, cognitive or psychosocial disability.[31] In this way, care will be able to integrate protection and autonomy simultaneously, dissolving the false dichotomy between care and respect for rights.[32]

4. VULNERABILITY, RELATIONAL AUTONOMY AND LEGAL CAPACITY

Our current legal systems, as well as the legal rights that derive from them, are strongly oriented towards protecting individuals against all undue forms

---

N. BEKKEMA, A. J. E. DEVEER, C. M. P. M. HERTOUGH and A. L. FRANCKE, "Respecting autonomy in the end-of-life care of people with intellectual disabilities: a qualitative multiple-case study" (2014) 58(4) *Journal of Intellectual Disability Research* 368–380.

[29] Cf., European Court of Human Rights –ECHR–, *Salontaji-Drobnjak v. Serbia*, Application No. 36500/06, judgment of 13 October 2009, para. 144; *X & Y v. Croatia*, Application No. 5193/09, judgment of 3 November 2011, para. 84; *D.D. v. Lithuania*, Application No. 13469/06, judgment of 14 February 2012 and; Supreme Court of Justice of the Nation of Mexico –SCJN–, First Chamber, *Amparo en Revision 1368/2015*, March 13, 2019, para. 34.

[30] T. CARNEY, S. THEN, C. BIGBY, I. WIESEL, J. DOUGLAS and E. SMITH, "Realizing 'will, preferences and rights': reconciling differences on best practice support for decision-making?" (2019) 28(4) *Griffith Law Review* 357–379.

[31] Take into account, in this sense, the way in which the SCJN resignifies the figure of the guardian of the person with a disability by stating: "[the guardian] has the function of assisting the person in making the corresponding decisions, but he cannot substitute their will, [...] the state of interdiction must be conceived as an institution of assistance so that the person makes their own decisions, which must be respected even when they may be considered inaccurate [...] the support model is not based on wisdom for decision-making, but simply in the freedom of people to carry them out and assume them, since the freedom to make one's own decisions forms part of the core of issues inextricably linked to respect for the inherent dignity and individual autonomy and independence of people" – Supreme Court of Justice of Mexico (SCJN), First Chamber, *Amparo Directo en Revisión 2805/2014*, January 14 2015, para. 42.

[32] "Care not administered in such a way as to preserve and respect a person's dignity is not care that most of us would want. In fact, it is a form of care that we fear [...] it is not care at all." E. F. KITTAY (n. 1), p. 211.

of interference and respecting the freedom of the subject in the choice of those ends that give meaning to the chosen life project.[33] In this framework, the law presupposes that people are independent, rational and reasonable, self-interested subjects and that, as adults, they act following their individual autonomy.[34] More specifically, the law presupposes that people can exercise their autonomy to the extent that they demonstrate their *mental capacity*. This idea of "mental capacity" is, in turn, built based on a simple intuition: human beings must exhibit a certain level of competence in making decisions so that these can be "respected". Among other aspects, this implies that people are capable of deciding *for themselves*, which will not happen if: (i) the person in question does not understand the information relevant to the decision; (ii) cannot retain said information; (iii) cannot use or "weigh" that information as part of a decision-making process; or (iv) is unable to communicate their decision, whether through speech, use of sign language, or otherwise.[35]

Thus, those who are outside this paradigm of normality or mental capacity are commonly described as "vulnerable", that is, people who (i) lack the capability to look after their own interests and needs; or (ii) are insufficiently equipped with skills to resist outside interference or irrational impulses that threaten their own well-being.[36] In this order of ideas, while independence and self-sufficiency are considered desirable ideals, dependency and vulnerability are presented to us as something that should be avoided. Those who lack the skills and capabilities to ensure their autonomy and individual freedom are identified as vulnerable. Their perceived vulnerability marks them as "lesser", "imperfect", "out of the ordinary", and places them in some way outside the protection of the social contract, as it is applied to other people. By operating in this way, those classified as vulnerable are subject to monitoring, supervision and regulation, as occurs in the case of the responses designed by the State for the so-called *vulnerable populations*, such as the "young people at social risk", those who are "dependent on the welfare state" or "persons with disabilities".[37]

---

[33]   While it is true that many constitutional systems protect more than individual liberty, the predominant role played by this principle and right is a central constant in most Western legal systems.

[34]   J. HERRING, *Vulnerable Adults and the Law*, Oxford University Press, Oxford 2016, p. 18.

[35]   In this sense, see, for example, Mental Capacity Act 2005 (England and Wales), s. 2(4), and Assisted Decision-Making (Capacity) Act 2015 (Ireland), s. 3.

[36]   D. BEDFORD, "Introduction: Vulnerability refigured", in D. BEDFORD and J. HERRING (eds), *Embracing vulnerability. The challenges and implications for Law*, Routledge, London and New York 2020, p. 1.

[37]   M. A. FINEMAN, "Equality, Autonomy, and the Vulnerable Subject in Law and Politics", in M. A. FINEMAN and A. GREAR (eds), *Vulnerability. Reflections on a New Ethical Foundation for Law and Politics*, Routledge, London and New York 2013 p. 16.

4.1. UNIVERSAL VULNERABILITY

The scepticism around the use of vulnerability and the dependency among many advocates of the equal recognition of legal capacity is understandable. Historically, many groups have fought for full recognition of their rights in opposition to the stigmatising dependency status. The dependence of women on men – as a restriction internalised by the former –,[38] the oppressive dependence of girls and boys and derived from the exercise of the "rights of control" exercised by their parents,[39] the emancipation of the "inevitable dependency of persons with disabilities" and the counter-narrative of an independent life[40] account for this well-documented fear.

However, there are other possible ways of understanding and responding to vulnerability and dependency. Focusing the analysis on vulnerability in specific populations leads to a severe error: believing that some of us are not vulnerable or that there is such a thing as "invulnerability".[41] The reality of our human experience, however, is very different. As Dodds has suggested:

> We are all vulnerable to the demands of our bodily, social, and relational existence, and by recognising this inherent human vulnerability, we can become aware of the ways in which a range of social institutions and structures protect us against some vulnerabilities while exposing us to risk others.[42]

In other words, vulnerability is a part of the human condition and a constant in the relationships between people and social institutions and structures. This vulnerability can derive from different sources; In life's course, it is possible to encounter: (i) *vulnerabilities inherent* or intrinsic to the human condition and emanating from human corporality; (ii) *situational vulnerabilities* of a contextual nature that arise in response to short-term, intermittent or permanent conditions faced by the subjects; and (iii) *pathological vulnerabilities*, which stem from interpersonal, social, and socio-political sources, affecting autonomy or exacerbating the sense of powerlessness that vulnerability generates.[43]

The complexity of vulnerability sources allows us to notice something fundamental: while a person or a group of people can be identified as "vulnerable"

---

[38] S. D. Beauvoir, *The second sex*, trans. by C. Borde and S. Malovany-Chavallier, Vintage, New York 2011.

[39] S. Godwin, "Against Parental Rights" (2015) 47(1) *Columbia Human Rights Law Review* 1–83.

[40] H. Lindemann, *Damaged Identities: Narrative Repair*, Cornell University Press, Ithaca, New York 2001.

[41] M. A. Fineman (n. 37) p. 16.

[42] S. Dodds, "Depending on Care: Recognition of Vulnerability and the Social Contribution of Care Provision" (2007) 21(9) *Bioethics* 507.

[43] C. Mackenzie, D. Rogers and S. Dodds, *Vulnerability: New Essays in Ethics and Feminist Philosophy*, Oxford University Press, Oxford 2014, pp. 3–4 and 7.

due to a particular characteristic of their body, their gender, ethnicity, social class, migratory status, cognitive functioning or other individual or group characteristics, it is the distribution of institutional, economic and social support that ultimately generates that vulnerability. To put it another way, the existence or absence of supports provides us – or not – with resources in the form of advantages or coping mechanisms, helping us cope with misfortune, disaster, or violence.[44] In particular, and considered cumulatively, these supports provide individuals with the necessary *resilience* to face our shared and universal vulnerability and demand a "reactive State" – *a responsive State* –. That is, a State that, although unable to eradicate our vulnerability, can at least mediate it, compensate it or reduce it through programs, institutions and structures.[45]

4.2. SITUATED VULNERABILITIES

A universal understanding of vulnerability should not make us lose sight of the fact that specific forms of vulnerability also inhabit it. Alongside the universality and constancy of the various forms of vulnerability that people experience in the course of their lives, particular, specific or situated forms of vulnerability coexist. This is a significant claim since the very affirmation of our universal vulnerability can lead to an oversight regarding certain specific or particular forms of human vulnerability. In particular, arguing that we are all vulnerable can hide the existence of inequitable dependencies experienced by certain groups, such as children, the elderly, the sick and persons with disabilities.[46]

The fact is that, while we are all vulnerable, we are not all *equally* vulnerable. Vulnerability is not distributed equally, and how we experience our vulnerability will largely depend on factors such as ethnicity, sexuality, gender, age, health, social class, employment status, and caregiving responsibilities, among others.[47] This is especially relevant in the case of people with disabilities. As a consequence of the affirmation of the universal and constant character of vulnerability, persons with disabilities may be ignored in their lives particularities and suffer the minimisation of their disability.[48] Vulnerabilities make people with disabilities dependent on external supports of one kind or another: their unique vulnerabilities lead to *exceptional dependencies*. Conversely, a dependency creates a new vulnerability. Whatever the reason for dependency, its existence

---

[44]   J. HERRING (n. 34), p. 19.

[45]   M. A. FINEMAN (n. 37), pp. 19, 24 et seq.

[46]   E. F. KITTAY, *Love's Labor: Essays on Women, Equality and Dependency*, Routledge, New York 1999, p. xi.

[47]   J. WALLBANK and J. HERRING, "Introduction", in J. WALLBANK and J. HERRING (eds), *Vulnerability, Care and Family Law*, Ashgate, Aldershot 2014, p. 8.

[48]   B. HUGHES, "Being Disabled: Towards a Critical Social Ontology for Disability Studies" (2007) 22 *Disability & Society* 673.

immediately inserts the risk of what could happen in that person's life if the support they depend on were withdrawn.[49]

Two additional examples illustrate the need for specificity in the field of vulnerability and disability. One in three people with intellectual disabilities has suffered some form of sexual abuse during their adult life, a rate that is even higher in institutionalised contexts.[50] This suggests a specific relationship between the situation of disability and the particular vulnerability to sexual abuse, whether committed by peers – which constitutes the majority of cases –[51] or by other adults. In turn, the global level of vulnerability experienced by adolescents and women is particularly acute when they suffer the imposition of guardianship and, with it, their sexual and reproductive health and autonomy are seriously affected. This manifests itself, among other things, in substantial limitations on their reproductive choice, higher rates of substitution in decision-making, and forced mental health practices.[52] Thus, the general rules that enable – and restrict – the exercise of legal capacity generate differentiated effects on the vulnerability that men and women experience in exercising the rights to freedom and sexual and reproductive health.

Specifying the particular vulnerabilities of people with disabilities should not make us lose sight of the need to apply an *intersectional approach* to them. This approach to vulnerability is not satisfied by the fact of making visible or adding "layers of danger" or "multiple discriminations" to the subject with disabilities, that is, adding "additional" categories such as race, class or gender to the general vulnerability that a person with intellectual, cognitive or psychosocial disability may experience.[53] A serious intersectional approach requires understanding that factors such as class, race, sex, gender, national origin, age, or immigration status *intersect* with disability.[54] These factors modify the experience of the person with intellectual, cognitive and psychosocial disability; similarly, the disability modifies the racial, sexual or class experience.

---

[49]   J. L. SCULLY, "Disability and Vulnerability: On Bodies, Dependence, and Power", in C. MACKENZIE, W. ROGERS and S. DODDS (eds), *Vulnerability. New Essays in Ethics and Feminist Philosophy*, Oxford University Press, New York 2014, p. 211.

[50]   R. TOMSA, S. GUTU, D. COJOCARU, B. GUTIERREZ-BERMEJO, N. FLORES and C. JENARO, "Prevalence of Sexual Abuse in Adults with Intellectual Disability: Systematic Review and Meta-Analysis" (2021) 18(4) *International Journal of Environmental Research and Public Health* <https://www.ncbi.nlm.nih.gov/pmc/articles/PMC7921934/> accessed 18.01.2023.

[51]   Ibid.

[52]   V. ARSTEIN-KERSLAKE, "Gendered denials: Vulnerability created by barriers to legal capacity for women and disabled women" (2019) 66 *International Journal of Law and Psychiatry* 101501.

[53]   On the limits of an approach to intersectionality based on a model of sums of multiple systems of oppression, see A. CARASTATHIS, *Intersectionality. Origins, Contestations, Horizons*, University of Nebraska Press, Lincoln US, paperback edition 2019, p. 35.

[54]   A.-M. HANCOCK, *Intersectionality: An Intellectual History*, Oxford University Press, New York 2016.

4.3. SUPPORT DECISION-MAKING AND RELATIONAL AUTONOMY

It would be a great mistake to believe that *vulnerability* and *autonomy* are opposite terms. An adequate ethics of vulnerability gives a central place to the obligation not only to respect but also to promote autonomy. Otherwise, the vulnerability and protection approach may open the door to objectionably paternalistic and coercive forms of intervention.[55] The question, then, lies not in seeking an alternative to personal autonomy, but in specifying this concept, in such a way as to make it compatible with the central role that vulnerability plays when it comes to respecting and promoting the will and preferences of people with intellectual, cognitive and psychosocial disabilities.

The cognitive-functional conceptualisation of capability hides the interpersonal dimensions that make up capacity itself. This obviates a fundamental fact: relationships are essential for the development of capabilities, whether the person has an intellectual, cognitive or psychosocial disability. In particular, relationships can enable – or seriously affect – the development of a person's specific capability to make decisions throughout their life.[56] This is because the development of the self is a process in relationships with other people. Therefore, autonomy should not be understood solely in terms of independence and self-determination. The formation of a person's emotional desires, beliefs, and attitudes is influenced by social norms, social institutions, cultural practices, and relationships.[57] This explains, among other things, the importance, in the context of intellectual, cognitive or psychosocial disability, that support mechanisms acquire for decision-making by third parties within the framework of interpersonal relationships, enforceable duties and practices.

A *relational* conception of autonomy seeks to do justice to three central convictions:[58]

- The capability to exercise some degree of self-determination is crucial to leading a prosperous life.
- The development and sustained exercise of this capability require extensive and continuous institutional, social and interpersonal scaffolding and can be frustrated by social domination, oppression and disadvantage.

---

[55] C. MACKENZIE, "The Importance of Relational Autonomy and Capabilities for an Ethics of Vulnerability", in C. MACKENZIE, W. ROGERS and S. DODDS (n. 43), p. 33.

[56] C. KONG, *Mental Capacity in Relationship. Decision-Making, Dialogue, and Autonomy*, Cambridge University Press, Cambridge 2017, pp. 4–5.

[57] C. MACKENZIE and N. STOLJAR (eds), *Relational Autonomy: Feminist Perspectives on Autonomy, Agency, and the Social Self*, Oxford University Press, Oxford, New York 2000, p. 4.

[58] C. MACKENZIE (n. 55), pp. 41–42.

- Such frustration constitutes a social injustice; therefore, the State has an obligation to develop social, political and legal institutions that promote citizen autonomy.

In other words, in a relational conception of autonomy, the analysis of will necessarily implies paying attention to the permanent interaction between the personal exercise of autonomy and the elucidation of the ethical characteristics, obligations and duties that arise in the framework of the relationships with whom one interacts. And if disability – according to the social model – is located at the interface of deficiency – *impairment* – and the environment with which a person comes into contact, then it makes sense to look at the relationships between people with disabilities and those with whom they interact.[59]

In my view, this is precisely what is at the basis of the second – positive – obligation derived from Article 12 of the CRPD: the duty to recognise, regulate and facilitate a system in which third parties support the decision-making of a person with a disability, be it helping them to obtain and understand the information relevant to the decision, talking about the pros and cons of the different options available or helping them to communicate with other people.[60] In this perspective, support systems for decision-making strengthen the resilience of persons with intellectual, cognitive and psychosocial disabilities to face the specific vulnerabilities derived from the difficulties in respecting – and exercising – their individual autonomy.

4.4. SAFEGUARDS AND VULNERABILITY

Looking at relationships also implies not failing to see the abuses that they can generate. Every human relationship, including relationships between those who support and/or care for a person with an intellectual, cognitive or psychosocial disability, entails risks and potential harm. Such risks are particularly concrete and manifest in a series of violations of the rights of those who make up the family nucleus, especially those in a position of greater dependence or vulnerability.[61] Indeed, human relationships based on care can become harmful or manipulative without rights.[62] Therefore, there can be no care without rights.

---

[59] S. DOWLING, V. WILLIAMS, J. WEBB et al., "Managing relational autonomy in interactions: People with intellectual disabilities" (2019) 32(5) *Journal of Applied Research in Intellectual Disabilities* 1059.

[60] On decision-making supports and relational autonomy, see L. SERIES, "Relationships, autonomy and legal capacity: Mental capacity and support paradigms" (2015) 40 *International Journal of Law and Psychiatry* 80–91.

[61] J. HERRING (n. 27), pp. 64–68.

[62] P. A. MEYERS, "The 'Ethic of Care' and the Problem of Power" (1998) 6(2) *The Journal of Political Philosophy* 142.

Nicolás Espejo-Yaksic

The specific rights and guarantees recognised in the CRPD do not replace the core of ethical relationships among those who support and/or care for a person with a disability but operate as a guarantee of protection when such care becomes oppressive, violent or unjust. In this lieu, rights provide a position of *support* and *security* in case the other constitutive elements of that social relationship disintegrate or distort.[63]

Aware of the need for protection and care against possible abuse, the CRPD recognises the importance of a series of *adequate and effective safeguards* to exercise legal capacity. Although all people can be subject to "undue influence", this risk can be exacerbated for those who depend on the support of others to make decisions. Pursuant to Article 12.4 of the CRPD, the main objective of safeguards is to ensure

> that the measures related to the exercise of legal capacity respect the rights, will and preferences of the person, that there is no conflict of interest or undue influence, that they are proportional and adapted to the circumstances of the person, and that they are applied in the shortest possible time and that they are subject to regular review by a competent, independent and impartial authority or judicial body. The safeguards will be proportional to the degree to which said measures affect the rights and interests of the persons.

As has been specified by the doctrine, these safeguards can be classified into three groups: (i) those aimed at guaranteeing the rights, will and preferences of a person; (ii) those that seek to avoid undue influence by third parties; and (iii) those that concern conflicts of interest.[64] Its fundamental meaning, as Constantino Caycho and Bregaglio Lazarte explain elsewhere in this volume, is to lessen the *relational* vulnerability faced by people with intellectual, cognitive or psychosocial disabilities linked to the possibility of manipulation within the support framework. Safeguards are aimed at verifying whether the statement made by the person with disabilities responds to their *true will* or if it is vitiated by the influence of a person who provides support or by the counterpart in a legal transaction. And not, instead, to determine if the person "understands or not" the legal act.

The analysis of the safeguards in the framework of Article 12.4 of the CRPD and how these have been duly or unduly regulated by the legal systems that have advanced towards decision-making support systems exceeds my remit. Instead, I am interested in highlighting here the role that safeguards play

---

[63]   J. Waldron, *Liberal Rights: Collected Papers 1981–1991*, Cambridge University Press, Cambridge 1993, p. 374.

[64]   W. Martin, S. Michalowski, J. Stavertn et al., *Three jurisdictions report. Towards Compliance with CRPD Art. 12 in Capacity/Incapacity Legislation across the UK*, An Essex Autonomy Project Position Paper, 2016, p. 38. <https://autonomy.essex.ac.uk/resources/eap-three-jurisdictions-report/> accessed 19.01.2023.

within the framework of a system of recognising the rights of persons with intellectual, cognitive and psychosocial disabilities based on both a capability and a vulnerability approach. Safeguards are not a mere "appendix" to the recognition of the legal capacity of persons with disabilities but rather an essential component that takes into account not only the interests of individual autonomy. In a relational framework, the safeguards give visibility and allow responding to the unwanted dynamics of said relationships, helping respond to the specific vulnerabilities generated around such relationships.

5. CONCLUSIONS

To recognise the equal right to legal capacity for all people is to accept the intrinsic value of all human life, its equal capacity to flourish, regardless of the limitations generated by the vulnerabilities associated with disability. A focus on justice and "support for the exercise of legal capacity" is aimed at facilitating a better understanding of the role played by people other than the individual agent of a given decision in the decision process. Through such supports, a person transforms an abstract good – as the equal right to legal capacity – into a specific operation, i.e., decision-making. In other words, in a relational conception of autonomy, the development and a sustained exercise of this capacity require extensive and continuous institutional, social, and interpersonal scaffolding. Such scaffolding counterbalances the specific vulnerabilities that arise in the context of disability. In particular, and considered cumulatively, these supports provide people with an intellectual, cognitive or psychosocial disability with the necessary *resilience* to face the barriers of their environment and project their personal autonomy.

The reformulation of legal capacity in the terms prescribed by Article 12 of the CRPD is not only relevant for specific regulation of the exercise of rights, will and preferences of persons with intellectual, cognitive or psychosocial disabilities. The model of equal recognition of the legal capacity of all people and the establishment of a support system for decision-making, including the necessary safeguards for its exercise, make it possible to test essential assumptions of political or moral theory and the law. By problematising the ontological assumptions of both disciplines and opening a central space to vulnerability and human relationships, equal respect for legal capacity moves from an *irrelevant* case to a *hard* case that allows us to re-signify our notions of social justice and radically enrich our appreciation of the role of law.

PART II
LAW REFORM
Country and Regional Perspectives

EMERGING JUDICIAL PRECEDENTS RELATED TO LEGAL CAPACITY IN LATIN AMERICAN HIGH COURTS

Agustina PALACIOS*

Al andar se hace camino
Y al volver la vista atrás
Se ve la senda que nunca
Se ha de volver a pisar.

Antonio Machado, *Caminante no hay camino*[1]

1. Introduction 110
2. Legal Capacity in Court Precedents: Making the Path as We Walk. 110
   2.1. Recognition of Legal Capacity without Discrimination Based on
        Disability 110
        2.1.1. Precedents that Support Legal Capacity Reforms. 111
        2.1.2. Precedents that Refer to the Legal Concept of
               Interdiction 112
   2.2. The Guarantee of Accessibility, Reasonable Adjustments and
        Support for the Exercise of Legal Capacity. 115
   2.3. The Right of Access to Justice and the Adoption of Procedural
        Adjustments 116
   2.4. Self-Determination, Mental Capacity, and Informed Consent 118
   2.5. The Right to Exercise Sexual and Reproductive Rights 121
   2.6. The Right to Family Life and the Exercise of Parental
        Responsibility 124
3. Conclusions. 127

---

* Doctor of Law from the Universidad Carlos III de Madrid. Adjunct Researcher of the CONICET (Spanish-language acronym meaning "National Board of Scientific and Technical Research of Argentina").

[1] In English "By walking you make the path before you, and when you look behind you see the path which after you will not be trod again".

1. INTRODUCTION

This chapter presents an overview of some precedents considered ground-breaking for the evolution of jurisprudence concerning legal capacity in Latin American courts. This text does not attempt to be an exhaustive study of jurisprudence as it pertains to legal capacity in the Latin American region; instead, it provides an initial approach to its current status by identifying the precedents considered to have set the trend in the last decade. To that end, a series of emerging central themes have been identified, making up the content and scope of international law standards on the subject, as they refer to:

- recognition of legal capacity without discrimination due to disability;
- the guarantee of accessibility, reasonable adjustments, and support for the exercise of legal capacity;
- the right of access to justice and adoption of procedural adjustments;
- self-determination, mental capacity, and informed consent;
- the right to exercise sexual and reproductive rights;
- the right to family life.

2. LEGAL CAPACITY IN COURT PRECEDENTS: MAKING THE PATH AS WE WALK

The Latin American region has been undergoing a process of law reform to incorporate the standards of the United Nations Convention on the Rights of Persons with Disabilities (hereinafter UNCRPD) regarding legal capacity.[2] The justice system is a fundamental actor in this process. It is possible to identify precedents that have been accompanying the implementation of this change, as well as others that have been driving it forward. However, there is still a long way to go towards deepening a disability perspective and a human rights-based approach to legal capacity.

2.1. RECOGNITION OF LEGAL CAPACITY WITHOUT DISCRIMINATION BASED ON DISABILITY

The recognition of legal capacity on an equal basis with others requires, among other things, that legal capacity be recognised and can be exercised without

---

[2]   Reform and Unification of the Nation's Civil and Commerce Code, Argentina, 2015; Law on Personal Autonomy of Persons with Disabilities, Costa Rica, 2016; Legislative Decree 1348 and DR, Peru, 2018 and 2019; Law for the Exercise of Legal Capacity of Persons of Legal Age with Disability, Colombia, 2019; and currently under study in other countries of the Latin American region.

discrimination on the basis of disability. On this point, the jurisprudence in the Latin American region is quite dissimilar.

2.1.1. Precedents that Support Legal Capacity Reforms

Some judicial precedents have supported legal reforms. For example, in Peru, the Constitutional Court has affirmed the constitutionality of the reform, stating that a law "that recognises and regulates the legal capacity of persons with disabilities under equal conditions, [...] presents us with a new reality given what is proposed by the current standards in terms of protection of the rights of persons with disabilities, vindicating this group of people and giving them back the status of true subjects of law".[3] Also supporting the reform, the Constitutional Court of Costa Rica has raised the inadmissibility of specific requirements by the Ministry of Finance that imposed a substitute model of legal capacity, expressing that such proceeding "contradicts the provisions in this regard in the Convention on the Rights of Persons with Disabilities [...] as well as in the Law for Promotion of Personal Autonomy of Persons with Disabilities".[4] Also, in Colombia, in relation to provisions of recent legal reforms, the Constitutional Court has stated "that the presumption of the legal capacity of persons with disabilities provided in [... Law 1996 is constitutional since it supports a perspective that is respectful of human dignity and real and effective equality in the exercise of fundamental rights".[5] It also found that "the positive impacts of the support system are in harmony with respect for the rights to human dignity and equality" and that the State should recognise legal capacity of persons with disabilities and provide the support necessary to enable its exercise on equal basis with others.[6]

It should be noted that prior to the legal reform, the Colombian Constitutional Court had understood that legal capacity should not be assimilated to mental capacity, since the latter "refers to the ability to make decisions, which naturally varies from one person to another and can be different for a given person based on many factors, including environmental and social factors".[7] It also references General Comment No. 1 of the Committee on the Rights of Persons with Disabilities (hereinafter CRPD), which states that the functional criterion is "incorrect for two main reasons: a) because it is applied in a discriminatory manner to persons with disabilities; and b) because it presupposes that the inner

---

3   Constitutional Court of Peru, STC, File. No. 00194-2014-PHC/TC AREQUIPA.
4   Constitutional Court of Costa Rica, Judgment No. 2019009287 of the Constitutional Court, 24/05/2019.
5   Colombian Constitutional Court, Judgment C-025 of 2021, subsection 55.
6   Ibid., subsection. 73.
7   Colombian Constitutional Court, Judgment C-182 of 2016.

workings of the human mind can be accurately assessed and, when the person fails the assessment, it denies him a fundamental human right – the right to equal recognition as a person before the law".[8] More recently, in relation to persons with disabilities "who are unable to express their will by any means", the Colombian Constitutional Court has found that:

> the exercise of legal capacity for these cases must be accompanied by a judgment of judicial adjudication of support as a necessary mechanism for decision-making. [...] The role of support is not to replace the will of the person with disabilities, validate it or enable entering into legal acts. The role of support, in contrast, is to help the person with a disability to formulate will give the possibility of carrying out a legal act and externalising it, or in such case, to represent it when executing it. In this way, in cases in which the person is unable to express their will, the support must be directed toward materialising the decision that is most harmonious to the life, context and/or social and family environment of the person in question, which are elements that will aid in "interpreting the will" of the holder of the legal act.[9]

2.1.2. Precedents that Refer to the Legal Concept of Interdiction

In countries where the substantive law has not yet been modified, it is possible to identify precedents from higher courts in which the figure of interdiction is understood as a violation of the right to equality and non-discrimination. This has been expressed by the Supreme Court of Justice of Mexico (SCJN) when it finds that "guardianship (*interdicción*) violates the right to equality and non-discrimination, among other rights [...] because it restricts the legal capacity of individuals based on disability, which is established as an undue distinction and contrary to Article 12 of the United Nations Convention on the Rights of Persons with Disabilities".[10] For the SCJN, full or total guardianship violates Article 12 of the UNCRPD since that treaty "does not allow legal capacity to be denied based on deficiency, that is, in a discriminatory manner, but rather it requires the provision of the necessary support for its exercise. [...] Therefore, denying or limiting legal capacity violates the right to equal recognition as a person before the law and constitutes a violation of Articles 5 and 12 of the UNCRPD the 1st Article of the Constitution".[11]

Likewise, it is interesting to analyse a precedent of the SCJN which declared invalid an electoral norm that restricted the right to vote of people

---

[8] Ibid.

[9] Colombian Constitutional Court, Judgment C-025/21, subsection 661.

[10] Supreme Court of Mexico (SCJN), Primera Sala, Amparo en Revisión 1368/2015, para. 34, March 13, 2019.

[11] Ibid., para. 87.

"subject to judicial interdiction" or referred to as "mentally ill." It did so on the understanding that "the rules that establish discriminatory criteria based on suspicious categories cannot expect a consistent interpretation because they are considered openly contrary to the dignity of people".[12]

Additionally, the SCJN has insisted on the need to distinguish between "legal capacity" and "mental capacity". For the Mexican court, "the right to legal capacity is not a question of intelligence in the adopted decisions, nor should it be linked to mental conditions. It is simply based on recognition of the will of every human being as a central element of the system of rights".[13] In the same line of thought aimed at clarifying and specifying essential concepts and categories for implementing Article 12 of the UNCRPD, the SCJN has also delved into the content, scope and function of *decision-making support*:

> the guardian of a person with a disability has the function of assisting him in making the corresponding decisions, but this cannot replace his will ... the state of interdiction (guardianship) must be conceived as an institution of assistance so that the person makes his own decisions, which must be respected even when they may be considered inappropriate ... [It was emphasised that] the support model is not based on wisdom in making decisions, but simply on the freedom of people to carry them out and assume them since the freedom to make one's own decisions goes to the heart of issues inextricably linked to respect for the inherent dignity and individual autonomy and independence of people.[14]

More recently, due to an *Amparo*[15] that demanded the declaration of unconstitutionality of the civil and procedural regulations on interdiction for Mexico City, the Supreme Court of Mexico has reaffirmed the above-mentioned concepts and has gone into more depth in others.[16] In this case, it was explained in detail that the interdiction system, provided for persons of legal age with disabilities in the Federal District law, substitutes a person's free will, which is discriminatory in light of Article 1 of the Constitution and the UNCRPD and is therefore unconstitutional. The Court also concluded that the current interdiction system violates human dignity, which prescribes that people be treated "in accordance with their volitions, and never in relation to other

---

[12]   SCJN, Plenario, Acción de Inconstitucionalidad 38/2014 and its accumulated case 91/2014, 92/2014 and 93/2014, subsection 88, October 2, 2014.

[13]   SCJN, Primera Sala, Amparo en Revisión 702/2018, September 11, 2019.

[14]   SCJN, Primera Sala, Amparo Directo en Revisión 2805/2014, subsection 42, January 14, 2015.

[15]   An "amparo" is a judicial remedy in Spanish law issued by a supreme or constitutional court to protect individual rights.

[16]   SCJN, Primera Sala, Amparo Directo (Public fragment of the draft decision, 2021).

properties over which they do not have control".[17] Furthermore, it stated that the current system,

> does not take into account the human dignity of the person with disabilities, who only becomes the object of study with respect to their mental health, their intellectual or sensory condition, or any psychosocial functional diversity, in order to declare their natural and legal incapacity, questioning everything that, in the opinion of medical experts, they can or cannot do in terms that are considered "normal" for the rest of the people.[18]

The Court explained that "the right to legal capacity is not a question of intelligence in the decisions that are adopted, nor should it be linked to mental conditions. It is simply based on recognition of the will of every human being as a central element of the system of rights".[19]

The Court required the recognition of and guarantee that every person enjoys "the right to govern their own life, including making decisions about what life is a good life to live."[20] It also stressed that the violation of legal capacity goes hand in hand with the violation of several rights that are inextricably linked to it, including "the rights to property, to work, to self-determination to choose the place of residence, where and with whom to live; the freedom of contract, to procreate, to leave any country, including one's own, to live independently and in the community, primarily".[21]

Contrary to the above, the Chilean Constitutional Court intervened in a case in which the inapplicability of an interdiction rule was at stake, alleging that it violated the right to equality and also invoking the UNCRPD.[22] In this context, it was understood that the contested norms would not produce results contrary to the Constitution and that any eventual adaptation of national legislation to the parameters derived from the Convention should be carried out by the co-legislative bodies.[23] It was also affirmed that there is a difference in treatment between capable and incapable persons that obliges the legislator to design the necessary mechanisms to protect the latter, while ensuring the protection of the social interest, which does not mean that their capacity to enjoy is not recognised.[24]

---

[17] Ibid., para. 110.
[18] Ibid., para. 124.
[19] Ibid., para. 80.
[20] Ibid., para. 109.
[21] Ibid., para. 39.
[22] Constitutional Court of Chile, Rol No. 2703, 26 January 2016. The request was rejected, arguing that the nature of the action of inapplicability due to unconstitutionality would prevent making value or merit judgments on the legislation.
[23] Ibid., para. 27.
[24] Ibid., para. 15.

2.2. THE GUARANTEE OF ACCESSIBILITY, REASONABLE ADJUSTMENTS AND SUPPORT FOR THE EXERCISE OF LEGAL CAPACITY

Persons with disabilities face structural discrimination in all spheres of life. This also takes the form of barriers to the exercise of legal capacity, which translate into a lack of accessibility conditions – communicational and/or attitudinal – as well as a lack of adoption of reasonable accommodation and/or provision of support systems or measures.

The Supreme Court of Argentina has specified that in this area, the applicable norms – together with the UNCRPD – "are centred not only on the recognition of the exercise of legal capacity, but also on the implementation of support mechanisms, safeguards and reasonable accommodation, so that those affected by these conditions can exercise that legal capacity under the same conditions as others".[25]

Thus, not only is the standard for the recognition of legal capacity under the same conditions as other persons strengthened, but it also recognises that for such equality to truly exist, support mechanisms, safeguards in the implementation of such support, and reasonable adjustments etc. must be guaranteed.[26]

Along the same lines, the SCJN has stated that "effective application of conventional law in the notary public's performance requires that [the notary] provide access to the system of supports and safeguards [...] as well as any tool that is suitable for helping the person to communicate their will, always ensuring that there is no conflict of interest or manipulation".[27] Assisted decision-making:

> means that the person with disabilities should not be deprived of their ability to exercise their will by way of another person who substitutes for them: they are simply assisted in making decisions in various areas, like any other person [...], providing them with the support and necessary safeguards thereof so that in this way the rights, will and preferences of the person with disabilities are respected.[28]

More recently, the Colombian Constitutional Court understood that:

> within the framework of the social model of disability, it is understood that the exercise of legal capacity must include assistance that eliminates the social, cultural and environmental barriers that do not allow for expressing one's will ... [for this purpose] the supports can be interpreted as different measures aimed at achieving materialisation of the will and preferences of the person with disabilities. These supports can include

---

[25] Supreme Court of Justice of Argentina (CSJN), B., J.M. s/insania, 12/06/2012, p. 7.
[26] Ibid.
[27] SCJN, Primera Sala, Amparo en Revisión 702/2018, September 11, 2019 *[sic]*.
[28] SCJN, Primera Sala, Amparo en Revisión 1043/2015, March 29, 2017, para. 93.

being accompanied by a trusted person in carrying out a legal act, communication methods other than conventional ones, and they can be measures related to universal design or accessibility, among others. The types of support and their degrees of intensity will depend on [each person] and will vary considerably from one person to another due to the diversity of persons with disabilities and their needs.[29]

The Colombian Constitutional Court has also addressed the obligation to guarantee accessibility and adopt adjustments in higher education through a precedent that originated from the request of a student with a psychosocial disability. The court ordered the educational institution to evaluate him differently through presentations and written work that better accommodated his needs and circumstances due to his disability.[30] It has also been recognised that persons with disabilities must be provided with "the necessary support to face the physical or social barriers that limit their possibilities to function normally." And that these:

(i) must vary in type and intensity according to the diversity of persons with disabilities [...]; (ii) they can be waived so that the person with a disability can refuse to exercise their right to receive the planned support [...]; (iii) they must not excessively regulate the lives of persons with disabilities [...] and (iv) the implementation of support measures must [sic] be consulted with and have the participation of the population with disabilities.[31]

2.3. THE RIGHT OF ACCESS TO JUSTICE AND THE ADOPTION OF PROCEDURAL ADJUSTMENTS

The content and scope of the right of access to justice require the guarantee of accessibility and procedural adjustments that enable the true, effective participation of the person going through a judicial process; that is, all those provisions that are part of the guarantees of due process.

The SCJN has stated that due process and the right to a hearing have effects of particular importance since "the condition of disability has historically represented a factor of imbalance for the exercise of their rights under equal conditions, [...] and has been the pretext so that, under a supposed protection, their right to due process is violated, specifically, the right to a hearing".[32] The SCJN has made an interpretation that requires the adoption of procedural adjustments even when the procedural law itself does not provide for it. More specifically, the SCJN has stated that:

---

29 Colombian Constitutional Court, Judgment T-231/20 App. 4.6.1.
30 Colombian Constitutional Court, Judgment T-097 of 2016.
31 Colombian Constitutional Court, Judgment C-182 of 2016.
32 SCJN, Primera Sala, Amparo en Revisión 1043/2015, March 29, 2017, para. 72.

although the contested procedure does not expressly establish the right for persons on whom the eventual declaration of disability falls to appear before the judge to express their decision or opinion during the processing of voluntary jurisdiction proceedings, [...], the condition of disability establishes in the judges the obligation to make reasonable adjustments so that persons with disabilities can exercise their rights under equal conditions with other people, and thus make the Convention effective in resolving the specific cases they are faced with in order to eliminate the barriers that impede the enjoyment and exercise of their rights.[33]

In this context, the SCJN has emphasised that in cases in which persons with disabilities are involved, the judge must make the necessary adjustments to the judicial procedures through accessible formats and with the necessary support so that they can express whatever they have the right to express, in order to satisfy their right to be heard.[34] This is due to the essential role played by knowledge of the will and preferences of the person with disabilities and enabling their participation in the judicial process, whatever it may be.[35] Therefore,

it cannot in any way be accepted that when a person with a disability is involved, that, under the pretext of their disability, the possibility of hearing them is not even contemplated, thus violating the essential formalities of the procedure – the right of access to justice and the principle of equality and non-discrimination.[36]

The inescapable requirement that the person with a disability must participate in the process and that it is mandatory to guarantee accessibility and adjustments to make this possible has recently been highlighted by the Superior Court of Rio Negro in Argentina. In this case, the sentence of the lower instance was annulled precisely because of the lack of participation of a child with a disability during the judicial procedure.[37] The case was ordered to be sent back to the Court so that, after fulfilling the obligation to hear the young person, it could issue a new ruling in accordance with the law. The Superior Court of Rio Negro found that the contested judgment, "contrary to what was due and expected, legitimises an approach to disability based on a medical perspective that prevents the application of the principle of real equality, as it does not recognise persons with disabilities as holders of rights, reduces them to their impairment and judges them as incapable of expressing themselves".[38]

---

[33] Ibid., para. 92.
[34] Ibid., para. 90.
[35] Ibid., para. 83.
[36] Ibid., para. 86.
[37] STJ Rio Negro, Civil Court Clerk No.1, G-3BA-1525-F2017 L. H., M. A. C/ F., A. E. S/ PERSONAL CARE(f) (S / CASACION), 21/10/2020 37 P 5/9.
[38] Ibid.

As good practice in the context of the right of access to justice, it is helpful to recall the first Spanish-language judgement in plain language issued by the SCJN.[39] This practice has been subsequently replicated by the same court and by courts and tribunals of other countries in the Latin American region. The Colombian Constitutional Court issued one of the latest resolutions on 15 January 2020.[40] Without ignoring the merit of the above-cited precedents, it should be noted that these advances continue to be isolated cases and, for the time being, it is impossible to affirm that any of the countries in the region have full incorporated accessibility provisions in the justice system. In this regard, it should not be forgotten that the *Revised Brasilia Rules* have gone into great detail on these requirements.[41]

Deepening the criterion of substantive equality with its four dimensions of redistribution, recognition, participation and accommodation, a recent judgment of a High Court in Argentina requires that the model of inclusive equality required by General Comment 6 (2018) of the CRPD be adopted in the area of legal capacity Understanding that the first instance ruling did not respect the standards set forth in the UNCRPD regarding the right to participate in the judicial process, the Court found that:

> contrary to what is due and expected, it has legitimised an approach to disability based on a medical perspective that prevents the principle of real equality from being applied since it does not recognise persons with disabilities as holders of rights, reducing them to their deficiency and judging them incapable of expressing themselves ... and that] inclusion is not inserting persons with disabilities within existing structures; instead, it means transforming systems to include everyone.[42]

2.4. SELF-DETERMINATION, MENTAL CAPACITY, AND INFORMED CONSENT

Replacing or impeding individuals' decision-making based on a disability diagnosis or condition constitutes a clear violation of the UNCRPD. However, the obligation to guarantee and enforce the right to decision-making and informed, participative consent of persons with disabilities requires much more than "not impeding". In the first place, the right to exercise legal capacity on an equal basis must be fully recognised. Secondly, and as part of this recognition, – it is necessary to guarantee accessibility, reasonable adjustments, and provision of support measures with appropriate safeguards as necessary. In addition to this,

---

[39] SCJN, Primera Sala, Amparo en Revisión 159/2013, October 16, 2013 (condensed reading).
[40] Colombian Constitutional Court, T-607 of 2019 Bogota, January 15, 2020.
[41] *Rules of Brazil regarding Access to Justice of Persons in Conditions of Vulnerability* (Update approved by the Plenary Assembly of the XIX Edition of the Iberoamerican Judicial Summit, Quito-Ecuador, April 2018).
[42] STJ Rio Negro (n. 37), 42 P 5/9.

Legal Capacity in Latin American High Courts

attitudinal barriers must be confronted, which are the product of stereotypes and prejudices that both underestimate disabled persons, their preferences, and life stories, and also imposing evaluation parameters – which on their face are neutral – are absolutely discriminatory.

A precedent that reflects the arbitrariness and injustice regarding the establishment of evaluations for the exercise of legal capacity is illustrated in the interpretation made by the Argentine Supreme Court in the appeal case mentioned above which disqualified a person with a disability from exercising his right to vote. Although the right was recognised for the petitioner in this case, when justifying the reasons, the Court stated that as a consequence of the aforementioned regulations:

> the restriction of the right to vote provided for in article 3, subparagraph a), of the National Electoral Code [...] must be applied under the principles and guarantees applicable to persons with disabilities. It imposes a detailed and specific assessment of the ability to vote, including the appointment of supports if the person is in a position to exercise that right autonomously but presents some difficulty in being able to do so. [... and that] in order to validly restrict Mr. [...] 's right to vote – and his consequent exclusion from the electoral roll –, it should have been determined that he lacked the capacity to carry out that specific political act, through evaluations that provided specific reasons why he was not in a position to exercise his right to vote autonomously; that is, he could not vote even with some support measure that would allow him without substituting his will.[43]

In another case, even when this meant a significant advance in terms of sexual and reproductive rights of women in general, the Argentine Supreme Court reflected a common prejudice against women with disabilities by interpreting their inability to consent to sexual relations. The Court stated that:

> since all sexual access to a mentally disabled woman is already considered a form of rape (the improper one), it is impossible to maintain that when she initially says "rape" it also refers to the same type of victim. [...] The same applies to minors under thirteen years of age--their statement is unnecessary because the law rules out the validity of their consent and declares that any sexual intercourse with them is already a (improper) violation.[44]

The restriction of capacity to consent has also been wrongly held by the Constitutional Court of Peru. In a decision regarding a claim against the

---

[43] Ibid., subsection. 8 and 9.

[44] Supreme Court of Justice of Argentina (CSJN), Case F.A.L. (2012), subsection 18. In the case, the Court analysed the issue from an international human rights law perspective and made a broad interpretation of the Penal Code that decriminalises abortion when the pregnancy is the product of the rape of any woman, and not only women with disabilities, as the Court wanted to understand from a restrictive interpretation of the rule.

Intersentia

119

National Health Insurance, requesting that a person be ordered to re-enter a mental health centre, the Court affirmed that:

> the requirement in the feasibility of granting informed consent by a person with a disability due to a (severe) mental disorder must logically have as a condition that they have, at least episodically, sufficient intellectual maturity, power of reflection and sense of responsibility to decide for himself the best treatment to follow, including a decision regarding hospitalisation or outpatient care, unless there is a psychiatric emergency or he is in a delusional, psychotic, paranoid state, etc., in a highly prolonged or permanent manner.[45]

Here it is worth asking the following: what is meant by "sufficient intellectual maturity, power of reflection and sense of responsibility"? And, for whom is this assessment made and under what parameters?

Concerning the involuntary internment and forced treatment of persons with disabilities, the absence of precedents that comprehensively and conclusively incorporate UNCRPD standards on the matter is notable. In this sense, and apparently contrary to current regulations, the opinion of the Peruvian Constitutional Court has expressed the following:

> in order to decide whether hospitalisation is necessary – for the amount of time strictly necessary and in the health facility closest to the user's home – or whether outpatient care that includes the community model is appropriate, the following factors must be considered: first, medical diagnosis; secondly, the need to guarantee the safety and integrity of the user himself and that of third parties, through a possible hospitalisation (according to the intensity and recurrence of signs of aggressiveness and violence); thirdly, the characteristics of the family environment, which will include assessment of the economic and social aspect; and, finally, fourth, the expression of the will of the person with mental disability. Therefore, the situation of disability, the guarantee of patient and third party safety, and the economic, medical and social situation of the person or persons on whom the responsibility for the support will fall, will not be the only criteria for restricting the personal liberty of the person with disabilities through the confinement method.[46]

More recently, the Peruvian Constitutional Court intervened in a case caused by the deprivation of liberty of a person with a disability in his own home, i.e., a home confinement.[47] It was understood that the right to personal liberty had been violated in the case, and the court ordered the mother to remove the obstacles that prevented his free movement from his room. It was also ordered that the

---

[45] Constitutional Court of Peru, EXP. No. 05048-2016-PA/TC LAMBAYEQUE ODILA YOLANDA CAYATOPA VDA. DE SALGADO, 2020, subsection 38.

[46] Ibid., subsection. 39.

[47] Constitutional Court of Peru, Guillén Domínguez, STC Exp. No. 00194-2014-PHC/TC, 2019.

Legal Capacity in Latin American High Courts

corresponding court adapt the interdiction process into a process of supports and safeguards under the new Peruvian regulations and in which framework the appropriate security measures must be adopted.[48] The Court also established that parents must adopt measures to ensure their child's adequate living and health conditions.[49] Furthermore, it ordered that the Public Prosecutor's Office "adopt a more active role in the exercise of its functions, in order to avoid endangering the life or integrity of persons with disabilities. Therefore, with this sentence, the Public Prosecutor's Office must be notified of this judgment so that it can take the appropriate actions to that end".[50] Finally, the decision ordered that, given the nature of the case, the executing judge must inform the Court periodically about the conditions in which the person is living to monitor compliance with its decision.[51] However, the Constitutional Court of Peru does not seem to have based the decision on the person's voice nor, therefore, on "the expression of the will of the person with disabilities", which is established as a requirement in previous precedents.[52]

2.5. THE RIGHT TO EXERCISE SEXUAL AND REPRODUCTIVE RIGHTS

As Constanza López Radrigán explains in detail in her chapter in this volume, the exercise of sexual and reproductive rights by persons with disabilities faces barriers rooted in prejudices and stereotypes about their ability to consent, as well as in relation to their experiencing their own sexuality.

In this regard, the Constitutional Court of Colombia has issued various rulings that reflect conflicting positions. A clear illustration of this situation has been the precedent of the Colombian Constitutional Court that endorsed, in 2014, the sterilisation of girls with disabilities without their consent.[53] It involved a claim of unconstitutionality against Article 7 of Colombian Law 1412 of 2010, whereby "the performance of the vas deferens ligation or vasectomy and the ligation of fallopian tubes is authorised free of charge and promoted as ways to promote responsible fatherhood and motherhood". Article 7 provided that "under no circumstances is the practice of surgical contraception allowed to minors." To analyse whether or not the provision demanded was in accordance with the Constitution, it was up to the Court to address two questions. First, whether

---

[48] Ibid., resolution item 3.
[49] Ibid., resolution item 2.
[50] Ibid., resolution item 4.
[51] Ibid., resolution item 5.
[52] Constitutional Court of Peru, Judgment C-025/21, subsection 661.
[53] Colombian Constitutional Court, Judgment C-131 of 2014. Through which the constitutionality of Article 7 of Law 1412 of 2010 was analysed. <http://www.corteconstitucional.gov.co/relatoria/2014/C-131-14.htm> accessed 23.01.2023.

Intersentia

121

the absolute prohibition of surgical sterilisation for adult minors constituted a measure that violated their rights to human dignity, equality, free development of the personality, and the exercise of sexual and reproductive rights. Second, whether the same prohibition violated the sexual and reproductive rights of children with disabilities.[54]

After inquiring about children's rights and their relationship with legal capacity, the Constitutional Court of Colombia declared the prohibition of practising definitive surgical contraception constitutional.[55] However, it introduced two exceptions to this legal prohibition: the first, for girls whose pregnancy would be an imminent risk to their lives, and the second, for minors with "profound or severe mental disability" who would not be able to give their consent in the future. In these two cases, definitive surgical sterilisation was understood to be constitutional as long as it was judicially authorised.

The incorporation of the second exception was based on the fact that,

> constitutional jurisprudence has established that, when it comes to minors with disabilities for whom it has been proven impossible for them to give their consent to undergo sterilisation in the future, the parents or, in any case, the legal representative must request authorisation from the judge to practice surgical contraception. In this sense, jurisprudence has established that a person who is unable to understand what sterilisation consists of and the consequences thereof, as in the case of mental disabilities, will hardly be in a position to understand the responsibility that motherhood or fatherhood entails, and therefore, the implications of being able to procreate or not.[56]

To this, the Colombian Constitutional Court added an unfortunate argument, which is exposed in the following way: "[...] the decision to undergo surgical contraception ensures more dignified living conditions for those who cannot make decisions related to the exercise of their reproductive freedom and who may be exposed to forced pregnancies in detriment to their dignity and personal integrity".[57]

It is important to clarify that, sometime later, the same Court modified its position by incorporating the social model of disability and the standards of

---

[54]   I. OTERO SUÁREZ, "The constitutionality of definitive surgical sterilization applied to minors with mental disabilities in Colombia". Paper presented at the 1st. International Virtual Conference on Disability and Human Rights, 04.12.2014, pp. 10–13. <http://repositoriocdpd.net:8080/bitstream/handle/123456789/741/Pon_OteroSuarezI_ConstitucionalidadEsterilizacionQuirurgica_2014.pdf?sequence=1> accessed 23.01.2023.

[55]   It considered that there was a legitimate purpose from the constitutional point of view, based on the preservation of the right of young people to found a family and the possibility that in the future they may decide freely and in an informed manner regarding this aspect.

[56]   Colombian Constitutional Court, Judgment C-131 of 2014, para. 6.4.2.i.

[57]   Ibid.

international human rights law on the matter.[58] In a new case where the practice of sterilisation was requested for an adolescent with a disability, the Court affirmed that "the doctor did not indicate that he had consulted the opinion of [...] regarding the possibility of submitting her to the surgical procedure. In fact, the medical consultation history does not even mention that an attempt was made to inquire about it".[59] After an analysis applying Article 23 of the UNCRPD, it was understood that her rights to human dignity and the free development of her personality were violated, for a variety of reasons. The adolescent had not had access to age-appropriate information and education about reproduction and family planning, nor had she been given guidance regarding the appropriate methods of contraception. Moreover, she had not been provided with the necessary support, adjustments and safeguards so that she could express her will and make an informed, voluntary decision about whether she wished to submit to any contraceptive method and, if so, choose according to her preference. Also, her right to equality was denied and she faced discrimination in violation of the UNCRPD because she lacked the reasonable adjustments needed to make her own decision.[60]

More recently, the Colombian Constitutional Court reiterated the prohibition against sterilising minors under Article 7 of Law 1412 of 2010.[61] In particular, the Court stated that exceptions can only be made to the prohibition in cases where a possible pregnancy implies a risk to the life of the minor, in which case it is necessary to have the free and informed consent of the minor with the adjustments and support that this implies. Notably, the Court ruled that:

> in the case of minors with disabilities who, despite the necessary support and adjustments, cannot provide their free and informed consent, the performance of this type of medical procedure is prohibited, and exceptions can only be made by judicial decision, after a procedure in which, based on presumption of the capacity of the minor to exercise her reproductive autonomy, it is verified: 1) that the person had been declared interdicted through a different and prior judicial process; 2) that there is a scientifically proven risk that justifies the medical necessity of the surgical intervention, 3) that there is no other less invasive alternative than definitive sterilisation; 4) that the minor is in a situation of profound and severe disability; 5) that every support and reasonable adjustments have been provided so that the minor can express her decision, and yet these have been unsuccessful for this purpose; and 6) that there is no possibility that the minor will be able to provide her consent in the future.[62]

---

[58]   Colombian Constitutional Court, Judgment T-665 of 2017.
[59]   Colombian Constitutional Court, Judgment T-573 of 2016.
[60]   Ibid.
[61]   Colombian Constitutional Court, Judgment T-655 of 2017.
[62]   Colombian Constitutional Court, Judgment T-231 of 2019, subsection 4 in fine.

Along the same lines, precedents can be cited in Brazil, which point out the impossibility of subjecting a person with a disability to forced surgical sterilisation under supervision. For example, the Court of Justice of Rio Grande do Sul[63] expressed that "the Statute of Persons with Disabilities, in Art. 6, states that disability does not affect the full civil capacity of the person, including with regard to their reproductive rights and fertility, thus establishing an express prohibition of compulsory sterilisation". And it concluded: "it is evident that the judgment under attack does not deserve reparations because, as can be seen, the claim of the plaintiff does not find support in the current legislation".[64] In the same vein, the Sao Paulo Court of Justice[65] affirmed that the performance of sterilisation surgery is allowed only with the free and informed consent of the person under custody, pursuant to Article 12 of the Statute of Persons with Disabilities. In another noteworthy judgment, the Court of Justice of São Paulo warned that the generic statement of the person with a disability and consent for the medical procedure is not enough to comply with the legal requirements of surgical sterilisation, requiring "the verification of a more complete informed consent".[66]

2.6. THE RIGHT TO FAMILY LIFE AND THE EXERCISE OF PARENTAL RESPONSIBILITY

The Supreme Court of Argentina had the opportunity to rule on the claim of a mother with an intellectual disability who had been separated from her new-born child since it was assumed that due to her disability, the child was in danger. During the process, the Court highlighted the rights violations suffered by the mother and the child. The precedent not only identifies discrimination based on disability founded on the separation of a new-born child from his mother due to disability but also highlights the right of this mother to have a support system for exercising the right to maternity.[67] In the case, the Court emphasises the State's obligation to guarantee "appropriate assistance to persons with disabilities in the performance of their child-rearing responsibilities".[68] This framework for analysis highlights the notion of "reasonable adjustments whose assurance is the responsibility of the States and which, in the logic of the UNCRPD, is aimed not only at the accessibility of the physical environment but, primarily, at the

---

[63] Court of Justice of Rio Grande do Sul, in Civil Appeal No. 0431052-80.2016.8.21.7000.

[64] TJRS, Civil Appeal No. 0431052-80.2016.8.21.7000, 09/03/2017.

[65] São Paulo Court of Justice, TJSP, Apelação Cível núm. 1006852-85.2017.8.26.0597, 28/01/2020.

[66] TJSP, Primeira Câmara de Direito Privado, Apelação Cível núm. 0006336-97.2012.8.26.0099, 06/02/2018.

[67] C.S.J.N, l., J. M. s/ special protection, 07/06/2016, adhering to the Attorney General's Opinion.

[68] Ibid., paragraphs Lb and 2.

exercise of all human rights".[69] It also highlights that such a "paradigm supposes that the legal capacity – recognised by Article 12 of the UNCRPD – not only refers to ownership of the rights but, centrally, to their complete exercise by the individual himself. Therefore, it brings with it the inclusion of those reasonable adjustments, whose effective implementation must be guaranteed by the States".[70]

More recently, the Supreme Court of Chile adopted similar grounds in a case in which it was decided to annul a declaration of the adoption status of a young girl.[71] On legal grounds, it was established that the contested resolution violated both the rights of the girl and the mother's rights. The Court also notes that:

> it is necessary to highlight the context in which the controversy unfolds [...], which flows from the facts established in the process, and which evidences the multiple forms of discrimination to which the girl's mother has been exposed throughout her life, as a disabled woman in a situation of poverty and a victim of violence, which has seriously damaged her dignity as a person and prevented her from being able to fully and equally enjoy all the rights and freedoms that the International Convention on Human Rights of persons with disabilities today aims to ensure.[72]

For the Chilean Supreme Court, the State's obligation was not exhausted with the offer of programs aimed at strengthening her parenting skills – which in fact, she fully carried out without achieving the expected standards to consider her qualified to take care of the girl – but it was crucial to work on those particular aspects that, given her condition, she needed to strengthen, and, given the lack of a social environment that could collaborate in child upbringing, it was crucial to directly provide the necessary assistance to carry out that responsibility. This dimension is not known to have been explored by the intervening bodies.

Similarly, and highlighting the need to have support in the exercise of childcare and the exercise of parental responsibility, the SCJN has determined that:

> when the judicial authorities notice that, due to conditions of disability, a person may have difficulties in caring for minors, especially in the case of a neurobiological or psychosocial disability in a guardianship and custody trial where it is decided which of the two parents is the more capable of caring for their children, and where there may be a suspected risk for minors: yes, support alternatives can be offered that, as a preventive measure, facilitate the parent with a disability in the tasks of safeguarding and caring for infants.[73]

---

[69]   Ibid., 2 and 5.

[70]   Ibid., subsection IV.

[71]   Supreme Court of Chile, RIT RUT of the Second Family Court of Santiago, 19/02/2020.

[72]   Ibid.

[73]   SCJN, Primera Sala, Amparo Directo en Revisión, 5904/2015, of 28/09/2016.

Additionally, concerning the constitutionality of a norm of the Code of Childhood and Adolescence, the Constitutional Court of Colombia referred to the legal conditions for granting informed parental consent when offering a male or female biological descendant for adoption. The norm regulated cases in which parental consent could be dispensed with. In particular, the norm stated that "the absence of the father or mother shall be understood not only when they have died, but also when they are afflicted by a mental illness or serious mental anomaly certified by the National Institute of Legal Medicine and Forensic Sciences".[74] The Court had to resolve whether the grounds referring to "suffering from a mental illness" were compatible with the Constitution. For the Court:

> what is at stake is the requirement to achieve a weighting or balance between the guarantee of the rights of children, guided above all by the primary, prevailing criterion of the best interests of the minor, an element that must be incorporated as the central axis of the constitutional analysis, as well as the right to have a family and to not be separated from them, pursuant to Articles 42 and 44 CP; and the rights of parents, in this case, of those who are in a situation of disability, especially the right to equality –art.13 CP– and the specific rights of this population, under Article 47 CP, and international treaties on the subject, particularly the Convention on the Rights of Persons with Disabilities –CRPD–.[75]

In its analysis, the Colombian Constitutional Court stated that the legal norm under review:

> makes an *a priori* discriminatory differentiation regarding legal status and the legal capacity to consent to adopt between fathers and mothers with a mental illness versus those who do not. [...] the accused provision would contradict the understanding of disability from the social model adopted by constitutional jurisprudence, which was highlighted by the majority of the interveners; this model recognises (a) the effective guarantee of the right to equality and the prohibition of discrimination; (b) the implementation of social inclusion measures in favour of these people, and the recognition of the rights to legal status and legal capacity of people with mental disabilities; and (c) the adoption of reasonable measures and adjustments to guarantee the exercise of the rights of persons with disabilities, per Articles 13, 14, 47 CP.[76]

The Court also observed that:

> the accused provision does not include the obligation to adopt reasonable measures and adjustments for exercising the rights of parents who are in a state of disability [...] nor does it include measures to support autonomous and independent decision-making

---

[74] Law 1098/06, para. 3, art. 66.
[75] Colombian Constitutional Court, Judgment T-741/2015, app. 5.
[76] Ibid.

to grant valid, suitable consent for their children's adoption, in order to remove all social barriers that prevent their social inclusion, recognise their legal status and capacity as moral and legal subjects – measures that in the opinion of this Court should be adopted in each case in particular and depending on the type and level of limitation.[77]

3. CONCLUSIONS

The case law of high and constitutional courts in Latin America shows progress in recognising and guaranteeing rights for persons with disabilities. This has been developing, specifically, in the area of recognition of Article 12 of the UNCRPD, referring to equal recognition of legal capacity. However, an overall reading of the precedents illustrates dissimilar interpretations, not only among the decision-making bodies but even regarding the content and scope of the rights analysed. It seems that these standards still need to be expanded, not only in conceptual terms (the social model and human rights approach) but also in normative (i.e., UNCRPD) and interpretive terms, incorporating the work of the bodies that make up the human rights protection system.

Thus, regarding recognising legal capacity without discrimination on the grounds of disability, justice systems have yet to delve deeply into the different dimensions of disability that affect the recognition of legal capacity and, therefore, the exercise of rights. Although some courts have made progress in recognising that the interdiction of persons with disabilities is discriminatory, a complete understanding of the reasons or the tools to eradicate these violations has not been fully understood. This has led some courts, for example, to authorise exceptions to this guarantee in the specific exercise of certain rights – such as suffrage and informed consent – based on the condition of disability which, with some exceptions, continues to be addressed from a purely medical-rehabilitative point of view.

This approach risks reducing the person's identity to their condition, and also reinforces a normalising and stigmatising view of disability, based on diagnoses that describe a "mental or intellectual deficiency." To avoid these risks, it would be useful to critically examine three dimensions that interact with each other: (i) the condition of disability – that personal condition that is usually defined as a deficiency, but should be defined from a more evolved, point of view recognising the diversity of human life; (ii) the inter-relational construction of disability that reveals social barriers that come into play; and, finally (iii) the constructions of disability, which find their origins in our representations, in our values, and in our culture. A judicial process or a sentence that does not understand or enable a look at the condition of a person beyond a medical label can become the barrier

---

[77]   Ibid.

that places them in the situation and position where it is assumed that disability should be prevented or eradicated.[78]

In addition, it seems necessary to delve into the notion of *substantive equality* in terms of legal capacity. Intention is needed to respect and guarantee its various dimensions, not only through a court judgment but also in the judicial process itself. That is to say, a doctrine of the courts that: (i) guarantees a *redistributive dimension* that takes into account that persons with disabilities are one of the groups with the highest levels of social exclusion in terms of distribution of resources and assets; (ii) a dimension of recognition to combat stigma, stereotypes, prejudice and violence, and to recognise the dignity of human beings from an intersectional perspective; (iii) a dimension of participation to reaffirm the social character of people as members of social groups and the full recognition of humanity through inclusion in society; and (iv) a dimension of adjustments, to make room for difference as an aspect of human dignity.[79]

The latter has a determinative impact on two areas analysed above: the guarantee of accessibility conditions, reasonable adjustments and support for the exercise of legal capacity; and, the right of access to justice and the adoption of procedural adjustments. Although the precedents analysed in this chapter appear to advance recognition of the need for and right to support measures and/or systems as part of the right to non-discrimination, it is also imperative to conceive of these measures/systems as part of the essential content of each right to be exercised, and also as a subjective right. It is possible to find precedents that expose the discriminatory absence of accessibility conditions, support systems and procedural adjustments that enable participation within the judicial process. At the moment, these precedents are largely from lower courts without macro-level impact within the justice system, which could prevent these cases from being replicated in the future. Moreover, the precedents examined evidence barriers people face to participating in these processes, especially in terms of informed consent.

This leads to the fourth point discussed in this chapter. Confusion remains between *functional autonomy and moral autonomy* of people, which is also manifested in the equation of so-called mental capacity with legal capacity. The precedents continue – in some cases illustrating, and in others even manifesting – the existence of stereotypes and prejudices which deny the specific ways in which persons with disabilities are or exist in the world – more specifically, their choices, desires, preferences, and even their life narratives. This may be a consequence of the imposition, of and parameters for, assessing mental capacity, which are presented as neutral but are nonetheless absolutely discriminatory. This *medicalised* viewpoint is far from guaranteeing rights and

---

[78]   See Colombian Constitutional Court, Judgment T-525 of 2019.
[79]   CRPD Committee, General Comment No. 6, 04/26/2016.

respect for dignity. The question that governs this perspective is whether the person "can" meet some ableist standard, when what is actually incumbent on the justice and other systems is to know what the person *requires* to exercise and enjoy their rights on an equal basis.

The chapter also analysed the right to exercise *sexual and reproductive rights* in the context of people with disabilities. As we have seen, there are entrenched barriers both regarding consent and in relation to the experience of sexuality of persons with disabilities, particularly women. It is possible to observe an evolution of jurisprudence regarding the prohibition of forced sterilisations, which unfortunately was forged from precedents that enabled them. In contrast, it is also possible to find precedents establishing the impossibility of consenting to sexual relations for adult women with disabilities. This is worrying from an intersectional perspective since it illustrates an evident absence of gender and disability perspectives in the reasoning and judging of cases. These restrictive perspectives on disability must be broadened.

The last point analysed in this chapter dealt with the right to *family life* – specifically to exercising parental responsibility. There is no doubt that one of the most severe violations in this area is the one that results in the division of family ties due to disability. In this sense, the precedents analysed are encouraging, given that they not only express this understanding but also understand that the right to exercise responsibility and care requires an accompanying support system – through benefits, accessibility conditions, reasonable adjustments, and personal supports. Much less encouraging are the rulings of lower courts that gave rise to these precedents, in which one can note the absence of recognition of the essential role that support and benefits play in exercising the right. They also fail to apply human rights standards, and clearly interfere with rights to liberty, motivated and justified by medical diagnoses from which an imminent danger is deduced. In these cases, the absence of an intersectionality perspective, denial of the right to support for mothering, and the invisibility of situations of poverty is striking.

Despite the limitations of the evolving jurisprudence, it is possible to deduce and identify – in general terms – an *emerging but insufficient perspective of disability*, which is leading to modifications in the mechanisms, norms, practices and values that reproduce the structural inequality of persons with disabilities. In order for this perspective to progress, it is necessary to understand and apply the *social model of disability*. Accessibility in all its meaning and scope must guide analysis. The right of persons with disabilities to participate at the public policy level, in judicial processes, and in the development of their personality is essential. We must not lose sight of the fact that this situation of structural inequality intersects with sources of marginality, and is the consequence of physical, communicational, attitudinal, and even legal barriers which prevent the exercise of rights in conditions of inequality. Although there are judgments where the courts state they are adopting the social model, the perspective on the individual condition continues to be pathologising, and the diagnosis continues to colonise people's lives and judicial decisions.

The precedents analysed in this chapter were selected because their reasoning and interpretations most closely follow the standards of the UNCRPD. They are the beacon that aims to light the way for lower courts and even influence social change. However, even in those countries that have achieved legal reform in terms of legal capacity, there remains a need to broaden and even transform judicial *praxis*. Along this path, the perspective of disability is a necessary and obligatory tool for the justice system to achieve progress towards inclusion and transforming the patters of inequality that affect the identity, projects and narratives of people's lives. We cannot forget that many continue to be restricted in the right to make their own path.

LEGAL CAPACITY REGIME REFORMS IN COSTA RICA, PERU AND COLOMBIA

A Comparative and Critical Analysis

Alberto Vásquez,* Federico Isaza** and Andrea Parra***

1. Introduction 132
2. Article 12 of the CRPD and its Impact in Latin America 132
   - 2.1. Costa Rica 132
     - 2.1.1. Situation before Reform 132
     - 2.1.2. Reform Process 133
     - 2.1.3. Content of the Reform 134
     - 2.1.4. Implementation...................................... 136
   - 2.2. Peru 137
     - 2.2.1. Situation before Reform 137
     - 2.2.2. Reform Process 139
     - 2.2.3. Content of the Reform 140
     - 2.2.4. Implementation...................................... 142
   - 2.3. Colombia.. 143
     - 2.3.1. Situation before Reform 143
     - 2.3.2. Reform Process 145
     - 2.3.3. Content of the Reform 147
     - 2.3.4. Implementation...................................... 148

---

* Lawyer specialising in the rights of persons with disabilities (Pontifical Catholic University of Lima-Peru and University of Galway-Ireland). Co-Director at the Center for Inclusive Policy (CIP), consultant to the United Nations and President of Society and Disability (SODIS).

** Human Rights Activist and Lawyer with Specialisation in Justice, Victims and Peacebuilding. Since 2016, he has been linked as a legal advisor to the Action Program for Equality and Social Inclusion-PAIIS of the Universidad de Los Andes in Bogotá, Colombia.

*** Lawyer (U de los Andes) Colombia and LL.M. (Boston University). Activist, feminist, experiential workshop facilitator and translator. Co-coordinator of the Latin American Network Art. 12, Co-director of the ALCE initiative (Abolition of Logics of Punishment and Confinement) and Director of Talleristas por la Justicia Trainers for Justice.

3. Challenges of Reform on Legal Capacity in Latin America 149
    3.1. Legislative Challenges 150
    3.2. Administrative Challenges 151
    3.3. Social, Cultural, Interpretive and Contextual Challenges 151

1. INTRODUCTION

Since the adoption of the United Nations Convention on the Rights of Persons with Disabilities (hereinafter CRPD) the right of persons with disabilities to legal capacity has experienced an unprecedented boost in Latin America. In 2015, Argentina carried out an important reform to its Civil and Commercial Code; very significant reforms have also been carried out in Brazil, and in the last five years, three countries in the region – Costa Rica, Peru and Colombia – have completed ground-breaking legislative reforms that have pointed a path forward for other countries within and outside the region. These reforms are considered an international benchmark due to their comprehensive nature and for the active participation of persons with disabilities in their design and drafting.

In this context, this chapter seeks to analyse comparatively and critically the legislative reforms in legal capacity carried out by Costa Rica, Peru and Colombia. To this end, the processes and contents of the reforms achieved in each country will be described. Then their elements will be analysed comparatively in light of the standards developed by the Committee on the Rights of Persons with Disabilities (hereinafter CRPD Committee). Finally, the challenges and limitations in implementing these reforms will be described and analysed. Thus, this chapter will provide valuable lessons for the new reform processes that are underway.

2. ARTICLE 12 OF THE CRPD AND ITS IMPACT IN LATIN AMERICA

2.1. COSTA RICA

2.1.1. Situation before Reform

The Costa Rican Civil Code established in 1996 that "legal capacity is inherent to persons throughout their existence" and, for natural persons, "it is modified or limited, according to the Law, by their marital status, their volitional or cognitive capacity or their legal capacity".[1] Likewise, the Civil Code makes express reference

---

[1]   Civil Code Costa Rica, Art. 36.

to the possibility of judicially declaring a person's incapacity and annulling "acts or contracts that are carried out without volitional or cognitive capacity".[2] Although the capacity to act is presumed, it is an *iuris tantum* presumption.[3] The Civil Code also establishes specific restrictions for those "who are not of sound judgment" to make a will.[4] These provisions were maintained after reform was achieved.

The Civil Procedure Code, until its modification in 2016, regulated the process of "insanity" or interdiction. Under this abbreviated process, a judge could declare a person's state of legal incapacity.[5] The determination of incapacity was made through medical expertise[6] and the interview of the presumed "insane person" was optional for the judge.[7] The Family Code regulated the designation of the subsequent curator. According to this legal body, adults with an "intellectual, mental, sensory or physical disability that prevents them from attending to their own interests" could be subject to curatorship.[8] Curatorship involved both the care of the person and the individual's assets.[9] The curator held legal representation in all areas of the life of the person declared incapacitated. The Civil Procedure Code also provided a "rehabilitation" process for the person declared incapacitated, which was subject to a medical opinion.[10]

There is no available information on the number of persons with disabilities subject to conservatorship at the time of the reform.

2.1.2. Reform Process

The reform process in Costa Rica began in 2009 with the presentation of draft legislation No. 17,305, Law of Autonomy of Persons with Disabilities.[11] The proposal was prepared at the initiative of the Accessibility Commission of the Judiciary, with the participation of an interdisciplinary group of professionals with and without disabilities.[12] The draft legislation was modelled on the Law for the Promotion of Personal Autonomy and Care for Persons in a Situation

---

2   Ibid., Art. 41.
3   Ibid., Art. 628.
4   Ibid., Art. 591.
5   Civil Procedure Code of Costa Rica, Art. 851.
6   Ibid., Art. 848.
7   Ibid., Art. 849.
8   Family Code of Costa Rica, Art. 230.
9   E. M. ALVAREZ and M. VILLAREAL ARROYO, "Análisis de la curatela y la capacidad de actuar de las personas con discapacidad en Costa Rica, a la luz de la Convención sobre los Derechos de las Personas con Discapacidad, Tesis para optar por el grado de Licenciatura", Thesis to opt for the Bachelor Degree, Law School, University of Costa Rica, 2010, p. 184.
10   Civil Procedure Code, Art. 853.
11   Draft Legislation No. 17,305, Law of Autonomy of Persons with Disabilities, presented on 3 March 2009.
12   E. M. ALVAREZ and M. VILLAREAL ARROYO (n. 9), p. 211.

of Dependency in Spain.[13] Although the proposal differs from the text finally approved, it proposes repealing several provisions related to the interdiction process.

The draft legislation was sent for procedure and opinion to the Permanent Commission of Social Affairs in accordance with the Legislative Information System, where consultations and hearings were held, but little progress was made. In 2014, the proposal was transferred for study to the recently created Special Commission on Issues Related to Persons with Disabilities.[14] In July 2015, this commission issued a unanimous affirmative opinion proposing a law to promote the personal autonomy of persons with disabilities. The opinion incorporates a chapter referring to the legal equality of people with disabilities, the safeguard and the guarantor of legal equality.[15]

This project was approved on First Reading by the Legislative Plenary on 9 May 2016, and Second Reading on 30 June 2016. The text underwent minor modifications during the discussions.[16] Law No. 9379, Law for the Promotion of the Autonomy of Persons with Disabilities, was published on 30 August 2016. At the time of its enactment, one of the authors of the initial proposal, former deputy Ana Helena Chacón Echeverría, held the position of Vice President of the Republic.

2.1.3. Content of the Reform

Law No. 9379 aims to promote and ensure that persons with disabilities exercise the right to personal autonomy in full and on equal terms with others.[17] The Law recognises the legal capacity of persons with disabilities, eliminates the figures of interdiction, insanity and guardianship from the Costa Rican legal system, and introduces the institution of the safeguard for the legal equality of persons with disabilities. The reform also introduces the institution of personal assistance in Costa Rican legislation.

Law No. 9379 states that "all persons with disabilities fully enjoy legal equality."[18] This supposes the recognition of their legal personality, their legal capacity and their capacity to act; the ownership and legitimate exercise of all their rights and attention to their own interests; and the exercise of parental authority, which may not be lost for reasons based merely on the person's

---

[13]   Law 39/2006, of 14 December on the Promotion of Personal Autonomy and Care for Persons in a Situation of Dependency, BOE-A-2006-21990, published on 15 December 2006.

[14]   More information available at <https://www.larepublica.net/noticia/lopez_logra_comision_para_discapacitados%20/> accessed 11.04.2023.

[15]   Opinion available at <http://www.asamblea.go.cr/Centro_de_informacion/Consultas_SIL/SitePages/ConsultaProyectos.aspx> accessed 11.04.2023.

[16]   Ibid.

[17]   Law No. 9379, Art. 1.

[18]   Ibid., Art. 5.

disability related condition.[19] Following this recognition, various articles of the Civil Procedure Code and the Family Code referring to insanity and guardianship were repealed and reformed.

The Law also establishes safeguards for the guarantee of legal equality of persons with disabilities. The purpose of this provision is to ensure the safe and effective exercise of the rights and obligations of "persons with intellectual, mental and psychosocial disabilities" within a framework of respect for their will and preferences.[20] The judge is the only one competent to review and process safeguard requests, which can be requested by the persons with a disability and, exceptionally, by family members and non-governmental organisations.[21] The person appointed by the judge to exercise the safeguard is called the guarantor of the legal equality of persons with disabilities. It can be a natural person or a legal entity.[22] When the person with a disability cannot indicate the person of their preference, the judge will consider the relatives of the person with a disability as an option to exercise the safeguard.[23]

Law No. 9379 establishes an extensive list of obligations of the guarantor of legal equality,[24] many of which function as safeguards. Among them: (i) not to act without considering the rights, the will and the capacities of the person; (ii) support them in the protection and promotion of all their rights; (iii) assist them in making decisions in a proportional and adapted manner; (iv) guarantee that the person has access to complete and accessible information so that they can decide on their sexual and reproductive rights; (v) provide support to the person in the exercise of their maternity or paternity; (vi) not to exert any type of pressure, coercion, violence or undue influence in the decision-making process; (vii) not to provide informed consent in place of the person; (viii) not to allow the person to be subjected to torture, cruel, inhuman or degrading treatment; (ix) not to allow the person to be subjected to medical or scientific experiments without their free and informed consent, and (x) protect the privacy of the person's personal information and data.

The Regulation of Law No. 41087–MTSS,[25] approved on 30 April 2018, specifies many of the Law's scopes and gaps. Thus, the Regulation refers to the importance of reasonable accommodations and the principle of universal design to exercise legal capacity.[26] It specifies that the safeguard is optional and may

---

[19]   Ibid.
[20]   Ibid.
[21]   Ibid., Art. 8.
[22]   Ibid., Art. 18.
[23]   Ibid., Art. 10.
[24]   Ibid., Art. 17.
[25]   Regulations to the Law for the Promotion of the Personal Autonomy of Persons with Disabilities No. 41087-MTSS, 30 April 2018.
[26]   Ibid., Art. 4, nos. 4 and 14.

not be imposed against the person's will.[27] The Regulation also clarifies that the safeguard is not a type of legal representation[28] and that several people may act as guarantors.[29] Additionally, it is pointed out that family members and non-governmental organisations may request the safeguard only when there is an "absolute impossibility that limits the person with a disability to present the request individually or with the support of another person or to sign – with their signature or fingerprint – the requesting document".[30] Finally, the Regulation includes the standard of best possible interpretation of the will and preferences of the person, indicating that when a person with a disability is in a "situation of compromised state of consciousness", the determination of support must be based on the will and preferences of the person, for which it is necessary to resort to "multidimensional procedures, such as life trajectory or family history, social context, and even the express manifestations that the person would have made in advance of receiving this type of support."[31]

Some provisions of the Law and Regulation are problematic in light of the CRPD. The Law allows *sterilisation without the person's consent* "when it is necessary and essential for the preservation of life or physical integrity."[32] The Regulation states that, exceptionally, the guarantor may take action in acts beyond what is determined in the judicial resolution establishing the safeguard, "as long as it is urgent and essential for the security and benefit of the person receiving the support."[33] Likewise, the Regulation specifies that the prohibition on the guarantor to provide informed consent for the person with a disability is not applicable when the person is "under imminent risk due to an emerging and unforeseen situation."[34]

2.1.4. Implementation

The implementation of Law No. 9379 has been slow. The Regulation took more than a year and a half. In the meantime, the courts have continued to rule and order interdiction and curatorship measures.[35] According to civil society

---

27   Ibid., Art. 7, nos. 2 and 4.
28   Ibid., Art. 7, no. 8.
29   Ibid., Art. 9.
30   Ibid., Art. 12.
31   Ibid., Art. 8.
32   Ibid., Art. 11, para. d.
33   Ibid., Art. 17, para. b.
34   Ibid., Art. 17, para. h.
35   See P. AMEY GÓMEZ and A. C. FERNÁNDEZ ACUÑA, "Los derechos humanos de las personas con discapacidad, desde la perspectiva de la Ley para la Promoción de la Autonomía Personal número 9379 y su reglamento", in *Revista de la Sala Segunda*, No. 16, Supreme Court of Justice, 2019, pp. 23–32.

commentators, the Law has generated resistance and rejection in some sectors, especially within family law, although little has been written about it.[36]

In this regard, the Family Court of the First Judicial Circuit of San José promoted a consultation on constitutionality before the Constitutional Chamber of the Supreme Court of Justice regarding several articles of Law No. 9379 and its Regulation.[37] In the opinion of the consulting court, such regulations could be unconstitutional since they do not respond to the needs or protection of persons with disabilities who "do not have the capacity to exercise their rights or be subject to obligations." The Supreme Court ruled by majority that there was no violation of the provisions of the Constitution and the CRPD.[38] According to the Court, the CRPD represents a paradigm shift in recognising the legal capacity that reaches all persons with disabilities. When it is not feasible to determine the will and preferences of a person, following the criteria of the CRPD Committee, the best possible interpretation of their will and preferences should be used.

According to Law No. 9379, curators immediately became guarantors of legal equality upon its entry into force. The judge has to conduct an ex officio review of these safeguards within two years. No information is available on the progress of the implementation of these processes. According to civil society commentators, training judicial operators – judges, prosecutors, defenders and public defenders, experts – it is still a pending task.[39]

Adopting the reform has also led to an important advance in restoring the right to vote. For the 2018 electoral process, the Civil Registry of the Supreme Electoral Tribunal had already incorporated all persons with disabilities who had been excluded from it by the declaration of insanity into the electoral roll.[40]

2.2. PERU

2.2.1. Situation before Reform

Until 2012, when the first reform related to the legal capacity of persons with disabilities was made, the Peruvian Civil Code declared the incapacity of a

---

[36] See IIDI, the Forum and REDODICEC, Alternative Report, Costa Rica, 2018. <https://tbinternet.ohchr.org/_layouts/15/treatybodyexternal/Download.aspx?symbolno=INT%2fCRPD%2fICS%2fCRI%2f30084&Lang=en> accessed 19.01.2023.

[37] File No. 19-018477-0007-CO.

[38] Supreme Court of Costa Rica, Sentence: 016863-20 of 4 September 2020. <https://nexuspj.poder-judicial.go.cr/document/sen-1-0007-1001746> accessed 19.01.2023.

[39] See IIDI, the Forum and REDODICEC (n. 36).

[40] Costa Rica, Second and Third Combined Report of Costa Rica on Compliance with the Convention on the Rights of Persons with Disabilities, February 2020.

number of persons with and without disabilities. Thus, according to Article 43 of the Civil Code, the following persons were absolutely incapable: (i) minors under 16 years of age; (ii) persons "deprived of discernment"; and (iii) "deaf-mutes, blind-deaf and blind-mute persons who cannot express their will in an indubitable manner". Also, according to Article 44, the following were relatively incapable: (i) those over 16 and under 18 years of age; (ii) the "mentally retarded"; (iii) those "suffering from mental deterioration that prevents them from expressing their free will"; (iv) prodigals; (v) those who incur in mismanagement; (vi) "habitual drunkards"; (vii) "drug addicts"; and those who have a criminal conviction that has a civil interdiction attached to it. All these persons could be declared judicially incompetent through an interdiction process.

The declaration of interdiction was made through a summary proceeding and, in practice, without legal defence. In such proceedings, the judge determined on the basis of medical expertise that the person required a guardian for rehabilitation and protection. Once the incapacity was determined, the judge restricted the exercise of the person's civil rights, including rights such as voting, contracting or marriage. In practice, such restrictions were absolute. On the other hand, although in principle the Civil Code regulated the "rehabilitation" of the person declared incapacitated (Article 610), because the system did not promote the rehabilitation of the person or the review of sentences, being declared interdicted meant the civil death of a person. Until 2012 persons with disabilities who were not declared legally incompetent were also subject to a series of limitations on legal capacity. Legal operators, public and private, presumed the incapacity of many people with disabilities even when not declared judicially.[41] The Civil Code established specific limitations to marrying, exercising parental authority, making a will or acting as a testamentary witness apart from the interdiction.[42]

There is no precise information on the number of interdicted disabled persons under this system. According to the National Superintendence of Public Registries (SUNARP) between 1998 and 2018, 12,197 interdiction orders were made.[43] Most of these orders were obtained for the purpose of continuing to receive social security or collecting an orphan's pension for incapacity to work

---

[41] See C. VILLAREAL LÓPEZ, *El reconocimiento de la capacidad jurídica de las personas con discapacidad mental e intelectual y su incompatibilidad con los efectos jurídicos de la interdicción y la curatela: Lineamientos para la reforma del Código Civil y para la implementación de un sistema de apoyos en el Perú*, Thesis presented to opt for the degree of Master in Human Rights, PUCP, Lima, 2014.

[42] Civil Code of Peru, Arts. 241, para. 3 and 4; 389; 466, paras. 1 and 3; 580; 687, paras. 2 and 3; and 705, para. 2.

[43] Request for information made by Society and Disability – SODIS – to the National Superintendence of Public Registries, with an electronic response dated 30 January 2020.

and, to a lesser extent, the protection of inheritance and property and the completion of various formalities.[44]

2.2.2. Reform Process

After ratifying the CRPD, the disability movement and allied organisations drafted and presented a citizen initiative to adopt a new legal framework on disability, Draft Law No. 04707/2010-IC. This process resulted in the approval of Law No. 29973, General Law for Persons with Disabilities, published on 24 December 2012. Article 9 of this Law generally recognises that persons with disabilities enjoy legal capacity in all aspects of life on an equal basis with others. In addition, the Law repealed Article 43(3) of the Civil Code on the incapacity of the "deaf-mute, blind-deaf and blind-mute who cannot indubitably express their will". However, the Law postponed the implementation of Article 12 of the CRPD to a second reform, providing for the creation of a special commission in charge of revising the Civil Code concerning the legal capacity of persons with disabilities.[45]

The Special Commission for the Reform of the Civil Code (CEDIS) began its activities in March 2014, made up of representatives of the three powers of the State, the Ombudsman's Office, universities and civil society. The latter included organisations for people with intellectual disabilities and psychosocial disabilities.[46] In February 2015, after several public sessions, the CEDIS approved a preliminary bill proposing the reform of more than 80 provisions of the Civil Code, in line with the majority of civil society proposals. This bill faced resistance in the Justice and Human Rights Commission and was shelved without an opinion in July 2016.

In January 2017, a new multi-party bill was introduced, supported by a broad coalition of disability and human rights organisations, Draft Law No. 00872/2016-CR. This proposal, drafted by civil society based on the work of the CEDIS, included modifications to the Code of Civil Procedure and the Legislative Decree of Notaries. Despite the advocacy undertaken, which included lobbying efforts, events, courses, pilot projects, art exhibitions and campaigns in the media and social networks, the proposal was not passed. Faced with this delay, the Executive, whose governing party had promised to push the reform, requested legislative powers[47] and adopted it through Legislative Decree

---

[44]   See A. Vásquez Encalada, *El camino a la libertad. La capacidad jurídica de las personas con síndrome Down en el Perú*, Peruvian Down Syndrome Society, Peru, 2012.

[45]   Law No. 29993, Second Final Complementary Provision.

[46]   Peruvian Society of Down Syndrome, Alamo Family and Society and Disability (SODIS).

[47]   Law No. 30823 delegated to the Executive Branch the power to legislate, among other things, in order to establish measures to guarantee the right of persons with disabilities to exercise their legal capacity under conditions of equality.

No. 1384, which recognises and regulates the legal capacity of persons with disabilities under equal conditions. It was published on 4 September 2018. The text approved by the Executive is similar to Draft Law No. 00872/2016-CR.

2.2.3. Content of the Reform

Legislative Decree No. 1384, which has the same status as a law, modified the Civil Code, the Civil Procedure Code and the Legislative Decree of Notaries concerning the legal capacity of persons with disabilities. This legislative decree recognises the total legal capacity of all persons with disabilities, abolishes disability-related guardianship and other restrictions on the legal capacity of persons with disabilities, and introduces supported decision-making regimes. Likewise, it recognises the right to reasonable and procedural adjustments in courts and notaries.

The amended Civil Code recognises the legal capacity of persons with disabilities on equal terms with others.[48] It clarifies that adults with disabilities have full legal capacity in all aspects of life, regardless of whether they need reasonable adjustments or support to express their will.[49] The legislative decree abolished the provisions that provided for the interdiction of various groups of persons with disabilities,[50] and the restrictions on marrying, exercising parental authority and making a will.[51] In addition, the possibility for a curator to admit a person with a disability to an institution was removed from the Civil Code.[52]

Despite these advances, restrictions on legal capacity were maintained for "habitual drunkards", "drug addicts", "prodigals", "bad managers", people with criminal convictions and people in comas; the latter is an assumption that had never been considered. The reason for maintaining these grounds was practical; the Law that delegated powers to the Executive made express reference to the legal capacity of persons with disabilities.

The modified Civil Code also recognises the right to reasonable accommodation to exercise legal capacity.[53] These include accessibility measures related to the environment, communications or information, the use of informal supports and other adaptations necessary to exercise legal capacity. In line with the CRPD and Law No. 29973, the denial of reasonable accommodation constitutes an act of discrimination based on disability, except when a disproportionate or undue burden is verified.[54]

---

[48]   Civil Code of Peru, Art. 3.
[49]   Ibid., Art. 42.
[50]   Ibid., Arts. 43 no. 2 and 44 no. 2 and 3.
[51]   Ibid., Arts. 241, 274, 466, 687, 693, 694 and 697.
[52]   Ibid., Art. 578.
[53]   Ibid., Art. 45.
[54]   Supreme Decree No. 016-2019-MIMP, Art. 5, para. 1.

Legislative Decree No. 1384 introduced decision-making supports into the Civil Code. These are defined as forms of assistance to facilitate the exercise of legal capacity, including support in communication, in understanding legal acts and their consequences, and in the expression and interpretation of volition.[55] The support measures are voluntary and can be accessed by anyone of legal age. The person requesting the support determines its form, identity, scope, duration and amount of support, which may fall to one or more natural persons, public institutions or non-profit organisations.[56] The beneficiary of the support is responsible for their own decisions, including those made with support, and is entitled to recover the damages that result from actions by supporters.[57] Supporters do not have powers of representation except in cases where this is expressly established.[58]

The reform provides for three support schemes. First, a person can designate their support before a court or a notary.[59] This designation is made directly by the natural person and does not imply a waiver of their legal capacity. Secondly, a person can designate "future supports" notarially in anticipation of requiring assistance in the future to exercise their legal capacity.[60] The person can determine to which individuals or institutions such designation should or should not fall, as well as the form, scope, duration and guidelines of the support. The notarial document must state the time or circumstances for the designation of future support to be in force. Thirdly, in exceptional cases where the person cannot express their will by any means and the appointment of supports is necessary to exercise and protect their rights, the judge can designate the necessary supports.[61] In line with the standard proposed by the CRPD Committee, when implementing this exceptional measure, the judge and the supporters must be guided by the best interpretation of the person's will and preferences.

The reform introduced a flexible system of safeguards to ensure that the rights, will and preferences of the individual are respected and to prevent abuse and undue influence.[62] The beneficiary of the support establishes the safeguards they deem appropriate, indicating, at a minimum, the deadlines for reviewing the support. The judge decides on safeguards only for exceptional support designations. The Regulation has established an open list of possible safeguards people can choose from, including accountability, audits, periodic

---

55 Legislative Decree No. 1384, Art. 659-B.
56 Ibid., Art. 659-C.
57 Ibid., Art. 1976-A.
58 Ibid., Art. 659-B.
59 Ibid., Art. 659-D.
60 Ibid., Art. 659-F.
61 Ibid., Art. 659-E.
62 Ibid., Art. 659-G.

unannounced supervision, unannounced home visits, interviews, and information requirements.[63]

Finally, the reform modified the Code of Civil Procedures and the Legislative Decree of Notaries to guarantee the legal capacity of people with disabilities in judicial and notarial procedures. In the Civil Procedure Code, limitations on the participation of persons with disabilities in judicial proceedings were abolished,[64] and their right to procedural fairness in all judicial proceedings was expressly recognised.[65] In addition, judicial decisions on the designation of supports must be written in easy-to-read formats.[66] The Legislative Decree on Notaries was also amended to include the obligation of notaries to provide accessibility measures, reasonable accommodations and safeguards.[67]

2.2.4. Implementation

The implementation of the Peruvian reform has been messy and uneven. The modified provisions entered into force the day after publication, generating uncertainty among legal operators, people with disabilities and their families. In addition, although the debate on the reform went practically unnoticed in academic circles, once it was approved several articles were published by civil lawyers strongly questioning the reform.[68] The initial criticism focused mainly on the elimination of provision for declaring absolute incapacity of persons considered "deprived of discernment", which was perceived as a threat to legal security and detrimental to people with intellectual and psychosocial disabilities themselves. Other criticisms related to the legislative technique, the regulation of the transition process, reforms to contracts and the civil liability regime.[69]

---

[63] Ibid., Art. 21, no. 3.

[64] Civil Procedure Code, Arts. 61, 66 and 207.

[65] Ibid., Art. 119-A.

[66] Ibid., Art. 847.

[67] Ibid., Art. 16.

[68] See J. Espinoza, "Las nuevas coordenadas impuestas en el Código Civil en materia de capacidad (o el problema de la' falta de discernimiento en una reforma legislativa inconsulta y apresurada)", in (2018) 64 Gaceta Civil & Procesal Civil, 13–25; Y. Vega-Mere, "La reforma del régimen legal de los sujetos débiles made by Mary Shelley: notas al margen de una novela que no pudo tener peor final", in Civil & Procedural Civil Gazette, No. 64, 2018, pp. 27–45; M. Castillo and J. Chipana, "La pésima nueva regulación de la capacidad jurídica de las personas con discapacidad", (2018) 65 Civil Gazette and Civil Procedure, 45–50.

[69] See J. W. Duran Vivanco, "¿Realmente el sistema de apoyos y salvaguardias implementado en el Código Civil cumple con su función de apoyar a las personas con discapacidad?" (2020) 12(14) Official Magazine of the Judicial Power, 323–351; R. Constantino Caycho, "The Flag of Imagination: Peru's New Reform on Legal Capacity for Persons with Intellectual and Psychosocial Disabilities and the Need for New Understandings in Private Law" (2020) 14 The Age of Human Rights Journal, 155–180; C. Garcia, "El impacto de la Convención de los Derechos de las Personas con Discapacidad en el Código Civil de Perú" (2021) Capacidad

The Judiciary, more familiar with the reform due to its participation in the CEDIS and previous training courses in the Judiciary Academy, approved, in a relatively short time, a transition regulation,[70] which regulates, among other things, the restoration of the legal capacity of persons under guardianship. The Executive Branch would not approve the regulations of Legislative Decree No. 1384 until August 2019.[71] There is no information on the review of interdiction sentences and their conversion into processes for support designation.

Despite these limitations, the Judiciary, in collaboration with the Ombudsman's Office and non-governmental organisations, has conducted various training courses for justice system actors. Likewise, civil society has raised awareness and trained other actors, including notaries and families. According to SUNARP, up to January 2020, 608 new support measures were registered.[72]

The reform has also made it possible to address respect for the legal capacity of persons with disabilities in mental health services. Although the legislative decree does not refer to such services, the Regulation of Law No. 30947, Mental Health Law, includes a series of provisions that recognise the legal capacity of users of mental health services and the role that supports can play in decision-making in that context. Significantly, the Regulation rethinks the traditional approach to "psychiatric emergencies", recognising the legal capacity of people in such cases and channelling the provision of support through the procedure established in Legislative Decree No. 1384 and its regulations.[73]

2.3. COLOMBIA

2.3.1. *Situation before Reform*

In 2009, the Colombian Congress enacted Law 1306 dated 5 June 2009, "By which rules are issued for the Protection of Persons with Mental Disabilities

---

      jurídica, discapacidad y derecho civil en Latinoamérica, Indaiatuba, Editorial Foco, SP; G. Castillo, "Modificaciones introducidas por el Decreto Legislativo 1384 al Código Civil peruano de 1984: especial referencia en materia de Derecho de las personas, Negocio jurídico, Derecho de familia y Derecho de sucesiones" (2021) 1(2) *Revista Cubana de Derecho*, 600–647.

[70]   Executive Council of the Judiciary, Administrative Resolution No. 046-P-CE-PJ, Regulations for the Transition to the Support System in Compliance with the Social Model of Disability, 23 January 2019.

[71]   Supreme Decree No. 016-2019-MIMP, Supreme Decree that approves the Regulation that regulates the granting of reasonable adjustments, designation of supports and implementation of safeguards for the exercise of the legal capacity of persons with disabilities, published on 25 August 2019.

[72]   Request for information made by Society and Disability – SODIS – to the National Superintendence of Public Registries, with an electronic response dated 30 January 2020.

[73]   Legislative Decree No. 1384, Art. 36, para. 6. In this regard, see A. Vasquez Encalada, "The Potential of the Legal Capacity Law Reform in Peru to Transform Mental Health Provision", *Mental Health, Legal Capacity, and Human Rights*, Cambridge University Press, Cambridge, 2021.

and the Regime of Legal Representation of Emancipated Disabled Persons is established."[74] This Law repealed and replaced titles XXII and XXXV of the Civil Code.[75] This would be the most significant reform to the legal capacity regime for people with disabilities in Colombia up to that time. Law 1306 of 2009, despite reforming the Civil Code, maintained the incapacitation scheme that was already enshrined in the Colombian Civil Code.[76]

The Law defined "subjects with mental disabilities" as people who "suffer mental or behavioural limitations, which do not allow them to understand the scope of their actions, or assume excessive or unnecessary risks in the management of their assets."[77] Regarding the legal capacity status of the individuals impacted by this Law, the norm classified persons into two groups: "with absolute mental disability" and "with relative mental disability", using the terms "disability" and "incapacity" interchangeably. The Law defined "subjects with absolute mental disability" as "those who suffer from a severe or profound learning, behavioural or mental deterioration condition or pathology". It established that those who "suffered" absolute mental disability were absolutely incapable before the Law and should be declared interdicted, understood as a measure to re-establish rights and, as such, could be requested by any person.

The legal duty to initiate the interdiction was established for some individuals,[78] as well as the legitimation of forced psychiatric internment for persons "with absolute mental disabilities" for up to two months by medical order and for one year with a judicial authorisation that could be extended indefinitely. The interdiction process was of voluntary jurisdiction. Once started, the family judge requested an expert opinion of forensic psychiatry, generally at the National Institute of Legal Medicine and Forensic Sciences, where it was determined whether the person had an absolute or relative mental disability. This procedure was very questionable since a forensic scientist was being asked to determine if a legal category applied to a person. Law 1306 of 2009 also established the category of "Subject with relative mental disability", which stated that:

> People who suffer from behavioural deficiencies, prodigality or business immaturity and who, as a result, may put their assets at serious risk, may be barred from entering into some legal transactions at the request of their spouse, permanent partner, relatives up to the third degree of consanguinity and even by the affected person.[79]

---

[74]   Colombian Congress. Law 1306 of 2009, *Official Gazette* No. 47,371 of 5 June 2009.
[75]   From Article 428 to Article 632.
[76]   Sanctioned in 1873 and later adopted in 1887, it states in its Article 1502 the requirements for a person to be bound by another.
[77]   Law 1306 of 2009, Art. 2.
[78]   Ibid., Arts. 25 and 26.
[79]   Ibid., Art. 32.

Legal Capacity Regime Reforms in Costa Rica, Peru and Colombia

If a judge determined that a person fell into this category, he or she could declare the person disqualified and established a partial restriction of legal capacity, limiting it to certain specific legal acts and appointing a third person as an advisor.

Finally, the Law contained a rehabilitation process through which interdiction and incapacitation measures could be lifted on the basis of an expert opinion[80] and provided that the person could recover administration of their assets.[81] However, this was not a tool that had a significant effect, especially since the same scheme was used that sought to prove that the person had not been able, initially, to demonstrate their capacity to act and therefore had been declared interdicted. In short, a different scenario was sought under the same evidentiary method that had demonstrated the alleged incapacity. In Colombia, there is no clarity about the number of persons declared interdicted today. Available information shows, for example, that as of May 2018, based on registration starting only in 2011, there were 9,346 people under guardianship throughout the country.[82]

2.3.2. Reform Process

The legislative reform in Colombia, which culminated in Law 1996 of 2019, was undoubtedly the result of mobilisation stemming from civil society, with actions that can be traced back to 2010, before the ratification of the CRPD in 2011.[83] In 2013, two important events occurred, which served as background for the reform. First, Statutory Law 1618 was approved,[84] which specifies the duties of the different territorial and national entities in light of the obligations of the CRPD and indicates in Article 21.2 the obligation to propose reforms to align regulations with Article 12 of the CRPD. The second was the start of pilot

---

[80]   Ibid., Arts. 30 and 38.

[81]   Constitutional Court, Judgment T-362-2017. <https://www.corteconstitucional.gov.co/relatoria/2017/T-362-17.htm> accessed 19.01.2023.

[82]   See ASDOWN COLOMBIA, NODO COMUNITARIO DE SALUD MENTAL and PAIIS, "El Ejercicio de la Capacidad Jurídica: Guía práctica para su aplicación", p. 22. <https://asdown.org/wp-content/uploads/2019/09/Guia-para-implementacion-Cap_Juridica.pdf> accessed 31.07.2023.

[83]   In 2010, Inclusion International, the Action Program for Equality and Social Inclusion organizations – (PAIIS) – the Legal Clinic of the Faculty of Law of the Universidad de los Andes, Asdown Colombia and the Saldarriaga Concha Foundation, organised a regional meeting on the right to legal capacity and the rights of persons with disabilities in light of the CRPD. The conferences of said meeting can be seen on the Universidad de los Andes PAIIS YouTube channel. Available at <https://www.youtube.com/channel/UCm18dBeJv9NqDD6UuIE80sw>. Welcome message from the founder, Natalia Ángel Cabo <https://www.youtube.com/watch?v=3KrG-c8xW1M> accessed 18.01.2023.

[84]   Colombia. Congress of the republic. Law 1618 of 2013. *By which the provisions are established to guarantee the full exercise of the rights of persons with disabilities.* <http://www.secretariasenado.gov.co/senado/basedoc/ley_1618_2013.html> accessed 18.01.2023.

Intersentia

145

projects led by civil society organisations and academia[85] that sought to identify, in real cases, barriers to decision-making and opportunities to generate support mechanisms for the exercise of autonomy. The lessons learned from this process can be found in a document published in 2019.[86]

In 2015, a technical working group was formed in coordination with the Presidential Council for the Inclusion of Persons with Disabilities and different organisations to advance the reform process. It was comprised of public entities that would have a role in implementing the reform, academia, civil society organisations[87] and independent activists with psychosocial disabilities. The working group held monthly meetings for two years to discuss a draft bill. In 2016, the CRPD Committee conducted the first review of Colombia and, in its recommendations to the State, advocated for repealing all normative provisions that totally or partially restricted the legal capacity of persons with disabilities.[88]

Various legislators supported and became key drivers of the bill in Congress. The first version was presented on 3 June 2017, in co-authorship with 24 congress members from the entire spectrum of political parties and the Ombudsman.[89] This bill was withdrawn on 21 June 2017 due to end of the legislative period. A second version of the bill was tabled on 25 July 2017, and went through the entire four legislative debates before the House of Representatives and the Senate.[90] The public hearing at the time of its presentation was attended by

---

[85] ASDOWN COLOMBIA, NODO COMUNITARIO DE SALUD MENTAL and PAIIS (n. 82).

[86] Ibid., p. 77.

[87] The workgroup included the Ministry of Justice and Law, the Ministry of Health and Social Protection, the Ministry of the Interior, the Prosecutor General's Office, the Attorney General's Office, the Ombudsman's Office, the Administrative Unit for Reparation and Comprehensive Attention to victims (UARIV), the Colombian Institute of Family Welfare and the National Institute of Legal Medicine and Forensic Sciences, in addition to the Universidad de los Andes, the Externado University of Colombia and the civil society organisations Asdown Colombia and the Mental Health and Coexistence Node.

[88] CRPD Committee, Concluding Observations on Colombia's Initial Report, CRPD/C/COL/CO/1, paras. 30–33 <https://undocs.org/en/CRPD/C/COL/CO/1> accessed 18.01.2023.

[89] This group of congressmen were part of what became known as the "Bancada IN *[IN caucus]*" (IN for Inclusion), made up of congressmen from all political parties who publicly committed themselves to promoting the inclusion of people with disabilities. This process was promoted by then Presidential Advisor for the Participation of Persons with Disabilities, Juan Pablo Salazar. The congressional teams received training from PAIIS. See Visible Congress, legislative trajectory of bill 248 of 2017. <https://congresovisible.uniandes.edu.co/proyectos-de-ley/ppor-medio-de-la-cual-se-establece-el-regimen-para-el-ejercicio-de-la-capacidad-legal-de-las-personas-con-discapacidad-mayores-de-edad-capacidad-legal-de-adultos-con-discapacidad/8823/#tab=2> accessed 18.01.2023. Published in the *Legislative Gazette* No. 222 of 2017 <http://svrpubindc.imprenta.gov.co/senado/index2.xhtml?ent=Camara&fec=7-4-2017&num=222&consec=47650> accessed 18.01.2023.

[90] The legislative history of the project can be consulted at <https://congresovisible.uniandes.edu.co/proyectos-de-ley/ppor-medio-de-la-cual-se-establece-el-regimen-para-el-ejercicio-de-la-capacity-legal-of-persons-with-disabilities-of-full-age-legal-capacity-of-adults-with-disabilities/8979/#tab=2> accessed 24.03.2023. It was registered under project number 27/17 in the House of Representatives and number 236/19 in the Senate.

Legal Capacity Regime Reforms in Costa Rica, Peru and Colombia

self-advocates who expressed, in their own words, what interdiction meant in their lives.[91] Law 1996 of 2019 was enacted by the Presidency of the Republic on 26 August of that year.

2.3.3. Content of the Reform

Law 1996 of 2019, "Which establishes the regime for the exercise of the legal capacity of persons with disabilities of legal age",[92] reforms the content of Law 1306 by repealing 54 articles related to disability and including nine chapters and 63 articles. From its legal nature, this is an ordinary and not a special law. Article 6 states the presumption of the legal capacity for all persons with disabilities of legal age.[93] In addition, it recognises that capacity is established "without any distinction and regardless of whether or not they use supports to undertake legal acts." This recognition is completed with the fact that "in no case may the existence of a disability be a reason for restricting a person's capacity to act."

The Colombian reform recognises and builds on the voluntary nature of the supports. Article 4, concerning the autonomy and primacy of the person's will and preferences, states that "the supports used to enter into a legal act must always respond to the will and preferences of the holder thereof". The Law proposes an interpretive sequence: first, it builds on the use of supports based on the will and preferences of the person; secondly, it requires making reasonable accommodations and adopting support measures that allow expressing a person's will and preferences; thirdly, it allows resort to the guidance principle of "best interpretation of the will and preferences of the person," under a specific process and very clear conditions, starting from the situation where "the holder of the legal act is absolutely unable to express their will and preferences, by any possible mean, mode and format of communication."[94]

The Law provides three mechanisms to establish supports to exercise legal capacity.[95]

- The execution of a support agreement between the holder of the act and the natural or legal persons designated as supports. This can be done by public

---

[91] The video of Sergio Araque's intervention on the day of the discussion of the bill in the House of Representatives is available at <https://www.youtube.com/watch?v=szY7FsUiR3I> accessed 18.01.2023.

[92] Congress of the republic. *Official Gazette* No. 51,057 of 26 August 2019. Law 1996 of 2019, Colombia.

[93] Article 7 of the Law states, for legal acts that minors can undertake in the Colombian legal system, that minors with disabilities can, in general terms, use the mechanisms of the law to guarantee that they can undertake said acts with the necessary support.

[94] Law 1996 of 2019, Art. 38.

[95] This despite the fact that Art. 9 only mentions support agreements and judicial adjudication processes as mechanisms. Advance directives should also be understood as one of the mechanisms provided by law.

Intersentia

147

deed before a notary or before a mediation centre and will have a maximum duration of five years.

- The judicial designation of support by a family court, at the initiative of the holder of the act, or in cases in which all reasonable accommodations have been exhausted, and the person's will cannot be unequivocally known. A third party may initiate the request for support designation with legitimate interest and under specific conditions.
- The implementation of advance directives where third parties, who acquire obligations to act, are designated.

Regarding who can act as a supporter, the Law allows both natural persons and legal entities. It establishes a specific chapter indicating the requirements for a support person, the restrictions on being a support person, obligations and general actions, and the responsibility it entails.[96] Chapter 8 establishes a transitional regime that automatically suspends interdiction processes in progress and provides family judges with the power to dictate nominated or unnominated measures to protect the property interests of the person with a disability. Additionally, it provides a transitional process for appointing a support system in cases where the unequivocal will of the person with a disability cannot be known.

The implementation of the measures have occurred in stages. Advance directives came into effect first on 26 August 2019; followed by support agreements – 26 August 2020; and finally on 26 August 2021 – the judicial adjudication processes for permanent support came into force. For persons who had already been placed under guardianship, a review process must be conducted by judicial initiative or at the request of a party.

2.3.4. Implementation

Implementing Law 1996 of 2019 encountered multiple resistances from civil lawyers,[97] notaries and families of persons with disabilities. However, it has also seen important actors championing the cause for adequate implementation, from civil society, academia and the Colombian government. For example, the Ministry of Justice was diligent in starting the draft decree that regulates the actions of notaries and mediation centres. For this, a participatory technical working group was convened, comprised of different entities, notaries, conciliators, and civil society and academia members.

---

[96] Ibid., ch. 6, Arts. 44–50.

[97] See for instance: <https://www.elpais.com.co/opinion/columnistas/jose-felix-escobar/el-derecho-otra-victima.html; https://www.ambitojuridico.com/noticias/columnista-impreso/civil-y-familia/la-muerte-de-la-incapacidad> accessed 18.01.2023.

As a result of this process, Decree 1429 of 2020 was issued, which regulates the process to formalise support agreements and advance directives before notaries and mediation centres.[98] The Ministry of Justice promoted the training of more than 2,000 justice system actors throughout the country on the content of the Law. It issued various informational documents about its content.[99]

In December 2020, the Office of the Presidential Advisor on Disability published the Guidelines and National Protocol for conducting support assessments within the framework of Law 1996 of 2019, "Decision-Making Supports Assessment", with funding provided by the Inter-American Development Bank (IDB).[100] On 1 April 2022, Decree 487 was issued, which regulates the support assessment service enshrined in the Law,[101] which came into effect a year late. To this day, the main challenges continue to be widespread ignorance and the deep and persistent hold of the medical paradigm over the meaning of disability. There have been documented cases of notaries refusing to carry out a support agreement without a supports assessment report, a requirement without a legal basis. The other significant challenge is the need for capacity to assess the quality and non-medicalised supports, which is still in a very early phase. While the judicial appointment of supports formally began on 26 August 2021, its application by the Judiciary has been very uneven. For its part, the Ombudsman's Office has not delimited the personal defence process for people lacking a support network.

3. CHALLENGES OF REFORM ON LEGAL CAPACITY IN LATIN AMERICA

Based on the experiences of these three Latin American countries in implementing reforms of their legal capacity regimes in the region, it is possible to highlight three important challenges for the full recognition of the right to legal capacity

---

[98] Colombia. Presidency of the Republic. Decree 1429 of 2020, by which Articles 16, 17 and 22 of Law 1996 of 2019 are regulated and Decree 1069 of 2015, Sole Regulatory of the Justice and Law Sector, is added. <https://www.funcionpublica.gov.co/eva/gestornormativo/norma.php?i=144938> accessed 18.01.2023.

[99] Available at <https://www.minjusticia.gov.co/programas-co/tejiendo-justicia/Paginas/publicaciones-discapacidad.aspx> accessed 18.01.2023.

[100] Presidency of the Republic. Presidential Council for the Participation of Persons with Disabilities, "Guidelines and national protocol for the assessment of support". <http://snd.gov.co/documentos/lineamientos-valoraciones-apoyo.pdf> accessed 18.01.2023.

[101] Presidency of the Republic, Decree 487, Colombia, 2022. Whereby Part 8 is added to Book 2 of Decree 1081 of 2015, in the sense of regulating the provision of the support assessment service conducted by public and private entities under the terms of Law 1996 of 2019. <https://www.funciónpública.gov.co/eva/gestorrmativo/norma.php?=185226> accessed 18.01.2023.

3.1. LEGISLATIVE CHALLENGES

This first challenge seems to imply only the introduction of legislation to reform the regulations for the countries in the region that do not comply with the standards of Article 12 of the CRPD. However, the resulting analysis of what has been learned in the three countries studied must incorporate a series of elements that are not necessarily obvious.

The first one, inexorably linked to legislative reforms, is the advocacy and political support required for recognising legal capacity as a necessary reform linked to the human rights movement in each country. In the three countries analysed, the reform processes began from civil society, with the active participation of persons with disabilities' organisations. They managed to consolidate high-level political support that allowed final adoption of the reforms. This confluence of factors appears to have enabled the achievement of comprehensive reforms in line with the standards of the CRPD Committee.

The second has to do with the nature of the Law that originates the reform. In Colombia, for example, two lawsuits were filed a few months after the Law was enacted, which sought to declare the provisions unenforceable in their entirety for not having been processed as a Statutory Law. However, the Constitutional Court declared their constitutionality as it interpreted that, since it did not regulate the essential core of a right, it should not have been processed as statutory measure.[102] In addition, it should be noted that while Costa Rica and Colombia adopted specific laws on the legal capacity of persons with disabilities and the provision of support, Peru carried out a substantial reform of the Peruvian Civil Code which relied on the issuance of an Executive decree to overcome the difficult parliamentary debate. This process of reform in Peru has generated significant interest from academia and other sectors.

The third and last one is linked to the scope of the reform. In some countries, the reform was carried out specifically in relation to civil legislation regulating legal capacity and aspects that had a direct and indirect effect on the rights of persons with disabilities, while in others, the reform was used to repeal other regulations other than civil legislation, such as procedural legislation, sexual and reproductive health, childhood and adolescence, among others. The scope of the reform will of course depend on each country's regulations, on opportunities

---

[102] Constitutional Court, Sentences C-022 of 2021, M.P: Cristina Pardo Schlesinger and C-118 of 2021, M.P: Gloria Stella Ortiz Delgado.

within existing processes, allies, the strength of the organisations and movements that are promoting it, and the political context, among others.

3.2. ADMINISTRATIVE CHALLENGES

These kinds of challenges seem to arise after the reform is in place. In reality, it must be analysed within it, along with the undertaken process. Although it may seem obvious, it is important to include in the debate, for example, the transition regime once the law enters into force, who will be the public officials whose functions and duties will change significantly, as well as possible new obligations to ensure the availability and accessibility of support. For example, the Peruvian reform legislative decree did not establish positive obligations for the State concerning the provision of support, which has been subsequently and incompletely addressed in the regulatory process. In general, the challenges encountered in the reform processes highlight the importance of appointing governing bodies to lead implementation.

It is also important to identify the entities with responsibilities regarding eventual regulations and specific guidelines to allow effective and easy implementation of the norm. The same is true for all training and instruction that must be provided. For example, in Colombia, the Law granted the Ministry of Justice one year to design and implement a training plan for notaries and conciliation centres on the content of the Law and the obligations derived from it, and 18 months for the public disability policy governing body – since 2019 attached to the Office of the Presidential Advisor for the Participation of Persons with Disabilities – to provide training to the entities which are required to provide the support assessment service.

Of course, over the course of ongoing implementation innumerable challenges will arise that require further development of regulations and guidelines.

3.3. SOCIAL, CULTURAL, INTERPRETIVE AND CONTEXTUAL CHALLENGES

Although the Law can change, which in itself is very important, the truth is that society must do the same. In this sense, the daily practices that lead to marginalisation and discrimination, based on the non-recognition of the person with disabilities as a subject who can and must be supported to make decisions, will undoubtedly continue. It is with an understanding of this broader context that the standard should be implemented.

This presents many challenges with different implications. On the one hand, one can see the social challenge of no longer recognising as necessary legal institutions that have functioned for decades in our countries and have generated so much acceptance in society, and the challenge of creating and consolidating new ones. As an important effect of this, multiple interpretations of what the norm seeks to do can be generated. For example, in Colombia, since the law was passed, eight lawsuits of unconstitutionality have been filed against it,[103] and, for now, the Constitutional Court has ratified the Law's constitutionality in its decisions.[104] For its part, the Supreme Court of Justice has issued more than 20 judgments interpreting the 1996 Law, enabling the acceptance of the norm as a legal reality in the country. Similarly, in Costa Rica, faced with resistance from the justice system itself, the Costa Rican Supreme Court of Justice had to ratify the constitutionality of the reform. A paradigm shift as significant as the one required by Article 12 of the CRPD requires a cultural change within the institutions, something challenging to achieve in the short term.

On the other hand, challenges have arisen from a lack of consolidated public policies. These policies must enable the necessary provision of support services for persons with disabilities since the reforms have sought to guarantee the provision of the necessary support for the exercise of legal capacity in a social context where other supports are not provided – such as those necessary for independent living in the community – which would allow this right to be effective in helping to secure and protect citizenship. Without addressing the social determinants that determine the *de facto* denial of the legal capacity of persons with disabilities within their families and their communities, the processes run the risk of becoming formal exercises, far removed from social reality.

---

[103] Lawsuits filed under filings: D-13525, D-13575, D-13585, D-13658, D-13738, D-13743, D-14076 and D-14077.

[104] Constitutional Court, Sentences C-022 of 2021, M.P: Cristina Pardo Schlesinger. Available at <https://www.corteconstitucional.gov.co/Relatoria/2021/C-022-21.htm>; Judgment C-025 of 2021, MP: Cristina Pardo Schlesinger. <https://www.corteconstitucional.gov.co/Relatoria/2021/C-025-21. htm> accessed 18.01.2023.

A CRITICAL REVIEW OF LEGAL CAPACITY REFORM IN THE U.S.

Kristin Booth GLEN*

1. Introduction 154
2. Context.. 155
   2.1. U.S. Hostility to Human Rights Treaties........................ 155
   2.2. The Deep-Rooted and Continuing Commitment to
        Guardianship and the Beginning of Reform 157
3. The Rise of Supported Decision-Making............................ 158
   3.1. The Concept of Supported Decision-Making.................... 158
   3.2. Supported Decision-Making and Guardianship Laws:
        The First Reform Effort 159
   3.3. Supported Decision-Making "in Practice" 160
   3.4. Supported Decision-Making Agreement (SDMA) Laws 160
        3.4.1. Coverage, or "who can Make an SDMA?"............... 161
        3.4.2. "Capacity" to Make an Agreement? 162
        3.4.3. Definition of SDM.................................... 163
        3.4.4. Effect of Agreement on Other Capacity Determinations ... 163
        3.4.5. Other Protections for those who Make SDMAs.......... 164
        3.4.6. Who can be Supporters: Statutory Disqualifications 164
        3.4.7. What Supporters *can* do............................. 165
        3.4.8. Supporter Access to Information 166
        3.4.9. Supporter Obligations, Liability, and Immunity.......... 166
        3.4.10. Amending or Terminating the SDMA................... 167
        3.4.11. Third Party Obligation under the Agreement............ 167
        3.4.12. Immunity from Liability 168
        3.4.13. Third Party Reporting of Abuse, Neglect, and/or
                Exploitation 169
        3.4.14. Education/Training................................. 170
        3.4.15. Monitoring.. 170

---

* University Professor and Dean Emerita, City University of New York School of Law; Justice
  of the New York Supreme Court and the Appellate Term, First Judicial Department, and
  Surrogate Judge, New York County, (ret.) Director, Supported Decision-Making New York.

Intersentia

153

4. Critiques of Existing Statutes 170
    4.1. Mixed Motives: The Case of Texas............................. 170
    4.2. What is (but should not be) in the Statutes 171
    4.3. What is Missing from the Statutes.............................. 172
5. Supported Decision-Making New York (SDMNY): A Successful
    Empirical Model Advancing the Right of Legal Capacity............... 173
    5.1. The Model... 173
    5.2. Learnings from the Project.................................... 173
6. Challenges and Barriers to Advancing Legal Capacity through SDM 174
7. The Future of an Equal Right to Exercise Legal Capacity in the U.S. 175

1. INTRODUCTION

Legal capacity, generally – and mistakenly – understood as "mental capacity" is deeply ingrained in U.S. law, resulting in the denial of the human right of legal capacity to people with intellectual/developmental, psychosocial, and cognitive disabilities. The most common and visible legislative manifestations of this denial are guardianship laws, which apply primarily to persons with intellectual/ developmental disabilities and older persons with cognitive decline, dementia, etc., and involuntary commitment and medication laws affecting persons with psychosocial disabilities/mental illness. In addition to guardianship, there is a vast body of laws, regulations and judicial decisions that impose differing tests of mental capacity for such activities as contracting, marrying, voting, serving as a witness or juror, giving consent for health care treatment, making a will, etc., allowing private and public third parties, like doctors, bankers, landlords, voting commissioners and marriage licence clerks to deny legal capacity to persons with disabilities.[1]

To date there has been little U.S. attention to the ways in which denial of legal capacity discriminates against persons with disabilities, and even less attention to any affirmative *right* to legal capacity.[2] The U.S. has not ratified the UN Convention on the Rights of Persons with Disabilities (CRPD), consistent with a long history of antipathy to human rights conventions, and other than an ever-growing body of legal scholarship, there is no public awareness of, or discussion about it.

Current reforms implicating legal capacity are tied to the use of supported decision-making (SDM), itself inconsistently understood and defined.[3] They

---

[1] K. B. GLEN, "Supported Decision-Making From Theory to Practice: Further Reflections On An International Pilot Project" (2020) 13 *Albany Government Law Review* 1.

[2] L. SALTZMAN, "Using Domestic Law To Move Toward a Recognition of Universal Legal Capacity for Persons with Disabilities" (2017) 39 *Cardozo L. Rev* 521.

[3] T. CARNEY, "Prioritising Supported-Decision-Making: Running on Empty or a Basis for Glacial-to-Steady Progress" (2017) 6(4) *Laws* 18.

take two forms: modest efforts to limit, but not repeal, guardianship laws through recognition of SDM as a "less restrictive alternative" to guardianship; and, more recently, laws recognising and regulating SDM Agreements (SDMAs) that purport to require legal recognition of decisions made pursuant to such agreements.

The impetus for even these limited efforts is mixed, resulting in the lack of any truly principled attack on substituted decision-making, and often leaving the door open for continuing imposition of mental capacity tests. In the absence of any popular movement advocates for the human right of legal capacity are almost all academic. With few exceptions, SDM advocates have pursued an incrementalist legislative strategy with few empirically based efforts to demonstrate how SDM might actually work "on the ground".

While reform efforts around guardianship potentially affect both persons with developmental and cognitive disabilities, there is currently no viable movement for reform of the involuntary hospitalisation (commitment) and medication laws that deny people with psychosocial disabilities their right to legal capacity.

Understanding why legal capacity reforms are so limited in the U.S. requires knowledge of the context in which they exist This includes the deeply rooted tradition of guardianship as "protection" for people with developmental and cognitive disabilities, and U.S. hostility to human rights treaties, including the CRPD.

2. CONTEXT

U.S. law is a mixture of common (judge-made) law, statutes, and regulations. As a federal system, the "police power" is largely reserved to the states, including guardianship and involuntary commitment and medication statutes, while the federal government has exclusive treaty power. The lack of interest in/commitment to any right of legal capacity in both jurisdictions reinforces the difficulty of creating significant reform, unlike countries that have ratified the CRPD and either domesticate its provisions or have responsibility for implementation.

2.1. U.S. HOSTILITY TO HUMAN RIGHTS TREATIES

Although the U.S. was a pioneer in international human rights, beginning with the aspirational Universal Declaration of Human Rights in 1948,[4] the

---

[4]   Universal Declaration of Human Rights, G.A. Res. 217A (III), UN Doc. A/810 (10 December 1948).

politics of anti-communism (and, to some degree, support for continuing racial segregation) led to backlash against later conventions that might require U.S. compliance with international norms.[5] Even when signing or ratifying, the U.S. does so only with significant formal reservations.[6]

Of four conventions that further elucidate human rights for "vulnerable groups", the U.S. has signed three: Convention on the Rights of the Child (1989),[7] Convention on the Elimination of Discrimination Against Women (1980)[8] and the CRPD (2009),[9] but has ratified only one, the International Convention on the Elimination of All Forms of Racial and Ethnic Discrimination (1994).[10] Despite commitment by the Obama administration, and broad bi-partisan support, in 2012, amidst a flurry of right-wing misinformation the Senate withheld its consent to the ratification of the CRPD by just five votes.[11] The subsequent Trump presidency prevented any possibility of ratification and, with current hyper-partisanship in Washington, the future is not promising.[12]

Another important, somewhat perverse reason, accounts for the U.S.'s disappointing failure to ratify the CRPD. In 1990 Congress passed the Americans with Disabilities Act (ADA), often trumpeted as a model for the CRPD and cited for why the U.S. needs no further legal protections for people with disabilities. The ADA is, however, a comparatively limited, traditional anti-discrimination law, dealing primarily with employment and public accommodations; its provisions have been further narrowed by conservative judicial decisions. Originally advanced as a cost-saving measure, as the actual cost of needed accommodations has become apparent, support has diminished.[13] This issue of cost-saving versus the need for, and cost of, increased services continues to impact legislative efforts, however modest, related to legal capacity.

---

[5] A. C. HARFIELD, "Oh Righteous Delinquent One: The United States' International Human Rights Double Standard – Explanation, Example, and Avenues for Change" (2001) 4 *N.Y.City L. Rev.* 59.

[6] L. HENKIN, "U.S. Ratification of Human Rights Conventions: The Ghost of Senator Bricker" (1995) 89 *Am J. Int'l. L.* 341.

[7] Convention on the Rights of the Child, 20 November 1989, 1577 UNTS 3.

[8] Convention on the Elimination of All Forms of Discrimination Against Women, 18 December 1979, 1249 UNTS 13.

[9] Convention on the Rights of Persons with Disabilities, 13 December 2006, 2515 UNTS 3.

[10] International Convention on the Elimination of All Forms of Racial Discrimination, 21 December 1965, 660 UNTS 195.

[11] R. JONES, "U.S. failure to ratify the Convention on the Rights of Persons with Disabilities" (2013) <https://www.awid.org/news-and-analysis/us-failure-ratify-convention-rights-persons-disabilities> accessed 21.10.2021.

[12] A. S. KANTER, "Let's try again: Why the United States should ratify the United Nations convention on the rights of people with disabilities" (2019) 35 *Touro L. Rev.* 301.

[13] S. R. BAGENSTOS, "Disability rights and the discourse of Justice" (2020) 73(1) *SMU Law Review Forum* 26–34.

2.2. THE DEEP-ROOTED AND CONTINUING COMMITMENT TO GUARDIANSHIP AND THE BEGINNING OF REFORM

Guardianship has been a part of the common law since at least the sixteenth century, adopted by the colonies, and then by individual states after the establishment of a federal republic.[14] Every state had at least one guardianship (sometimes called "conservatorship") law, covering "incompetence" no matter the cause or population; a few had, and still have, statutes specifically for persons with developmental disabilities.[15] These laws were almost entirely diagnosis-driven, plenary in nature, removing all legal capacity upon a finding of "incompetence", lacking the most basic procedural protections, and with no time limitation.

A series of financial scandals in 1987 spurred the first round of guardianship reform, resulting in many procedural protections and a presumption of competence that, in theory, could only be overcome by clear evidence. Capacity was understood as "functional", with removal of rights tied to specific inabilities. Although most statutes required "tailored" guardianships, enabling wards to retain all rights in areas where their specific "incapacities" were unproven, courts have continued to grant plenary guardianships in most cases, totally and permanently removing all the person's legal capacity.[16]

The 1990 ADA adopted a social, rather than medical model of disability. This, despite its limitations, has resulted in shifting public perception of people with disabilities, although primarily for those with mobility, visual and hearing disabilities. Other laws, including those related to "special education" for children (through the age of 21) with intellectual/developmental disabilities also expanded possibilities for social inclusion.[17] A 1997 U.S. Supreme Court decision (*Olmstead*, 1999)[18] interpreted the ADA to require that persons with disabilities receive services in the least restrictive setting meeting their needs, spurring a community living movement with greater possibilities for inclusion. Finally, judicial decisions based in the Due Process clause of the U.S. Constitution have required that, when the state employs its police power civilly to "protect" individuals (rather than criminally, to protect society) it must do so by the "least restrictive means" available.[19]

---

[14]   F. A. JOHNS, "Ten Years After: Where is the Constitutional Crisis with Procedural Safeguards and Due Process in Guardianship Adjudication?" (1999) 7 *Elder L. J.* 33.

[15]   National Council on Disability, *Beyond guardianship: Toward alternatives that promote greater self-determination*, Washington, DC: National Council on Disability 2018.

[16]   R. DILLER, "Legal capacity for all: Including older persons in the shift from adult guardianship to supported decision-making" (2016) 43 *Fordham Urb. L.J* 495.

[17]   *Individuals with Disabilities Education Improvement Act*, 20 USC 400 et seq. 2004.

[18]   *Olmstead v. L.C.*, 527 U.S. 581, 595 (1999).

[19]   R. DILLER, "Legal capacity for all: Including older persons in the shift from adult guardianship to supported decision-making" (2016) 43 *Fordham Urb. L.J* 495.

These social and legal changes, together with public scandals involving financial (and less frequently, personal elder abuse by guardians,) has spurred interest, if not yet commitment to, a "better way." Primarily academic rights discourse offered the possibility that SDM could be that "better way". Unfortunately, the recent media circus around Britney Spears' conservatorship has re-focused the conversation almost entirely to abuse of power by guardians/conservators.[20] Proposals for reform, including those made in Congressional hearings, have been limited to making guardianship "better", while reinforcing its legitimacy for people who, unlike rich, white, multi-millionaire pop stars, are clearly "disabled".

3. THE RISE OF SUPPORTED DECISION-MAKING

SDM is not a full manifestation of the *right* of legal capacity; it is a *means* to that end. Because legal capacity requires both the right to *make* one's own decisions and have them *legally recognised*, there is dissonance between the common practice by which everyone, including most people with developmental disabilities, use support from others in *making* decisions, and barriers to legal recognition of those decisions because of disability.[21] This has led to significant lack of clarity in the discourse around SDM and related legislative efforts for recognition and implementation. It is also at least partially responsible for the overwhelming emphasis on SDM as a practice, rather than on legal capacity as a human right.

3.1. THE CONCEPT OF SUPPORTED DECISION-MAKING

Although persons with developmental, psychosocial and/or cognitive disabilities have, like others, always used supports in making decisions, the concept of "SDM" is relatively recent. An oft-cited definition that recognises its many manifestations states that it is "a series of relationships, practices, arrangements, and agreements, of more or less formality and intensity, designed to assist an individual with a disability to make and communicate to others decisions about the individual's life".[22]

---

[20] J. Coscarelli and L. Day, "Judge frees Spears from father's control", *The New York Times*. <www.nytimes.com/2021/09/29/arts/music/britney-spears-court-decision-conservatorship.html> accessed 17.03.2023.

[21] CRPD Committee: Committee on the Rights of Persons with Disabilities, *General Comment No. 1*, 11th Session, 50(a) UN Doc. CRPD/C/GC/;1 (19 May 2014).

[22] R. D. Dinerstein, "Implementing Legal Capacity Under Article 12 of the UN Convention on the Rights of Persons with Disabilities: The Difficult Road from Guardianship to Supported Decision-Making" (2012) 19 *Hum. Rts. Brief* 8, 10.

The first formal meeting and exploration in the U.S. on SDM, was held in New York City in 2012, convened by two Commissions of the American Bar Association with support from the federal government's Administration for Community Living. The briefing paper for that interdisciplinary round table drew directly from the CRPD and focused on the necessity of legal recognition for decisions made by persons using SDM, while also promoting SDM as an alternative to guardianship. These distinct but related goals have informed how SDM is conceptualised and employed in legislative efforts that implicate legal capacity.

3.2. SUPPORTED DECISION-MAKING AND GUARDIANSHIP LAWS: THE FIRST REFORM EFFORT

Recognition of SDM as an alternative to guardianship has proceeded both in case law and legislation. In 2012, a New York court terminated the guardianship of a young woman with a developmental disability because she had developed a support system enabling her to make her own decisions, obviating the need for guardianship. Beside "least restrictive means", the decision explicitly cited the human right of legal capacity, CRPD Article 12, and the term SDM.[23] Since then, courts in New York and other states have employed similar reasoning, both to deny and terminate guardianships, though few have cited the CRPD.[24]

The New York decision and 2012 meeting spearheaded efforts to amend existing guardianship laws to include SDM as a "less restrictive alternative" to be attempted before guardianship could be imposed.[25] The Uniform Law Commission, a highly respected national organisation that drafts model statutes, revised its model guardianship statute, to do so.[26] Several states including Maine[27] and Virginia[28] have since amended their guardianship statutes, incorporating this revision.

---

[23]   *Matter of Dameris L.*,956 N.Y.S. 2d 848 (Surr. Ct. N.Y. Co. 2012).

[24]   For an example of a recent decision that does both, see *Matter of Grace J.*,176 N.Y.S.3d 450 (Surr. Ct. Kings Co 2022).

[25]   American Bar Association, Commission on Disability Rights, Section of Civil Rights and Social Justice, Section of Real Property Trust and Estate Law, Commission on Law and Aging, "Report to the House of Delegates and Resolution 113" (14 August 2017), online: <https://www.americanbar.org/content/dam/aba/administrative/law_aging/supported-decision-making-resolution-final.pdf> accessed 31.03.2023.

[26]   National Conference of Commissioners On Uniform State Laws, "Uniform Guardianship, Conservatorship, and other Protective Arrangements Act" (2017), online: <https://www.uniformlaws.org/HigherLogic/System/DownloadDocumentFile.ashx?DocumentFileKey=de9bae9e-0b4e-0781-12b5-f5305569bf19&forceDialog=0> accessed 31.03.2023.

[27]   18-C M.R.S. §5-102(14).

[28]   VA ST §37.2-1200.

3.3. SUPPORTED DECISION-MAKING "IN PRACTICE"

The 2012 round table also led to official support for SDM by the federal Administration for Community Living, including a five-year grant to the National Resource Center on SDM (NRCSDM). That entity took a broad view of SDM, embracing it as "everyone's right to make their own decisions," without requiring written agreements by which a key component of legal capacity, legal recognition of decisions, could be achieved. Nor did it interrogate what supports might be necessary to ensure an authentic decision-making process.

Unlike countries like Bulgaria,[29] the Czech Republic,[30] and some Australian states,[31] there was no effort to create empirical pilot projects to experiment with models for making SDMAs that reflect a learned process of using and giving support. Instead, most energy and resources were directed toward legislative reform, lacking any evidentiary base of how to actually "do it." One critic of SDMA legislation notes the false comparison between a "descriptive account of guardianship with an idealized, normative account of supported decision-making".[32]

3.4. SUPPORTED DECISION-MAKING AGREEMENT (SDMA) LAWS

Since 2012, 16 states (Texas,[33] Delaware,[34] Indiana,[35] Wisconsin,[36] Alaska,[37] Nevada,[38] Rhode Island,[39] North Dakota,[40] Louisiana,[41] Washington,[42] Colorado,[43]

---

[29]   Bulgarian Center for Not-for-Profit Law, Supported Decision-Making or How People with Intellectual Disabilities or Mental Health Problems Can Live Independent Lives, Bulgarian Association for Persons with Intellectual Disabilities, Sofia 2014.

[30]   I. LEMANE-VELDMEIJERE, *Study Visit to Czech Republic Was Carried Out, to Explore Supported Decision Making Model in the Czech Republic*, ZELDA (2 September 2015), <http://zelda.org.lv/en/arh%C4%ABvi/2150> accessed 31.03.2023.

[31]   C. BIGBY et al., "Delivering decision making support to people with cognitive disability – what has been learned from pilot programs in Australia from 2010 to 2015" (2017) 52(3) *Australian Journal of Social Issues* 222–240.

[32]   N. KOHN, "Legislating Supported Decision-Making", (2021) 58 *Harvard Journal on Legislation* 313, 326.

[33]   TX EST §1357.001(A).

[34]   16 Del.C. §9405A.

[35]   IN ST §29-3-14.

[36]   W.S.A. §52.01-32.

[37]   AS §13.56.150.

[38]   N.R.S. §162C.320.

[39]   RI ST §42-66.13-5.

[40]   ND ST §14-09-31.

[41]   LA RS §13-4261.101.

[42]   WA ST §11.130.020.

[43]   C.R.S.A. §15-14-801.

Oregon,[44] Virginia,[45] New Hampshire,[46] Illinois[47] and New York[48]) and the District of Columbia[49] have passed some form of SDMA statutes. At the time of writing, additional statutes are pending in states including Massachusetts,[50] which like New York, is the only jurisdiction with empirical evidence to draw on.[51] Most statutes involve written/form agreements that require or permit third parties to accept decisions of (or "give legal recognition to") people who have executed SDMAs. Most also give third parties (who enter a contract or agreement with a person) immunity from liability for doing so in good faith.

In a limited way, these statutes guarantee legal capacity to some number of persons whose decisions might otherwise be questioned or ignored. As such, they advance legal capacity, although limitations on who can make valid SDMAs, who they can choose as supporters, how agreements can be terminated, etc. make that problematic. Equally concerning from the standpoint of CRPD Article 12(4) safeguards compliance, is the absence any educational or training requirements for those making SDMAs and their supporters that ensure the integrity of the process and guard against exploitation or misuse of the SDMAs.

Differing in particulars, these laws follow a similar pattern, with roughly similar components, including defining SDM, establishing a "capacity" standard, who can make an agreement, who can be supporters and what they can and cannot do, required third party recognition with corresponding immunity, and a number of more "procedural" provisions including the form of the agreement, formalities for execution and revocation, supporter access to information, alternate supporters, choice of law provisions, etc. Given space constraints, only those provisions that bear most directly on advancing legal capacity are considered here.

3.4.1. Coverage, or "who can Make an SDMA?"

Some statutes allow any adult to make the agreement, using terms including "the Principal" (Rhode Island, 2019, s.1),[52] "the Supported Person" (District of Columbia, 2018, s. 301(13)),[53] the "Named Individual" (North Dakota, 2019, s. 1(2)).[54] Others are limited to persons with disabilities, variously defined.

---

[44] ORS 343.181-2.
[45] VA ST §37.2-1200.
[46] NH ST §563–B:17.
[47] 210 I.L.C.S. §9/5-9/99.
[48] NY CLS Men. Hyg. Art. 82 (2022).
[49] DC ST §7-761.01-13.
[50] 2019 MA S.B. 64 (NS); 2021 MA S.D. 1746 (NS).
[51] C. Constanzo, K. Glen and A. Krieger, "Supported Decision-Making in Practice: Lessons from Pilot Projects" (2022) 72 *Syracuse Law Review* 99, 154.
[52] RI ST §42-66.13-3(7).
[53] DC ST §7-761.01-13.
[54] ST §14-09-31, S. 1(2).

Only New York's statute[55] is limited to persons with developmental, psychosocial and/or cognitive disabilities, whose legal capacity is most likely to be questioned. One statute refers to an adult who "doesn't need a guardian but would benefit from decision-making assistance" (Delaware)[56] raising the separate problem of capacity to make the agreement.

Use of the category "people with disabilities" also raises issues. There has been a long and unfortunate tendency in the U.S. to divide the disability rights community *by disability*, which use of this broad term avoids, intentionally or otherwise. Conversely, and linked to the issue of "capacity" to make a "supported decision-making agreement", there is potential to exclude persons with developmental, psychosocial and/or cognitive disabilities from the very protections the statute is meant to offer.

The New York[57] statute refers to the person making an agreement as the "Decision-Maker", recognising their centrality to the process. That term is now widely used in the U.S., and will be employed here.

3.4.2. "Capacity" to Make an Agreement?

This is obviously a critical issue, at least as the UN Committee sees it, since almost any effort to define capacity, including a "functional test", is deemed to violate Article 12.[58] The various approaches of most U.S. statutes are, at best, problematic, and at worst, simply a continuation of the old "mental capacity" standard.

Some statutes are silent, some begin with a presumption of capacity for all adults, (e.g., Rhode Island,[59] New Hampshire);[60] "unless otherwise determined by "a court" (Illinois[61]) or "legal proceedings" (Colorado[62]) or may permit the presumption to be rebutted by clear and convincing evidence (North Dakota).[63] Texas limits those who can make agreements to "adults with disabilities who need assistance with decisions regarding daily living but who are not considered incapacitated persons for purposes of establishing a guardianship" (Texas).[64] Others require that the agreement must be entered into voluntarily, without coercion, and that the adult must understand the nature and effect of the

---

[55]   NY CLS Men. Hyg. Art. 82 (2022).
[56]   16 Del.C. §9401A(1).
[57]   2021 NY S.B. 7107(B) (NS).
[58]   UN Committee on the Rights of Persons with Disabilities, "General Comment No. 1 – Article 12: Equal Recognition Before the Law," UN Doc. No. CRPD/C/GC/1 (April 2014) [General Comment No. 1], para. 15 <https://tbinternet.ohchr.org/_layouts/15/treatybody external/Download.aspx?symbolno=CRPD/C/GC/1&Lang=en> accessed 11.11.2022.
[59]   RI ST §. 33-15.3-4(a).
[60]   NH ST §464–D:3.
[61]   210 I.L.C.S. §9/5-9/99, S. 15(a).
[62]   C.R.S.A. §15-14-801(1)(c).
[63]   ND ST §30.1-36-04(1).
[64]   TX EST §1357.003.

agreement (Nevada,[65] Rhode Island,[66] Delaware[67]). A few, like New York and Alaska, require that "capacity" be judged not in a vacuum, but with support(s), ("a person is considered to have capacity even if the capacity is achieved by the person receiving decision-making assistance") (Alaska[68]).

To the contrary, as in Nevada,[69] the traditional legal standard seems still to apply ("an adult should be able to live in the manner in which he or she wishes and to accept or refuse support, assistance for protection as long as the adult does not harm others *and is capable of making decisions about such matters*"[70] (emphasis added)). The initial presumption disappears in states where a court may subsequently abrogate an agreement based on a finding that the person lacked capacity to make the agreement (Indiana[71]) or decision "despite the existence of a supporter (Delaware).[72]

3.4.3. Definition of SDM

With minor variations, most statutes have followed the Texas definition:

> Supported decision-making means a process of supporting and accommodating an adult with a disability to enable the adult to make life decisions including decisions related to where the adult wants to live, the services, supports, and medical care the adult wants to receive, whom the adult wants to live with, and where the adult wants to work, without Impeding the self-determination of the adult.[73]

3.4.4. Effect of Agreement on Other Capacity Determinations

Several states specifically provide that existence of an SDMA may not be used as evidence of the adult's incapacity (e.g., Rhode Island,[74] Delaware,[75] Indiana,[76] Nevada,[77] Alaska[78] Colorado,[79] New York[80]) or in a "proceeding" (Illinois;[81]

---

[65] N.R.S. §162C.320, S. 12(b).
[66] RI ST §42-66.13-10.
[67] 16 Del.C. §9405A.
[68] AS §13.56.160(d).
[69] N.R.S. §162C.320, S. 11.2(a).
[70] N.R.S. §162C.320, S. 11.2(a).
[71] C.R.S.A. §15-1.5-110.
[72] 16 Del.C. §9405A(i).
[73] TX EST §1357.002.
[74] RI ST §42-66.13-4(c).
[75] 16 Del.C. §9405A(c).
[76] IN ST §29-3-14, S. 4(c).
[77] N.R.S. §162C.320, S. 15.
[78] AS §13.56.160(d).
[79] C.R.S.A. §15-14-803(4).
[80] NY Men, Hyg. L. S. 82.01(e).
[81] 210 I.L.C.S. §9/5-9/99, S. 15 (c).

New Hampshire[82]). As a separate and potentially significant matter, an SDMA does not preclude the adult from acting independently of the agreement (e.g., Rhode Island,[83] Delaware,[84] Indiana,[85] Nevada[86])

3.4.5. Other Protections for those who Make SDMAs

To avoid negative and unintended consequences, statutes may provide that a SDMA does not relieve an entity otherwise legally obligated to provide services and required accommodations (e.g., North Dakota,[87] New York[88]).

3.4.6. Who can be Supporters: Statutory Disqualifications

Although critical for the Decision-Maker's autonomy, virtually all statutes limit who can be chosen by imposing statutory disqualification on various classes of persons, including employees and employers of the Decision-Maker (e.g., Rhode Island,[89] Delaware,[90] Alaska[91]), service providers (Delaware,[92] Alaska,[93] District of Columbia[94]) and employees of governmental agencies with financial responsibility for the person's care (Illinois[95]), although there is often an exception for the Decision-Maker's relatives.

Most statutes disqualify persons who might present a danger to the Decision-Maker, including persons against whom there is an order of protection (Rhode Island,[96] Delaware,[97] Alaska[98]); governmental finding of abuse (Wisconsin[99]); abuse, neglect, or exploitation of the supported person (District of Columbia);[100] convictions based on such findings (Wisconsin);[101]

---

[82]   NH ST §464–D:3.
[83]   RI ST §42-66.13-4(c).
[84]   16 Del.C. §9404A(c).
[85]   IN ST §29-3-14, S. 4(c).
[86]   N.R.S. §162C.320, S. 15.
[87]   ND ST §14-09-31, S. 1, p.4 (5).
[88]   NY Men. Hyg. L. 82.01(c).
[89]   RI ST §42-66.13-6, b(1).
[90]   16 Del.C. §9405A(e)(2).
[91]   AS §13.56.020(1).
[92]   16 Del.C. §9406A(b)(1).
[93]   AS §13.56.020(2).
[94]   DC ST §7-761.01-13, S. 302(a)(1).
[95]   210 I.L.C.S. §9/5-9/99, S. 20(3).
[96]   RI ST §42-66.13-6(b)(3).
[97]   16 Del.C. §9406A(b)(3).
[98]   AS §13.56.020(3).
[99]   W.S.A. §52.30(1).
[100] DC ST §7-761.01-13, T. III, S. 302(b)(A)(i).
[101] W.S.A. §52.14(2)(a).

or, an enumerated series of crimes, primarily involving physical violence and financial malfeasance (District of Columbia).[102]

3.4.7. *What Supporters* can *do*

Most states provide that supporters can assist the Decision-Maker in gathering information, understanding the information, considering alternatives, weighing the consequences of a decision, and communicating the decision to third parties (i.e., Texas[103]).

Other statutes include provisions that are, or are perceived as problematic because they permit supporters to actually do things *for* the Decision-Maker, rather than supporting them in making decisions, e.g., "assist[ing] in making appointments, implementing a service plan and monitoring support services" (Nevada, [104] Illinois[105]) or "keep[ing] track of future necessary or recommended services" (Delaware).[106] Critics argue that granting more extensive powers to supporters may, or does, transform them into substitute decision-makers, or what I would refer to as "guardians on the cheap".[107] That argument, has intensified as New Hampshire's[108] recent statute includes, in its statement of legislative purpose, "giv[ing] legal status to supporters of ... people[with disabilities]."

Questions about actual or assumed independent powers and legal status of supporters are troubling because of the potential for abuse or exploitation of the Decision-Maker; that potential is greatly exacerbated by the absence of any requirements for educating or facilitating Decision-Makers and supporters discussed below.

The danger of conferring legal status on supporters is not only about abuse or exploitation of the relationship. Most statutes attempt protection by imposing various kinds of responsibilities, discussed below. Those protections – whose efficacy and enforceability are problematic at best – fail to deal with a real threat to legal capacity, the possibility or likelihood that supporters, especially those with actual or assumed power, will slip back into substitute decision-making and paternalism, the very antithesis of support for the exercise of autonomy and legal capacity.

---

[102] DC ST §7-761.01-13, T. III, S. 302(b)(B).
[103] TX EST §1357.051(1).
[104] N.R.S. §162C.320, S. 13.1.(c).
[105] 210 I.L.C.S. §9/5-9/99, S. 30(4).
[106] 16 Del.C. §9406A(a)(4).
[107] N. KOHN, "Legislating Supported Decision-Making", (2021) 58 *Harvard Journal on Legislation* 313, 336–337.
[108] NH ST §464-D:1.

Kristin Booth Glen

3.4.8. Supporter Access to Information

Although important to support, especially in areas of health and education, provisions concerning supporter access are primarily relevant to CRPD legal capacity in protections they provide, including imposing a duty of confidentiality, (e.g., Rhode Island,[109] North Dakota,[110] Wisconsin[111]) and/or requirements "properly dispose of such records when appropriate".[112]

3.4.9. Supporter Obligations, Liability, and Immunity

Statutes impose a variety of obligations on supporters, including the traditional duty of care, (e.g., Nevada[113]), or, in two states, the heightened obligations of a fiduciary (Texas,[114] New Hampshire[115]) A number require/limit supporters to acting within "the scope of the agreement" (e.g., Indiana[116]). Statutes also commonly contain prohibitions against exerting undue influence (e.g., Delaware,[117] Indiana,[118] Alaska[119]) but also, relevant to legal capacity, "making decisions on behalf of" the adult (Delaware,[120] Alaska[121]), signing agreements or binding the person to a legal agreement (e.g. Alaska,[122] Wisconsin[123]) or requiring supporters to "[s]upport the will and preference of the adult, and not the supporter's opinion of the adult's best interests" (Indiana[124]). Notably, procedures for enforcing such obligation are entirely lacking. Indiana prohibits supporters from receiving a fee for services performed in the role of supporter (Indiana[125]). These limitations are controversial, and bear on legal capacity because many Decision-Makers, especially older persons without natural supports, have no one *but* direct service providers, with whom they may have long and trusting relationships, to support them in their exercise of legal capacity.

---

[109]   RI ST §42-66.13-8(b).
[110]   ND ST §14-09-31, Chapter 30.1-36, Code 30.1-36-06.
[111]   W.S.A. §52.16(4).
[112]   N.R.S. §162C.320, S. 14.2(c).
[113]   N.R.S. §162C.320, S. 13.3.
[114]   TX EST §1357.052(b).
[115]   NH ST §563–B:4(a)(2).
[116]   IN ST §29-3-14, S. 4, c, 14, s. 5(a)(1).
[117]   16 Del.C. §9405A(a)(1).
[118]   IN ST §29-3-14, S. 4 (a)(1).
[119]   AS §13.56.110(1).
[120]   16 Del.C. §9406A(c)(1).
[121]   AS §13.56.110(2).
[122]   AS §13.56.110(2).
[123]   W.S.A. §52.10(2).
[124]   IN ST §29-3-14, S. 5(a)(1).
[125]   IN ST §29-3-14, S. 5, (c)(2).

A Critical Review of Legal Capacity Reform in the U.S.

Finally, a few statutes provide supporters immunity against the Decision-Maker so long as they act in good faith and compliance with the SDMA (Wisconsin[126]).

3.4.10. Amending or Terminating the SDMA

Among existing statutes, only New York provides for changing terms of the agreement such as the areas in which the Decision-Maker wishes support, or the kinds of support they wish to receive. New York speaks explicitly of the Decision-Maker's right to *amend* or terminate the agreement at any time, setting out requirements for both.[127]

The fragility of legal capacity conferred by SDMA statutes is underscored by the many grounds upon which those agreements can be terminated by, or because of, the actions of others. Although lacking any stated procedure or authorisation, statutes provide for termination or revocation based on a supporter's criminal conviction (on any number of enumerated crimes) or issuance of a restraining order against a supporter (Illinois,[128] North Dakota[129]); or a court finding that a supporter has used the agreement to commit financial exploitation, abuse, or neglect of the adult (Indiana,[130] Texas[131]), or if the named supporters withdraw their participation without naming successor supporters (Indiana[132]). Most disturbing, one statute provides for termination on a retroactive finding that the Principal lacked capacity to enter into the agreement (Indiana[133]).

3.4.11. Third Party Obligation under the Agreement

The legally imposed obligation that third parties must accept decisions made pursuant to an SDMA, cannot impose their own view of a person's legal capacity, and are bound by the decision is the primary means to ensure legal capacity for persons with developmental, cognitive, and psychosocial disabilities. A typical provision reads:

> A decision or request made or communicated with the assistance of a supporter in conformity with this chapter shall be recognized for the purposes of any provision of law as the decision or request of the principal and may be enforced in law or equity on the same basis as a decision or request of the principal. (N.H. 464-D:11)

---

[126] W.S.A. §52.30(2).
[127] NY Men. Hyg. L, 82.07.
[128] 210 I.L.C.S. §9/5-9/99, S. 70, (b)(2).
[129] ND ST §14-09-31, S. 1, p.3.3.b.
[130] IN ST §29-3-14, S. 4, c, 14, s. 9(a)(5).
[131] TX EST §1357.53(b)(1).
[132] IN ST §29-3-14, S. 4, c, 14, s. 9(a)(3).
[133] C.R.S.A. §15-1.5-110.

Intersentia

Kristin Booth Glen

There is, however, a considerable, if unintended split in what states are actually recognising: the *agreement*, or *decisions* made pursuant to the agreement. SDMAs frequently contain a provision that the Decision-Maker is not required to use the support provided for in the agreement in making any particular decision. If the state requires recognition of a decision *because of* the use of supports, how does a third party know if the Decision-Maker actually utilised the support described in the agreement?

In requiring recognition of a decision, some statutes require third parties to rely on (presumably the existence of) the agreement (Texas,[134] Colorado,[135] Illinois[136]). A common provision, requiring recognition of a "decision or request made or communicated with the assistance of a supporter in conformity with [this law]" (e.g., Delaware,[137] Rhode Island,[138] Alaska,[139] Indiana[140]) leaves ambiguous the issue of whether or not the Principal used the support set forth in the SDMA.

Any guarantee of legal capacity is undermined by eschewing mandatory recognition, instead substituting the discretionary "may" (Delaware,[141] Indiana[142]). Furthermore, in some states, third parties may decline to recognise a decision if they believe in good faith that the agreement is "invalid" or has been terminated (e.g., Texas,[143] Wisconsin,[144] Indiana[145]).

Some statutes provide "conscience" or religious belief, and "medical judgment" exceptions, like Delaware[146] and Alaska[147] which permit third parties to "declin[e] to comply with authorizations related to health care contrary to conscience, or good faith medical judgment or the provisions of a written institutional policy on conscience."

3.4.12. Immunity from Liability

Because the U.S. is so litigious and liability-conscious, immunity from liability for good faith recognition of decisions is a *sine qua non* for ensuring legal capacity. If third parties see a person's disability as raising the possibility that their capacity

---

[134]   TX EST §1357.101(a).
[135]   C.R.S.A. §15-14-806.
[136]   210 I.L.C.S. §9/5-9/99, S. 55(a).
[137]   16 Del.C. §9407A.
[138]   RI ST §42-66.13-7.
[139]   AS §13.56.030.
[140]   IN ST §29-3-14, S. 4, c, 14, s. 6.
[141]   16 Del.C. §9401A(c).
[142]   IN ST §29-3-14, S. 4, c, 14, s. 10.
[143]   TX EST §1357.101(b).
[144]   W.S.A. §52.30(3).
[145]   IN ST §29-3-14, S. 4, c, 14, s. 11(a).
[146]   16 Del.C. §9408A(3).
[147]   AS §13.56.040(a)(3).

A Critical Review of Legal Capacity Reform in the U.S.

could be challenged later, and the transaction (including "informed consent" for medical care) undone, statutory relief from liability is essential.

Most statutes specifically relieve third parties from civil and criminal liability and/or professional discipline for good faith reliance on an SDMA or decision made pursuant to it (e.g., District of Columbia,[148] Texas,[149] Delaware,[150] Alaska,[151] Illinois,[152] Colorado[153]), or against potential claims of medical malpractice (Wisconsin[154]). There are exceptions: Indiana[155] denies immunity if the third party's "act or omission amounts to fraud, misrepresentation, recklessness, or willful or wanton misconduct". New Hampshire,[156] however, makes no provision for immunity, effectively undercutting any guarantee of legal capacity.

3.4.13. Third Party Reporting of Abuse, Neglect, and/or Exploitation

One important argument for SDMA statutes is that they create many "watchful eyes", permitting third parties to disregard decisions where there may be abuse, neglect or exploitation, (Texas,[157] North Dakota[158]), or the person "is in need of protective services" (District of Columbia[159]), and permitting or requiring third parties to notify the appropriate government entities (e.g., Texas,[160] Rhode Island,[161] Illinois,[162] New Hampshire[163]). There is, however, an unexamined confusion between the purpose of these provisions. Are they intended to protect the *decision*, and the decision-making process, as CRPD Article 12(4) requires? Or, are they a new, additional, mostly private system to protect the *person* with a SDMA? If the former, undue influence, abuse and/or exploitation may be relevant, while neglect in general is not. If the former, only persons actually asked to accept or honour a decision should be included; if the latter, anyone with knowledge that a person with a SDMA is being abused or neglected is empowered to report to the appropriate state agency and be protected for doing

---

[148]   DC ST §7-761.01-13, S. 303(e).
[149]   TX EST §1357.101(b).
[150]   16 Del.C. §9408A.
[151]   AS §13.56.040(a).
[152]   210 I.L.C.S. §9/5-9/99, S. 55(b).
[153]   C.R.S.A. §15-14-806(2).
[154]   W.S.A. §52.30(1).
[155]   IN ST §29-3-14, S. 4, c, 14, s.11(c).
[156]   NH ST §563–B:17.
[157]   TX EST §1357.053(b)(1).
[158]   ND ST §14-09-31, S. 1, p.3(1)(a).
[159]   DC ST §7-761.01-13, T. III, S. 303(c)(1).
[160]   TX EST §1357.102.
[161]   RI ST §42-66.13-9.
[162]   210 I.L.C.S. §9/5-9/99, S. 65.
[163]   NH ST §464–D:14.

Intersentia

so. (e.g., Texas,[164] Rhode Island,[165] Illinois,[166] New Hampshire[167]). Expansion of voluntary reporters raises real possibilities for misuse, including by vindictive former spouses who use claims of abuse or neglect to punish or control, or seek financial or other advantage, undermining or disincentivising the use of SDMA.

3.4.14. Education/Training

Until recently, no statute contained any provision for educating/training either Decision-Makers or supporters. Virginia and Illinois have modest provisions for creating materials and/or training opportunities, thus far undeveloped, while New York, alone, conditions legislative recognition on agreements made pursuant to a meaningful facilitation process.[168] See section 4.3 below.

3.4.15. Monitoring

Although the prototype for all SDMA statutes, the British Columbia Representation Act (B.C. 1990) provided, in considerable detail, for appointment of "monitors", no U.S statute included any provision for such role until New Hampshire which permits Decision-Makers to "designate a monitor" to ensure that supporters are complying with statutory provisions on "Authority of Supporters" and "Duties of Supporters," including duties deriving from a fiduciary relationship.

4. CRITIQUES OF EXISTING STATUTES

4.1. MIXED MOTIVES: THE CASE OF TEXAS

As an extensive study demonstrated, Texas, the first state to pass a SDMA statute, was driven not by human rights, but concern about courts' ability to process and monitor the enormous influx of guardianship cases predicted to accompany an aging population. This "ma[de] supported decision-making an attractive policy to pursue for stakeholders like state legislators, judges, and court administrators … [and] to conservatives who favor small government".[169]

---

[164]   TX EST §1357.102.
[165]   RI ST §42-66.13-5.
[166]   210 I.L.C.S. §9/5-9/99, S. 65.
[167]   NH ST §464–D:14.
[168]   NY Men. Hyg. L. 82.11.
[169]   E. J. Theodorou, "Supported decision-making in the lone-start state" (2018) 93 *NYUL Rev.* 973.

A coalition of disability rights activists and these more conservative, cost-driven stakeholders, resulted in compromises, including adoption of a "moderate position on [SDM]" and an apparent concession that a more traditional standard of mental capacity, similar to that required for a power of attorney would be necessary for a valid SDMA.[170] This understanding has been confirmed by the only reported judicial decision to date. An appellate court held that, in a guardianship proceeding, SDM was not an alternative because the "[Respondent was] incapacitated and cannot make important life decisions for herself."[171] The lesson here is that when SDMA legislation is primarily driven by prospective cost-saving, the result is unlikely to achieve legal capacity for anyone who does not already possess it.

4.2. WHAT IS (BUT SHOULD NOT BE) IN THE STATUTES

A recent article by the most prominent U.S. interrogator of SDM and critic of related legislation,[172] reads existing statutes as legally empowering supporters, giving them legal status, and creating a kind of "guardianship on the cheap" that deprives people with disabilities of autonomy, and potentially subjects them to abuse and exploitation.[173] The critique relies on provisions in Alaska and Delaware statutes permitting supporters to independently enforce a decision made by the Decision-Maker (Alaska, 2017; Delaware, 2016).

Kohn also charges that, rather than expanding the rights of people with disabilities to make their own decisions, SDMA statutes limit those rights by imposing restrictions on who can be supporters, how agreements can be revoked, etc. To make clear that informal supported decision-making is *not* being curtailed, New York's statute provides

> The availability of [SDMAs] is, in no way, intended to limit the use of informal supported decision-making, or to preclude judicial consideration of such informal arrangements as less restrictive alternatives to guardianship.[174]

---

[170] E. J. THEODOROU, "Supported decision-making in the lone-start state" (2018) 93 *NYUL Rev.* 973.

[171] In *re Guardianship of A.E.*, 552 S.W.3d at 879, 880 (Texas S. Ct., 2018).

[172] N. COHN, J. BLUMENTHAL and A. CAMPBELL, "Supported decision-making: A viable alternative to guardianship" (2013) 117 *Penn St. L. Rev.* 1111.

[173] N. KOHN, "Legislating Supported Decision-Making" (2021) 58 *Harvard Journal on Legislation* 313.

[174] 2021 NY S.B. 7107 (NS).

4.3. WHAT IS MISSING FROM THE STATUTES

Aside from the indeterminate, minimal education/training requirements still to be developed pursuant to Virginia and Illinois statutes, and with the exception of New York, existing statutes require neither meaningful training nor education for Decision-Makers and/or supporters. Yet every pilot project internationally[175] and the U.S.[176] has utilised a facilitation process through which trained facilitators assist Decision-Makers to understand how decisions are made, and the steps to go into them, determine areas in which they desire support and the kinds of support they wish. Similarly, supporters learn to move from their pre-existing roles with Decision-Makers, understand the "dignity of risk", and commit to supporting Decision-Makers in making their own decisions, rather than substituting a paternalistic "best interest" test. An authentic facilitation process is the only means that has been demonstrated to "offe[r] genuine support rather than being surrogate decision-making in disguise."[177]

The facilitation processes already developed have been used almost exclusively for persons with developmental disabilities; there is no similar body of empirical work demonstrating what might constitute adequate supports for members of any other groups whose legal capacity is denied or at risk, including older persons with cognitive decline, dementia, etc.,[178] and persons with psychosocial disabilities, or traumatic brain-injuries,[179] yet all of them are presumptively included among those who can make SDMAs.

The experience of all these pilot projects, especially the large New York pilot (see below), has demonstrated that it takes real work, over time, to create a process by which persons with developmental disabilities come to see themselves as decision-makers, understand what goes into making a decision, and where and how they need support from others. Similarly, amplified by empirical studies in Australia,[180] it is clear that without training or substantial capacity-building, even the most well-intentioned supporters can quickly fall back into a more familiar and paternalistic role of substitute decision-making.

---

[175] K. GLEN, "Not Just Guardianship: 'Supported Decision Making From Theory To Practice: Further Reflections On An Intentional Pilot Project'" (2020) 13 *Albany Government Law Review* 94.

[176] E. PELL and V. MULKERN, "Supported decision making pilot: Pilot program evaluation year 1 report" (2015) *Human Service Research Institute*, Boston, MS, USA.

[177] E. LARGENT et al., "Supported Decision-Making in the United States and Abroad" (2021) 23 *J. Health Care L. & Pol'y* 271.

[178] R. DILLER, "Legal capacity for all: Including older persons in the shift from adult guardianship to supported decision-making" (2016) 43 *Fordham Urb. L.J* 495.

[179] K. GLEN, "Supported Decision-Making: What You Need to Know and Why" (2018) 23 *NYSBA Health L. J.* 93.

[180] C. BIGBY et al., "Delivering decision making support to people with cognitive disability – what has been learned from pilot programs in Australia from 2010 to 2015" (2017) 52(3) *Australian Journal of Social Issues* 222–240.

5. SUPPORTED DECISION-MAKING NEW YORK (SDMNY): A SUCCESSFUL EMPIRICAL MODEL ADVANCING THE RIGHT OF LEGAL CAPACITY

5.1. THE MODEL

Supported Decision-Making New York (SDMNY) is a large pilot project funded by state agencies and private foundations in New York state. Since 2016 it has drawn on legal capacity work by pilot projects around the world to develop and pilot a three-phase facilitation model to enable people with developmental disabilities to make their own decisions with the support and supporters they choose, and to memorialise that process in a SDMA.[181] Based on its experience, SDMNY developed "Principles for Supported Decision Making Agreement Legislation"[182] that has been essentially incorporated in New York's statute; designed a cost-effective service delivery model through which the state could enable SDM facilitation for anyone who wants it;[183] and been awarded a $4 million, three-year grant to pilot that model.

5.2. LEARNINGS FROM THE PROJECT

Although funding focused on promoting SDM as an alternative to guardianship, the project has always been based on the human right of legal capacity, and participants are inspired by being part of a world-wide movement.[184] SDMNY's facilitation model is about much more than reaching a signed agreement that confers legal recognition. It is about spending the necessary time and effort to empower Decision-Makers to understand and make their own decisions, and to become agents in their own lives, entitled to dignity, equality, and non-discrimination.

While, at least in the U.S., it may be politically advantageous to characterise SDM as an alternative to guardianship, or related legislation as "civil rights" or "anti-discrimination" laws for people with developmental disabilities, SDMNY's

---

[181] K. GLEN, "Not Just Guardianship: 'Supported Decision Making From Theory To Practice: Further Reflections On An Intentional Pilot Project" (2020) 13(1) *Albany Government Law Review*.

[182] See Supported Decision Making New York, "Principles for Supported Decision Making Agreement (SDMA) Legislation" <https://sdmny.org/supported-decision-making-legislation/principles-for-supported-decision-making-agreements-in-new-york/principles-for-a-supported-decision-making-agreement-sdma-law-long/> accessed 06.07.2022.

[183] STOUT RISIUS ROSS, *The Estimated Economic Impact of Facilitated Supported Decision-Making in New York*, 2022.

[184] K. GLEN, "Supported Decision-Making: What You Need to Know and Why" (2018) 23 *NYSBA Health L. J.* 93.

strategy and experience demonstrate and embody the necessary conditions for legal capacity as defined by the CRPD: state-provided support for *making decisions* (the facilitation process) and state-provided support (through recognition in legislation) to ensure that those decisions are *legally recognised*.

Another important learning is the importance of changing the educational system to include SDM to advance legal capacity for many people with developmental disabilities. If, from an early age, children were taught how to make decisions, where they need support, and how to get it, guardianship would disappear for the vast majority of those on whom it might have been imposed, and people with developmental disabilities would develop the self-determination, autonomy and skills to enable them to exercise legal capacity and live good, inclusive lives.

6. CHALLENGES AND BARRIERS TO ADVANCING LEGAL CAPACITY THROUGH SDM

1. There are no well-developed, empirically tested models for giving authentic decision-making support to older persons with cognitive decline and dementia, persons with psychosocial disabilities, and those with traumatic brain injuries. The extensive work done to create and pilot models for people with developmental disabilities shows that there is no "one-size-fits-all" model easily transferable to other at-risk populations. Time and resources are required to develop appropriate disability-specific supports as the New York statute specifically notes, urging government and civil society to undertake that work "... so that full legislative recognition can also be accorded to the decisions made with [SDMAs] by persons with such conditions, based on a consensus about what kinds of support are most effective and how they can best be delivered."[185]

2. There is enormous and pervasive scepticism about the ability of persons with severe impairments to make their own decisions with support, and no empirical models exist to disprove that scepticism or provide the basis for their credibly entering into supported decision-making agreements.

3. To the extent that full, or near-full, recognition and/or enabling of legal capacity is tied to SDM, the existence of a social network from which supporters can be drawn is critical. Yet many persons who could benefit from SDM and related agreements lack any such network or social capital sufficient to create one.

---

[185] NY Men. Hyg. L. 82.01(d).

7. THE FUTURE OF AN EQUAL RIGHT TO EXERCISE LEGAL CAPACITY IN THE U.S.

Modest changes in guardianship statutes, and/or SDMA statutes that may decrease guardianship, but lack provisions for effective decision-making supports do not meaningfully advance the right of legal capacity in the U.S.

The New York experience, however, offers a potential blueprint. It demonstrates the importance of initiating and building on incremental projects to promote SDM as an alternative to guardianship, encouraging and incentivising a facilitation model leading to SDMAs, providing state funding for that model, and granting legislative recognition to decisions made pursuant to facilitation-enabled SDMAs.

Substantial pent-up demand exists for a viable SDM model for older persons with cognitive disabilities and dementia.[186] There is more nascent attention to how SDM could address the unique issues facing persons with psychosocial disabilities. Progress in these areas depends on SDMA legislation that requires meaningful, disability-specific supports.

Such legislation can potentially limit or end denial of legal capacity to persons to whom it would otherwise be denied in numerous situations where some form of "mental capacity" is required for legal transactions.[187] The existence of legislation alone, however, is not enough. Comprehensive education reaching all who are potentially involved – persons with SDMAs, private and public third parties with whom they deal, lawyers and judges – is also necessary.

As more people use SDM and SDMAs, guardianship will presumably decline, especially for young adults with developmental disabilities. Public consciousness about their abilities should increase, as it has for persons with mobility, visual and hearing disabilities who utilise accommodations. Increased consciousness should also, albeit slowly, decrease discrimination against, and denial of legal capacity to, people with "mental" disabilities by third parties, both public and private.

Finally, a small but growing understanding that "Disability Rights are Human Rights", together with increased attention to the rights of vulnerable populations (who are racialised, ethnically diverse, living in poverty, LGBTQ+ community members, and/or gender-diverse) provides opportunities for coalition-building that can begin to focus attention on a human rights agenda that includes legal capacity for everyone, regardless of disability.

---

[186] M. S. WRIGHT, "Dementia, autonomy, and supported healthcare decision making" (2020) 79 *Md. L. Rev.* 257.

[187] K. GLEN, "Not Just Guardianship: Uncovering The Invisible Taxonomy Of Laws, Regulations And Decisions That Limit Or Deny The Right Of Legal Capacity For Persons With Intellectual And Developmental Disabilities" (2020) 13(1) *Albany Government Law Review*.

A CRITICAL REVIEW OF LEGAL CAPACITY REFORMS IN THE AFRICAN REGION

Dianah Msipa*

1. Introduction 177
2. Legal Capacity and the Role of Support............................. 179
3. The Right to Legal Capacity in Kenya, Zambia and South Africa 181
4. Reviewing the Reforms in Kenya, Zambia and South Africa............ 185
   4.1. How the Decided Cases Show Insufficient Understanding of
        Legal Capacity... 185
        4.1.1. Kenya 185
        4.1.2. Zambia 188
   4.2. Old Wine in New Skins: How the Legislative Reforms have
        Reproduced the Outdated Understanding of Legal Capacity 190
        4.2.1. Kenya 190
        4.2.2. Zambia 192
        4.2.3. South Africa.. 195
5. Conclusion.. 197

1. INTRODUCTION

The majority of African countries have signed and ratified the CRPD and its
Optional Protocol indicating a willingness to be bound by its norms and
standards.[1] Of the 54 African countries, 48 have ratified the CRPD and 49 have
ratified the Optional Protocol to the CRPD.[2] Article 12, which is regarded as

---

[*]   Dianah Msipa is the Manager of the Disability Rights Unit at the Centre for Human Rights,
University of Pretoria. She is currently completing a Doctor of Laws (LL.D) degree at the
Centre for Human Rights, Faculty of Law, University of Pretoria. Her doctoral research is on
recognising the sexual autonomy of women with intellectual disabilities. Dianah wishes to
thank Mr Paul Juma for his invaluable and masterful research assistance in the preparation of
this book chapter. dianahmsipa@gmail.com.

[1]   United Nations Treaty Collection Convention on the Rights of Persons with Disabilities,
<https://treaties.un.org/Pages/ViewDetails.aspx?src=TREATY&mtdsg_no=IV-
15&chapter=4&clang=_en> accessed 17.03.2023.

[2]   Ibid.

"emblematic of the paradigm shift of the Convention",[3] requires States Parties to "recognize that persons with disabilities enjoy legal capacity on an equal basis with others in all aspects of life."[4] Notably, the CRPD recognises "universal" legal capacity for all persons with disabilities, regardless of severity[5] and requires States Parties to "take appropriate measures to provide access by persons with disabilities to the support they may require in exercising their legal capacity."[6] The African Charter on Human and Peoples' Rights on the Rights of Persons with Disabilities in Africa (the "African Disability Protocol") also requires the recognition of legal capacity and the provision of support to exercise legal capacity.[7]

In spite of having ratified the CRPD, many governments, including African governments, remain opposed to the idea of "universal" legal capacity for all persons with disabilities.[8] Nonetheless, there have been sporadic legal capacity reform efforts aimed at closing this chasm by aligning domestic legislation with the CRPD. Kenya, Zambia and South Africa have all taken steps to reform domestic law on legal capacity with varying levels of success. Reform efforts in these countries have taken place through the courts and through the legislature.

After ratifying the CRPD on 5 May 2008,[9] Kenya has two bills currently before Parliament, namely the Persons with Disabilities (Amendment) Bill 2015 and the Mental Health (Amendment) Bill 2018, both of which seek to domesticate the CRPD.[10] Zambia ratified the CRPD on 2 February 2010,[11] and two years

---

[3]   G. Quinn, "Personhood and legal capacity: Perspectives on the paradigm shift of article 12 CRPD, Address at Harvard Law School" (2010) *Harvard Law School Library* 4.

[4]   CRPD Art. 12(2).

[5]   G. Quinn and A. Rekas-Rosalbo, "Civil Death: Rethinking the Foundations of Legal Personhood for Persons with a Disability" (2016) 56 *Irish Jurist (N.S.)* 286, 289.

[6]   CRPD, Art. 12(3).

[7]   Protocol to the African Charter on Human and Peoples' Rights on the Rights of Persons with Disabilities in Africa (hereinafter African Disability Protocol) adopted by the thirtieth ordinary session of the Assembly, held in Addis Ababa, Ethiopia on 29 January 2018, Arts. 7(2) (a) and 7(2)(c). Although the African Disability Protocol is not yet in force, this article will make reference to it because after its adoption by the African Union, it became part of the African human rights framework. Once it enters into force, is likely to be the most influential regional instrument on the rights of persons with disabilities. The African Disability Protocol will enter into force thirty days after the deposit of the fifteenth instrument of ratification in accordance with its Article 38. So far, nine African states have signed the African Disability Protocol, but none have ratified it. The nine states that have signed the African Disability Protocol are Angola, Burkina Faso, Cameroon, Central African Republic, Gabon, Mali, Rwanda, South Africa and Togo.

[8]   G. Quinn and A. Rekas-Rosalbo (n. 5), at 289.

[9]   <https://tbinternet.ohchr.org/_layouts/15/TreatyBodyExternal/Treaty.aspx?Treaty=CRPD> accessed 17.03.2023.

[10] Persons with Disabilities (Amendment) Bill 2015. Mental Health (Amendment) Bill 2018 (Kenya).

[11] <https://tbinternet.ohchr.org/_layouts/15/TreatyBodyExternal/Treaty.aspx?Treaty=CRPD> accessed 17.03.2023.

later, enacted the Persons with Disabilities Act 2012, which domesticates the CRPD.[12] In 2019, Zambia also enacted the Mental Health Act to which the right to legal capacity is directly relevant.[13] South Africa ratified the CRPD on 30 November 2007[14] and is instituting legal capacity reform through the Supported Decision-Making Bill.[15]

This chapter critically appraises the legal capacity reforms in Kenya, Zambia and South Africa showing how, to a large extent, the reform efforts have been unsuccessful, particularly in Kenya and Zambia. The chapter is divided into four sections. The first section summarises the meaning of the right to legal capacity and the role of support in its exercise. The second section addresses the position of the right to legal capacity in the law in Kenya, Zambia and South Africa. The third section critically appraises the legal capacity reforms in Kenya, Zambia and South Africa.

2. LEGAL CAPACITY AND THE ROLE OF SUPPORT

The CRPD recognises universal legal capacity to be enjoyed by all persons with disabilities regardless of the severity of the disability.[16] Cognisant of the fact that persons with severe disabilities may not be able to exercise their legal capacity unaided, the CRPD requires the provision of support in exercising the right to legal capacity.[17] It provides that "[s]tates Parties shall take appropriate measures to provide access by persons with disabilities to the support they may require in exercising their legal capacity."[18]

Prior to the coming into force of the CRPD in 2008, the distinction between legal standing and legal agency was prominent. Lawmakers were ready to recognise the legal standing of persons with severe disabilities, but they were not prepared to recognise their legal agency. Where a person with a disability was deemed to lack legal agency, persons known as "substitute" decision-makers were appointed to exercise rights on behalf of the person with a disability.[19] Guardianship laws are an example of substitute decision-making.[20]

---

[12]   Persons with Disabilities Act 2012 (Zambia).
[13]   Mental Health Act 2019 (Zambia).
[14]   <https://tbinternet.ohchr.org/_layouts/15/TreatyBodyExternal/Treaty.aspx?Treaty=CRPD> accessed 17.03.2023. South Africa is one of the nine African countries that have signed the African Disability Protocol. <https://au.int/en/treaties/protocol-african-charter-human-and-peoples-rights-rights-persons-disabilities-africa> accessed 17.03.2023.
[15]   Supported Decision-Making Bill (South Africa).
[16]   CRPD, Art. 12(2).
[17]   Committee on the Rights of Persons with Disabilities General Comment 1 on Article 12: Equal recognition before the law, para. 15.
[18]   CRPD, Art. 12(3).
[19]   G. Quinn and A. Rekas-Rosalbo (n. 5), at 288.
[20]   Ibid., at 289.

Guardianship is "a form of surrogate decision-making, usually imposed after a court proceeding, that substitutes as decision-maker another individual (the guardian) for the individual in question (called variously the ward or the allegedly incapacitated person)."[21] The decisions that are made by the substitute decision-maker may not necessarily be in accordance with the actual wishes of the person but will be justified on the basis that they are in the person's best interests.[22] Essentially the argument is that they are "protecting" the person from themselves.[23] In the past, these regimes were criticised for being too inclusive in that they affected persons with intellectual disabilities who were capable of exercising their rights.[24] In recent years however, the argument has shifted from challenging the breath of such laws to challenging their very existence.[25] The CRPD requires the elimination of guardianship regimes in favour of systems of support to enable all persons with disabilities to exercise their legal capacity.[26] Persons with disabilities should not be denied legal capacity to act based on the fact that they require support.[27]

Accordingly, states must not only refrain from denying persons with disabilities their legal capacity, but must also ensure that they have access to the support they require in order to exercise their legal capacity.[28] Any support that is provided, "must respect the rights, will and preferences of persons with disabilities and should never amount to substitute decision-making."[29] The nature of support is broad and includes formal and informal support arrangements such as peer support or assistance with communication.[30] Furthermore, due to the diversity of persons with disabilities, the type and intensity required will vary and should be decided on a case by case basis.[31] The concept of support is therefore, central to the new supported decision-making paradigm.

To date, no African country has made the transition from substituted to supported decision-making. There are still laws in Kenya, Zambia and South Africa that deny persons with disabilities the right to legal capacity and make no provision for support in order to exercise one's legal capacity.

---

[21] R. DINERSTEIN, "Implementing Legal Capacity under Article 12 of the UN Convention on the Rights of Persons with Disabilities: The Difficult Road from Guardianship to Supported Decision-Making" (2012) 19 *Human Rights Brief* 8, 9.

[22] G. QUINN and A. REKAS-ROSALBO (n. 5), at 288.

[23] Ibid., at 289.

[24] Ibid.

[25] Ibid.

[26] CRPD, Art. 12(3).

[27] A. DHANDA, "Legal Capacity in the Disability Rights Convention: Stranglehold of the Past or Lodestar for the Future?" (2016) 34 *Syracuse Journal of International Law and Commerce* 429, 439.

[28] Committee on the Rights of Persons with Disabilities General Comment 1 on Article 12: Equal recognition before the law, para. 16.

[29] Ibid., at para. 17.

[30] Ibid.

[31] Ibid., at para. 18.

3. THE RIGHT TO LEGAL CAPACITY IN KENYA, ZAMBIA AND SOUTH AFRICA

The right to equality before the law, which is the equivalent of the right to equal recognition before the law, is recognised at domestic level as a fundamental right in the Constitutions of Kenya, Zambia and South Africa. The Constitution of Kenya recognises the right to equality before the law stating that "[e]very person is equal before the law and has the right to equal protection and equal benefit of the law."[32] The phrase, "every person" may be interpreted to include persons with disabilities within the ambit of this constitutional provision, particularly since the Kenyan Constitution prohibits direct and indirect discrimination on various grounds including disability.[33]

Similarly, the Constitution of South Africa also enshrines the right to equality before the law.[34] The South African Constitution states that "[e]veryone is equal before the law and has the right to equal protection and benefit of the law."[35] Discrimination is prohibited on various grounds including disability.[36] Therefore, the phrase, "everyone" includes persons with disabilities.

Although the Constitution of Zambia does not have a specific provision on equality before the law, the right is implicit in the anti-discrimination clause, which states that "no law shall make any provision that is discriminatory either of itself or in its effect."[37]

The right to equal recognition before the law is also enshrined in various other international human rights instruments that have also been ratified by Kenya, Zambia and South Africa. Article 12(1) of the CRPD "re-affirms" the right to equal recognition before the law indicating that it is not a new right, but one that already exists in other international human rights instruments such as the Universal Declaration of Human Rights.[38] At global level, the right to equal recognition before the law is protected in the International Covenant on Civil and Political Rights (CCPR), which provides that everyone "shall have the right to recognition everywhere as persons before the law."[39] Furthermore, Article 26 of the CCPR states that all "persons are equal before the law and are entitled

---

[32] Constitution of Kenya, 2010, Art. 27(1).

[33] Ibid., at Art. 27(4).

[34] Constitution of the Republic of South Africa, 1996, sec. 9.

[35] Ibid., at sec. 9(1).

[36] Ibid., at sec. 9(3).

[37] Constitution of Zambia 1991, Art. 23(1).

[38] A. ARSTEIN-KERSLAKE, "A Call to Action: The Realisation of Equal Recognition under the Law for People with Disabilities in the EU" (2014) 5 *European Year Book of Disability Law* 75,84. Universal Declaration of Human Rights, G.A. Res. 217 (III), U.N. Doc. A/RES/217(III), Art. 7 (10 December 1948).

[39] International Covenant on Civil and Political Rights, Art. 16, (16 December1966), 999 U.N.T.S. 171, 6 I.L.M. 368 (1967) (hereinafter ICCPR).

without any discrimination to the equal protection of the law."[40] All the three countries under review have ratified the CCPR. Kenya ratified the CCPR on 1 May 1972,[41] Zambia on 10 April 1984[42] and South Africa on 10 December 1998.[43] The right is also enshrined in the Convention on the Elimination of All Forms of Discrimination against Women (CEDAW), which recognises women's equality before the law and requires States Parties to ensure that women enjoy legal capacity on an equal basis with men.[44] The three countries under review have also ratified CEDAW. Kenya ratified CEDAW on 9 March 1984,[45] Zambia on 21 June 1985[46] and South Africa on 15 December 1995.[47]

At Regional level, the right to equal recognition before the law is also enshrined in a number of African human rights instruments. The African Charter on Human and Peoples' Rights (Banjul Charter) enshrines the right in Article 3 which states that "every individual shall be equal before the law" and "shall be entitled to equal protection of the law".[48] Article 3 forms part of the anti-discrimination and equal protection provisions of the Banjul Charter.[49] In interpreting and applying this provision in the *Purohit and another v. The Gambia*, the African Commission on Human and Peoples' Rights (the African Commission) held that "article 3 is important because it guarantees fair and just treatment of individuals within a legal system of a given country."[50] Kenya ratified the Banjul Charter in 1992,[51] Zambia in 1984[52] and South Africa in 1996.[53]

The right to equal recognition before the law is also enshrined in the Protocol to the African Charter on Human and Peoples' Rights on the Rights of Women in Africa (Maputo Protocol).[54] Article 8 of the Maputo Protocol provides for women's right of access to justice and equal protection before the law and declares that women and men are equal before the law and have the right to

---

[40] Ibid.
[41] <https://tbinternet.ohchr.org/_layouts/15/TreatyBodyExternal/Treaty.aspx?Treaty=CRPD> accessed 17.03.2023.
[42] Ibid.
[43] Ibid.
[44] Convention on the Elimination of All Forms of Discrimination Against Women, G.A. Res. *34/180*, U.N. Doc. A/RES/34/180, Art. 15 (18 December 1979).
[45] <https://tbinternet.ohchr.org/_layouts/15/TreatyBodyExternal/Treaty.aspx?Treaty=CRPD> accessed 17.03.2023.
[46] Ibid.
[47] Ibid.
[48] African Charter on Human and Peoples' Rights, 27 June 1981, OAU Doc. CAB/LEG/67/3/ Rev.5 (1981), Art. 3 (entered into force on 21 October 1986).
[49] *Purohit and another v. The Gambia* 2003 AHRLR 96 (ACHPR 2003) 49.
[50] Ibid.
[51] <https://achpr.au.int/en/states> accessed 28.03.2023.
[52] Ibid.
[53] Ibid.
[54] Protocol to the African Charter on the Rights of Women in Africa (Maputo Protocol) Adopted on 11 July 2003, (entered into force on 25 November 2005).

A Critical Review of Legal Capacity Reforms in the African Region

equal protection and benefit of the law.[55] Kenya ratified the Maputo Protocol on 13 October 2010, Zambia on 2 May 2006 and South Africa on 17 December 2004.

Despite having Constitutional provisions that protect the right to equality before the law, the countries under review also have provisions that deny persons with disabilities the right to legal capacity. The Constitution of Kenya states that a person of "unsound mind" may not be elected as president, governor, senator, member of parliament or member of county assembly.[56] The concept of unsound mind is problematic for a number of reasons. First, the Constitution does not define the term "unsound mind."[57] Second, there are no parameters set out for determining who is of "unsound mind" and whether one may appeal or challenge such a finding.[58] This ambiguity leaves the concept of "unsound mind" open to abuse.[59]

In its concluding observations on the initial report submitted by Kenya, the Committee on the Rights of Persons with Disabilities also raised concern about the existence of various laws that deprive persons with disabilities, particularly persons with intellectual and psychosocial disabilities, of the right to legal capacity.[60] Examples of these laws include the Children's Act 2001, the Mental Health Act 1991 and the Marriage Law 2014. The Committee also expressed concerns about the existence and prevalence of *de facto* guardianship within families that operates to deprive persons with disabilities choices when buying food, renting a house or with regards to issues of inheritance, for example.[61]

Zambia also has legal provisions that deny persons with disabilities the right to legal capacity. For example, persons with "mental or physical disability that would make the person incapable of performing the legislative function" may not be elected as members of Parliament.[62] Similarly, a person who has "a mental or physical disability that would make the person incapable of performing the executive functions" is ineligible for nomination as candidate for election as President.[63] The Speaker of the National Assembly can be removed from office if he or she has "a mental or physical disability that makes the Speaker or Deputy Speaker incapable of performing the functions of the office of Speaker or Deputy Speaker."[64] A minister may also be removed from office if he or she has

---

[55]   Equality Now "A Guide to Using the Protocol on the Rights of Women in Africa for Legal Action" <https://d3n8a8pro7vhmx.cloudfront.net/equalitynow/pages/303/attachments/original/1527598602/Manual_on_Protocol_on_Women_Rights_in_Africa_EN.pdf?1527598602> accessed 17.03.2023.

[56]   Constitution of Kenya, 2010, Arts. 99(2)(e), 137, 180 and 193.

[57]   P. OYUGI, "The Implementation of Article 12 of the Convention on the Rights of People with Disabilities in Kenya" (2018) 3 *Journal of Law and Ethics* 21, 30.

[58]   Ibid., at 30–31.

[59]   Ibid., at 30.

[60]   Committee on the Rights of Persons with Disabilities, Concluding Observations on the initial report of Kenya, CRPD/C/KEN/CO/1 para. 23.

[61]   Ibid.

[62]   Constitution of Zambia, 1991, at Art. 70(2)(d).

[63]   Ibid., at Art. 100(2)(f).

[64]   Ibid., at Art. 83(1)(b).

"a mental or physical disability that makes the Minister incapable of performing the functions of that office."[65] Similarly, Provincial Ministers may be removed from office on the same grounds.[66] The Constitution permits the deprivation of personal liberty where a person is, or is "reasonably suspected to be, of unsound mind."[67] The Constitution also permits the possession or acquisition of any property or interest therein belonging to a person of "unsound mind."[68] There are other laws as well which deny persons with disabilities the right to legal capacity. For example, it is an offence under the Penal Code to have sexual intercourse with a woman or girl with intellectual or psychosocial disabilities.[69] The Penal Code uses the derogatory terms "idiot" and "imbecile" to refer to women with intellectual and psychosocial disabilities stating that:

> Any person who, knowing a woman or girl to be an idiot or imbecile, has or attempts to have unlawful carnal knowledge of her in circumstances not amounting to rape, but which prove that the offender knew at the time of the commission of the offence that the woman or girl was an idiot or imbecile, is guilty of a felony and is liable to imprisonment for fourteen years.[70]

Women and girls with intellectual and psychosocial disabilities, therefore, cannot exercise the right to enter into sexual relationships. From 18–28 April 2016, the then Special Rapporteur on the rights of persons with disabilities, Ms Catalina Devandas Aguilar, visited Zambia at the Government's invitation. In her report, she raised some concerns about the rights of persons with disabilities in Zambia, including the right to legal capacity.[71] She raised concerns about provisions in the Constitution that deprive legal capacity, such as Article 16(2)(i) which allows the deprivation of property.[72] She also raised concerns about the provisions of the Mental Disorders Act depriving of liberty persons who are "dangerous to himself or others" or "wandering at large and unable to take care of himself."[73]

In South Africa, legal capacity is denied through substituted decision-making schemes in the form of the common law curatorship scheme and under the legislative process of appointing administrators pursuant to the Mental

---

[65]   Ibid., at Art, 116(3)(f).
[66]   Ibid., at Art. 117(2)(e).
[67]   Ibid., at Art. 13(1)(h).
[68]   Ibid., at Art. 16(2)(i).
[69]   Sec. 39 Penal Code Act Chapter 87 (Zambia).
[70]   Sec. 39 Penal Code Act Chapter 87 (Zambia).
[71]   Report of the Special Rapporteur on the rights of persons with disabilities on her visit to Zambia (2016) A/HRC/34/58/Add.2.
[72]   Ibid., para. 64.
[73]   Ibid., para. 65.

Health Care Act of 2002.[74] Under the Mental Health Care Act, an administrator may be appointed by the Master of the High Court to "care for and administer" the property of a mentally ill person or a person with "severe or profound intellectual disability".[75]

As shown above, the main barrier to the right to equal recognition before the law is laws that deny persons with disabilities, especially cognitive disabilities, the right to legal capacity.[76] As the following analysis shows, this remains a contested area of law reform and a matter of significant urgency in the Africa region.

4. REVIEWING THE REFORMS IN KENYA, ZAMBIA AND SOUTH AFRICA

Attempts have been made to reform legal capacity law in Kenya, Zambia and South Africa. These have been made through the courts and through the legislature. This section evaluates these reforms using Article 12 of the CRPD as a standard.

4.1. HOW THE DECIDED CASES SHOW INSUFFICIENT UNDERSTANDING OF LEGAL CAPACITY

The courts in Kenya and Zambia have decided cases that are pertinent to the right to legal capacity after their respective countries had ratified the CRPD. This section demonstrates how the cases decided by the courts in these countries show a lack of understanding about legal capacity. The cases in each country are outlined in turn as follows.

4.1.1. Kenya

Any international law instrument ratified by the government of Kenya forms part of the law of Kenya.[77] The Constitution of Kenya states that "[a]ny treaty or convention ratified by Kenya shall form part of the law of Kenya under this

---

[74] W. HOLNESS and S. RULE, "Legal capacity of parties with intellectual, psycho-social and communication disabilities in traditional courts in KwaZulu-Natal" (2018) 6 *African Disability Rights Yearbook* 27, 42. Mental Health Care Act 17 2002, sec. 59 (South Africa).

[75] Mental Health Care Act 17 2002, sec. 59(1).

[76] A. ARSTEIN-KERSLAKE, (n. 38), at 75.

[77] Constitution of Kenya, 2010, Art. 2(6).

Constitution."[78] So, upon its ratification by the Kenyan Government, the CRPD became part of the law of Kenya. The High Court of Kenya expressly mentioned Article 12 of the CRPD in *Wilson Morara Siringi v. Republic* (hereinafter *Siringi*).[79] The appellant, Wilson Morara Siringi, was tried and convicted of rape and was sentenced to 15 years' imprisonment.[80] The complainant was a 34-year-old woman with an unspecified mental disability. The appellant appealed against his conviction and sentence on the grounds that he did not rape the complainant and that he had an alibi defence. On appeal, the court found that the prosecution had proved that the appellant had sexual intercourse with the complainant.[81] At issue, was whether the complainant had consented to the sexual intercourse. According to the law in Kenya, "a person consents if he or she agrees by choice, and has the freedom and *capacity* to make that choice."[82] The law goes on to enumerate the various circumstances that make an act intentional and unlawful. For instance, an act is intentional and unlawful where it is committed "in respect of a person who is incapable of appreciating the nature of an act which causes the offence."[83] It is further clarified that the "circumstances in which a person is incapable in law of appreciating the nature of an act referred to in subsection (1) include circumstances where such a person is, at the time of the commission of such an act *mentally impaired*".[84] According to the law in Kenya therefore, persons with mental disabilities cannot lawfully consent to sexual intercourse. The approach that is taken is a functional approach to the denial of legal capacity whereby one is considered to lack capacity if he or she as a result of the disability, cannot perform a specific function (e.g., inability to understand the nature of a contract).[85] In this case, complainants with mental disabilities are considered as lacking capacity because of a perceived inability to understand the nature of the sexual act. The prosecution in *Siringi* relied on the fact that the complainant had a mental disability to prove lack of consent. The court in *Siringi* clarified that the "issue is not whether the complainant was mentally impaired generally but whether ... the complainant exercised freedom and capacity to make the choice of having sexual intercourse and whether at the time the act took place the complainant was incapable of consenting by reason of mental impairment."[86] Prior to the commencement of the original trial, the magistrate conducted a *voir dire* to determine whether the complainant could give evidence in court.[87] He concluded that she was "able to give coherent testimony and answer questions

---

[78] Ibid., at Art. 2(6).
[79] *Wilson Morara Siringi v. Republic*, Criminal Appeal No. 17 of 2014.
[80] The offence of rape is found in the Sexual Offences Act 2006, sec. 3(1)(b) and (3) (Kenya).
[81] *Siringi* (n. 79), at para. 9.
[82] Sexual Offences Act 2006, sec. 42.
[83] Ibid., at sec. 43(1)(c).
[84] Ibid., at sec. 43(4)(e). Emphasis added.
[85] A. DHANDA (n. 27), at 431.
[86] *Siringi* (n. 79), at para. 12.
[87] Ibid., at para. 13.

put to her in cross-examination" and allowed her to testify based on that finding.[88] On appeal, the court took the magistrate's conclusion from the *voir dire* together with the lack of medical evidence proving that she was "at any time unable to appreciate the nature of the act or consent to it" to mean that there were instances where she could make independent decisions in spite of the mental disability.[89] The appeal court therefore, concluded that the prosecution had failed to prove lack of consent beyond a reasonable doubt and quashed the appellant's conviction.[90]

The court only made reference to Article 12 of the CRPD in its conclusion and dedicated only one paragraph out of the 17 paragraphs in the judgment to discussing Article 12. The court's dealing with Article 12 was therefore minimal and superficial. The court stated that "the approach taken by the prosecution and the learned magistrate is that the complainant is an object of social protection rather than a subject capable of having rights including the right to make the decision whether to have sexual intercourse."[91] It is submitted that it is not the approach that is taken by the prosecution that is incompatible with Article 12, rather it is the legislative provision in the Sexual Offences Act itself that sanctions a functional approach to capacity to consent to sexual relations. In spite of these shortcomings the decision in *Siringi* remains an important step in the right direction in as much as it condemns an approach treating the mere fact that a complainant has a mental disability as meaning that he or she cannot consent to sex (status approach). The approach that was encouraged by the appeal court, one of requiring the court to prove whether in the particular circumstances, the person understood the nature of the act is tantamount to a functional approach, which may also result in a denial of legal capacity.

Prior to *Siringi*, Kenya had conceded that Article 12 of the CRPD was "one of the most misunderstood provisions of the CRPD."[92] This explains why, before *Siringi*, the Courts in Kenya evaded applying the CRPD. Two cases were brought before the Courts in Kenya in which the petitioners alleged violations of the CRPD.[93] In both cases, the court did not address the CRPD, but focused on domestic legislation.[94] *Siringi* was decided after government officials were

---

88   *Siringi* (n. 79), at para. 13.
89   Ibid., at para. 13.
90   Ibid., at para. 14.
91   Ibid., at para. 15.
92   Committee on the Rights of Persons with Disabilities, Replies to the List of Issues: Kenya, 10 July 2015, CRPD/C/KEN/Q/1Add.1 para. 39. <https://www.globaldisabilityrightsnow. org/sites/default/files/related-files/260/Response_to_LOIs_from_Kenya.pdf> accessed 17.03.2023.
93   *Cradle – Children Foundation (suing through the Trustee Geoffrey Maganya) v. Nation Media Group Limited ex parte Cradle – Children Foundation (suing through Geoffrey Maganya)* [2012] eKLR and *Satrose Ayuma & 11 others v. Registered Trustees of the Kenya Railways Staff Retirement Benefits Scheme & 2 others* [2011] eKLR.
94   P. OYUGI, "The Implementation of Article 12 of the Convention on the Rights of People with Disabilities in Kenya" (2018) 3 *Journal of Law and Ethics* 21, 28.

Dianah Msipa

sensitised about Article 12 by civil society.[95] For example, in April 2014, civil society held an event in Nairobi to launch a report on legal capacity at which various government officials were sensitised.[96] The Kenya National Commission on Human Rights made recommendations on implementing Article 12 in a briefing paper.[97] While the sensitisation was indeed helpful, the court still failed to provide a detailed analysis of the right to legal capacity in *Siringi*, indicating that there is still a knowledge gap in relation to the right to legal capacity.

4.1.2. Zambia

Prior to the coming into force of the Mental Health Act 2019, the High Court of Zambia delivered a judgment in the case of *Gordon Maddox Mwewa & Others v. Attorney-General & Another* (hereinafter *Mwewa*) in October 2017.[98] *Mwewa* challenged the constitutionality of the Mental Disorders Act. The petitioners in *Mwewa*, filed a suit in the High Court of Zambia pursuant to Article 28 of the Constitution of Zambia challenging the constitutionality of the Mental Disorders Act. The petitioners also sought a declaration protecting persons with mental disabilities from unlawful detention, ensuring their rights including the right to give informed consent to medical treatment and admission to medical facilities. The petitioners, therefore, argued that the Mental Disorders Act violated their Constitutional rights to dignity through its use of derogatory terms,[99] to freedom from torture and inhuman or degrading treatment,[100] and to freedom from discrimination.[101] The petitioners were unsuccessful and the Court declined to declare the Mental Disorders Act unconstitutional.

One of the arguments advanced by the petitioners in *Mwewa* is that subjecting them to forced treatment without their informed consent violated their right to legal capacity in health matters, thereby violating their right to health. The Court had this to say:

> It is not in every case that an affected person might be able to appreciate the severity of their illness so as to voluntarily give consent to medical treatment. However, in

---

[95] Manyara Reginald Mworia, Criminal Appeal No. 17 of 2004 on the Capacity of Persons with Mental or Psychosocial Disabilities to Consent to Sex, 2016 E. AFR. L.J. 96, 99 (2016–2017).

[96] Report available at <http://mdac.org/sites/mdac.org/files/mdac-kenya legal-capacity_9apr2014_0.pdf> accessed 28.03.2023.

[97] Kenya National Commission on Human Rights, "How to Implement Article 12 of Convention on The Rights of Persons with Disabilities regarding Legal Capacity in Kenya: A Briefing Paper", 2014. <https://www.knchr.org/Portals/0/GroupRightsReports/Briefing%20Paper%20on%20Legal%20Capacity-Disability%20Rights.pdf> accessed 28.03.2023.

[98] *Gordon Maddox Mwewa & Others v. Attorney-General & Another (Mwewa case)* 2017/HP/204 (unreported).

[99] Constitution of Zambia, Art. 8.

[100] Ibid., at Art. 15.

[101] Ibid., at Art. 23.

188

Intersentia

cases where patients have minor conditions, such persons should be allowed to consent to medical treatment. By saying so, I do not hold that the Mental Disorders Act is unconstitutional because it removes the right to informed consent to medical treatment. I can only hold to the contrary if there was medical evidence adduced to assist me in making an informed finding. In my view, this issue is more complex than it appears and I cannot on the basis of the petition as the only evidence make a finding. This claim accordingly fails.[102]

The High Court agreed with the petitioners that section 5 of the Mental Disorders Act which uses derogatory language is unconstitutional. However, the Court did not declare the entire Act unconstitutional.

The petitioners further argued that the Mental Disorders Act deprived them of their right to liberty by allowing forced admission. The right to liberty in the Constitution is not absolute, so the petitioners argued that their case did not fall into the circumstances in which the right could be lawfully deprived. The High Court found that the Mental Disorders Act did not contravene the right to liberty guaranteed by Article 13 of the Constitution. The Court had this to say:

By this I mean to say that there needs to be a balance between the competing considerations on detention and admission to mental health institutions which appear to be involuntary on the one hand and the affected persons (sic) rights. In my view, there may be instances where it is necessary for the family, community or law enforcement agencies to have a mental patient admitted without their consent especially where they suffer from severe disabilities or where is obvious that an affected person is not capable of making an appropriate decision for their care and treatment. The decision to determine the detention or admission of mental patients to prisons or medical institutions is a medical question, and cannot be determined by this Court.[103]

It is not surprising that this case failed because it was based on a Constitution which permits the denial of legal capacity.

In recent years, legal capacity reform has been made through legislative reform with varying levels of success. The following section contains a critical review of the legislative legal capacity reforms in Kenya, Zambia and South Africa.

---

[102] *Mwewa* (n. 98) at 40.
[103] Ibid.

Intersentia

189

4.2. OLD WINE IN NEW SKINS: HOW THE LEGISLATIVE REFORMS HAVE REPRODUCED THE OUTDATED UNDERSTANDING OF LEGAL CAPACITY

4.2.1. *Kenya*

There are two Bills currently before the Kenyan Parliament that are pertinent to the right to legal capacity of persons with disabilities: the Persons with Disabilities (Amendment) Bill 2015 and the Mental Health (Amendment) Bill 2018.

The Persons with Disabilities (Amendment) Bill 2015 seeks to repeal and replace the pre-CRPD Persons with Disabilities Act 2003, which makes no provision for the right to legal capacity.[104] The Bill's provisions on legal capacity are very much in line with Article 12 of the CRPD and Article 7 of the African Disability Protocol. The Bill provides for the right to legal capacity stating that every person with a disability has the right to "recognition of legal capacity before the law"[105] and "protection and benefit of the law on an equal basis with others."[106] The Bill defines legal capacity in the same way that the CRPD and the African Disability Protocol do. It states that legal capacity means "the ability to hold rights and duties under the law and to exercise these rights and duties."[107] Furthermore, the requirement to provide support is also part of the right to legal capacity. The Bill states that "[e]very person with disability is entitled to the support services he or she may require in exercising the right to legal capacity."[108] Like the CRPD and the African Disability Protocol, the Bill also expressly provides that every person with a disability has "equal right to own or inherit property, to control his or her own financial affairs and to have equal access to bank loans, mortgages and other forms of financial credit."[109] The Bill also provides for other rights which are normally denied when a person's legal capacity has been taken away, such as the right to marry and form a family,[110] right to documents of registration or identification,[111] the right health, which includes the right to enjoyment of sexual and reproductive health rights,[112] and the right to "information that will enable him or her to make responsible and informed choices about their sexual and reproductive health."[113] The Bill also states that "[n]o person shall subject a person with disability to any medical

---

[104]   Persons with Disabilities (Amendment) Bill 2015 (Kenya).
[105]   Ibid., at sec. 13(1)(i).
[106]   Ibid., at sec. 13(1)(ii).
[107]   Ibid., at sec. 2(2).
[108]   Ibid., at sec. 13(2).
[109]   Ibid., at sec. 13(3).
[110]   Ibid., at sec. 14.
[111]   Ibid., at sec. 20.
[112]   Ibid., at sec. 30(2)(a).
[113]   Ibid., at sec. 30(2)(b).

procedure which leads to or could lead to infertility without that person's express consent."[114] It also provides for civil and political rights[115] as well as the right of persons with disabilities to access credit.[116]

The Kenyan government's reform efforts exhibited in the Persons with Disabilities (Amendment) Bill are to be applauded as they are consistent with the right to legal capacity as it is formulated in the CRPD and include additional provisions relevant to the African context, such as the right to documents of registration or identification.[117] Curiously, the position is not the same in the later Mental Health (Amendment) Bill 2018.

The Mental Health (Amendment) Bill 2018 exhibits a reluctance to fully recognise universal legal capacity for persons with mental disabilities. The result is a document that embraces some, but not all, aspects of the supported decision-making approach, whilst simultaneously holding on to the substitute decision-making framework.

In terms of the right to legal capacity, the Bill provides that a person with "mental illness has a right to recognition before the law and shall enjoy legal rights on an equal basis with other persons in all aspects of life."[118] However, the Bill does not recognise universal legal capacity and states that "[u]pon application, the court may make a determination whether a person with mental illness has legal capacity"[119] and where "the court determines that a person lacks legal capacity, the court shall appoint a representative to manage that person's affairs."[120] The term "representative" is defined in the Bill as the "spouse, parent, guardian, next of kin, or court appointed representative of the person suffering from mental illness, having legal capacity to make decisions on behalf of the person with mental illness."[121] This is suspiciously similar to the guardianship framework. The Bill also provides for the "right to representation".[122] The Bill states that, a person with "mental illness is entitled to choose and appoint another person to represent them in any manner, including in any complaint procedure or appeal."[123] The Bill further states that, where a person with "mental illness is unable to exercise the right under subsection (1) the representative of the person may appoint a person to represent the person with mental illness in any manner, including in any compliant procedure or appeal."[124]

---

[114]   Ibid., at sec. 30(5).
[115]   Ibid., at sec. 31(F).
[116]   Ibid., at sec. 37.
[117]   Ibid., at sec. 20.
[118]   Mental Health (Amendment) Bill 2018, sec. 3K(1).
[119]   Ibid., at sec. 3K(2).
[120]   Ibid., at sec. 3K(3).
[121]   Ibid., at sec. 3(d).
[122]   Ibid., at sec. 3J.
[123]   Ibid., at sec. 3J(1).
[124]   Ibid., at sec. 3J(2).

The right to consent to treatment is not absolute but only applies where "a person with mental illness is capable of making an informed decision on the need for treatment."[125] In circumstances where the person is capable of making an informed decision, health care providers are required to "obtain the written consent of such person before administering any treatment."[126] Where the person is deemed incapable of making an informed decision on the need for treatment, "such consent shall be sought and obtained from the representative of that person."[127] Furthermore, such consent shall be valid if "the person with mental illness or the person's representative is competent to give consent."[128] Similarly, the right to participate in treatment planning is not absolute.[129] In circumstances where "a person with mental illness is incapable of exercising the right under subsection (1) due to the nature of the illness, the representative shall be entitled to participate in the formulation of treatment plans."[130]

The inconsistent approach to legal capacity in the two Bills indicates that there is a mistaken and pervasive belief that persons with mental disabilities are simply not capable of enjoying the right to legal capacity. The Mental Health (Amendment), in particular, fails to reform legal capacity law and reproduces the old substituted decision-making framework in a new law.

4.2.2. Zambia

The legislative reforms that have taken place in Zambia also show a reluctance to accept the concept of universal legal capacity and depart from the substituted decision-making regime. Because Zambia is a dualist state, international law has to be incorporated into domestic law through an Act of Parliament.[131] The CRPD was incorporated into domestic law in Zambia through the Persons with Disabilities Act 2012. Further legal capacity reform took place through the enactment of the Mental Health Act 2019.

---

[125] Ibid., at sec. 3B(1)(a).
[126] Ibid., at sec. 3B(1)(b).
[127] Ibid., at sec. 3B(2).
[128] Ibid., at sec. 9D(2)(a).
[129] Ibid., at sec. 3C(1).
[130] Ibid., at sec. 3C(2).
[131] F. Viljoen, *International Human Rights Law in Africa*, Oxford University Press: Oxford 2007, pp. 1, 18. Sec. 2 of Zambia's Ratification of International Agreements Act 34 2016. The Act confirms the position stated by case law before its enactment; see *Zambia Sugar PLC v. Fellow Nanzaluka* Supreme Court Appeal 82 of 2001, where it was held that international instruments on any law, although ratified and assented to by the state, cannot be applied unless they have been domesticated. The Courts in Zambia have, however, made reference to undomesticated international law instruments as persuasive authority (*Attorney-General v. Roy Clarke* (2008) 1 ZR 38. (Zambia)). In *Sarah Longwe v. Intercontinental Hotel*, the High Court indicated that the fact that a state ratifies international legal instruments without reservation is indicative of its willingness to be bound by the provisions of the ratified instruments. (*Sarah Longwe v. Intercontinental Hotel* 1992/HP/765 (HC)).

On 21 July 2012, Zambia adopted the Persons with Disabilities Act (hereinafter PWDA), which domesticates the CRPD.[132] The Act provides for a number of rights including the right to education,[133] health care and facilities,[134] habilitation and rehabilitation,[135] employment and social protection,[136] accessibility and mobility,[137] political and public life.[138] However, equal recognition before the law is not expressed as a right. Instead, "recognition as persons before the law" is mentioned as one of the general principles in the PWDA.[139] The Act does, however, provide for the right to legal capacity.[140] It states that persons with disabilities "shall enjoy legal capacity on an equal basis with others in all aspects of life."[141] However, the rights necessary for the enjoyment of legal capacity are not provided for. The PWDA is silent about the provision of support in order to exercise one's legal capacity.[142] Without support, it may be difficult, if not impossible, for persons who require intensive support to exercise the right to legal capacity. This omission is therefore, detrimental to persons with severe disabilities whose right to legal capacity is often challenged. Furthermore, it does not explicitly mention the right of persons with disabilities to own and inherit property and manage their own financial affairs as the CRPD does.[143]

Similarly, the Mental Health Act 2019 fails to adequately protect the right to legal capacity.[144] The Mental Health Act replaced the Mental Disorders Act, which dates back to 1949.[145] The Mental Disorders Act used dated and derogatory terminology such as "mentally infirm", "idiot", "imbecile", "feeble-minded", and "moral imbecile".[146] It also allowed for forced detention and treatment[147] and provided for substituted decision-making which was achieved through "control orders."[148] Disability rights activists who were hopeful that the Mental Health Act 2019 would uphold the right to legal capacity for persons with intellectual and psychosocial disabilities in Zambia would be disappointed. The Mental Health Act does not subscribe to the idea of universal legal capacity.

---

[132]   Persons with Disabilities Act No. 6 2012, Zambia.
[133]   Ibid., at sec. 22–26.
[134]   Ibid., at sec. 27–31.
[135]   Ibid., at sec. 32–34.
[136]   Ibid., at sec. 35–39.
[137]   Ibid., at sec. 40–50.
[138]   Ibid., at sec. 51.
[139]   Ibid., at sec. 4(c).
[140]   Ibid., at sec. 8(1).
[141]   Ibid.
[142]   CRPD, Art. 12(3) and African Disability Protocol, Art. 7(2)(c).
[143]   CRPD, Art. 12(5) and African Disability Protocol, Art. 7(2)(g) and (h).
[144]   Mental Health Act, No. 6 of 2019 (Zambia).
[145]   Mental Disorders Act Chapter 305 (Zambia).
[146]   Ibid., at sec. 5.
[147]   Ibid., at secs 6, 7 and 8.
[148]   Ibid., at sec. 13.

Although the Act acknowledges that "a mental patient shall enjoy legal capacity,"[149] this right is not absolute and the Act leaves room for a court to make a declaration that a person lacks legal capacity. It states that "[w]here a court declares that a mental patient does not have legal capacity, that person is legally disqualified under subsection (4) and any other written law."[150] Crucially, the Act does not require the provision of support in order to exercise legal capacity. Instead, the Mental Health Act also introduces a "supporter" who is a "person who represents a mental health service user or mental patient's rights or interests".[151] The Act states that "[w]here a mental patient lacks legal capacity, a court may appoint a supporter."[152] The supporter is permitted to consent to admission and treatment.[153] The Mental Health Act requires consent to be obtained before admission, treatment, care, rehabilitation or palliation can take place.[154] The Act states that where "a mental patient is unable to give consent to the treatment, the consent may be given by a supporter."[155] There is no requirement for the supporter to ascertain the patient's will and preference before making decisions on his or her behalf. The supporter is, therefore, analogous to a substituted decision-maker. Furthermore, it is not clear what constitutes inability to give consent and this ambiguity leaves the Mental Health Act dangerously open to abuse.

Contrary to the standard in the CRPD, the Mental Health Act also provides for involuntary admission.[156] Voluntary admission is provided for in aspirational terms rather than as a duty. The Mental Health Act states that a mental health facility shall "endeavor" to ensure that there is voluntary admission.[157] Involuntary admissions are permitted in an "emergency situation where it is not possible or reasonable to comply with a procedure for voluntary admission and treatment."[158] Furthermore, the Mental Health Act permits the Board of the mental health facility to authorise "admission, treatment, care, rehabilitation or palliation" in circumstances where if not done this may result in "death or irreversible harm to a mental patient", "a mental patient inflicting serious harm to oneself or another person" or "a mental patient causing serious damage to, or loss of, property."[159] Involuntary admission is therefore, permitted in violation of the right to legal capacity enshrined in the CRPD and the African Disability Protocol.

---

[149] Mental Health Act (n. 144), at sec. 4(1).
[150] Ibid., at sec. 4(5).
[151] Ibid., at sec. 2.
[152] Ibid., at sec. 4(3).
[153] Ibid., at sec. 23(1).
[154] Ibid., at sec. 22(1)(a).
[155] Ibid., at sec. 23(1).
[156] Ibid., at sec. 26.
[157] Ibid., at sec. 2(1)(a).
[158] Ibid., at sec. 26.
[159] Ibid., at sec. 22(1)(b), (c)(i)(ii) and (iii).

The failure in the Persons with Disabilities Act to require the provision of supports in order to exercise legal capacity compromises the potential for persons with disabilities to actually enjoy the right to legal capacity enshrined therein. Similarly, the Mental Health Act allows the court to declare that a person lacks legal capacity, introduces the role of supporter who makes decisions on behalf of the patient (substitute decision-maker), and allows involuntary treatment. This waters down the transformative potential of the provision on the right to legal capacity and indicates that the Mental Health Act has not in fact reformed the law on legal capacity in Zambia.

4.2.3. South Africa

Of the countries under review, South Africa is unique in that it is the only country that is developing specific legislation on supported decision-making in the form of the draft Assisted Decision-Making Bill.

The White Paper on the Rights of Persons with Disabilities, which is a policy document focusing on persons with disabilities in South Africa preceded the Assisted Decision Bill.[160] The White Paper is based on the Constitution of South Africa along with various international legal instruments including the CRPD.[161] It is a "call to action for government, civil society and the private sector to work together to ensure the socio-economic inclusion of persons with disabilities."[162] The White Paper provides for the right to equal recognition before the law.[163] It calls for a review of all relevant legislation to ensure equal recognition before the law for persons with disabilities.[164] Furthermore, it stipulates that the "development of supported decision-making legislation, in particular for persons with intellectual, psychosocial and neurological disabilities, must coincide with the review of substitute decision-making regimes."[165] Closely, related to that, it calls for the development of supported decision-making services.[166]

The Assisted Decision-Making Bill was first drafted in 2004. The South African Law Reform Commission subsequently revised the Assisted Decision-Making Bill of 2004 which predates South Africa's ratification of the CRPD in order to bring it in line with the CRPD, particularly Article 12 of the CRPD.[167] The Supported Decision-Making Bill aims to "provide for measures to enable

---

[160]   White Paper on the Rights of Persons with Disabilities, No. 39792, 9 March 2016.
[161]   Ibid., at foreword by the Minister at 7.
[162]   Ibid.
[163]   Ibid., at 77.
[164]   Ibid.
[165]   Ibid., at 78.
[166]   Ibid., at 102.
[167]   W. HOLNESS, "Equal Recognition and Legal Capacity for Persons with Disabilities: Incorporating the Principle of Proportionality" 30 *South African Journal on Human Rights* 313, 316.

persons with disability to access the support they may require in exercising their legal capacity on an equal basis with others."[168] This is done by "recognising and regulating informal support"[169] and "introducing and regulating alternative measures of formal support."[170] The Bill therefore, provides for both informal and formal support in exercising legal capacity.

In order for informal support to be lawful, it must be "reasonable for such support to be provided by the person who does so"[171] and the person with a disability must have been consulted "to the extent reasonably possible with regard to his or her need for the support, and has to the extent reasonably possible consented to the support being provided."[172] The Bill also provides for several safeguards relating to the provision of informal support. The use of threat or force on the person with a disability is prohibited.[173] Furthermore, the person providing support may not "detain or confine the person with a disability."[174] There are also restrictions with regard to property, namely, that informal support may not be provided with regard to "the alienation, mortgaging of a servitude over or conferring of any other real right in immovable property" belonging to a person with a disability.[175] Informal support may also not be provided when "entering into any credit agreement"[176] and with regard to the "investment or reinvestment of funds, or the withdrawal of an investment," on behalf of a person with a disability.[177] Informal support does not extend to giving or refusing consent with regard to personal welfare in terms of the National Health Act 2003.[178] The person providing informal support is also required to "keep sufficient records thereof for at least five years."[179] The person providing informal support does not need to be appointed by the Master[180] and is entitled to claim expenses incurred during the course of the support from the person with a disability.[181]

The Bill also makes provision for formal support in exercising legal capacity in the form of a financial supporter[182] and a welfare supporter.[183] A financial supporter assists a person with a disability "in exercising legal capacity with regard

---

[168]   Supported Decision-Making Bill (Republic of South Africa), sec. 2(a).
[169]   Ibid., at sec. 2(a)(i).
[170]   Ibid., at sec. 2(a)(ii).
[171]   Ibid., at sec. 6(1)(a).
[172]   Ibid., at sec. 6(1)(c).
[173]   Ibid., at sec. 8(a).
[174]   Ibid., at sec. 8(b).
[175]   Ibid., at sec. 9(a).
[176]   Ibid., at sec. 9(b).
[177]   Ibid., at sec. 9(b).
[178]   Ibid., at sec. 10.
[179]   Ibid., at sec. 11.
[180]   Ibid., at sec. 6(3).
[181]   Ibid., at sec. 7.
[182]   Ibid., at Chapter 3.
[183]   Ibid., at sec. 45.

to his or her property."[184] In order to become a financial supporter, one must submit an application and be appointed by the Master.[185] The financial supporter is subject to certain restrictions such as the prohibition on using threat or force[186] and restrictions on conducting specified transactions involving immovable property without the written consent of the Master.[187] The appointment of the financial supporter is subject to periodic review.[188] Furthermore, the resignation, termination and withdrawal of a financial supporter are regulated in the Bill.[189]

The Bill also provides for the formal appointment by the Master of a personal welfare supporter "to support a person with disability in exercising legal capacity with regard to his or her personal welfare."[190] The personal welfare supporter is required to keep written records of the support provided[191] and report to the Master on the support provided.[192] The supporter may be remunerated "out of the property of the person with disability."[193] The supporter is also subject to restrictions including the prohibition on using threats or force[194] and the prohibition on substituting "any other person to act as personal welfare supporter" in their place.[195] The appointment of the personal welfare supporter is subject to periodic review by the Master[196] and the resignation, termination and withdrawal of the supporter is regulated in the Bill.[197] The Bill also provides for other forms of support such as enduring power of attorney[198] and agents.[199]

Reforms that have taken place in South Africa are consistent with the requirements in Article 12 of the CRPD and are to be applauded.

5. CONCLUSION

The legal capacity reform efforts in Kenya and Zambia have been largely unsuccessful. In part, this is due to a lack of adequate understanding of the right to legal capacity as exhibited in the cases of *Siringi* and *Mwewa*. Furthermore,

---

[184]   Ibid., at sec. 16.
[185]   Ibid., at sec. 16.
[186]   Ibid., at sec. 34.
[187]   Ibid., at sec. 35(1).
[188]   Ibid., at sec. 38.
[189]   Ibid., at sec. 39.
[190]   Ibid., at sec. 45.
[191]   Ibid., at sec. 52.
[192]   Ibid., at sec. 53.
[193]   Ibid., at sec. 55.
[194]   Ibid., at sec. 56.
[195]   Ibid., at sec. 58.
[196]   Ibid., at sec. 59.
[197]   Ibid., at sec. 60.
[198]   Ibid., at Chapter 5.
[199]   Ibid., at sec. 73.

the legislative reforms exhibit a reluctance to accept universal legal capacity and shift from substituted to supported decision-making. The reason for this reluctance is unclear. Consequently, the legislation has either dealt with the right to legal capacity on a superficial level or legitimised the denial of legal capacity. Ultimately, the legislation has failed to achieve the desired goal of legal capacity reform.

South Africa is the exception in that the Supported Decision-Making Bill exemplifies a CRPD compliant approach to supported decision-making. If the Bill is passed into law, it is likely to be the first legislation dealing with supported decision-making on the African continent.

Nevertheless, all the three countries under review need to abolish existing laws that permit the denial of legal capacity and substituted decision-making.

CHANGING THE PARADIGM OF SUBSTITUTED DECISION-MAKING IN BULGARIA

The Tipping Point

Nadia SHABANI and Marieta DIMITROVA

1. The Bulgarian Concept of Supported Decision-Making.............. 200
    1.1. Guardianship According to the Bulgarian Legislation: Concept,
        Background, and Case Law................................. 200
    1.2. Supported Decision-Making: Rationale for the Pilot Program and
        the Draft of the Natural Persons and Support Measures Act....... 203
2. Changes in Jurisprudence and the Practice of the Courts 207
    2.1. The Legislative Paradigm 207
    2.2. Poverty: Not a Legal Risk 210
3. Changes in the "Social Laws" which Introduce Supported
    Decision-Making 210
    3.1. Consent to Placement in a Residential Service 210
    3.2. Support Measures for Ensuring Access to Justice in Conformity
        with the Persons with Disabilities Act........................ 212
4. Lessons Learnt and Main Conclusions for the Way Forward........... 215
    4.1. The Focus of Change 215
    4.2. Leadership... 215
    4.3. The Central and Eastern European Context: Social and Political
        Factors 216
    4.4. Changing the Law versus Changing Communities.............. 217
5. Conclusion.. 218

Intersentia

1. THE BULGARIAN CONCEPT OF SUPPORTED DECISION-MAKING

1.1. GUARDIANSHIP ACCORDING TO THE BULGARIAN LEGISLATION: CONCEPT, BACKGROUND, AND CASE LAW

The effective Bulgarian legislation and the case law of the Supreme Court of Cassation[1] require that two criteria must be met to place a person under guardianship: (i) weak-mindedness or a mental health condition (medical criterion); (ii) incapacity (i.e., limited capacity) of the person to take care of their affairs (legal criterion); and that a causal link is established between the medical criterion and the legal one. Pursuant to the provisions regulating the legal status of individuals and the possibilities for the restriction thereof, guardianship, as regulated:

- is imposed for an indefinite period of time;
- covers all legal areas of an individual's activity;
- is effective in the future, and, in practice, it is difficult to revoke it in the context of the established case law[2] where the precondition thereof is that the person under guardianship prove their recuperation with a medical document or protocol issued by a medical consultative committee;
- does not take into consideration the dynamics of the individual's state, and does not recognise that their inability or difficulties in terms of taking care of their affairs may change over time and vary in respect of the legal spheres;
- shall not be subject to periodic review;
- the individuals under guardianship are deprived of any access to the court or redress for their fundamental rights and interests, the legal consequences from partial guardianship in the Bulgarian context being the same as the ones from full guardianship;[3]
- is entirely a form of substitute decision-making: the person under guardianship is assigned a substitute in all civil matters who makes decisions

---

[1] Judgment No 596 of 28.08.2006 in civil case No 1342/2005, 2nd C.D.

[2] Decree No 5/79 of 13.02.1980 г. of the Plenary of the Supreme Court.

[3] Judgment of the European Court of Human Rights (ECtHR) in the case *Stanev v. Bulgaria*. While in accordance with Decree No 5/79 of 13.02.1980 of the Plenary of the Supreme Court, the person under partial guardianship can, on their own or with the consent of their custodian, including the one under Article 108 of Personal and Family Act, request the revocation of their guardianship, Mr. Stanev who had been placed under partial guardianship had not been able to access the court. After ECtHR judgments in the cases *Stanev v. Bulgaria* and *Stankov v. Bulgaria* were delivered, the Civil Code of Procedure was amended accordingly (Article 340 (2) of CCP, amended – SG No 86 of 2017), which allowed a person under partial guardianship to request independently the revocation of guardianship.

based in their "best interest", as understood by third parties (where the person under guardianship is turned into an "object" who is fully subordinated to their guardian and does not have any mechanism available to ensure respect for their wishes and preferences).

The Persons and Family Act, as well as the institution of guardianship and custodianship regulated in the Family Code of Bulgaria reflect the old paradigm which defines persons with intellectual disabilities or mental health conditions as "objects of care" who are unable to express their will, and who should have a substitute (guardian/custodian) in all civil matters. This legislation dates back to the middle of the 20th century.[4] In conformity with the new paradigm of legal capacity under Article 12 of the UN Convention on the Rights of Persons with Disabilities (CRPD), legal agency is an abstract possibility to hold rights and obligations, which is acquired by means of being a subject of law. This can be defined as a *static* element of legal capacity.[5] Capacity to act, on the other hand, is determined by additional prerequisites: attaining a state of intellect and will that allow understanding and managing behaviour (cognitive/intellectual maturity and the ability to express will). These states are acquired, i.e., they depend on specific factors (maturity, existence of a disease or disability which determines the behaviour). Hence, capacity to act can be defined as the *dynamic* element of legal capacity.

While legal capacity is said to be relevant mostly to the legal actions carried out by an individual,[6] its broader social meaning and impact cannot be denied. Indeed, legal capacity determines the overall autonomous life of an individual in all areas of life.[7] Legal capacity, being the possibility to exercise rights through personal actions, is, in effect, the legal instrument, the key, for the implementation of legal agency and any right. Therefore, in terms of the outcome and consequences for the individual, restrictions on legal capacity result in diminishing their legal status. Such limitation, in addition to being a protective measure, also implies the deprivation of rights because a person is thus unable to exercise them in person: the exercise of legal agency is assigned to other natural persons or authorities.

---

4   The Persons and Family Act (PFA) was passed in 1949, and the relevant provisions thereof have not been amended since 1953.
5   N. SHABANI, P. ALEXIEVA, P. DIMITROVA, A. GENOVA and V. TODOROVA, "New Formula for Legal capacity: article 12 from UNCRPD" (2014) 1 *Legal Thoughts* 91.
6   M. PAVLOVA, Civil Law General Part (Sofia R, 2002), p. 233.
7   Legal capacity and delictual capacity (the possibility for legal subjects to bear the consequences of legal liability) must be differentiated. Delictual capacity is the prerequisite for making the individual a subject of offence. As of the time of carrying out the offence, the individual must be aware of the characteristics and meaning of their deed and be able to manage his/her actions. This must be proven by means of a medical expert report and is examined for each individual case. R. TASHEV, General Theory of Law (SIBI, 2010), p. 303–304, and M. PAVLOVA, Civil Law General Part (2002), pp. 233–234.

Pursuant to Article 5 (4) of the Constitution of the Republic of Bulgaria any international treaty which has been ratified, promulgated, and entered into force, shall be part of the domestic law of the land. Such treaties have priority over any conflicting standards of domestic legislation. The new legal framework for the full exercise of human rights by people with disabilities introduced by the CRPD, which determines the foundation for a brand new regulation of legal relations, has existed in parallel with the rule regarding legal incapacity laid down in Article 5 of the Persons and Family Act. It is paramount to ensure that the goals of the Convention are met (to promote, protect and ensure the full and equal enjoyment of all human rights and fundamental freedoms by all persons with disabilities, and to promote respect for their inherent dignity). Where there is an absence of legal rules to recognise and protect these rights or existing legal rules allow the denial or infringement of the rights recognised in the Convention, the relevant state should take all the necessary measures to ensure their exercise and enjoyment by any individual.[8] The need to do so is also recognised by Bulgaria's Constitutional Court in judgment No 12 in the constitutional case No 10/2014. This judgment explicitly emphasises the need to protect the rights of people with disabilities, given the current limitations and consequences of the overall legal regime with respect to legal incapacity, and states that this should be remedied by adopting the relevant legislation on the regime of legal capacity.

In Bulgaria, there is now a parallel existence of two legal frameworks regarding the legal status of persons with disabilities (i.e., the CRPD and the Draft Natural Persons and Supports Measures Act of Bulgaria which is based on the CRPD[9]) which are an entirely different paradigm than the current law. In this context, and with the established priority of international legal instruments over domestic legislation, and the absence of specific national legal rules regulating equality before the law for people with disabilities, the Bulgarian court is confronted with a serious challenge in judicial proceedings with respect to placing persons with disabilities under guardianship, or the revocation thereof. Despite these general legal provisions, and irrespective of some court decisions recognising informal supports for decision-making, the prevailing case law still reproduces the old paradigm, as regulated in current legislation.

---

[8]   Judgment No 226 of 31.10.2016 in civil case No 4922/2015 of SCC, 4th civil div.

[9]   For a presentation of the Draft Natural Persons and Supports Measures Act, commentaries on the draft, and analysis of similar provisions in an international context, see BULGARIAN CENTRE FOR NOT-FOR-PROFIT LAW, *Deficiency of Law, Deficiency of Rights: The Legal Capacity to Act as a Universal Standard of Being Human, The International Perspectives and the Bulgarian Legal Reform*, Sofia, 2015.

1.2. SUPPORTED DECISION-MAKING: RATIONALE FOR THE PILOT PROGRAM AND THE DRAFT OF THE NATURAL PERSONS AND SUPPORT MEASURES ACT

Contrary to the current legal framework, a series of supported decision-making pilot programs – "The Next Step Program" – were initiated in Bulgaria in 2012.[10] Furthermore, a draft law, the Natural Persons and Support Measures Act, introduced an entirely new concept of legal capacity based on supported decision-making.[11] Through the pilot projects, and regardless of the effective legislation, the individual participants with mental health conditions and/or intellectual disabilities, while being *de facto* under guardianship, were treated as equal subjects who can express wishes and preferences. The pilot projects observed the following fundamental principles:

1. Any individual, irrespective of whether he/she has a disability and of how serious it is, has wishes and preferences.
2. The wishes, preferences and will should always be respected, regardless of any issues with communication; the legislation should recognise all forms of communication, including alternatives ones.
3. Any individual, irrespective of whether he/she has a disability and of how serious it is, can build a trusting relationship with another individual.
4. Any individual, irrespective of whether he/she has a disability and of how serious it is, at some point in time needs support for making decisions and receives it from the people whom he/she trusts.
5. The legal capacity of individuals cannot be denied or restricted based on an assessment of their intellectual abilities.

The Next Step Program aimed to design and recognise in a systematic manner decision-making support measures for people with intellectual disabilities or mental health problems, to monitor the outcomes and to document specific conclusions. This experience and its findings were to be the basis for law reform proposals, taking into consideration the contextual features in various areas

---

[10] For an overview of the Next Step Program and the supported decision-making pilot initiatives introduced in Bulgaria, see BULGARIA CENTRE FOR NOT-FOR-PROFIT LAW, *Supported Decision Making: Guidebook for rights enforcement*, Sofia, 2014.

[11] We recall once again that the law was drafted based on the results from the pilot programs – the social interventions applied under the programs were transformed into measures and legal instruments for preserving legal capacity and providing support in conformity with the persons' needs. In this connection, the value-based approach of the pilot programs aimed at ensuring equality for persons with mental health conditions and/or intellectual disabilities was incorporated in the draft law.

across Bulgaria, and the specifics of the individual groups of persons targeted by the Program.

The Program covered over 150 persons with intellectual and mental health disabilities and over 1,500 family members and friends. It was implemented in Sofia (Autism Association and Global Initiative on Psychiatry - Sofia), Vidin (Regional Society for the Support of People with Intellectual Disabilities), Plovdiv (Parallel World Association), Dobrich (St. Nikolay the Wonderworker Foundation), Lovech (Protection Association), and Bobovdol (Innovation Association). The pilot projects were incorporated within the framework of social services – and are operational and have accumulated experience over time – for people with intellectual and developmental disabilities or mental health problems. The new approach was based on person-centred planning and the provision of social support to the persons involved in the project and aimed to support the individual's functioning in everyday self-care and in identifying and prioritising personal wishes and needs.

Within the framework of the pilot projects, a new formula for legal capacity was developed and applied in practice. Outcomes demonstrated that whether people are "normal" or diagnosed with mental health problems or intellectual disabilities, they all have similar values, dreams and expectations – they want to have a job, start a family, have the possibility to do things their way, be self-sufficient. The pilot programs introduced supported decision-making as a process of social intervention in which supporting persons assist adults with mental health conditions or intellectual disabilities in making decisions about their private life, health, finances, and property. The supported participants, irrespective of the seriousness of their disability, chose the persons to support them, usually family, friends, community members and advocates whom they trusted. This person-centred approach helped draw a broad picture of a person's life, their aims and wishes, to determine the scope of the support needed. It also focused on working with third parties to accommodate decision-making processes and provided information resources and easy-to-read formats.

A variety of social interventions were developed, which resulted in incorporating the following support measures into the draft law:

- Building support networks for persons based on person-centred planning, which was subsequently the basis of the supported decision-making agreement, and for recognising specific support measures;
- Creating a mechanism for developing a crisis response plan;
- Providing for the person in need of support to voluntarily choose restrictions on the disposition of their property above a certain value;
- Procedures for facilitating crisis response, including a mechanism to ensure the best interpretation of the person's wishes and preferences by involving all the parties who have some knowledge of the person's history, to determine protection measures in crisis situations and to prevent serious risk of harm.

The principles of the pilot program were incorporated in the draft Natural Persons Supports Measures Act which laid down the irrebuttable presumption that any individual has legal capacity, whether they have a disability and irrespective of how serious it is. An assessment of the individual's intellectual capacity is admissible only to assess decision-making support needs and to tailor them accordingly. The draft law also contains a legal definition of the concept of "supported decision making": a support measure whereby the supporting person approved by the court shall, under the conditions of a relationship of trust, assist the supported person with expressing his/her wishes and preferences in making a decision and carrying out related legal actions. Supported decision-making is to be applied for a certain period and for specific legal actions. The main components of the Bulgarian understanding are as follows:

- This is a new legal status for exercising legal capacity;
- Individuals benefit from this status only where they need support to make decisions;
- Using the above assumption is conditional: it applies only to a person with disabilities who has specific difficulties in terms of specific legal spheres/ actions;
- This is a form of support which is used for specific legal actions and does not cover the full scope of a person's legal capacity;
- It is based on a relationship of trust;
- The support is focused on the expression of a person's wishes and preferences;
- A person's wishes and preferences must always be recognised and respected, regardless of communication challenges;
- It excludes substitution in the process of decision-making;
- The support is time-limited, it is tailored to the person's needs, and is subject to regular review.

No one is (or can be) protected against making wrong decisions and choices. Anyone can make a "wrong" decision, regardless of their physical or mental status, when the decision concerns issues requiring specialised competence. The potential for persons with mental health problems or intellectual disabilities to make a mistake or what others may perceive to be an incorrect or unreasonable decision should not serve as grounds for restricting their rights, just as it should not serve as grounds to restrict the rights of persons without disabilities in similar circumstances. Not everyone can make complex financial or medical decisions for the simple reason of not fully understanding relevant information and appreciating all the potential consequences. We all draw on informal support networks or seek professional advice in making decisions. The draft law aims to regulate a set of instruments for providing support to persons with intellectual disabilities and mental health problems on this same basis: use of informal decision-making support as used by people without disabilities and access to professional advice as needed. The difference is that under the draft law the person with a disability would go through a fair procedure for designating support measures, and thereby obtain formal legal recognition of this informal support as the basis of their new legal status. This process does not concern the issue of whether the decision is correct or not (which would imply another paradigm, that of "best interest").

The relationship of trust between the supported person and the supporting one is the basis of the Bulgarian supported decision-making model. The supporting person should be trusted by and have significance for the supported person and is obliged to communicate the supported person's decision in the most credible way, acting exclusively in their interest and based on their wishes and preferences. By definition, a relationship of trust should exclude undue influence, violence, or abuse by the supporting person. The quality of the relationship is assessed by the court which rules also on the support measures with various degrees of intensity. The supporting person is obliged to perform their obligations in person, which may include: (i) providing assistance by explaining in an accessible way the information needed to make the decision, and providing assistance with consultations with specialists, meetings and communication with persons affected by the decision, and other persons; (ii) providing assistance with receiving in an accessible format any information, consultations and documents needed to make the decision; (iii) providing help with clarifying the supported person's wishes and preferences, and with formulating and expressing the decision; (iv) taking responsibility where appropriate for implementation of the supported person's decision; and (v) informing the persons affected by the legal action that it is carried out via supported decision-making.

A specific feature of the Bulgarian understanding of supported decision-making is its reliance on the concept of "wishes and preferences," rather than the concept of "will", which is used in the CRPD Article 12. According to conservative legal doctrine in Bulgaria, will is mainly inherent to a rational person. This doctrine understands that a cognitive deficit results in vices or weakness of will. In order to break out of this paradigm, the draft law refers to expressing "wishes and preferences" as a stage in the decision-making process. In view of the specifics and the complexity of certain legal actions, the person concerned does not need to understand the very essence of these legal actions; it suffices that he/she expresses a wish and preference to be supported by a specific person and shows that he/she understands this supportive role.

The existing legal framework justifies restricting legal capacity as a safeguard to prevent harmful consequences that could arise from poor decisions. In contrast, the draft law aims to change the legal framework by ensuring, through means of tailored support, that people with disabilities can exercise their rights on an equal basis with others. In relation to safeguarding the rights of people with disabilities, the current legislation uses the term "protection," which is also used in the Constitution and in the judgment of the Constitutional Court delivered in case No 10/2014. The meaning[12] of the word "protection" in the Bulgarian language is "prevention, provision, patronage". It implies relations of authority and subordination between two subjects, with the subordinated one receiving prevention, provision and patronage from the one in authority; in other words, a vertical, hierarchical relationship. It denotes people with disabilities as passive objects. The draft law and the concept of supported decision-making introduce the term "support" whose meaning[13] in the Bulgarian language is "assistance, foundation, aid". This meaning implies active steps taken by a subject for which he/she is assisted by another subject, i.e., interaction between two subjects who relate and act in a mutual, horizontal relationship. In this context, the understanding of supported decision-making introduced by the draft law challenges the existing paradigm that people with disabilities are objects of protection, and, in contrast, demonstrates an understanding that any individual, irrespective of whether they have a disability and of how serious it is, can exercise their rights in person if they receive the necessary support to help them cope with the challenges of the outside world.

2. CHANGES IN JURISPRUDENCE AND THE PRACTICE OF THE COURTS

Although the draft law was not passed in 2016, a change of the paradigm has been observed in jurisprudence. The main court cases affected by this change are: cases related to mandatory and forced medical treatment under the Healthcare Act; cases related to placement under guardianship under the Persons and Family Act; and cases related to accommodation under the Social Services Act (before 2020, under the Social Assistance Act[14]).

2.1. THE LEGISLATIVE PARADIGM

The Bulgarian judiciary, being part of the continental system, is not easily influenced by provisions of general principle (even ones adopted within international legal instruments which, following ratification, become part of

---

[12] Dictionary of the Bulgarian Language.
[13] Dictionary of the Bulgarian Language.
[14] In response to the recommendations of the Court of Human Rights in Strasbourg in the cases *Stanev v. Bulgaria* 2012 and *Stankov v. Bulgaria* 2015, in 2016 Bulgarian law amended the procedure for the placement of persons under full guardianship in residential services: judicial review over such placement was introduced only in respect of persons under full guardianship (as for persons under partial guardianship who can express their will together with the custodian, it was considered that their consent was always taken into account); the procedure includes receiving the person's consent, and the guardian expressing an opinion on the

the domestic law). Courts tend to apply these general provisions (for instance, the standards laid down in Article 12 of CRPD) only as they are developed in specific legal norms and instruments of the material and procedural law. A more substantial change occurs when the law offers specific mechanisms recognising a person's expressed wishes. For example, the new Social Services Act, contains a requirement to review the placement of persons under full guardianship in residential care, as discussed below.

Persons with mental disabilities who are involved in these cases should be regarded as vulnerable, and the provision of information about their rights, as well as the efficient guarantees of these rights should be ensured by taking into consideration their specific needs, including the need for support. In such proceedings, the court should act as a guarantor of the person's rights and interests. The discussion on all the facts and evidence regarding the person's state and functioning are, in combination, crucial for the assessment of the existence of the legal criterion for restricting legal capacity (i.e., the existence of a risk), and for the analysis of the necessity and proportionality of the measure. Therefore, the court should draw an overall picture, not just a partial perspective based only on the expert report. Rather, the court should receive evidence about the environment in which the person lives, and the need for social support, its intensity and effect – these assessments are generally not incorporated (except in a very few cases) in the practice of the court. Providing additional support to the court in this regard will assist it in making the analysis essential to determining support measures.

A serious obstacle to such analyses continues to be the tools used by the court (including by the other auxiliary professions) which reproduce the old models of disability and incapacity. Of primary concern is the medical expert assessment of the disability, which is mostly carried out by doctors and psychiatrists, and which does not provide any answers to the questions that are fundamental for the court (i.e., how does the persons act in relation to decision-making areas in question and under various conditions, and what supports would assist the person?). Instead, it reaffirms the person's helplessness and sums up the absence of capacity as a result of the disability. The context in which these judgments are made is not analysed. However, against this predominant trend, there has been a "breakthrough" in the practice of the Bulgarian courts as a result of the new Social Services Act, which makes it possible for the court, irrespective of the restricted general legal capacity (i.e., when placed under guardianship following the procedure of PFA) for the person to seek and use new options for communicating their will.

---

issue. Bulgarian law introduced this judicial review in order to address the risk of breaching Article 5 of the ECHR – Deprivation of liberty – which the ECtHR had found in the cases of *Stanev* and *Stankov*, who had not expressed *de facto* and *de jure* their consent to being accommodated at the said institutions.

While the new law lays down minimum safeguards for participation in person and for fair court proceedings (including, the court reviewing the consent of the person under guardianship to be placed in a residential care facility, ensuring the person's consent regardless of the position of the guardian, the three-year time limit of the placement, etc.), practical experience shows that the formality of the procedures continues to be the main barrier. In many cases, subjects are vulnerable persons who are, on the one hand, poor and socially dependent and, on the other hand, limited in their active communication. As a result, they are often defended via legal aid. However, lawyers providing legal aid often lack specialised knowledge and preparation for working with this group.

A related issue is limited capacity to support communication. The court is obliged to get a "personal impression" of the individual. Except for a hearing/interview conducted by the judge, there are almost no other means and options used in practice to assist the court in acquiring these personal impressions such as, for example, involving social service providers who have specific expert knowledge and skills to analyse the factors determining the individuals' behaviour, which is crucial in terms of medical, social, and behavioural interventions.

In this respect, an interesting element of the court practice in several court hearings of the Sofia Regional Court is using the interpretive support provided through the supporters in a supported decision-making arrangement. When the provisions of the Social Assistance Act regarding the supervision over placement became effective, the initial approach of the court was a formal one: the court usually relied on the opinion of the social services which does not focus much on the person's consent but rather on the statement that declares that the relevant institution is a good place for the person to live, and he/she has nowhere else to go. In the case 516916/2018 and 524739/2018 (the first of this kind) the judge held that the law is clear in terms of what it stipulates. The court applies two new analyses which help it decide the extent to which the conditions for consent exist: (i) the court appoints an expert assessment by a psychiatrist which includes an analysis of the environment and the conditions in which the person functions; and (ii) appoints a supported decision-making interpreter (which is an innovation in court proceedings) whereby it accepts that the said person has difficulties communicating. This innovation of interpretive support involves development of a special procedure before the court, including a general protocol to be applied in respect of the person, and a special/individualised protocol showing the specific characteristics of the person's communication.

In some of the subsequent cases, this practice was further developed, including by means of a new type of expert tasked with assessing the person's communication capacities and needs and, most importantly, providing recommendations on how to ensure the needed conditions are in place in the proceedings for supporting and interpreting this communication. This is a major innovation in implementing a multi-disciplinary approach to ensuring fair access to judicial proceedings, particularly because it offers more safeguards for ensuring the person's participation and judicial respect for their expressed will.

2.2. POVERTY: NOT A LEGAL RISK

Whatever the initiatives for amending the legislation or training the professionals involved in the process or its preparation, the outcome will be undermined unless the legitimate goal, and not the legal one, comes to the forefront: unless the person is provided with a real choice (not a choice between the street and the institution); unless attention is given to all those pre-trial matters which concern the person's life and the support he/she receives, and which, in spite of the person's wish, neither the court, nor the prosecutor or the defence lawyer can solve to the benefit of the individual.

3. CHANGES IN THE "SOCIAL LAWS" WHICH INTRODUCE SUPPORTED DECISION-MAKING

Although the National Persons Support Measures Act was not passed in 2016, several factors, such as the ratification of CRPD; the concept for changing the regime of legal capacity adopted by the Council of Ministers in 2012; the three public discussions of NLSMA; and the numerous workshops and conferences on the topic, changed[15] the discourse not only on how people with disabilities should exercise their rights in person, but also the meaning of legal capacity in the context of today, and the possibility to distinguish between the possibility to hold rights and the possibility to exercise them.[16]

3.1. CONSENT TO PLACEMENT IN A RESIDENTIAL SERVICE

The first change concerned the placement in residential care of persons under full guardianship. In 2016 the Ministry of Labour and Social Policy initiated a change in the Social Support Act. The provisions of Articles 16a, 16b, and 16c of the Act introduced judicial review for the placement in residential services of

---

[15] The Next Step Program initiated more than 100 events devoted to changing the paradigm, with more than 15,000 participants (Bulgaria Centre for Not-for-Profit Law, data from 2020).

[16] N. Shabani, P. Alexieva, P. Dimitrova, A. Genova and V. Todorova, "New Formula for Legal capacity: article 12 from UNCRPD" (2014) 1 *Legal Thoughts* 91; S. Stavru, "Incapacity of Natural Persons to Act: Contemporary Challenges" (2016) *Bulgarian Centre for Not for Profit Law: Sofia*; R. Yankulova, "Rights to vote and people with ID and MHP" (2016) 3 *Legal Thoughts* 20; S. Stavru, "Is there a legislative alternative to guardianship for persons considered incapable?" (2018) 2 *Legal Thoughts* 28; R. Yankulova, "The Guardianship in the legislation of the European constitutional courts" (2017) 3 *Legal Thoughts* 3.

persons under full guardianship. These legal norms were replicated in the Social Services Act (SSA).[17] Pursuant to this legislation, the provision of social services to individuals under full guardianship shall be in conformity with the person's wishes and the opinion of their guardian and, in the event of conflict, the wish of the person in need of a social service has priority.

Requests for the accommodation of a person under full guardianship in a specialised institution or a community-based residential social service are within the competence of the regional court with jurisdiction over the person's current residence address. Within this procedure, the court can gather evidence on its own initiative, and is obliged to examine the will of the person whose accommodation has been requested, including by means of expert witnesses. It is worth mentioning that the above-mentioned laws use the term "consent" only in relation to solving one single issue – does the person wish to be accommodated in a residential service? Despite its limited application, this requirement to attend to the wishes of the person is a significant innovation insofar as persons under full guardianship are recognised to have the ability to express a legally valid consent (will) on specific matters. Prior to the Act, such consent was entirely denied by the legal doctrine and the general norm under Article 5 of the Persons and Family Act. The new law provides for the person to participate in proceedings in person, including the legal option for the court hearing to take place outside the courthouse, at the whereabouts of the individual. During the proceedings, the possibilities for care in a family environment or placement in a community-based residential social service are considered. This conclusion reasonably ensues from the provision of Article 16c of the Social Support Act which stipulates that the request for accommodation in a specialised institution can be granted only where the proceedings do not identify a possibility for the individual to be taken care of in a family environment or placed in a community-based residential social service.

The request for accommodation is submitted by the Social Assistance Directorate based on the person's wish declared in writing and the guardian's opinion. The following are attached thereto: a report with an opinion on the possibilities to ensure care for the person in a family environment; an assessment of the person's needs; an individual support plan; and an information note on the existing appropriate community-based social services and specialised institutions in the territory of the region and the vacancies in them.

Similar provisions are contained in the Social Services Act which repealed the provisions of Articles 16a, 16b, and 16c of the Social Support Act. The legal provisions contain the following safeguards to assure the right of access by persons under full guardianship to an impartial court, and include:

---

[17] Enacted on 01.07.2020.

- an examination of the persons' will, their opinion, wishes, and preferences;
- participation of the person in the proceedings;
- examination of possibilities to ensure care for the person in a family environment or in the community;
- proportionality of the measures ruled by the court;
- preparing the court and the other participants in the proceedings for working with persons with intellectual disabilities and/or mental health problems who are under full guardianship;
- expeditious and efficient judicial proceedings.

As noted above, control over the placement and the requirement to obtain the person's consent, despite the full restriction of their legal capacity, was the first step, and an important one, towards the recognition of the full and unequivocal implementation of the paradigm of full legal capacity in compliance with the standards laid down in Article 12.

3.2. SUPPORT MEASURES FOR ENSURING ACCESS TO JUSTICE IN CONFORMITY WITH THE PERSONS WITH DISABILITIES ACT

A new Persons with Disabilities Act was passed in 2018 (effective as from 2019). For the first time, the law made a clear and systematic attempt to introduce some of the standards of Articles 12 and 13 of CRPD with the purpose of changing the legal and social paradigm for people with disabilities. Also, for the first time, "supported decision making" is defined in law, stipulating that any person with a disability who has serious difficulties with the individual exercise of rights in relation to specific legal actions shall be entitled to supported decision-making, which is determined under the procedure laid down in the law for the provision of support measures.

The law explicitly stipulates that supported decision-making is a combination of social interventions with the aim to provide support for making decisions which have legal consequences and will yield specific results for the person with a disability. The law clarifies "serious difficulties" to refer to situations where a person with a disability:

1. does not understand the information on which the decision to perform a specific legal action is based;
2. does not assess the nature and the consequences of the specific legal action;
3. is unable, in the process of making a specific decision, to link the information under point 1. to the assessment of consequences under point 2.

An important point is that the law does not consider it to be a "serious difficulty" where the person is unable to independently express their wishes and preferences via generally accepted means of communication, provided that the person uses ways and means appropriate to their state, including non-verbal forms of communication, for example utilising visual representations, etc.

It should be highlighted that the Persons with Disabilities Act introduces the possibility for special support to be provided to persons with intellectual disabilities to enable them to communicate their wishes and preferences. Furthermore, the law explicitly stipulates that support measures be designed to facilitate the person seeking support in exercise of their rights. In summary, the provisions require that for a support measure to be provided: (i) the persons concerned must have difficulties understanding information, appreciating consequences and communicating with a third party, and (ii) the support measures should provide the person with means to express their wishes and help them better understand and appreciate information relevant to the decision.

Moreover, the support provided must not result in undue influence on the part of the supporting person, nor substitute the supported person's will with the supporting person's will. This means that where family members/relatives act as supporting persons, their potential conflicts of interest in decisions they are supporting must be considered (e.g., where a supported person's property would be transferred to their supporting person on whom they are reliant for communication). Additionally, providing supportive communication measures must not be used to override the supported person's expressed wishes by conveying instead the perspectives and messages of supporters.

Recognised support measures include:

1. consultations with a trained professional;
2. provision of specialised services for supported decision-making;
3. ensuring a mentor for assistance with the decision-making;
4. developing an anti-crisis plan;
5. supported decision-making via appropriate supporting measures;
6. applying protection and safeguarding measures.

These types of interventions are aimed at assisting the person to communicate and express their wishes, and are to be designed to:

1. explain the essence of the legal action and the consequences therefrom;
2. assist the supported person with understanding the role of other participants in the decision-making process, or those affected by it;

3. assist the supported person with expressing their wishes and preferences in a way understandable to the others;
4. provide any other assistance related to carrying out the legal action.

Recognising support measures for a specific person must be done in compliance with the following principles:

1. the need for each measure;
2. respect for the wishes and preferences of the supported person;
3. proportionality, timeliness, and flexibility;
4. avoiding conflicts of interest, and undue influence;
5. exhausting support measures prior to applying any protective measures which may restrict legal capacity.

The law also requires that the designated supporting person shall be a person with whom the supported person has a relationship of trust.

Underlying all these provisions is a general obligation on the judicial authorities and all government institutions to ensure that people with disabilities have the same access to justice as any other individuals, including by providing procedural and age-appropriate measures for support in all court proceedings and support determination. To this end, training programs for working with people with disabilities have been included in the curricula of the National Institute of Justice and the Academy with the Ministry of Interior.

Thus, the changes made to date offer a very good opportunity to introduce supported decision-making as an alternative social intervention to restrictions on legal capacity. We emphasise, however, that this is a *social* intervention, and does not allow for the full and unequivocal application of Article 12 to ensure that people with disabilities can exercise their right to legal capacity on an equal basis with others.

In summary, we can say that the public awareness and political campaigns associated with efforts to secure adoption of the Natural Persons Supports Measures Act contributed to changing the policy environment and the institutional culture of disability in Bulgaria. However, the passage of time has weakened political momentum for this more substantive reform. While the legislative reforms under the Social Services Act and the Social Support Act are important and decisive for recognising the entitlement of people with disabilities to exercise their rights in person, they remain palliative in nature and fall short. They do not transform the general regime of legal capacity, as would be accomplished with the adoption into law of the draft Natural Persons Supports Measures Act. Nevertheless, the changes in the social sphere, currently outstripping those in the legal domain, indicate a greater sensitivity to the rights of persons with disabilities than has otherwise been seen to date.

4. LESSONS LEARNT AND MAIN CONCLUSIONS FOR THE WAY FORWARD

Given that transformational change in the legal status and rights of persons with disabilities with respect to legal capacity has not yet been secured despite enormous efforts, it is helpful to step back and reflect on lessons learnt about how change can happen. Four main aspects of the change process are considered: (i) the essence of the change sought; (ii) the leadership for making the change happen; (iii) the contextual possibilities for change; and (iv) how you get to the "tipping point" which signals the beginning of substantial and transformational change.

4.1. THE FOCUS OF CHANGE

In terms of the change to be advocated for, it is essential to move beyond the level of principle as articulated in the Convention itself and the General Comment on Article 12, which guides its interpretation. Human rights organisations often make the mistake of restricting their calls for change to this level – making claims to implement the CRPD, for example. Instead, we have learnt that the claims need to be more specific, proposing a more detailed interpretation applicable to the national context. In our case, this was accomplished through the development of the pilot programs. However, one does assume a huge risk in advancing interpretations, because they can be rejected by the interpretive decisions of constitutional courts.

4.2. LEADERSHIP

The second factor – leadership – often becomes the cornerstone of the reform. Who is the major agent of the change, its planning, involving other stakeholders, and communicating it? The answers to this question will have a significant impact on the outcome of the change efforts. As for the Bulgarian context, the strongest natural driving force were the parents' organisations. What is unique about the Bulgarian program is that it built a strong core of collaboration and synchronising of efforts among the legal team (the think-tank behind the legal reform and the proposals), the professionals (who had the knowledge and the motivation to do the Next Step Program) and the parents (who believed that, without the reform, all their efforts aimed at the well-being of their children would have only partial effect and eventually, in particular after their death, their children would be left without control over their lives and could experience serious hardship as a result). It is the synergy of these three elements that produced the fuel to keep the engine running over these eight years along all the lines of activity which together achieved the overall effect. Had we missed one of these elements, we certainly would not have achieved as much as we have to date. However, we must reiterate that it was the dedication of the parents' group and their refusal to back down in the most difficult moments (like the discussions at the National Assembly, and the attacks from other organisations) that fuelled the motivation and commitment of the legal team and the professionals. The strongest motivation for the Bulgarian parents were the dilemmas they confronted and accepted: (i) if guardianship remained in place, the effect of everything they have achieved in terms of social inclusion (social services, education, employment) for their family members would become pointless (because *de facto* and *de jure* guardianship results in isolation and substitution of the person); (ii) unless strong legal foundation and recognition could be secured for the informal forms of support in the community which the team had created, these forms of support could easily be "taken over" by other legal instruments (with guardianship continuing to be effective as the option of last resort). The strongest driver which will keep the Bulgarian movement going – at present and in the future – is the parents' movement.[18]

4.3. THE CENTRAL AND EASTERN EUROPEAN CONTEXT: SOCIAL AND POLITICAL FACTORS

Several broad trends in Central and Eastern Europe contributed to the challenges we faced and have strongly influenced the effectiveness of our change efforts. Poverty and social exclusion affect large groups of the population (not only people with disabilities), which severely constrains the social and community capacity to create and implement support measures for people with disabilities. In addition, there are immense barriers to accessing to all the systems which are relevant to health and social well-being – for example, healthcare, social assistance, and employment. Discriminatory attitudes towards people with disabilities as "different", combined with family-oriented values which justify exclusion and restrictions on the rights of persons with disabilities are endemic, posing huge barriers to overcome.[19]

In addition to these trends over the last 30 years, we must also mention: (i) the rising political (and constitutional) populism which undermines the values of social solidarity and support for marginalised groups, values which

---

[18] We clarify that when we use "parents" we mean the parents of children with an intellectual disability; the community of parents of persons with mental health difficulties had weak representation.

[19] Public attitudes toward people with intellectual disabilities and mental health problems, Alpha research, 2018.

are elemental to our proposals for change; and (ii) the growing anti-human rights and the anti-NGO rhetoric which has very serious consequences in a less developed environment, where NGOs are fewer and have more limited resources, including for mobilising activities to counter these attacks. Unless these issues of the broader environment are addressed, it will not be possible to achieve the balanced solutions we are after.

We have confronted these negative trends by prioritising the pilot program approach in order to demonstrate that here and now, in the Bulgarian context, solutions other than guardianship are possible, regardless of how underdeveloped the systems are, and how insurmountable the obstacles to inclusion seem. We have learnt that our efforts will eventually be successful to the extent that we can continue working to change the broader context, while making sure that our calls for change are not so strong that they are doomed in an environment still structurally unable to address the problems we raise.

4.4. CHANGING THE LAW VERSUS CHANGING COMMUNITIES

There is an important tension that should be highlighted in this part of the world generally, as well as in the context of our initiative. That is, the wish to strategically use law reform to more quickly drive needed changes in social and legal practice, while at the same time requiring social transformations to take hold in practice in order to build the momentum, leadership, and public support on which substantial law reform is dependent. It is a classic "chicken and egg" problem. Which comes first? We found that pushing too hard and too quickly on law reform can breed rejection and resistance (which, in turn, often fuels the populist political attitudes). A top-down approach by means of imposing new standards was applied both in Bulgaria's accession to the EU and in the advocacy strategy of the civil organisations and movements. This process contributed to accumulated disappointment at ground level since despite securing certain legislative changes, (including the ratification of CRPD), they did not lead to positive change in the daily lives of individuals. This challenge made it imperative for the Next Step Program to include and enhance several strategies to counter (or at least diminish) this negative effect. These included:

(a) public awareness campaigning and mobilising the community for to advocate for change;
(b) introducing and adopting action research on an ongoing basis to learn from participants at ground level, including not only the groups leading the change strategy but also other leaders in the community whose involvement is needed in order to reach the tipping point for structural change; and, above all

(c) enhancing the potential of community-based projects (through supporting the lead organisations, local leaders, outstanding jurists, bankers, and even a basketball club, among others, whose active role in advocacy was invaluable).

We have come to understand that the needed changes, top-down and bottom-up, may take more time to achieve than at first anticipated. But by creating solid community and legal foundations, the transformed social practices that enable equal rights of legal capacity will be more resilient over time. They will not be so dependent on changing political and social priorities on the public agenda. In this context, leaders of the initiative and those whose voices are at the forefront of the change process (the parents' and self-advocates' groups) will gain more self-confidence and determination to undertake efforts and actions to make a lasting difference in people's lives.

5. CONCLUSION

To what extent has everything achieved so far – the demonstration and scaling of supported decision-making practice, the initial legislative recognition of support measures, and increase in public awareness – been established securely enough to make the changes irreversible? And is it only a matter of time before the overall change of the legal capacity paradigm (the law, its application, the practice) will inevitably occur?

We can say for certain that the theoretical and practical implications of the new paradigm of legal capacity presented the legal community is a huge challenge. However, it has also become clear that maintaining and applying the guardianship regime exclusively is unthinkable. The reason is not so much that Bulgaria has ratified the CRPD, and so necessary changes should follow, but rather that members of the legal community increasingly experience that the old legislation cannot deliver on the legitimate goal for which it was developed – namely, the protection of individual rights. Nor does it meet the needs for protection of other parties, in particular, third parties who have an interest in ensuring the legitimacy of transactions with a person with a disability and of the legal consequences that follow from them. Moreover, the high price for society of the "civil death" of an increasing proportion of the population is evident.

With these developments, the opinion of the Bulgarian legal community has changed irreversibly. What is still in question and under discussion is what the alternatives to guardianship will be. Should guardianship be replaced with an alternative regime or is its revocation sufficient? And if an alternative regime of supported decision-making is adopted is this new legal construct possible on a systemic scale? And if so, should guardianship still be preserved as a measure of last resort for "serious" cases? These latter two options – an alternative regime of supported decision-making with guardianship as a last resort – are, indeed, at the centre of the philosophical and practical debate that the Bulgarian legal community continues to conduct in its attempt to develop a viable approach in the current context. Over the course of this debate, it is interesting to note that it is the younger jurists (judges, lawyers, etc.) who are predominantly bolder in their views and braver in believing that guardianship should be replaced with a legal regime of supported decision-making because it based on and consistent with a recognition of rights of the person.

Some key factors can explain this shift. In part, this younger generation in Bulgaria has more opportunities to travel, share professional knowledge and practice with colleagues from other countries, as well as apply legislation based on new values and approaches. Another factor to highlight is the change achieved in social services and interventions. The debates and the trainings have led professionals to begin applying a supported decision-making approach. Furthermore, the format of social interventions is changing from a focus on providing care to ensuring respect for rights and, above all, rejecting the "best interests" principle in favour of respect for a person's authentic wishes and preferences as the guide in supporting a person in decision-making processes. While introducing supported decision-making into social care needs further investments, new professional methods and standards in this area appear to be most quickly adopted and can help to drive change in the legal and other spheres.[20]

One of the most important changes that we have achieved is the organisational change of the actors leading this reform. Both organisational culture and their approaches to intervention have undergone a transformation (regardless of whether they are projects, social services, etc.). The change is manifested, first and foremost, in the approach to interacting with and engaging the individual with intellectual disabilities or mental health problems. Potential difficulties in communication are no longer regarded as an individual problem, but the result of barriers in the broader social context including perceptions of a person's history and behaviour, and the ways they have been interpreted by others over time.

Finally, what has irretrievably changed is the public perception of guardianship – now clearly recognised as a restriction on the person imposed by the external world, not the measure of protection it was assumed to be. That is the most important accomplishment of the Bulgarian campaign to

---

[20] One example of this is with the special expert witnesses in court proceedings who provide interpretive support to a person in their capacity as decision-making supporters.

date: shifting the cultural, social, and legal paradigm of legal capacity. The campaign succeeded in avoiding a reactive public response and discourse: "*Someone* from abroad is imposing it on us." Instead, having taken stock of the inadequacy and violations of the guardianship system, the need for change is now widely recognised especially considering the effectiveness of the supported decision-making alternative.

EVALUATING THE INDUCTION OF ARTICLE 12 JURISPRUDENCE IN INDIAN LAW

Is Half a Loaf Better?

Amita DHANDA[*]

1. Introduction 221
2. Indian Laws and Legal Capacity................................. 222
3. Reforming Legal Capacity....................................... 225
   3.1. Law Reform Process 225
       3.1.1. Persons with Disabilities Act 225
       3.1.2. The Mental Health Law 227
   3.2. The Many Incarnations of Legal Capacity 228
       3.2.1. Persons with Disabilities Act...................... 228
       3.2.2. The Mental Health Care Act 2017................... 230
4. Legal Capacity and the Courts: *Suchita Srivastav v. Chandigarh Administration*.. 233
5. So what is the Verdict?... 235

1. INTRODUCTION

All advocates for change have to battle with dilemmas on the pace and process of the change that is being demanded. Should it be gradual or radical? Is it acceptable to make concessions and carry everyone along or should an inflexible stance be adopted as every concession would only prolong the rule of the old and provide the semblance of change only? Robert Caro in his biography on Robert Moses has a telling paragraph documenting the impatience of a leading politician with idealism and the idealist's inability to compromise.[1] Such people, the politician

---

[*]   Professor Emerita, NALSAR University of Law, Hyderabad, India.
[1]   R. A. CARO, *The power broker: Robert Moses and the fall of New York*, Alfred A Knopf Incorporated, New York, 1974.

Intersentia

bemoans, "were willing to devote their lives to fighting for principle and wanted to make that fight without compromise or surrender of any part of the ideals with which they had started it",[2] even if the unwillingness to compromise causes real losses to those for whose mission they battle. The paragraph made me wonder, can idealists only be categorised as inflexible impediments? Also, if change is being visualised, is it enough only to agonise on the substance of the change, or is it also important to reflect on how the change should be executed?

Article 12 of the United Nations Convention on the Rights of Persons with Disabilities (hereinafter CRPD) has often been referred to as effecting a paradigm shift in the legal understanding of legal capacity by recognising that all persons with disabilities possessed it and the accessing of support to exercise legal capacity in no way negated the existence of capacity. I have elsewhere recounted the ebb and flow accompanying the adoption of this article in the United Nations.[3] Since India follows the dualist system of international law, the Convention becomes part of Indian law only after the enactment of domestic legislation. This chapter will analyse: the seven year-long process of inducting Article 12 into Indian law; the tension between the demands made by various stakeholders at different points in time and the final text adopted by the legislature. Since the motivations of the various stakeholders were different, the final text gives everyone a look in; but no one has got all that they wanted (it has not satisfied everyone). It is this final result, which causes me to ask, whether half a loaf is better?

2. INDIAN LAWS AND LEGAL CAPACITY

In this section I undertake a short description of the Indian laws which needed to be amended in order to fulfil India's commitment to the CRPD. These laws can be classified as general and special. The special laws which were laws made with special focus on disability included: the Persons with Disabilities Act of 1995;[4] the Mental Health Act of 1987;[5] the National Trust for (Persons with Autism, Cerebral Palsy, Mental Retardation and Multiple Disabilities) Act of 1999[6] and the Rehabilitation Council of India Act 1992.[7] The general laws are laws which

---

[2]   CARO (n. 1), p. 135.

[3]   A. DHANDA, "Legal capacity in the disability rights convention: stranglehold of the past or lodestar for the future" (2006) *Syracuse J. Int'l L. & Com.*, 34, 429.

[4]   An Act to give effect to the Proclamation on the Full Participation and Equality of the People with Disabilities in the Asian and Pacific Region, 1995, *Ministry Of Law, Justice And Company Affairs*, 1 January 1996, India.

[5]   The Mental Health Act 1987, *Ministry Of Law And Justice*, 22 May 1987, India.

[6]   The National Trust Act, No. 44, *Ministry Of Law, Justice And Company Affairs*, 30 December 1999, India.

[7]   The Rehabilitation Council of India Act, 1 September 1992, India.

have been made for non-disabled people but which may have a specific provision which impacts on persons with disabilities.[8]

The Persons with Disabilities Act of 1995 contains a detailed impairment-specific definition of disability, primarily provided for socio-economic entitlements for the impairments included in the statute.[9] The statute was silent on the question of civil-political rights and the exhaustive definition made the statute exclusionary. To bring the statute in harmony with the CRPD, its exclusionary perspective needed to be rectified. The Constitution of India guarantees civil-political rights to all persons or citizens as the case may be. Since discrimination on grounds of disability was not expressly prohibited[10] fundamental rights could be denied to persons with intellectual, psychosocial or developmental impairments without breaching the Constitution. To remedy this discriminatory situation the matter of universal legal capacity with support needed to be addressed to enable the Persons with Disabilities Act to conform to the CRPD.

The Mental Health Act of 1987 primarily addressed the matter of compulsory commitment to psychiatric institutions. The statute allowed voluntary treatment[11] but leaned towards compulsory care as it allowed medical judgment prevail over the will and preference of the person with mental illness.[12] The statute also provided for a procedure by which a person with mental illness could lose the right to manage property and a guardian could be appointed to take care of them.[13] The ratification of the CRPD made it imperative that the routine deprivation of life and liberty allowed by the Mental Health Act of 1987 be subject to scrutiny.

The National Trust Act was a law which only concerned itself with the four named impairments.[14] Although the statute contained a provision which allowed the designated authority to consider whether or not a person with the

---

[8]   For a detailed treatment of these other laws and the disqualifications imposed by them see A. DHANDA, *Legal order and mental disorder*, Sage, New Delhi, 2000.

[9]   Section 2(i) of the Act defines disability to mean "blindness, low vision, leprosy-cured, hearing impairment, mental retardation, locomotor disability and mental illness". An Act to give effect to the Proclamation on the Full Participation and Equality of the People with Disabilities in the Asian and Pacific Region (n. 4).

[10]   Art. 14 of the Indian Constitution prohibits the State from denying to any person "equality before the law and equal protection of the laws within the territory of India." Articles 15 and 16, however, only prohibit discrimination on grounds of religion, race, caste, sex, place of birth or any of them.

[11]   The Mental Health Act (n. 5), s. 15.

[12]   Ibid., section 18(3) authorised the medical superintendent of a hospital to refuse the discharge of a voluntary patient if they believed that such discharge was not in the interest of the voluntary patient.

[13]   Ibid., section 52.

[14]   Autism, Cerebral Palsy, Mental Retardation and Multiple Disabilities. The National Trust Act (n. 6).

named impairment needed a guardian, the statute, for the most part, endorsed the appointment of a guardian for persons with the included impairments.[15] Since the appointment was seen as unproblematic, the procedure of appointing a guardian did not have the fair process rigour found in the Mental Health Act 1987. The CRPD would again require that the unproblematic guardianship model of the National Trust Act be dismantled and a regime of capacity with support be constructed.

The Rehabilitation Council of India Act 1992 was primarily concerned with ensuring quality control in the services provided by professionals working in the field of disability. Although the statute needed to look at the matter of disability expertise and peer-to-peer support, the question of legal capacity was only obliquely relevant in this legislation.

In addition to these special laws, nearly all general laws contained provisions by which persons with intellectual and psychosocial disabilities were denied the right to contract, to manage property, to marry, be appointed guardian or retain custody of children. These special provisions in general laws undermined the recognition accorded to legal capacity of all persons with disabilities in the CRPD. In order to fulfil the commitments India had assumed by ratifying the CRPD, a repeal or amendment of all these provisions was also required.

A comprehensive harmonising of Indian Law with the CRPD would have required that all the aforesaid Indian Laws were put on the anvil of reform. However, as the following section will show, the law reform process was limited to the Disabilities Act 1995 and the Mental Health Act 1987. The National Trust did undertake several law reforms exercises, however. their efforts remained restricted to the offices of the Trust, with some deliberations in the administrative ministry. There was, however, no legislative proposal taken to Parliament.[16] And now as the amendments to the Trust Act are being taken up, Article 12 or the CRPD are not the reform triggers.[17] The impact of special provisions on general laws would now largely be an interpretative exercise.[18]

---

[15] The National Trust Act (India), s. 14(3), 30 December 1999.

[16] The various proposals considered by the National Trust were amongst the most imaginative efforts to make universal legal capacity with support the norm in India. However, the government largely remained cold to the initiative. For an analytical description of the proposals see A. Dhanda, "A Disability Studies Reading of the Laws for Persons with Disabilities in India" in A. Ghai (ed), *Disability in South Asia: Knowledge and Experience*, Sage, India, 2018.

[17] The National Trust for Welfare of Persons with Autism, Cerebral Palsy, Mental Retardation and Multiple Disabilities (Amendment) Bill 2018 (India), 20 December 2018.

[18] One of the important rules of statutory interpretation allows special laws to prevail over general laws. This would mean that in a situation of conflict the special laws which have been amended would prevail. However, this would require someone to take the matter to court. Otherwise, the pre-CRPD laws in the Indian statute book will continue to occupy the field.

Evaluating the Induction of Article 12 Jurisprudence in Indian Law

In the next section, I examine how legal capacity was understood in the Disabilities Legislation and the Mental Health Law. Since the perspective of persons with disabilities is at variance from the non-disabled, it is important to also examine the participation provided to persons with disabilities in this law reform process. The Ministry of Social Justice and Empowerment thought, at first, that the Persons with Disabilities Act 1995 could be harmonised with the CRPD simply by amending it. Only when the amendments required became too innumerable was this idea abandoned, and it was decided that a new statute would need to be enacted to usher in the new paradigm of disability rights. The Ministry of Health from the very start proposed to replace the Mental Health Act 1987 with a CRPD-consonant new statute.

3. REFORMING LEGAL CAPACITY

This section is divided into two subsections. In the first I outline the process by which the reform process was inaugurated and in the second I discuss the various legal capacity formulations, which were deliberated upon as the making of the statutes proceeded from the consultation to the enactment process.

3.1. LAW REFORM PROCESS

3.1.1. *Persons with Disabilities Act*

For the new Persons with Disabilities Act the Union Government set up a multi-sectoral committee to formulate a disabilities rights law.[19] This included representatives from key ministries and some States but most of the governmental members on the Committee came on an occasional basis and either kept silent or voiced opinions; they did not engage with the issues confronting the Committee. The responsibility for formulating the draft law largely resided on the Committee and the Centre for Disability Studies at the National Academy of Legal Studies and Research, the legal consultant to the Committee.

One of the critical concerns of the Committee was to conduct its affairs in a participative manner. Upon the insistence of the disability sector, the

---

[19] The Ministry of Social Justice and Empowerment, by notification F.No. 16-38/2006-DD. III dated 30 April 2010, constituted a Committee chaired by Dr Sudha Kaul with members representing persons with disabilities, NGO's and experts from the disability sector, to draft a new law to replace the Persons with Disabilities (Equal Opportunities, Protection of Rights and Full Participation) Act 1995 ("PwD Act").

Intersentia

225

membership of the Committee was expanded to ensure that all impairments and all sectors were represented on the Committee. The nominated members felt accountable to their community and the disability sector did not want to be informed of the decisions of the Committee after the fact but wanted to be kept in the loop even as issues were being discussed. This need for wide-ranging consultation largely drove the procedure adopted by the Committee.

This consultation was ensured in several ways. The Committee formed sub-groups for all major issues that needed to be addressed by the statute. A number of experts in the sector who were not part of the Committee were invited to deliberate on the issue in the sub-groups, so that the expertise available to the Committee was wider than that possessed by the members of the Committee. Even though the Committee had a legal consultant of their own, the draft law was also scrutinised by a range of legal experts in a special consultation with legal experts.

In order to keep the disability sector in the loop, the minutes of each Committee meeting were put up on the website of the Ministry of Social Justice and Empowerment and can still be found on the website of the Centre for Disability Studies.[20]

There were two drafts of the proposed law which were opened for deliberation, with the Ministry providing financial support to members from the sector who wished to attend the consultations that took place in Delhi before the final report was submitted to the government. Since the people who could come to the nation's capital were necessarily limited, the penultimate draft of the law was consulted in the length and breadth of the country in the language of the province.[21] Sign language and braille copies of the draft report were also circulated. The Committee members travelled in all parts of the country explaining the law as well as receiving representations from stakeholders. If the Committee accepted any stakeholder's suggestion, the fact of this acceptance was recorded in the footnotes of the final report.[22]

This bare bones description of the process adopted by the Committee shows that participatory deliberation was the driving force of the procedure adopted by the Committee. In fact there were times at which one felt that the Committee

---

[20] "The Rights of Persons with Disabilities Bill 2011." Law and Policy Reform: Centre for Disability Studies. <https://disabilitystudiesnalsar.org/newlaw.php> accessed 13.03.2023.

[21] India has 22 official languages which find mention in Schedule VIII of the Constitution of India. In addition, there are 121 languages and 270 mother tongues. "Statement-1 Abstract of Speakers' Strength of Languages and Mother Tongues" <https://disabilitystudiesnalsar.org/newlaw.php> accessed 13.04.2023.

[22] "Final Report of the Committee on Drafting the Rights of Persons with Disabilities Bill 2011" Law and Policy Reform: Centre for Disability Studies. <https://disabilitystudiesnalsar.org/finalnewlawreport.php> accessed 13.04.2023.

deliberated more than it decided. At certain critical junctures the Committee was compelled to opt for closed door meetings in order to arrive at drafts which could then be opened for consultation.

The value of the consultation became obvious when the drafting of the law moved from the Committee to the Ministry. If transparency was the ruling guideline for the Committee, then secrecy dictated the operations of the Ministry. After this widely consulted report was submitted to the Ministry, a draft was shared in 2012,[23] which largely accepted the Report of the Committee on substantive rights and duties except for requiring economic entitlements to be related to the severity of the impairment. The Committee's design on authorities was, however, totally rejected and the government preferred to take a more conservative approach.

It was then leaked that the Ministry planned to adopt a mutilated version of the law.[24] This resulted in country-wide street protests, compelling the government to defer its plans and refer the proposed legislation to a Joint Parliamentary Committee. The Committee acknowledged the dismay of the sector and tried to bring about a compromise between the government and the sector. It especially asked the government to re-examine the guardianship provisions, but this recommendations was not heeded by the Ministry.

3.1.2. The Mental Health Law

Unlike the Disabilities Law, a more technocratic process was adopted to reform the Mental Health Law. The Ministry of Health and Family Welfare which was the Ministry in charge of administering matters of health set up a Committee consisting of a psychiatrist and a law professor to formulate the first draft of the Mental Health Law. This two-member body came up with the first draft which was then circulated for suggestions and two oral consultations were held in the north and south of the country. In comparison to the Disabilities Law, the process of the making of the draft was more closely monitored by the Ministry, who saw the matter primarily as one of care and treatment while some persons with psychosocial disability and their organisations asked for the social dimensions to be also addressed, and the will and preference of the person with disability respected in substance and not just form. The expert and the Ministry

---

[23] "The Draft Rights of Persons with Disabilities Bill, 2012" *Department of Disability Affairs, India.* <https://cdn.nic.in/SJ/PDFFiles/DisabilityBill2012.pdf> accessed 13.04.2023.

[24] Except for increasing the number of impairments to be covered by the law, the Bill of 2013 had eliminated every progressive provision of the Committee Bill as also government's own version of 2012 as recorded in the following source: K. GANZ, "What Is Wrong with the Leaked 'Mincemeat' Disabilities Bill 2013? Annotated & Explained, Section by Section, by Nalsar" (2014) Home – Legally India – Career Intelligence for Lawyers, Law Students.

preferred to stay with the psychiatric perspective.[25] Since the proponents of the psychosocial approach found little traction with the consultants and the Ministry, they decided to boycott the consultation proceedings in order to make a visible demonstration of their disagreement. The Ministry kept renewing the invitation to participate but did not change its stance. The activists felt that participation would legitimise the process adopted by the Ministry and hence did not accept the invitation. This legislation was also referred to the Joint Parliamentary Committee which invited representations and provided hearing to various stakeholders and many changes were introduced in the legislation.[26] However, the legal capacity provisions largely remained unchanged.

3.2. THE MANY INCARNATIONS OF LEGAL CAPACITY

3.2.1. *Persons with Disabilities Act*

As already discussed, the draft legislation submitted to the government was finalised after intense consultations. During these consultations, two major approaches came before the Committee: one whereby the Committee was asked to unequivocally recognise the legal capacity of all persons with disabilities and to suggest the repeal of all legal provisions by which such capacity was being denied. Persons subscribing to this view wanted persons with disabilities to be released from the shackles of guardianship by suggesting the repeal of various laws which provided for plenary guardianship. Such a change, they contended, was dictated by the CRPD and any other option militated against the form and spirit of the Convention.

In contradistinction to the groups advocating total autonomy (which were largely self-advocates) there were groups led by families of persons with disabilities who made a case for protection and objected to the one-size-fits-all advocacy of the autonomy group. They agitated for the retention of guardianship so that persons with disabilities who needed the support could obtain it. Even as several members of the group agreed with the CRPD vision of moving from substitution to support, such support, they pointed out, was still not available. To replace guardianship without the support structures being in place would be callous to the needs of several persons with disabilities.

Both groups agreed that all persons with disabilities had legal capacity and also had a right to seek support whether high or minimal or none. The point of discord was on what to do about guardianship?

---

[25]   Mental Healthcare Act 2017. <https://prsindia.org/files/bills_acts/bills_parliament/2013/Mental%20Healthcare%20Act,%202017.pdf> accessed 15.11.2022.

[26]   Most significantly the provision by which all suicides were seen as evidence of mental disorder was dropped.

The provision that found inclusion in the Committee's final report was an attempt to find a middle ground. The Final Report incorporated a provision whereby all plenary guardianships were to be transformed into limited guardianships by the force of the law.[27] This provision, which was a transitory arrangement, came along with an unequivocal assertion of legal capacity of all persons with disabilities.[28] In limited guardianship, the guardian was obligated to act in close consultation with the ward, fully respecting their will and preference. This arrangement was to subsist for a short period to enable the State and society to put in place support arrangements. The idea was to use the institution of limited guardianship as a ramp to transition from substitution to support. Consequently, whilst all plenary guardianships were made limited, the movement from limited to plenary was impermissible. Furthermore any denial of legal capacity on grounds of disability was made void in law[29] and explicit duties were placed on the State for provisioning support.[30] These provisions were aimed at obtaining consensus in the Committee, which it failed to do as all the proponents of the immediate abolition position chose to resign from the Committee.

---

[27] After the commencement of this Act, any provision in any legislation, rule, regulation or practice which prescribes for the establishment of plenary guardianship shall be hereinafter deemed to be establishing a system of limited guardianship.

[28] *"18. Right to Legal Capacity and Equal Recognition before the Law*

(1) Notwithstanding anything contained in any other law to the contrary, persons with disabilities enjoy legal capacity on an equal basis with others in all aspects of life and have the right to equal recognition everywhere as persons before the law;

(2) Any express or implied disqualification on the grounds of disability prescribed in any legislation, rule, notification, order bye-law, regulation, custom or practice which has the effect of depriving any person with disability of legal capacity shall not be legally enforceable from the date of enforcement of this Act;

(3) Notwithstanding anything contrary contained in any other law, all persons with disabilities have right, on an equal basis with others, to own or inherit property; control their financial affairs; obtain access to bank loans, mortgages and other forms of financial credit, and not to be arbitrarily deprived of their property;

(4) All persons with disabilities have the right to access all arrangements and support necessary for exercising legal capacity in accordance with their will and preferences;

(5) The legal capacity of a person with disability shall not be questioned or denied, irrespective of the degree and extent of support, by reason of accessing support to exercise legal capacity;"

[29] Any act, order or proceedings which has the effect of denying the legal capacity of a person with disability in any matter or which questions the legal capacity of a person with disability on the grounds of disability shall be void.

[30] *"20. Duty to Provide Support*

(1) The appropriate governments shall establish or designate one or more authorities to mobilize the community and create social networks to support persons with disabilities in the exercise of their legal capacity. Such authorities shall:

a. take immediate steps to put in place suitable support measures for the exercise of legal capacity by persons with disabilities living in institutions and persons with disabilities who need to have high support;

The legal capacity provisions that were ultimately incorporated in the Rights of Persons with Disabilities Act 2016 drew from the Committee's report but the unequivocal tone and tenor of the Report's text was made more aspirational and section 13(2) of the Act required the appropriate government "to ensure that persons with disabilities enjoy legal capacity on an equal basis with others in all aspects of life and have the right to equal recognition everywhere as any other person before the law". The provision which made denial of legal capacity on grounds of disability void in law was not adopted. In the Committee's draft, limited guardianship was introduced to lessen the rigours of plenary guardianship, but section 14 of the Act of 2016 allowed for limited guardianship arrangements to be made "if a person with disability who has been provided adequate and appropriate support" is unable to take legally binding decisions then such person may be provided with "further support of a limited guardian". This limited guardianship graduated from being a transitory measure pending creation of support systems to a permanent fixture of the support system. And instead of explicitly imposing duties of providing support on the appropriate government as required in the Committee's draft, section 15 of the Act of 2016 only required the appropriate government to "designate one or more authorities to mobilise the community and create social awareness to support persons with disabilities to exercise their legal capacity". The statute incorporated provisions on legal capacity and support but as aspirational goals and not as non-negotiable legal measures aimed at obtaining the full inclusion of persons with disabilities.

3.2.2. *The Mental Health Care Act 2017*

As already mentioned, the drafting of the new Mental Health Care Act, unlike the Rights of Persons with Disabilities Act, was undertaken to improve the quality of mental health care available to persons with psychiatric illness and not to advance their will and preference. Since the competence of persons with a diagnosis to seek treatment, continue or discontinue it has always been suspect, the statute also addressed the issue of legal capacity. Legal capacity was of concern to the framers of the mental health law as its absence may impede

---

  b. take suitable steps including, where appropriate, mediation proceedings, in order to assist persons with disabilities who have exited from plenary guardianship to set up where required by such persons with disabilities suitable support arrangements other than limited guardianship for the exercise of their legal capacity;

  c. take steps to review how the system of deemed limited guardianship is operating for persons with disabilities including those living in institutions and to assist such persons with disabilities in establishing suitable support arrangements to exercise their legal capacity;

(2) The review process referred to in sub clause (1) (c) is facilitative in nature and no person with disability can be denied legal capacity or refused the benefit of limited guardianship arrangements due to the delay or non-occurrence of the review."

a person with psychiatric illness from obtaining treatment. Thus, even as the statute according to its preamble was being enacted to bring the Indian law in harmony with CRPD, it is not the CRPD but the UN's "Principles for protection of persons with mental illness" (Mental Illness Principles) of 1991[31] which seem to be driving the law. Section 3(1) of the Mental Health Act provides that mental illness shall be determined according to nationally or internationally accepted medical standards, including the latest edition of the *International Classification of Disease* of the World Health Organization, which are notified and accorded approval by the central government. And section 3(3), in line with the UN principles, places an embargo on diagnosing mental illness on the basis of political, economic or social status or membership of cultural, racial or religious group or any other reason not directly relevant to the mental health status of a person.

Having asserted the primacy of the medical paradigm, the statute then declares that every person, including a person with mental illness, shall be deemed to be competent to take their own care and treatment decisions, provided they possess the listed competencies, such as the ability to understand the information relevant to the treatment and the ability to understand the foreseeable consequences of taking or refusing treatment. If they lacked the aforesaid competence for treatment to happen, it was necessary that someone should be able to decide on their behalf. The Mental Health Care Act has addressed the issue of legal capacity by providing for this eventuality. Substitution has been provided in two ways: first where individual persons provide for who will act for them if they are unable to act for themselves. The Act allows individuals to register advance directives[32] or nominate representatives who will act on their behalf. Simply making a directive in no way ensures that the will of persons making it would be respected. Section 11 of the Act allows a mental health professional, relative or caregiver to apply to the competent Board seeking modification of the directive. Amongst the grounds on which such modification can be obtained is that the persons making the directive lacked capacity or free will or did not understand what they were doing. Just as mental health professionals have been granted the option to challenge the directive, in order to underscore "the at your own risk" dimension of advance directives, section 13 of the MHCA grants immunity from liability to both medical practitioners and mental health professionals for following a valid advance directive.

---

[31] "Principles for the Protection of Persons with Mental Illness and the Improvement of Mental Health Care." Office of the High Commissioner for Human Rights, 17 December 1991.

[32] Section 5 of the Mental Health Act allows the making of advance directives in writing where individuals can specify how they should or should not be treated. It will become active when persons lose the competence to decide for themselves but will be operable only if made in accordance with law and any directive in breach of legal requirements would be void *ab initio*.

The second option of nominating a representative operates in a similar fashion. Section 14 of the Act allows persons to nominate in order of preference a representative or representatives who would act on their behalf. In order to ensure that there is no vacuum for persons who had failed to appoint representatives, section 14(4) provides a statutory list of persons who would be deemed to be nominated representatives for such persons. These statutorily empowered nominated representatives would have the same authority as a self-appointed nominated representative. Section 17 specifies the considerations that are to be kept in mind by nominated representatives in how to perform their duties. In specifying these duties, no distinction is made between self-appointed and statutorily appointed nominated representatives. The statute provides no special guidance to the statutorily appointed representatives on how they are to fulfil responsibilities such as considering the current and past wishes of the person with mental illness, and providing or withholding consent for research. No distinction has been made even when the statute allows the Director of Social Welfare or their representatives to function as such nominated representatives.

Except for these two new introductions of advance directive and nominated representative, the Mental Health Care Act has retained the admission procedures of voluntary and involuntary admissions to psychiatric facilities provided in the Mental Health Act of 1987. Only the newer law requires the admissions to be carried out following all fair process safeguards. It has established Mental Health Review Boards as oversight bodies who can be appealed to for poor living conditions or the breach of any rights guaranteed by the Act. Appeals can be filed against the decisions of the Review Board to the High Court. Unlike the Mental Health Act of 1987, the 2017 Act asks for mental health care to be provided employing the least restrictive alternative.

Although these requirements have been incorporated, the Act is more intent on making treatment accessible and easily available to all. Thus it allows for ambulance services to be provided to persons with mental illness on the same terms as for physical illness,[33] even when the person with mental illness may not want such treatment. On similar rationale, persons with mental illness have been given a statutory right to procure essential medications on their own and seek reimbursement of such expenditure.[34] This access has been guaranteed only for medical services. Even when alternatives are provided they are limited to other systems of medicine.[35] Psychosocial interventions such as peer-to-peer support or open dialogue which have been found effective by persons with psychosocial

---

[33] Mental Healthcare Act 2017, 7 April 2017, *Ministry Of Law And Justice*, India, section 21(1)(c).
[34] Mental Health Act 2017 (n. 33), section 18(10).
[35] Proviso to subsection (10) of section 18 provides for access to medications prescribed by systems of medicine other than allopathy such as Ayurveda, yoga, unani, siddha and homeopathy.

disability and their peers are in no way recognised in the Act even when these may be the preferred options of the person with mental illness.

The CRPD was a step ahead of the least restrictive alternative and fair process safeguards of the Mental Illness Principles. In recognition of the same the preamble to the CRPD expressly omitted reference to the Principles in its recital of initiatives prior to the CRPD which signify progressive recognition of the rights of persons with disabilities. Yet the Indian law seems more guided by the Principles than the Convention. The Rights of Persons with Disabilities Act is ideologically closer to the CRPD but it has ensconced limited guardianship into the law even if masked as support. Also, the law would provide little protection against discrimination as the enforcement component of the text is weak.

Persons living with mental illness have been included in both laws but since the ideology of both statutes is far from similar, it is a matter of the moment as to which law would apply to them in which situation? Both laws are special laws if compared to other statutes relating to the non-disabled. Yet the Rights of Persons with Disabilities Act which includes 23 impairments and allows for the possibility of more inclusions that could be categorised as the general law for persons with disabilities; whereas the Mental Health Care Act which only provides for the care and treatment of persons with mental illness could be perceived as the special legislation. The continuance of the incompetence discourse in that Act could render difficult the realisation of the entitlements guaranteed to persons with mental illness in the Rights of Persons with Disabilities Act. The possibilities of these conflicts are real and how they will be resolved will depend to a great extent upon how Courts approach the matter of legal capacity and personhood. In order to complete this narrative on the current Indian law on legal capacity, I examine some judicial decisions which have addressed the issue of legal capacity after the adoption of the CRPD. No disputes around the two statutes have surfaced yet in the appellate courts. Hence in the last section I am primarily discussing the one judicial decision where the dispute resolved around the issue of capacity and choice and the CRPD was relied upon by the advocate for the appellant to seek judicial protection for the choice of her client with intellectual disability.

4. LEGAL CAPACITY AND THE COURTS: *SUCHITA SRIVASTAV v. CHANDIGARH ADMINISTRATION*[36]

This case relates to a young woman reportedly with "mild mental retardation" who whilst residing in a women's protective home was sexually assaulted by

---

[36] Supreme Court of India, "Suchita Srivastava & Anr vs Chandigarh Administration on 28 August, 2009". <https://indiankanoon.org/doc/1500783/> accessed 14.04.2023.

some unknown person and became pregnant. Keeping in view her impairment and poor financial status the Chandigarh Administration was of the view that the pregnancy should be terminated. A medical board was established and whilst reporting on her diagnosis and deficient understanding, the Board also recorded that the young woman wanted to carry the child to term. Since the legal position on the matter was tenuous the Chandigarh Administration approached the High Court of the State for permission to go ahead. A second medical Board was constituted which again noted the vulnerability of the woman and raised some concerns on the rearing capabilities of the woman, although it did not opine that the pregnancy must be terminated. The High Court, however, took the view that the mental state of the woman rendered her incompetent to raise a child and therefore, despite the advanced stage, the pregnancy should be aborted.

Since the woman wanted to retain the child, a young woman advocate moved the Supreme Court of India against the judgment of the High Court as she felt that the CRPD was meaningless if a woman with intellectual disability was denied her reproductive rights only because of her impairment. The Supreme Court admitted the case and allowed urgent hearing and even granted relief to the person with disability.

However, the reasoning for the decision primarily arose from the Court's reading of the Medical Termination of Pregnancy Act 1971 which required that except in the case of a minor or a woman with mental illness, an abortion could not be performed without the consent of the woman.[37] Since the woman was not a woman with mental illness and only had "mild mental retardation" she could not be considered incompetent and her choice had to be respected. The Supreme Court also did not find that the High Court had acted in the best interests of the woman with disability "as to terminate the victim's pregnancy was not in pursuance of her 'best interests'. Performing an abortion at such a late-stage could have endangered the victims' physical health and the same could have also caused further mental anguish to the victim since she had not consented to such a procedure". Also the Court refused to accept the interpretation of the High Court as it would dilute the requirement of consent and the same "would amount to an arbitrary and unreasonable restriction on the reproductive rights of the victim".

The woman before the Court had an intellectual disability and the Court did protect her choice but the protection was provided by relying upon the plain language of the Medical Termination of Pregnancy Act and not because of any

---

[37] Section 3(4)(a). The relevant section provided that "No pregnancy of a woman who has not attained the age of eighteen years, or, who, having attained the age of eighteen years, is a mentally ill person, shall be terminated except with the consent in writing of her guardian. (b) Save as otherwise provided in clause (a), no pregnancy shall be terminated except with the consent of the pregnant woman."

understanding of disability rights. Even so, the Court was moved because India had ratified the CRPD and the decision of the High Court was in breach of the international commitment. The Supreme Court of India whilst relying on international law chose to reproduce the entire text of the UN Declaration on the Rights of Mentally Retarded Persons and the existence of the CRPD was acknowledged in this solitary sentence which said "We must also bear in mind that India has ratified the Convention on the Rights of Persons with Disabilities (CRPD) on October 1, 2007 and the contents of the same are binding on our legal system". Perhaps if the Court had made a real and not notional connection to the CRPD, its treatment of the rights of persons with mental illness may have been more informed. As it stands the Court reinforced the stereotype of incompetence accompanying persons with mental illness.

The High Court had extended the incompetence imposed on persons with mental illness on the reasoning that intellectual disability and mental illness are often clubbed together. Differing from the High Court, the Supreme Court opined that while the "categories can be collapsed for the purpose of empowering the respective classes of persons, the same distinction cannot be disregarded so as to interfere with the personal autonomy that has been accorded to mentally retarded persons for exercising their reproductive rights."

This opinion was voiced by the Apex Court whilst pronouncing on the rights of persons with disabilities whose rights had also been protected by statute. It may be hoped that the same outlook will be adopted when the Court has to read conflicting statutory provisions relating to the rights of persons with mental illness. Ideally, the Court will read the entitlements of the Disabilities Act liberally and adopt a more strict construction of the provisions of the Mental Health Care Act which are negating the will and preference of persons with mental illness. At this point, however, the matter is still in the realm of speculation.

5. SO WHAT IS THE VERDICT?

The above narrative shows that neither the engagement with the State nor a boycott yielded the desired results on the matter of legal capacity. In both the Rights of Persons with Disabilities Act and the Mental Health Care Act, the concerned Ministries asserted their will. However in the case of the former, the government had to take back the severely mutilated legislation and mollify the sector. I believe that the wide consultation undertaken by the Committee made for an informed community, which protested because they knew the difference between the promise and the delivery. Also the Committee draft allowed people to understand that all their requirements could be accommodated in the law if there was the accompanying will. This realisation assisted the process of advocacy. It was no longer possible for the government to set the limits of what could be achieved through the law. Moreover, in the drafting of the Rights of Persons with Disabilities Act the government was responding to the civil society draft whereas in the Mental Health Care Act civil society had to make suggestions on the draft prepared by the technocrats with government support. Consequently, while the Ministry of Health agreed to make cosmetic changes, there was a total refusal to move out of the medical paradigm. And yet, I wonder whether more persistent engagement instead of a cold boycott could have yielded better results. So, is half a loaf better? Maybe.

LEGAL CAPACITY IN CHINA'S MAINLAND

Huang Yi and Chen Bo

1. Introduction 237
2. Status of the Convention at Domestic Level in China's Mainland 238
3. Legal Capacity and Adult Guardianship 239
    3.1. The Law on Legal Capacity 239
    3.2. The Adult Guardianship Mechanism 242
    3.3. Restrictions on Rights as the Consequence of the Denial of
        Legal Capacity and the Appointment of Guardianship 244
    3.4. Summary and Discussion 246
4. Legal Capacity and Mental Health Law 247
    4.1. Voluntary Principle and Dangerousness Standard 248
    4.2. Capacity and Guardianship 249
    4.3. Family's Responsibility and Liabilities 250
    4.4. Insufficient Safeguard and Lack of Independent Oversight 251
    4.5. Summary and Discussion 252
5. Conclusion 252

1. INTRODUCTION

This chapter reviews the normative framework of legal capacity in China's mainland. The primary focus includes China's adult guardianship system in the recently adopted Civil Code[1] and the provisions from the first national Mental Health Law (MHL)[2] that authorise detention and involuntary treatment. This chapter defines legal capacity, the equal recognition of which is central to the spirit of the United Nations Convention on the Rights of Persons with Disabilities (CRPD or Convention),[3] as both the capacity for having rights

---

[1]   Civil Code of the People's Republic of China (Adopted at the Third Session of the Thirteenth National People's Congress 28 May 2020; enters into force 1 January 2021).

[2]   Mental Health Law of the People's Republic of China (passed by the Standing Committee of the National People's Congress on 26 October 2012, entered into force on 1 May 2013).

[3]   United Nations Convention on the Rights of Persons with Disabilities (adopted 13 December 2006, entered into force 3 May 2008) 2515 UNTS 3.

and the capacity for exercising rights.[4] In China, as elsewhere, legal capacity, particularly the legal capacity of persons with intellectual disabilities and psychosocial disabilities, is denied through provisions for adult guardianship and the application of involuntary admission and treatment under Chinese non-criminal law. Following the adoption of the CRPD, the normative framework governing legal capacity has been subject to law reform, through which the respect for the autonomy of persons concerned has been strengthened. The chapter will outline the key points of this normative framework, with a view to highlighting the changes brought by the law reforms. It will also raise questions about the extent to which these changes have been translated into practice.

Before proceeding to a closer examination of the law regulating the exercise of legal capacity in China's mainland, we outline the approach that gives effect to CRPD Article 12 on legal capacity in this jurisdiction. Sections that follow discuss the law reforms related to the adult guardianship system in the Civil Code and the Mental Health Law respectively. We conclude with a discussion on the implementation of such law reforms.

2. STATUS OF THE CONVENTION AT DOMESTIC LEVEL IN CHINA'S MAINLAND

It is difficult to define whether the Chinese legal system, like most domestic legal systems, follows the theory of monism or dualism;[5] therefore, the status of international treaties in the Chinese legal system is a very complex issue. There is not an explicit rule that prescribes the status, hierarchy, or effect of Article 12 in Chinese law. Before the ratification of the CRPD, China has been a party to all the core human rights conventions except for the International Covenant on Civil and Political Rights, which has not been ratified. In most cases, these international human rights conventions are not regarded as automatically having effect in Chinese law.[6] The main approach to give effect to these international human rights instruments is to transform the rights and obligations prescribed

---

[4]   I. BATENKAS, M. A. STEIN and D. ANASTASIOU (eds), *The UN Convention on the Rights of Persons with Disabilities: A Commentary*, Oxford University Press 2018.

[5]   See M. D. EVANS, *International Law*, Oxford University Press 2006, p. 428; J. L. DUNOFF, S. R. RATNER and D. WIPPMAN, *International Law: Norms, Actors, Process: A Problem-Oriented Approach*, Aspen Publishers 2006, p. 267; M. CHENGYUAN, *Monograph on International Law*, China Citic Press 2003, p. 4.

[6]   H. XUE and Q. JIN, "International Treaties in the Chinese Domestic Legal System" (2009) 8 *Chinese Journal of International Law* 299.

therein into the domestic legal system by making changes to existing domestic law or creating new law.[7] This is also the case with domesticating Article 12.[8]

Accordingly, to give effect to Article 12 at the national level requires scrutiny of relevant domestic law in the context of Article 12, abolishing or modifying any domestic law that conflicts with Article 12, and enforcing the rights and obligations elaborated in Article 12 in domestic law and practice.

3. LEGAL CAPACITY AND ADULT GUARDIANSHIP

Given that CRPD Article 12 elaborates the right to equal recognition before the law, which further entails the right to legal capacity and the right to support in the exercise of legal capacity, the most relevant areas of domestic law to be scrutinised in the context of Article 12 is the law on legal capacity and adult guardianship.[9]

The legal framework for the exercise of legal capacity and adult guardianship is mainly contained in the Civil Code and Civil Procedure Law of the People's Republic of China[10] (the Civil Procedure Law). The following three subsections examine the legal standards of legal capacity and guardianship, and the legal consequences of being denied full legal capacity.

3.1. THE LAW ON LEGAL CAPACITY

Articles 13–22 of the Civil Code provide substantive perspectives on how to determine one's legal capacity. According to Articles 13 and 14, citizens have legal capacity as a right holder from birth to death,[11] and all citizens are recognised as a right holder before the law on an equal basis.[12] These two articles arguably reflect the legal capacity to be a right holder prescribed in Article 12. Article 18 provides that an individual aged 18 or over is an adult and is recognised by law as a person with full legal capacity to act under the law, which means they can independently participate in civil activities.[13] This article generally reflects

---

[7]   Ibid.

[8]   Ibid.

[9]   See Committee on the Rights of Persons with Disabilities, "Concluding Observations on the Initial Report of China, Adopted by the Committee at Its Eighth Session (17–28 September 2012)" (2012) CRPD/C/CHN/CO/1, para. 21.

[10]   Civil Procedure Law of the People's Republic of China (2012 Amendment) 1991 (Order No 59 of the President of the People's Republic of China).

[11]   Civil Code of the People's Republic of China 2020, Article 13.

[12]   Ibid., Article 14.

[13]   Ibid., Article 18.

the legal capacity to act under the law prescribed in Article 12 of the CRPD. Articles 21 and 22 then set out the exception to Article 18 that:

> An adult who is unable to account for his own conduct shall be a person having no capacity for civil conduct[14] ... An adult who is unable to fully account for his own conduct shall be a person with limited capacity for civil conduct.[15]

According to the Opinions of the Supreme People's Court on several issues concerning the implementation of the "General Principles of the Civil Law of the People's Republic of China" (Interpretation of the Civil Law), to determine to what extent a person can account for their own conduct, several factors need to be considered. This includes "the degree of connection of the conduct with his/her own life",[16] "whether they can understand the conduct and foresee the consequence",[17] whether they can understand "the amount or objects of the conduct"[18] and to what extent they have the ability of "judgment" and "self-protection".[19] Thus, together, Articles 21 and 22 provide the ground for denying an individual's legal capacity for disability-related reasons, and, to a great extent, conflates legal and mental capacity. This constitutes the central conflict with Article 12.

Articles 177–180 and 187–190 of the Civil Procedure Law provide the procedural requirements of cases determining an individual's legal capacity. It is stipulated in the current law that only the court can make the decision to deny an individual's full legal capacity. An individual's close relatives or other interested parties can initiate a case by applying to the court for a declaration that the individual is with limited or no legal capacity. The application should be submitted with facts and evidence.[20] After accepting this application, the court shall require judicial assessment on the individual's legal capacity. If the judicial assessment has already been completed, the court should examine the result of the assessment.[21] The case then goes to trial under the special procedure provided in Chapter 15 of the Civil Procedure Law.[22] According to Article 178, the case will be heard by one judge and the judgment of the first instance shall be final, which means there is no opportunity to appeal. According to Article 189, a close relative of the person concerned, other than

---

[14] Ibid., Article 21.
[15] Ibid., Article 22.
[16] Opinions of the Supreme People's Court on Several Issues concerning the Implementation of the General Principles of the Civil Law of the People's Republic of China (For Trial Implementation) 1988, para. 4.
[17] Ibid., para. 4.
[18] Ibid., para. 4.
[19] Ibid., para. 5.
[20] Civil Procedure Law of the People's Republic of China (2012 Amendment) (n. 10), Article 187.
[21] Ibid., Article 188.
[22] Ibid., Article 177.

the individual who submits the application, should act as the agent *ad litem* of the person concerned in the trial. The court may assign one of the person's relatives to be the agent *ad litem* if necessary. The court should also hear the opinion of the person concerned if their health condition permits.[23] If through the trial, the court finds that the application is based on relevant facts, the court will declare that the person is with limited or no legal capacity. Otherwise, the court will reject the application.[24]

The procedural dimensions of such cases raise two main concerns. First, considering that a case on an individual's legal capacity is heard by only one judge and there is no opportunity to appeal, there may be the potential danger that the right of access to justice of the person whose legal capacity is being challenged is not guaranteed. Second, Article 189 stipulates a compulsory requirement that the person whose legal capacity is being challenged and examined in the case should have close relatives as their agent's *ad litem*, whereas Article 58 of the Civil Procedure Law indicates that the appointment of agents *ad litem* is an individual's right rather than a compulsory requirement to be fulfilled in the court proceeding. Based on the comparison between Article 58 and Article 189, it can be further argued that in cases where a person's legal capacity is challenged and examined by the court, Article 189 may have the effect of denying the person's right and full legal capacity to participate in the court proceeding on their own behalf. This is the case even though the person's legal incapacity may only be suspected at the time of the court proceeding.

It should be noted that current Chinese law on legal capacity prescribes only the legal standards and procedures for the denial of one's full legal capacity. It does not specify whether the recognition of one's legal capacity, especially the legal capacity to act under the law, is an individual's right protected by the law. Neither does it manifest whether the arbitrary deprivation of one's legal capacity is an infringement of an individual's rights, or in which situation one would be liable for arbitrary interference in another's exercise of legal capacity. Article 12 of the CRPD and General Comment No.1, by contrast, make it much clearer that equal recognition before the law is an individual's right, based on which disabled people have the right to exercise legal capacity on an equal basis with others.[25] The failure to define the recognition of legal capacity as an individual's right, without discrimination based on disability, is one of the fundamental gaps between the Chinese law on legal capacity and Article 12 of the CRPD.

---

[23]   Ibid., Article 189.

[24]   Ibid., Article 189.

[25]   Committee on the Rights of Persons with Disabilities, "Convention on the Rights of Persons with Disabilities General Comment No. 1 (2014): Article 12: Equal Recognition before the Law" (2014) CRPD/C/GC/1, para. 11–13.

3.2. THE ADULT GUARDIANSHIP MECHANISM

According to Articles 21 and 23 of the Civil Code, once the person is determined as having no or limited capacity to act under the law, they shall be represented by their agent *ad litem* in some, or all civil activities,[26] and the guardian of the person is the agent *ad litem*.[27] The current law is clear that guardianship can be assigned only after a person is determined to have limited or no legal capacity by the court through due process. Without such a judicial decision, guardianship should not be imposed on any adult regarded as having full legal capacity before the law.

Article 28 of the Civil Code lists the categories of people that can be appointed as the guardian of a person found to have limited or no legal capacity:

> (1) spouse; (2) parent and adult child; (3) any other close relative; (4) any other person or organizations willing to bear the responsibility of guardianship and having approval from the unit to which the person belongs or from the neighbourhood or village committee in the place of his residence.[28]

Article 33 of the Civil Code provides that a person can pre-arrange guardianship for themselves when they have full legal capacity, and the guardianship arrangement will take effect when the person concerned is determined to be losing part or all of their legal capacity.[29] Article 26 of Law of the People's Republic of China on Protection of the Rights and Interests of the Elderly prescribes such pre-arrangement of guardianship for people at or above the age of 60.[30]

The pre-arrangement of guardianship could be argued to serve a similar function of power-of-attorney: a competent person appoints an agent to perform the duties of a substitute decisionmaker when the adult loses all or part of the capacity for civil conduct (or the capacity for performing "civil juristic acts," the term used in some translated versions). In the context of Chinese civil law, entering an agreement for health care services with a health care service provider, such as a hospital or clinic, deciding on a treatment plan, or signing documentation to signal informed consent are often considered as civil juristic acts.

---

[26] Civil Code of the People's Republic of China, Article 21.
[27] Ibid., Article 23.
[28] Ibid., Article 28.
[29] Ibid., Article 33.
[30] Law of the People's Republic of China on Protection of the Rights and Interests of the Elderly (2015 Revision) 2015 (Order No 24 of the President of the People's Republic of China), Article 26.

As a relatively new mechanism, the effect of pre-arranged guardianship is still largely unknown. From an optimistic perspective, it may be argued that the pre-arranged guardianship echoes the principle of maximum respect for the autonomy and will of the person under guardianship. However, the lack of clarity about how the pre-arranged guardianship can be enforced raises some concerns. It is clear in law that pre-arranged guardianship must be set up in writing;[31] less so is its enforcement. As noted earlier, the Civil Procedure Law contains a section on the special procedure for declaring full or partial loss of capacity,[32] and only after this procedure can a person be put under guardianship. However, the existing practice of using public notaries to effectuate pre-arranged guardianship, effectively bypasses court proceedings.[33] In such cases, the practice of pre-arranged guardianship may have the effect of arbitrary deprivation of one's autonomy.

Articles 34–37 and 1188–1189 of the Civil Code list the obligations of the guardian. Regarding the person under guardianship, the guardian has obligations to protect the person's health and take care of their personal needs and decisions, manage and protect their property, control and educate the person under guardianship, and act as their agent *ad litem* in civil activities and litigation.[34] Article 35 requires that the guardian be guided by the principle of acting in the best interests of the person and, to the greatest extent possible, respect the will and preference of the person under guardianship. As compared to the previous legal rules on adult guardianship, Article 35 arguably represents some progress in light of Article 12 of the CRPD by strengthening the requirements on the guardian to safeguard the person's interests and be guided by their will and preferences. However, so far no more detailed guidelines have been issued for evaluating the degree to which the will and preference of the person under guardianship is respected and acted upon.

In addition to the obligations to the person under guardianship, the guardian also bears obligations to others. According to Articles 1188 and 1189, the guardian is responsible for any damages caused by the person under guardianship.[35] Some more specific obligations of guardians are provided in other pieces of law, including: namely, caring for the person under guardianship, being the agent

---

[31]   Civil Code, Article 33.

[32]   The Civil Procedure Law of the People's Republic of China (Adopted by the Fourth Session of the Seventh National People's Congress 9 April 1991; amended 8 October 2007, 31 August 2012, and 27 June 2017), Chapter 14 Section 4.

[33]   Q. Bei, "The First Pre-arranged Guardianship in China is issued in Shanghai", Wenhui Bao, 8 December 2017 <whb.cn/zhuzhan/kandian/20171208/112574.html> accessed 24.03.2023.

[34]   Civil Code of the People's Republic of China, Articles 34–37,1188–1189; Interpretation of the Civil Law, para. 10.

[35]   Civil Code of the People's Republic of China, Articles 1188–1189.

ad litem for the person in civil activities, and bearing the responsibility for any damage caused by the person under guardianship.[36]

It should be noted that although the current law prescribes the obligation of the guardian, it is not clear to what degree the guardianship is monitored, and whether the person under guardianship can, on their own, file a complaint about their guardian.

Given the substantive and procedural standards for guardianship, as well as the legal obligations of the guardian, it can be argued that guardianship in most cases has the characteristics of the substitute decision-making regimes that are referenced in the UN Committee on the Rights of Persons with Disabilities' General Comment No.1.[37] Accordingly, the legal mechanism of adult guardianship in current Chinese law constitutes a conflict with the requirement of Article 12. Furthermore, in its Concluding Observations on China's initial report, the UN Committee expresses concern that provisions for a system of supports for exercising legal capacity is absent in current Chinese law.[38]

3.3. RESTRICTIONS ON RIGHTS AS THE CONSEQUENCE OF THE DENIAL OF LEGAL CAPACITY AND THE APPOINTMENT OF GUARDIANSHIP

In its General Comment No.1, the UN Committee recognises and affirms that the equal recognition of legal capacity is inextricably connected to the enjoyment of many other rights.[39] Under current Chinese law, once a person is denied full legal capacity, many restrictions will be imposed on the rights of the person. General restrictions are provided in Articles 143–145 of the Civil Code. According to Article 143, to make civil conduct legally valid, the actor must have relevant legal capacity for the civil conduct.[40] A civil conduct is not legally valid if it is performed by a person recognised as without legal capacity, or a person recognised as with limited legal capacity who cannot carry out this conduct independently.[41] These articles generally deny the participation of individuals without full legal capacity in civil activities.

---

[36] Mental Health Law of the People's Republic of China 2012 (Order No 62 of the President of the People's Republic of China), Articles 9, 36, 45, 49 and 59; Law of the People's Republic of China on the Protection of Disabled Persons (2008 Revision) (Order No 3 of the President of the People's Republic of China), Article 9.

[37] Committee on the Rights of Persons with Disabilities (n. 25), para. 27.

[38] Committee on the Rights of Persons with Disabilities (n. 9), para. 21.

[39] Committee on the Rights of Persons with Disabilities (n. 25), para. 31.

[40] Civil Code of the People's Republic of China, Article 143.

[41] Ibid., Articles 144–145.

In addition to these general restrictions, there are also other restrictions stipulated in various pieces of legislation at different levels. Some examples are given below to illustrate how people recognised as without full legal capacity may be directly or indirectly excluded from civil activities and the enjoyment of other basic rights.

A typical example is the direct exclusion from the right to access to justice. Article 57 of the Civil Procedure Law provides that for people without legal capacity to participate in a lawsuit, the guardian should participate in the lawsuit on their behalf as agent *ad litem*.[42] Individuals determined to have limited legal capacity may still have opportunities, although very limited, to present before the court on their own behalf. However, for individuals determined to have no legal capacity, their right to access to justice is to a large degree compromised by guardianship.[43] Moreover, Article 16 of Regulation on Legal Aid provides that if the applicant of legal aid has been denied full legal capacity, their agent *ad litem*, for example the guardian, can apply for the legal aid on the person's behalf.[44] However, if a person does not have an agent *ad litem* who makes such an application the person remains significantly restricted in accessing justice.[45]

Many other laws, policies, and rules also set explicit restrictions on the rights of people determined to be without full legal capacity. These cover a broad range of matters, for example, the right to select the beneficiary of the insurance,[46] the right of association,[47] and the right to get occupational qualifications.[48]

Moreover, restrictions can also be imposed in an indirect way by delegating power to the guardian. A typical example is Article 39 of the Mental Health Law of the People's Republic of China (Mental Health Law). It provides that when the treatment plans for patients with mental disability are formulated, the health care provider "shall inform the patients or their guardians about the treatment plan ...".[49] The term "patients or their guardians", to some degree, makes the person under guardianship and their guardians as one subject to the relevant duty bearer. Under Article 39, the health care providers can fulfil their obligation by providing information to the guardians only. In this case, the patient's right to

---

[42]   Civil Procedure Law of the People's Republic of China (2012 Amendment), Article 57.

[43]   See CRPD (n. 3), Article 13, access to justice, which requires states parties to facilitate disabled people's effective role as direct and indirect participants in all legal proceedings.

[44]   Regulation on Legal Aid 2003, Article 16.

[45]   See Committee on the Rights of Persons with Disabilities (n. 9) paras. 23 and 24. In evaluating China's performance under Article 13, access to justice, the Committee indicates concerns about the establishment of legal aid services.

[46]   Insurance Law of the People's Republic of China (2015 Amendment) 1995, Article 39.

[47]   Regulation on Registration and Administration of Social Organizations 1998 (Order No 250 of the State Council of the People's Republic of China), Article 13.

[48]   Lawyers Law of the People's Republic of China (2012 Amendment) 2012 (Order No 64 of the President of the People's Republic of China), Article 7; Law of the People's Republic of China on Certified Public Accountants (2014 Amendment) 1993, Article 10.

[49]   MHL, Article 39.

provide informed consent, and therefore the right to health, may be significantly compromised.

Based on terms similar to "patients or their guardians", the guardian is empowered to make substitute decisions for the person under guardianship on a wide range of issues, such as using the person's name or image in advertising,[50] consenting to treatment including surgeries that result in loss of function of body organs, and experimental clinical treatments of mental disorders,[51] consenting to disclose personal information of people who are HIV positive,[52] and consenting to the termination of pregnancy or performance of tubal ligation operations.[53] Although the law does not explicitly prevent the person under guardianship from making decisions, it delegates such a breadth of powers to the guardian that it, in fact, undermines the rights of the person to make decisions about virtually all aspects of their lives.

3.4. SUMMARY AND DISCUSSION

As examined above, in Chinese civil law, reforms recognising a "person having 'limited' rather than 'no' capacity for civil conduct" is a promising concept, although it is not fully consistent with Article 12. Nonetheless, it creates considerable room for a person who may be under guardianship for certain types of decisions to exercise their legal capacity in those decision-making areas where they are able to act legally independently. The newly adopted principle of "maximum respect" for the wills of persons under guardianship is another progressive change in the law. It requires the guardian to empower the person in engaging in civil activities as much as possible. In addition, the voluntary guardianship significantly expands the autonomy of persons under guardianship and moves the law in the direction of better respecting all persons' legal capacity.

However, the procedural requirement for declaring a person to have no legal capacity was established long before the introduction of law reform recognising "a person having limited capacity for civil conduct" and is thus deeply embedded in legal practice. Rarely are there declarations of "limited" rather than "no" capacity. The general ignorance about this important distinction raises doubts about the extent to which the positive law reform can be effectively translated

---

[50] Advertising Law of the People's Republic of China (2015 Amendment) 1994, Article 33.

[51] MHL, Article 43.

[52] Regulation on the Prevention and Treatment of HIV/AIDS 2006, Article 39.

[53] Law of the People's Republic of China on Maternal and Infant Health Care (2009 revision) (Order No 33 of the President of the People's Republic of China), Article 19. In two cases in 2005, the guardian consented and arranged for a woman with mental illness to have a hysterectomy. The guardian did so because of their concern that if the mentally ill woman was to have a child, the burden of care for the guardian would be increased. The guardian was then prosecuted by the procuratorate.

into practice. There is also little evidence that the voluntary guardianship has been widely utilised in practice.

In summary, the current law on legal capacity provides the ground for denying one's legal capacity for disability-related reasons, and largely conflates it with "mental capacity." Moreover, the current law fails to recognise the equal recognition before the law as an individual's right protected by the law. Such failure can be regarded as one of the fundamental gaps between the Chinese law on legal capacity and Article 12 of the CRPD. In addition, provisions for adult guardianship prescribed in the current law have the characteristics of substitute decision-making listed in the UN Committee's General Comment No.1 and are therefore not in compliance with requirements of Article 12.

In light of China's obligation under the CRPD to achieve the full implementation of Article 12 at the national level,[54] it is necessary to reconsider and modify the current law on legal capacity and guardianship in line with its requirements.

4. LEGAL CAPACITY AND MENTAL HEALTH LAW

China finally saw its first national Mental Health Law after a 28-year effort of law-making. It was passed by the Standing Committee of the National People's Congress of China on 26 October 2012 and then came into force on 1 May 2013. Before that, China, with one fifth of the world's population, only had six pieces of local legislation regulating mental health services in six cities. Given that Chinese society has rapidly developed and changed in the past number of decades, the old legal framework was clearly insufficient.[55]

On one hand, the new law was justified as necessary to facilitate effective treatment for the estimated over 170 million people who live with mental health disabilities in China, almost 160 million of whom it is estimated have never received any form of mental health services.[56]

On the other hand, the need for law reform became evident after several high-profile cases of psychiatric abuse were exposed by the media. Advocates for reform argued that stronger safeguarding measures were needed to ensure that people were not "wrongly" and involuntarily diagnosed, committed, and treated by psychiatric services. There was huge public concern about such cases and

---

[54] Committee on the Rights of Persons with Disabilities, "General Comment No. 1" (n. 25), paras. 24–30, 50.

[55] M. R. PHILIPS et al., "China's New Mental Health Law: Reframing Involuntary Treatment" (2013) 170 *American Journal of Psychiatry* 588.

[56] M. R. PHILIPS et al., "Prevalence, Treatment, and Associated Disability of Mental Disorders in Four Provinces in China during 2001–05: An Epidemiological Survey" (2009) 373 *The Lancet* 2041.

the phenomenon earned its own name "wrongly labelled with mental illness."[57] After many rounds of receiving public comments and revision made by the legislative body, reforms were adopted into law.

As a detailed account of the law and its provisions on coercive measures have been provided elsewhere,[58] this section will introduce only its key features and its connection to legal capacity.

4.1. VOLUNTARY PRINCIPLE AND DANGEROUSNESS STANDARD

The breakthrough of the Mental Health Law is commonly believed to be its principle of voluntary inpatient psychiatric treatment. However, perhaps more importantly, involuntary inpatient treatment is still permitted under the "dangerousness standard". Article 30 of the law reads: "[i]f the result of the psychiatric evaluation indicates that a person has a severe mental disorder, the medical facility may impose inpatient treatment if the individual meets one of the following conditions: (1) self-harm in the immediate past or current risk of self-harm; (2) behaviour that harmed others or endangered the safety of others in the immediate past or current risk to the safety of others."[59] This criterion is a result of considerable changes. "Necessity for treatment" and "disturbance of public order" was originally included but later deleted from earlier drafts of the Law, mainly because of its vagueness and openness to abuses.[60]

The reliance for involuntary inpatient treatment on a dangerousness standard draws criticism and concerns from both sides. Some commentators in psychiatry observe that many other jurisdictions include "inability of self-care" or "lack of insight" as criteria for involuntary treatment and suggest the most patients with mental disorders in China will be deterred from being treated solely by the dangerousness standard.[61] Meanwhile, there are also commentators in law focusing on the flaws of dangerousness standard, advocating a fusion model of mental health law that includes decision-making incapacity as a necessary criterion for involuntary commitment and treatment system.[62]

---

[57]   C. DING, "Involuntary Detention and Treatment of the Mentally Ill: China's 2012 Mental Health Law" (2014) 37 *International Journal of Law and Psychiatry* 581; X. ZHAO and J. DAWSON, "The New Chinese Mental Health Law" (2014) 21 *Psychiatry, Psychology and Law* 669.

[58]   B. CHEN, *China's Mental Health Law in Action*, Routledge, forthcoming.

[59]   MHL, Article 30.

[60]   Y. SHAO and B. XIE, "Approaches to Involuntary Admission of the Mentally Ill in the People's Republic of China: Changes in Legislation From 2002 to 2012" (2015) 43 *Journal of the American Academy of Psychiatry and the Law Online* 35.

[61]   B. XIE, "Impact of the New Mental Health Act on Mental Health Services in the Future" (2013) 13 *Journal of Neuroscience and Mental Health* 3.

[62]   Y. WANG, "Rethink of the Dangerousness Principle of Compulsory Treatment to Mental Disorders" [2014] *China Health Law* 4.

Interestingly, the law then differentiates people with mental disorders who are dangerous to themselves and those who are dangerous to others. In brief, if a person diagnosed with a severe mental disorder is dangerous to others, their guardian could apply for a re-examination and medical certification if the guardian disagrees with the decision of inpatient treatment made by the medical facility.[63] But if the person is dangerous to themself instead of others, their guardian would decide whether to impose inpatient treatment and when to discharge, and the person cannot challenge the guardian's decision except by going to court as provided for under the law.[64]

In both circumstances the law grants to a guardian immense power over people with mental disorders. It also offers its own definition in Article 83 defining "severe mental disorder" as a degree of condition that "results in serious impairments in social adaptation or in other types of functioning, in impaired awareness of objective reality or of one's medical condition, or in an inability to deal with one's own affairs."[65] But because there is no judicial or quasi-judicial review procedure over the assessment as well as the decision for involuntary inpatient treatment based upon it, this supposedly legal standard is in fact primarily, if not only, applied by medical professionals. Thus, they can impose involuntary admission and treatment based only on a category of diagnosis.[66]

4.2. CAPACITY AND GUARDIANSHIP

While capacity for medical decision-making by mental health services users and the potential for guardianship are central issues under the Mental Health Law, the law itself does not provide many provisions on how to determine capacity or appoint guardians. These provisions are covered in the civil law as examined above. Prior to the adoption of the Mental Health Law, the common practice was that a person would be automatically regarded as lacking capacity and represented by a guardian or family member if a psychiatric diagnosis was made, even though Chinese law explicitly ruled that such a determination should be made through a special civil procedure in court. However, in the eyes of some commentators the new Mental Health Law keeps these problematic presumptions in place. Zhao and Dawson observe:

> In the past, it has not been the mentally disordered individual who has been consulted about their hospital admission, but their family. Based on the naive thought that guardians are always "protectors of patients' interests", the new Law continues to

---

[63]   MHL, Article 32.
[64]   MHL, Article 31.
[65]   MHL, Article 83.
[66]   X. Qu, "The UN Convention on the Rights of Persons with Disabilities and Rights Protection of Persons with Disabilities" (2013) *Law Science* 105, 107.

give guardians key powers over the management of mentally disordered patients. For example, guardians are authorised to take patients to hospital and initiate their assessment for involuntary treatment. They have clear authority to veto involuntary hospitalisation of patients at risk of self-harm, and to take them home. They can give proxy consent to treatment and have important rights to receive information. They can apply for discharge of the patient from hospital.[67]

In this regard, Article 83 provides "[i]n this law, guardians of persons with mental disorders are persons *who may assume the role of guardian* as specified in the relevant regulations of the General Principles of the Civil Law" (emphasis added). As yet we have no evidence about how this provision operates in practice. However, its problematic nature is obvious when considering that a person may have multiple qualified "guardians" who have conflicting opinions. The law does provide for a close family member to be recognised by the adult guardianship system who could thus be empowered to exercise authority over a person with a psychiatric diagnosis.

4.3. FAMILY'S RESPONSIBILITY AND LIABILITIES

Another side of this immense discretionary power, however, is the full responsibility and liabilities that guardians or family members assume. Due to the lack of community-based mental health services, family members often bear the both the financial and emotional responsibility for mental health service users.[68] Article 21 of the Mental Health Law echoes and reinforces this "tradition", providing that:

> [f]amily members shall be concerned about each other, create a healthy and harmonious family environment, and improve their awareness of the prevention of mental disorders; if it appears that a family member may have a mental disorder, other family members shall help them obtain prompt medical care, provide for their daily needs, and assume responsibility for their supervision and management.[69]

Moreover, if guardians "fail to fulfil their responsibilities as guardian" and this causes harm to the patients or other people, the guardians are liable to pay compensation.[70] In a recent extreme case, for example, the court ruled that

---

[67]   X. Zhao and J. Dawson, "The New Chinese Mental Health Law" (2014) 21 *Psychiatry, Psychology and Law* 669.

[68]   B. Xie, "Experience and Lessons Draw from the Process of Mental Health Legislation in China" (2013) 27 *Chinese Mental Health Journal* 245.

[69]   MHL, Article 21.

[70]   MHL, Article 28.

the father, in his 60s, should pay a compensation of over 40,000 euros to the family members of the victim who was murdered by his adult son with a mental disorder, simply because he was seen as the guardian and failed to stop his son from killing the victim.[71] Unsurprisingly, respect for the autonomy of persons with mental disorders is vulnerable in the face of family members who exercise control out of fear for their own liability.

4.4. INSUFFICIENT SAFEGUARD AND LACK OF INDEPENDENT OVERSIGHT

Several ambiguities and potential abuses have been identified by commentators in relation to safeguarding the rights of people with mental disorders. For example, it is unclear how many psychiatrists are required to make a diagnosis and authorise involuntary inpatient treatment.[72] Equally unclear is what is meant in Article 40 of the Mental Health Law by the provision "behaviour that disrupts the facility's functioning of the medical facilities." Nor is it clear what is meant by the exceptions to the prohibition on measures like restraints and isolation when patients "engage in or are about to engage in self-harm, in behaviour that endangers the safety of others, or in behaviour that disrupts the facility's functioning of the medical facilities."[73]

More importantly, however, the law does not set up any independent body, such as Mental Health Tribunals used in many other jurisdictions, which provide oversight to the operation of involuntary inpatient treatment. Instead, Article 82 merely provides that "[p]ersons with mental disorders and their guardians and close relatives who believe that administrative bodies, medical facilities, other relevant agencies, or individuals have violated the provisions of this law and infringed on the legal rights and interests of persons with mental disorders may legally initiate a lawsuit."[74] Although it has been observed that, in practice, cases could be accepted by courts based on this provision,[75] it is still doubtful about how accessible and effective such recourse is if patients are involuntarily committed in institutions with no access to rights advice or oversight.

---

[71] No. 02826 Civil Case in the People's Court of Fulin in 2013.
[72] C. DING, "Involuntary Detention and Treatment of the Mentally Ill: China's 2012 Mental Health Law" (2014) 37 *International Journal of Law and Psychiatry* 581.
[73] C. DING, "Involuntary Detention and Treatment of the Mentally Ill: China's 2012 Mental Health Law" (2014) 37 *International Journal of Law and Psychiatry* 581.
[74] MHL, Article 82.
[75] B. CHEN, "Right to Litigate of Persons with Psychosocial Disabilities in China: From Mental Health Law to the UN Convention on the Rights of Persons with Disabilities", *Disability Rights Study in China*, Social Science Academic Press 2015.

4.5. SUMMARY AND DISCUSSION

Under the Mental Health Law, the only exception to the voluntary principle is that inpatient treatment must meet both a diagnostic threshold of a severe mental disorder and a dangerousness standard to oneself or others. It is a significant change in the law, compared to its predecessor law which supported the dominant practice of medical protective admissions, without any dangerousness criterion, even as problematic as such a criterion can be. The Mental Health Law does not adopt any general threshold for a service user in exercising his or her right to information and decision-making, (moving away from the old paradigm that relied on insight or capacity for civil conduct). This is a laudable reform and moves in the direction of maximising the respect for service users' autonomy and decision-making rights.

Nonetheless, there are several potential pitfalls with the legislation and practice that give cause for concern. The guardians and mental health facilities are still vested with the authority for imposing detention and involuntary treatment in violation of the CRPD. Very little guidance on the determination of severe mental disorders and dangerousness are provided for in the law. These provisions are especially vulnerable to abuse, as there is no independent oversight. Research suggests that the practices outlined above, in place before the law was adopted, and which were to be restricted with when it came into force, nonetheless persist and continue to be practised and accepted by both mental health professionals and judges in China.[76]

It is worth noting that no steps have been taken in law reform under the Mental Health Law or other legislation to recognise and provide for any form of support in decision-making, which state parties to the CRPD are obliged to provide under Article 12(3) of the CRPD. Without such recognition it is impossible to institute alternatives to the biomedical approach to mental health care. So far, law reform has not driven any real breakthrough in the practice of mental health care or increased respect for the autonomy of mental health users. Given this, it is reasonable to suggest that changing practice through pilot initiatives and training of mental health professionals about the rights of mental health users is needed before the initial and minimal reforms represented by the Mental Health Law, much less more radical reforms consistent with the CRPD, will have any substantive impact on the mental health system in China.

5. CONCLUSION

The practice of legal capacity and guardianship in China reflects not only the legal framework, as discussed throughout this chapter, but also the social and cultural

---

[76]   B. CHEN, *Mental Health Law in China: A Socio-legal Analysis*, Routledge forthcoming.

context. In most cases, it is the family member of a disabled person that plays the role of guardian. The legal status of the guardian and the moral authority granted to family members may, to a great extent, be conflated in practice. Whether or not they are formally recognised as guardians, family members are positioned in society to take on this decision-making role in the lives of family members with disabilities. This recognition and understanding of the legal, social, and moral context of guardianship are essential to a deeper and more comprehensive understanding of the concerns and issues underlying guardianship in practice.

The context in which guardianship operates in China can be highlighted from three main perspectives. First, guardianship should be understood in the context of family relationships and responsibilities. Family members of disabled people often take on the role of guardian even if they are not bound by any legally recognised guardianship status. Second, other social actors tend to presume that disabled people's families have the obligation, either moral or legal, to take care of the disabled person and to be responsible for their behaviour. Another normalised presumption is that a disabled person's family knows better than others what is best for the person concerned and that the family will always do what is best for them. Therefore, disabled people's family members are more likely to be recognised by other social actors as being authorised to make decisions for the disabled person concerned. Third, most disabled people understand and accept that their family members will take on a guardianship role over them as the way in which they can all best manage their life together.

The interaction between the social, legal, and moral context of guardianship shapes dual roles for disabled people's guardians and families in practice. On the one hand, disabled people's guardians or families who play the role of guardian are authorised to do so either by the law or by the publicly accepted understanding that it is their moral obligation to make substitute decisions for their disabled family member. On the other hand, they are legally or morally obliged to take most of the responsibility for the disabled person and their behaviour. Such responsibilities include, for example, protecting and taking care of the disabled person, supporting the disabled person's development, and deciding whether the disabled person's decisions or actions should be recognised as having legal effect. In cases where the person causes damage and cannot compensate for it, their family may have to compensate for it on their behalf even if the person concerned has not been denied full legal capacity under the law.

It is important to recognise and understand that in China disabled people's guardians or families play the role of both substitute decision-maker and responsibility bearer in practice. How the guardian or families treat the disabled person and balance these two roles is influenced by the complex interaction of several factors, such as the nature of the person's disability-related conditions, the culturally based understanding of disability, and the social barriers and disadvantages faced by disabled people. Recent trends suggest that most of the families of disabled people have the awareness and willingness to be more supportive to the disabled persons. Based on our field work, it is evident that some parents of disabled people have begun to think about the guardianship arrangements and alternatives to be put in place for after they pass away. Distinctions between substituted and supported decision-making are beginning to be recognised as awareness grows about the right to personal autonomy. However, because families are still bound by existing legal and moral responsibilities, and supported decision-making is not yet recognised in law or widely practised it is difficult to presume the degree to which they can turn away from substitute decision-making towards supported decision-making as a viable alternative.

The current practice of legal capacity and guardianship in China raises two main issues. First, since guardianship is rooted in or driven by moral and cultural imperatives, changes in the law, such as abolishing the legal status and authorisation of the guardian, may not be sufficient to bring about changes in practice. Second, considering the cultural and moral understanding of family relationships and responsibilities, it may be culturally and emotionally unacceptable to disabled people, and perhaps against their will and preference, for their family members to be completely excluded in a legal regime of support for exercising legal capacity. Therefore, some degree of conflation between the social and moral imperatives of the family relationship and the legal regime of support may be inevitable in future law reform efforts directed at achieving greater consistency with Article 12 of the CRPD. In other words, families will continue to assume substitute decision-making roles either in law or informally. Thus, at the same time as law reform efforts are advanced, it is critically important to encourage families (e.g., through public awareness and family support systems) to shift from acting as substitute decision-makers for disabled family members to instead become decision-making supporters who respect their family member's autonomy and are guided by their will and preferences.

To conclude, family members play a complex role in affording a disabled person the enjoyment and exercise of their legal capacity. All too often they restrict or deny it all together. Recent reforms to the Civil Code and Mental Health Law provide greater scope for maximising the autonomy of disabled people, yet there is little evidence to suggest satisfactory implementation. It is also clear that recent reforms did not incorporate needed provisions for recognising support in decision-making. Future development in this regard depends on reconfiguring the complex relationships among disabled people who are often denied legal capacity, their family members who are often seen as *de facto* guardians and potentially supporters, the government, and civil society and disabled persons organisations. The latter have played an increasingly important role in advancing awareness of the right to autonomy and self-determination. Its fuller realisation in the lives of disabled people in China will depend on how these tensions are resolved in both law and practice.

LESSONS FROM A REFORMIST PATH TO SUPPORTED DECISION-MAKING IN AUSTRALIA

Piers GOODING* and Terry CARNEY**

> *While Australia's moves in these legal fields have been rather slow, nevertheless in time most, if not all, jurisdictions will most likely adopt to varying degrees the paradigm change ushered in by article 12.*

Ron McCallum AO[1]

1. Background: Australia and Human Rights 257
   1.1. Australia and Article 12 CRPD 258
   1.2. Australian Law Reform Commission Report 2014 260
   1.3. The CRPD Committee's Assessment of Australia's Compliance 261
   1.4. Pilot Projects 262
2. Legal Developments 263
   2.1. "Guardianship and Administration" Law 264
        2.1.1. Victoria 264
        2.1.2. Law Reform Proposals in Tasmania and
               New South Wales. 266
   2.2. Mental Health Law 267
   2.3. Income Security and the National Disability Insurance Scheme. ... 268
3. Discussion 270
   3.1. The Federal Laboratory for Supported Decision-Making 270
   3.2. Hastening Slowly? 271
   3.3. Educative Impacts Towards Cultural Change?. 273
4. Conclusion. 274

---

* PhD. Senior Research Fellow, University of Melbourne Law School. Dr Gooding would like to acknowledge Dr Yukio Sakurai, Yokohama National University, Japan who provided feedback for this chapter.

** PhD, AO. Emeritus Professor, University of Sydney Law School.

[1] Prof Ron McCallum AO was the inaugural Chair of the UN Committee on the Rights of Persons with Disabilities, nominated to the Committee by the Government of Australia in

Australia has taken a gradual approach to reforming laws concerning legal capacity since the coming into force of the UN Convention on the Rights of Persons with Disabilities (CRPD) but an extensive one by global standards. Change has comprised statutory and non-statutory supported decision-making options, a growing body of conceptual and empirical research on the topic, and policy developments challenging the "best interests" principle behind longstanding substituted decision-making laws, policies and practices. Legislative reform has centred on guardianship and mental health laws but also criminal law,[2] and other areas in which legal capacity has been – and, in some cases, continues to be – restricted for persons with disabilities, such as marriage, estate law and contract law.

Law reform has not extended to abandoning "substituted decision-making". Guardianship and mental health laws appear likely to exist in some form for the foreseeable future, although the criteria for appointing a guardian or representative, or the imposition of involuntary psychiatric intervention, appears likely to narrow, with greater priority given to the actual and likely wishes of represented persons over the more paternalistic protection of their "best interests".[3] The duties of third parties to recognise legal capacity and adjust decision-making processes accordingly, also appear to be expanding, as do practical resources for individuals, families, supporters and service providers.

Australia can therefore be seen to have taken a *reformist* and *incrementalist* reform approach to legal capacity, equality and disability, but again one that is extensive by global standards. The breadth of change is somewhat paradoxical given Australia lacks a comprehensive legislative, administrative, or judicial framework for the protection of human rights, and given its interpretive declaration that restricts the scope of how Article 12 of the CRPD is to be applied, as discussed below. Australia's federalised system of government has seen reform initiatives and civil society activity concerning legal capacity vary between jurisdictions. Some jurisdictions within the patchwork have gone further than others in heading toward the "purist" approach to Article 12 envisaged by the Committee on the Rights of Persons with Disabilities (CRPD Committee). These

---

September 2008. R. McCALLUM, *The United Nations Convention on the Rights of Persons with Disabilities: An Assessment of Australia's Level of Compliance*, Royal Commission into Violence, Abuse, Neglect and Exploitation of People with Disability, Sydney 2020, p. 55.

[2] See, e.g., NSW Department of Communities and Justice, *Capacity Toolkit*, Part 6 "Assisted decision-making" <https://www.justice.nsw.gov.au/diversityservices/Pages/divserv/ds_capacity_tool/ds_capa_decision.aspx> accessed 11.11.2022.

[3] J. CHESTERMAN, "Adult Guardianship and Its Alternatives in Australia" in C. SPIVAKOVSKY, K. SEEAR and A. CARTER (eds), *Critical Perspectives on Coercive Interventions*, Routledge, Abingdon 2018; Victorian Mental Health Royal Commission, *Royal Commission into Victoria's Mental Health System: Final Report*, Melbourne 2021, vol. 4; M. BLAKE et al, "Supported Decision-Making for People Living with Dementia: An Examination of Four Australian Guardianship Laws" (2021) 28 *Journal of Law and Medicine* 389.

varied developments offer lessons for global efforts to improve legal responses, including in public law, private law and soft law, and other areas of policy, service provision and social life.[4] This chapter outlines some of the most striking developments, drawing on law and policy reform activity, advocacy work, scholarly and civil society research, and practical resources developed by service providers and others.[5]

1. BACKGROUND: AUSTRALIA AND HUMAN RIGHTS

Australia is a common law jurisdiction substantially derived from the English legal system. Australia has a federal system of government: six States have separate jurisdictions with their own system of courts and parliaments, and two Territories are granted a regional legislature by the Commonwealth. Guardianship and mental health legislation are State and Territory responsibilities; along with any supported decision-making; the day-to-day running of health, welfare and disability services; and the making and administration of general civil and criminal laws,[6] though there are multiple areas of federal law concerning citizens' Article 12 legal capacity such as voting[7] and marriage rights.

In 2008, Australia was among the first countries to ratify the CRPD, acceding to its Optional Protocol in 2009. Under Australian law, international treaty obligations do not become law until the treaty is specifically enacted into domestic law.[8] The constitutional ability of the national government to enact a Bill of Rights or legislate to enact the CRPD has not been exercised. Although Charters of Rights have been enacted in two States (Victoria and Queensland) and the Australian Capital Territory, these establish a "dialogue" model of human rights protection substantially based on their UK equivalent and do not directly engage the CRPD.[9] There is no comprehensive legislative, administrative, or judicial framework for the protection of human rights; formal protections

---

4   T. Carney, "Prioritising Supported Decision-Making: Running on Empty or a Basis for Glacial-to-Steady Progress?" (2017) 6 *Laws* 1.

5   For a recent review: C. Bigby et al, *Diversity, Dignity, Equity and Best Practice: A Framework for Supported Decision-Making*, Royal Commission into Violence Abuse Neglect and Exploitation of People with Disability, Sydney 2023 <https://disability.royalcommission.gov. au/policy-and-research/research-program> accessed 22.03.2023.

6   T. Carney, "Where Now Australia's Welfare State" [2013] *Diritto Pubblico Comparato ed Europeo* [*Journal of Comparative and European Public Law*] 1353.

7   For comparative analysis of autonomy and the right to vote, see T. Carney, "Australia" in K. N. Schefer et al (eds), *Persons with Disabilities' Right to Autonomy and Their Right to Vote*, Swiss Institute of Comparative Law, Lausanne 2019.

8   *Minister for Immigration and Ethnic Affairs v. Teoh* (1995) 183 CLR 273.

9   M. Groves and C. Campbell (eds), *Australian Charters of Rights a Decade On*, Federation Press, Sydney 2017.

remain narrow, piecemeal and ad hoc.[10] Nevertheless, human rights instruments may, and often do, influence the curial interpretation of legislative provisions and/or common law rules.[11] For example, although in no way binding, CRPD principles favouring supported decision-making have had some small influence on tribunal decisions to avoid making adult guardianship orders.[12]

1.1. AUSTRALIA AND ARTICLE 12 CRPD

When ratifying the CRPD in July 2010, Australia made an interpretive declaration concerning Articles 12, 17 and 18. Regarding Article 12, the government declared:

> Australia recognizes that persons with disabilities enjoy legal capacity on an equal basis with others in all aspects of life. Australia declares its understanding that the Convention allows for fully supported or substituted decision-making arrangements, which provide for decisions to be made on behalf of a person, only where such arrangements are necessary, as a last resort and subject to safeguards.[13]

Australia interpreted Article 12(4) as containing safeguards, which, if established, make substituted decision-making permissible in limited circumstances. As is well covered in the literature, this contradicts the CRPD Committee's position[14]

---

[10] P. GERBER and M. CASTAN (eds), *Critical Perspectives on Human Rights Law in Australia*, Thomson Lawbook Co, Sydney 2021. A rare exception under the Victorian Charter was a 2018 Supreme Court ruling limiting the circumstances where electroconvulsive therapy can be used in mental health treatment: *PBU & NJE v.* Mental Health Tribunal [2018] VSC 564. See further I. FRECKELTON, "Electroconvulsive Therapy, Law and Human Rights: *PBU & NJE v Mental Health Tribunal* [2018] VSC 564, Bell J" (2018) 26 *Psychiatry, Psychology and Law* 1.

[11] R. MCCALLUM, *The United Nations Convention on the Rights of Persons with Disabilities: An Assessment of Australia's Level of Compliance*, Royal Commission into Violence, Abuse, Neglect and Exploitation of People with Disability, Sydney 2020; *Dietrich v. The Queen* (1992) 177 CLR 292, 305 (Mason CJ and McHugh J). See further L. WADDINGTON, "Australia" in L. WADDINGTON and A. LAWSON (eds), *The UN Convention on the Rights of Persons with Disabilities in Practice: A Comparative Analysis of the Role of Courts*, Oxford University Press, Oxford 2018.

[12] M. BLAKE et al (n. 3); T. CARNEY, "From Guardianship to Supported Decision-making: Still searching for true north?" (2023) 30 *Journal of Law and Medicine* 70.

[13] United Nations Treaty Collection, *Convention on the Rights of Persons with Disabilities: Declarations and Reservations (Australia)*, opened for signature 30 March 2007, United Nations Treaty Series vol. 999, entered into force 3 May 2008, <https://treaties.un.org/Pages/ViewDetails.aspx?src=TREATY&mtdsg_no=IV-15&chapter=4&clang=_en#EndDec> accessed 13.11.2022.

[14] United Nations Committee on the Rights of Persons with Disabilities, *General Comment No. 1 – Article 12: Equal Recognition Before the Law* <https://documents-dds-ny.un.org/doc/UNDOC/GEN/G14/031/20/PDF/G1403120.pdf?OpenElement>, paras. [3], [7], [17], accessed 13.11.2022.

calling for full abolition of substitute decision-making,[15] which itself is subject to wide-ranging contestation.[16]

The Government declaration and lack of a formal human rights framework may imply a poor fit for the type of supported decision-making law and policy reform envisaged by the CRPD Committee. Yet, somewhat paradoxically, Australia has seen much domestic activity in this area, including wide-ranging law and policy reform of guardianship,[17] mental health,[18] and other areas of law,[19] as well as much research and civil society activity, including among disabled peoples' organisations and disability service providers.[20]

The remainder of the chapter outlines this activity, with attention to developments that appear novel to Australia.

---

[15]   See, e.g., E. CUKALEVSKI, "Supporting Choice and Control: An Analysis of the Approach Taken to Legal Capacity in Australia's National Disability Insurance Scheme" (2019) 8 *Laws* 8.

[16]   W. MARTIN and S. GURBAI, 'Surveying the Geneva Impasse: Coercive Care and Human Rights' (2019) 64 *International Journal of Law and Psychiatry* 117.

[17]   J. BRAYLEY, *Supported Decision Making in Australia*, Presentation Notes, Melbourne 2009; Victorian Law Reform Commission, *Guardianship: Final Report*, Melbourne 2012; New South Wales Law Reform Commission, *Review of the Guardianship Act 1987*, Sydney 2018; Tasmanian Law Reform Institute, *Review of the Guardianship and Administration Act 1995 (Tas): Final Report*, Hobart 2018.

[18]   S. CALLAGHAN and C. RYAN, "An Evolving Revolution: Evaluating Australia's Compliance with the Convention on the Rights of Persons with Disabilities in Mental Health Law" (2016) 39 *University of New South Wales Law Journal* 596.

[19]   Australian Law Reform Commission, *Equality, Capacity and Disability in Commonwealth Laws: Final Report*, Sydney 2014; Victorian Law Reform Commission, *Review of the Crimes (Mental Impairment and Unfitness to Be Tried) Act 1997: Report No. 28*, Melbourne 2014.

[20]   See, e.g., B. McSHERRY, "Legal Capacity under the Convention on the Rights of Persons with Disabilities" (2012) 20 *Journal of Law and Medicine* 22; T. CARNEY and F. BEAUPERT, "Public and Private Bricolage: Challenges Balancing Law, Services and Civil Society in Advancing CRPD Supported Decision Making" (2013) 36 *University of New South Wales Law Journal* 175; P. GOODING, "Supported Decision-Making: A Rights-Based Disability Concept and its Implications for Mental Health Law" (2013) 20 *Psychiatry, Psychology and Law* 431; M. BROWNING, C. BIGBY and J. DOUGLAS, "Supported Decision making: Understanding How Its Conceptual Link to Legal Capacity Is Influencing the Development of Practice" (2014) 1 *Research and Practice in Intellectual and Developmental Disabilities* 34; L. KNOX, J. DOUGLAS and C. BIGBY, "'The Biggest Thing Is Trying to Live for Two People': Spousal Experiences of Supporting Decision-Making Participation for Partners with TBI" (2015) 29 *Brain Injury* 745; S. CALLAGHAN and C. RYAN, "An Evolving Revolution: Evaluating Australia's Compliance with the Convention on the Rights of Person's with Disabilities in Mental Health Law" (2016) 39 *University of New South Wales Law Journal* 596; A. ARSTEIN-KERSLAKE et al, "Human Rights and Unfitness to Plead: The Demands of the Convention on the Rights of Persons with Disabilities" (2017) 17 *Human Rights Law Review* 399; T. CARNEY, "Supported Decision-Making in Australia: Meeting the Challenge of Moving from Capacity to Capacity-Building?" (2017) 35 *Law in Context* 44, 63; M. BYRNE, B. WHITE and F. McDONALD, "A New Tool to Assess Compliance of Mental Health Laws with the Convention on the Rights of Persons with Disabilities" (2018) 58 *International Journal of Law and Psychiatry* 122; I. WIESEL et al, "The Temporalities of Supported Decision-making by People with Cognitive Disability" [2020] *Social and Cultural Geography* (advance); J. CHESTERMAN, "The Future of Adult Guardianship in Federal Australia" (2013) 66 *Australian Social Work* 26; J. CHESTERMAN, "The Future of Adult Safeguarding in Australia" (2019) 54 *Australian Journal of Social Issues* 360.

1.2. AUSTRALIAN LAW REFORM COMMISSION REPORT 2014

In 2013, the Australian Government requested the Australian Law Reform Commission (ALRC) to conduct a comprehensive inquiry regarding the CRPD into:

> [T]he laws and legal frameworks within the Commonwealth jurisdiction that deny or diminish the equal recognition of people with disability as persons before the law and their ability to exercise legal capacity.[21]

This was perhaps the first national law reform agency in the world to consider the implications of the CRPD provision on legal capacity and equality – and not just for guardianship or mental health laws, but *all* national laws, including those concerning access to justice, contract law, consumer protection laws, electoral matters, company directorship and marriage.

The ALRC report, *Equality, Capacity and Disability* (2014), developed a novel and influential set of National Supported Decision-Making Principles, supported by guidelines, to direct the reform of all Commonwealth, State and Territory laws relating to decision making. The National Decision-Making Principles are:

- *Equal rights*: All adults have an equal right to make decisions that affect their lives and to have those decisions respected.
- *Support*: Persons who require support in decision-making must be provided with access to the support necessary for them to make, communicate and participate in decisions that affect their lives.
- *Will, preferences and rights*: The will, preferences and rights of persons who may require decision-making support must direct decisions that affect their lives.
- *Safeguards*: Laws and legal frameworks must contain appropriate and effective safeguards in relation to interventions for persons who may require decision-making support, including to prevent abuse and undue influence.

The ALRC recommended five framing principles for guiding the recommendations for reform: *dignity; equality; autonomy; inclusion and participation;* and *accountability.*[22] The Report also recommended the government adopt a "Commonwealth decision-making model" based on the positions of "supporter" and "representative" (rather than "guardian") under

---

[21]   M. Dreyfus (Attorney-General of Australia), *"Terms of Reference" to Undertake a Review of Equal Recognition before the Law and Legal Capacity for People with Disability*, Canberra 2013 <https://www.alrc.gov.au/inquiry/equality-capacity-and-disability-in-commonwealth-laws/terms-of-reference-16> accessed 13.11.2022.

[22]   Australian Law Reform Commission (n. 19), pp. 47–62.

Commonwealth legislation to encourage supported decision-making.[23] It also called for greater consistency of terminology, policy and data collection and increased cross-jurisdictional recognition of arrangements,[24] of relevance to federal systems internationally.

The *representative* model of decision-making would apply "only as a last resort" and would be guided by "the will, preferences and rights of persons [to] direct decisions that affect their lives".[25] Representatives may, however, have to give "effect to what the person would likely want" in the event that his or her will and preference were unclear.[26] Further, "[i]f it is not possible to determine what the person would likely want, the representative must act to promote and uphold the person's human rights and act in the way least restrictive of those rights".[27]

By employing the "best interpretation of will and preferences" standard advanced by the CRPD Committee, this proposal marks a significant break from the longstanding "best interests" approach to disability-related law – though perhaps not a complete break. Ultimately, the proposal retains elements of substituted decision-making, retaining a functional mental capacity assessment as the threshold for activating representative decision-making; and recommending a provision for overriding a person's will and preferences "to prevent harm".[28] More directly, the ALRC stated that "[s]ome system of appointment of others to act is a necessary human rights backstop".[29] New South Wales (NSW) may yet be the first jurisdiction to apply these recommendations, as discussed below.

1.3. THE CRPD COMMITTEE'S ASSESSMENT OF AUSTRALIA'S COMPLIANCE

For its part, the CRPD Committee broadly endorsed the ALRC's supported decision-making framework. In its 2019 Concluding Observation, the Committee called on Australia to "[i]mplement a nationally consistent supported decision-making framework, as recommended in the [ALRC]'s 2014 report ...".[30]

---

23   Ibid., pp. 91–125.
24   Ibid.
25   Ibid., rec 3-3(b).
26   Ibid.
27   Ibid., rec 3-3(c).
28   Ibid., rec 3-3(2)(d); P. GOODING, "Navigating the 'Flashing Amber Lights' of the Right to Legal Capacity in the United Nations Convention on the Rights of Persons with Disabilities: Responding to Major Concerns" (2015) 15 *Human Rights Law Review* 45; B. ALSTON, "Towards Supported Decision-Making: Article 12 of the Convention on the Rights of Persons with Disabilities and Guardianship Law Reform" (2017) 35 *Law in Context* 21; E. CUKALEVSKI (n. 15).
29   Australian Law Reform Commission (n. 19), p. 60.
30   Committee on the Rights of Persons with Disabilities, *Concluding Observations on the Second and Third Combined Reports of Australia*, 2019, para. [24].

The CRPD Committee have also recommended that Australia's interpretive declarations on Articles 12, 17 and 18 be rescinded,[31] a view supported by a coalition of Australian disabled people's organisations[32] and the Australian Human Rights Commission.[33] To date, Australia has indicated it will retain the interpretive declarations, and that it is still considering the ALRC's recommendations.[34]

Amid these tensions, McCallum[35] has observed that in the years since Australia ratified the CRPD, there has been a clear, if gradual move away from substituted decision-making in favour of various forms of supported decision-making, particularly in Australia's network of guardianship and mental health laws, which we will discuss below.

1.4. PILOT PROJECTS

The state of South Australia led non-statutory efforts to implement supported decision-making programs as an alternative to, or as supplementary to, guardianship.[36] This was a very early global initiative to operationalise supported decision-making in the lives of persons with intellectual and cognitive disabilities. Non-statutory efforts extended to encouragement for citizens to use informal forms of supported-decision-making under South Australia's 2013 legislation on advance care directives.[37]

During the second decade of the 21st century, Australia embarked on several other small-scale trials testing the viability of operationalising supported decision-making for people with selected disability and social profiles, such as social isolation. These pilots lacked the rigorous evaluation necessary to shed much light on program costs, effectiveness or design features,[38] but

---

[31]   Committee on the Rights of Persons with Disabilities, *List of Issues prior to the Submission of the Combined Second and Third Periodic Reports of Australia*, 2017, para. [13](a).

[32]   Disability Rights Now, *Australian Civil Society Shadow Report to the United Nations Committee on the Rights of Persons with Disabilities*, 2019, para. [13](b).

[33]   Australian Human Rights Commission, *Information Concerning Australia's Compliance with the Convention on the Rights of Persons with Disabilities*, 2019, p. 5.

[34]   Attorney-General's Department (Cth), *Combined Second and Third Periodic Reports Submitted by Australia under Article 35 of the Convention*, 2018, paras. [16], [147].

[35]   R. McCallum (n. 11).

[36]   J. Brayley (n. 17).

[37]   L. Barry and S. Sage-Jacobson, "Human Rights, Older People and Decision Making in Australia" (2015) 9 *Elder Law Review* 1; T. Carney, "Supported Decision-Making in Australia: Meeting the Challenge of Moving from Capacity to Capacity-Building?" (n. 20).

[38]   C. Bigby et al, "Delivering Decision-making Support to People with Cognitive Disability – What Has Been Learned from Pilot Programs in Australia from 2010–2015" 222.

Lessons from a Reformist Path to Supported Decision-Making in Australia

as the Victorian Office of Public Advocate (OPA) concludes, the pilots have demonstrated:[39]

> the potential … for increasing the role played by people even with significant cognitive impairment as authors of their own lives. They also point to the complexity involved in negotiating the relationships between supporters and the people being supported: important incremental developments need to occur before major "decisions" can be made. This developmental stage often involves pre-decision education about possibilities and the working through of the potential consequences of particular courses of action. People with cognitive impairments often have a history of marginalisation, so it is extremely rare for a person to come to a supported decision-making program with knowledge of a particular "decision" they simply want to be helped to make.

Similar small pilot projects in Colombia, Peru and Argentina are credited as giving confidence for the full repeal of substitute decision-making in those countries, though the real test is whether any permanent programs materialise given resources are scarce, and how effective they prove to be.[40] As a rich, first-world economy, Australian experience with program development and training has been more positive, but remains very patchy.[41] Unfortunately, too many Australian programs do not rise above provision of educative resources, little known to or understood by the audience of supporters to whom they are notionally directed.

2. LEGAL DEVELOPMENTS

The Australian Constitution confines national government responsibilities such as income support or universal health care benefit payments and aged care, or any grant funding of health and welfare services run by other levels of government or civil society, to specific "heads of power".[42] Everything not specifically mentioned is the responsibility of the States and Territories, including major laws explicitly concerning guardianship, mental health and broader health care decision-making.

Australia's second decade of the 21st century also proved moderately productive for legislating new supported decision-making avenues in the state of

---

[39] Office of the Public Advocate (Vic), *Decision Time: Activating the Rights of Adults with Cognitive Disability*, Melbourne 2021, p. 22.

[40] A. V. ENCALADA, K. BIALIK and K. STOBER, "Supported Decision-Making in South America: Analysis of Three Countries' Experiences" (2021) 18 *International Journal of Environmental Research and Public Health* 5204.

[41] Cognitive Decline Partnership Centre, *Supported Decision-Making in Dementia Care: Final Project Report*, Sydney 2019 <https://cdpc.sydney.edu.au> accessed 22.03.2023.

[42] *Australian Constitution* s. 51.

Intersentia

263

Victoria, and in the development of law reform blueprints set to be implemented in other jurisdictions. Arguably the largest achievement, however, was enshrining fundamental CRPD concepts and philosophies in legislative guiding principles of enactments. Early examples include the *National Disability Insurance Scheme Act 2013* (Cth) and the *Mental Health Act 2014* (Vic)[43] (notwithstanding the contested place of mental health law post-CRPD).

2.1. "GUARDIANSHIP AND ADMINISTRATION" LAW

Victoria and NSW, the two most populous states, have seen the most significant changes or planned changes to state laws concerning adult guardianship and administration of finances and property, including new statutory or non-statutory mechanisms for support to exercise legal capacity. These law reform efforts were the first concerning laws focused on mental capacity for over 30 years.

Victoria introduced the *Guardianship and Administration Act 2019*[44] (subsequently "*Victorian Act 2019*"). Despite its anachronistic title (which we discuss shortly), McCallum calls the *Victorian Act 2019* the most "far reaching reform" in Australia thus far.[45] The Act came off the back of 2014 legislative changes that ostensibly provide legislative alternatives to guardianship to support a person's decision-making,[46] discussed below. NSW was expected to go a crucial step further in a single consolidated Assisted Decision-Making Act, akin to say Ireland; however, this plan has stalled indefinitely.

2.1.1. Victoria

The *Victorian Act 2019*[47] was enacted in May 2019 and commenced in March 2020, superseding the pioneering *Guardianship and Administration Act 1986* (Vic). The *Victorian Act 2019* was based almost entirely on the 2012 recommendations of the Victorian Law Reform Commission (VLRC) that *predated* both the CRPD Committee's General Comment 1 and the ALRC's 2014 Report. Perseverance with the VLRC recommendations[48] missed the

---

[43]   Office of the Public Advocate (Vic) (n. 39), p. 23.

[44]   Ibid., pp. 21–24.

[45]   R. McCallum (n. 11), p. 54.

[46]   *Powers of Attorney Act 2014* (Vic) ss. 87–89; *Medical Treatment Planning and Decisions Act 2016* (Vic).

[47]   Section 3(1) (Definitions) indicates that "disability" means neurological impairment, intellectual impairment, mental disorder, brain injury, physical disability or dementia.

[48]   An earlier Guardianship and Administration Bill 2012 did not pass, but the 2018 Bill duly passed in May 2019.

opportunity – one taken up in NSW and Tasmania a few years later – to more fully reflect the interpretive contribution of these two influential documents.

The *Victorian Act 2019* retains a functional mental capacity approach, described in the act as "decision-making capacity", which is subject to a rebuttable presumption.[49] The "best interests" standard, at least in name if not substance, was replaced with the guiding notion of "promot[ing] the personal and social wellbeing of a person"[50] in which "the will and preferences of a person with a disability should direct, as far as practicable, decisions made for that person".[51]

"Supported decision-making" is included in the *Victorian Act 2019* and can arise in two ways. First the person themselves (the "principal") can designate a "supportive guardian" or "supportive administrator" to have legal authority to assist with decision-making in personal affairs and financial management respectively. Alternatively, the Victorian Civil and Administrative Tribunal (VCAT) can make an appointment.[52] In either case, it is deemed to be the decision of the principal, grounded in agreement between the principal and the supporter.[53]

An array of object statements,[54] general principles,[55] and decision-making principles,[56] widely reflect core CRPD values and the National Decision-Making Principles. A VCAT appointment of a guardian or administrator is permitted only as a last resort and is not warranted where someone such as a close relative is adequately discharging that role.[57] The person appointed as a "supportive guardian" or "supportive administrator" must respect the will and preferences of the principal, give effect to their decisions as far as possible,[58] and "must discuss anything relating to a supported decision with the supported person in a way that the supported person can understand" for the purposes of assisting with a decision.[59] Supportive guardians or supportive administrators must not "coerce, intimidate or in any way unduly influence the supported person into a particular course of action".[60] To safeguard against exploitation, penalties apply if a guardian or administrator engages in illegality such as financial misappropriation[61] and there is also an avenue for recouping losses.[62]

---

[49]   *Guardianship and Administration Act 2019* (Vic) s. 5.
[50]   Ibid., s. 4.
[51]   Ibid., s. 8.
[52]   Ibid., s. 87.
[53]   Ibid., pt. 4, s. 87(2).
[54]   Ibid., s. 7.
[55]   Ibid., s. 8.
[56]   Ibid., s. 9.
[57]   Ibid., s. 31.
[58]   Ibid., ss. 8–9.
[59]   Ibid., s. 94(f).
[60]   Ibid., s. 94(h).
[61]   Ibid., ss. 188–89.
[62]   Ibid., ss. 181–85.

Retention of terms like "guardianship" and "administration" in descriptors of supporters continues to be criticised as both confusing for the public and reflecting a poor grasp of CRPD requirements. As one of us has noted, "[m]uch of the good work in the package was undone by a *very unfortunate choice* of the terms", creating the "considerable risk of the public mistakenly assuming that supporters are actually proxy decision-makers, even though no such power is actually conferred".[63] The Tasmanian and NSW proposals avoid this misstep, removing the term "guardian" altogether, as discussed in the next section.

Importantly, the suite of legislation introduced to Victoria from 2014, includes several legislative alternatives to guardianship. The *Powers of Attorney Act 2014* (Vic), for example, introduced "supportive attorney" roles, allowing an individual to appoint someone to assist in making and implementing decisions but not exercising the ultimate decision-making authority. Supportive attorneys are authorised to collect information, "communicate" information and "give effect to" decisions (but not in relation to a "significant financial transaction"). Similarly, health care proxy powers were strengthened in the state's *Medical Treatment Planning and Decisions Act 2016* (Vic), enabling anyone with the ability to do so, even children, to appoint a support person to assist with the making of medical treatment decisions. This extends to accessing and communicating information in a way that privacy and health records legislation would ordinarily inhibit,[64] and the Act also strengthens advance care directives (though these can be overridden in the context of involuntary mental health interventions).

2.1.2. Law Reform Proposals in Tasmania and New South Wales

The 2018 NSW Law Reform Commission offers Australia's most advanced law reform blueprint; however implementation is distant and uncertain, and while Tasmania likewise envisages legislating to establish support roles, public education and longer lead-time is recommended.[65] Thus, neither is imminent.

The proposed NSW Assisted Decision-Making Act would minimise possible restrictions on the rights of the principal by confining appointment of a guardian (renamed as "the Advocate") to an absolute last resort. Instead, if any measure is needed for an adult (over 18), supported decision-making respecting the principal's will and preferences would be strongly favoured. Appointed to carry out decision-making support in accordance with the decision support agreements or a tribunal order, supporters would be over the age of 16, and without a criminal record (or bankruptcy order) if financial support is involved.

---

[63]   T. CARNEY, "Supported Decision-making for People with Cognitive Impairments: An Australian Perspective?" (2015) 4 *Laws* 37.

[64]   Office of the Public Advocate (Vic) (n. 39).

[65]   Tasmanian Law Reform Institute (n. 17), pt. 7.

When providing assistance, the supporter would be obliged to observe an extensive set of general principles. A standard form and witnessing protections would govern agreements for support. An independent statutory body as in Victoria, the Office of the Public Advocate, would cover assistance for supportive decision-making, problem-solving, information provision, aid and support, or issues of abuse and neglect.

The principal would be deemed to have decision-making capacity as per an "understand and appreciate" assessment: she or he must "understand the relevant information; understand the nature of the decision and the consequences of making or failing to make that decision; retain the information to the extent necessary to make the decision; use the information or weigh it as part of the decision-making process; communicate the decision in some way". On loss of capacity and where substituted decision-making is required as a last resort, the tribunal would be able to make a "representation order". If an enduring power of attorney exists, then the holder of that authority would be the substitute decision-maker.

2.2. MENTAL HEALTH LAW

Again, the Australian Government has resisted the CRPD Committee's call to repeal all involuntary mental health treatment provisions and withdraw its interpretive declaration allowing their use as a last resort.[66] However, some jurisdictions have recently sought to give more practical force to a fairly long-standing policy of making such measures a last resort.[67] The policy is embodied in the "least restrictive alternative" principle and recently reinforced by measures such as enacting a presumption of mental capacity and legislative injunctions against involuntary treatment or restrictive practices for anyone with mental capacity. Relying on mental capacity at all falls foul of the CRPD Committee's interpretation of Article 12, but in any event these provisions did little to reduce the incidence of involuntary measures,[68] an outcome in line with international experience.[69] Notably, the negligible impact on rates of coercion of replacing the diagnostic threshold (mental disorder) with mental incapacity extends

---

[66]   R. McCallum (n. 11), pp. 79–80.

[67]   T. Carney et al, *Australian Mental Health Tribunals: "Space" for Fairness, Freedom, Protection & Treatment?*, Themis Press, Sydney 2011.

[68]   T. Foley and C. J. Ryan, "The Frequency of References to Decision-Making Capacity in Reports to the NSW Mental Health Review Tribunal Did Not Change after Legislative Reforms That Promoted Them" (2020) 28 *Australasian Psychiatry* 171; C. J. Ryan, "Is Legislative Reform Translating into Recovery-Orientated Practice and Better Protection of Rights?" (2019) 53 *Australian and New Zealand Journal of Psychiatry* 382.

[69]   P. Gooding, B. McSherry and C. Roper, "Preventing and Reducing 'Coercion' in Mental Health Services: An International Scoping Review of English-Language Studies" (2020) 142 *Acta Psychiatrica Scandinavica* 27.

to involuntary community-based psychiatric intervention, or "community treatment orders",[70] contrary to what some had hoped.[71] Indeed, the rates of such interventions appear to be rising in most Australian jurisdictions.[72]

Provision in Victoria's *Mental Health Act 2014* for appointing a supporter to assist a person deal with the mental health system, particularly Tribunal hearings into involuntary in-patient or community treatment orders, was seen as another small advance. However, the contribution has been slight, with few people taking up the opportunity.[73] Further, a recent Victorian Royal Commission into Mental Health Services criticised the 2014 Act as being "no longer fit for purpose" given the aspirations behind it, "including embedding concepts such as supported decision making ... have not been realised".[74] Instead, the Victorian Royal Commission recommended a new Mental Health and Wellbeing Act with an explicit provision requiring services to implement coercion-reduction initiatives, and a legislative mandate to expand voluntary services. Benchmark indicators to this end are to be monitored and overseen by a new independent Mental Health and Wellbeing Commission comprising significant membership with lived experience.[75] Ensuring involuntary treatment is genuinely a last resort[76] and working for elimination of seclusion and restraint[77] are among other recommendations commendably framed in concrete rather than the usual platitudinous terms. An "opt-out" model of non-legal advocacy support for anyone under or at risk of compulsory services is also proposed.[78]

However, while the new legislation has been enacted, what the overall reform package ultimately looks like and how it plays out, remains unknown at the time of writing, beyond the Government's public commitment to fully implement all recommendations.

2.3. INCOME SECURITY AND THE NATIONAL DISABILITY INSURANCE SCHEME

At the national level, social security legislation contains widely used and long-standing substitute decision-making provisions for appointing someone else to

---

[70] E. M. LIGHT, "Rates of Use of Community Treatment Orders in Australia" (2019) 64 *International Journal of Law and Psychiatry* 83.

[71] G. NEWTON-HOWES and C. J. RYAN, "The Use of Community Treatment Orders in Competent Patients Is Not Justified" (2017) 210 *British Journal of Psychiatry* 311.

[72] E. M. LIGHT (n. 70).

[73] L. BROPHY et al, "Community Treatment Orders and Supported Decision-Making" (2019) 10 *Frontiers in Psychiatry* 1.

[74] Victorian Mental Health Royal Commission, *Royal Commission into Victoria's Mental Health System: Final Report*, Melbourne 2021, vol. 4, pp. 22–23.

[75] Ibid., recs 42(2)(e)–(f), 53(2)(a)–(b), 44 respectively.

[76] Ibid., rec 55.

[77] Ibid., rec 54.

[78] Ibid., rec 56(2).

manage a person's income payments (called "representative payees" in the USA). The more recent power to appoint a "correspondence nominee", authorised to supply or access information on the person's behalf, is more facilitative in nature; but even this is hardly fully CRPD compliant.[79] Reforms proposed by the ALRC in its 2014 Report would render these powers more compliant, renaming them as representation and support appointments. But provision of meaningful safeguards to ensure fidelity to purpose remains a serious challenge because of the large numbers of people who rely on such powers in managing pensions and routine day-to-day living.[80]

Rendering Article 12 support for decision-making meaningful for the mass of ordinary citizens with few resources is surely a very high priority. This is also true for the States and Territories. They too have carriage of laws pitched at the ordinary citizen. The most common of these are laws dealing with health care decisions. These include the laws establishing "pre-authorised" lists of relatives and others empowered to make health decisions for another, and powers for the person to themselves make advance care directives and appoint an enduring attorney to make such decisions in the event of future incapacity.[81] Safeguards are a challenge in this context as well.

Similar nominee powers to those for social security are written into a national scheme to support some 800,000 people with severe functional disabilities – the National Disability Insurance Scheme (NDIS), but these are lightly used. Reliance instead is placed on State and Territory adult guardianship powers,[82] which complicates cross-jurisdictional problems.[83] In late 2020, consultancy reports on how to progress supported decision-making were commissioned by both the NDIS and by the Department of Social Services (DSS, responsible for income security payments). The NDIS consultation had closed at the time of writing with the final report still pending, but its discussion papers do not auger well, failing to canvas concrete commitments to public funding or program development.[84] This is a worrying omission because having a supporter

---

[79]   T. CARNEY, "Adult Guardianship and Other Financial Planning Mechanisms for People with Cognitive Impairment in Australia" in L. Ho and R. LEE (eds), *Special Needs Financial Planning: A Comparative Perspective*, Cambridge University Press, Cambridge 2019.

[80]   T. CARNEY, "Supported Decision-making for People with Cognitive Impairments: An Australian Perspective?" (2015) 4 *Laws* 37.

[81]   B. WHITE, L. WILLMOTT and S.-N. THEN, "Adults Who Lack Capacity: Substitute Decision-Making" in B. WHITE, F. McDONALD, and L. WILLMOTT (eds), *Health Law in Australia*, 3rd ed., Thomson Reuters Lawbook Co., Sydney 2018.

[82]   T. CARNEY, "Adult Guardianship and Other Financial Planning Mechanisms for People with Cognitive Impairment in Australia" (n. 79).

[83]   J. CHESTERMAN, "The Future of Adult Guardianship in Federal Australia" (n. 20); Office of the Public Advocate (Vic) (n. 39).

[84]   National Disability Insurance Agency, *Companion Paper: Supporting You to Make Your Own Decisions*, 2021; National Disability Insurance Agency, *Consultation Paper: Supporting You to Make Your Own Decisions*, 2021.

currently is not accepted as one of the "reasonable and necessary" supports able to be funded under the NDIS.[85] The recently published DSS Report[86] at least identifies some of the elements involved in operationalising supported decision-making. However, as yet there is no indication of how any federal initiatives would mesh with existing or future exercise of State/Territory mainstream responsibilities for supported decision-making, or whether or how adequately they would be funded.

3. DISCUSSION

3.1. THE FEDERAL LABORATORY FOR SUPPORTED DECISION-MAKING

A feature of federal systems of government is fostering diversity and policy experimentation.[87] This is amplified in Australia because the national government has few ways of bringing about greater support for decision-making. National promotion of "uniform" laws by the States and Territories has theoretical appeal but few successes;[88] national-state Agreements for coordination of service provision are another,[89] but this mechanism has recently lost favour in disability services. The National Disability Agreement 2009–2020[90] was transitioned into but largely superseded by the NDIS. The associated National Disability Strategy 2010–2020 has been extended until its successor is drafted, but although the current Strategy references promotion of CRPD principles, safeguarding to date has largely been left to State and Territory agencies such as Offices of the Public Advocate.

One benefit of federal dispersal of authority for action is boosting the chances of one jurisdiction pioneering a bold and progressive legislative or program initiative. Victoria's commendable if still slightly flawed supported decision-making reforms to guardianship, enduring powers, medical treatment, and the new *Mental Health and Wellbeing Act 2022* are examples. The far-sighted

---

[85]   T. CARNEY, "Adult Guardianship and Other Financial Planning Mechanisms for People with Cognitive Impairment in Australia" (n. 79).

[86]   J. LAURENS et al, *Good Practice in Supported Decision-Making for People with Disability*, Social Policy Research Centre UNSW Sydney, Sydney 2021.

[87]   D. HALBESTRAM and M. REIMANN (eds), *Federalism and Legal Unification: A Comparative Empirical Investigation of Twenty Systems*, Springer, Dordrecht 2014.

[88]   L. MORAUTA, "Implementing a COAG Reform Using the National Law Model: Australia's National Registration and Accreditation Scheme for Health Practitioners" (2011) 70 *Australian Journal of Public Administration* 75.

[89]   J. MENZIES, "Blowing Hot and Cold–Intergovernmental Relations Capacity in the Commonwealth Government" (2011) 70 *Australian Journal of Public Administration* 408.

[90]   See here: <https://federalfinancialrelations.gov.au/sites/federalfinancialrelations.gov.au/files/2021-05/national-disability-agreement.pdf> accessed 18.07.2023.

blueprint for an Assisted Decision-Making Act from the NSW Law Reform Commission (2018) and worthy Tasmanian proposals (2018), along with the ALRC's (2014) as yet unactioned template for national leadership, are other such beacons. Certainly, those blueprints rate well for face validity on the test of international comparison.[91] Perversely, however, another benefit of inability to legislate a "national" reform may be greater attention to arguably more effective measures *outside* the law (overcoming undue faith in "legal" solutions to policy issues), as evidenced by the plethora of pilot programs and assessments of training.

Yet for such a comparatively small population, federal governance certainly magnifies risks of confusing relevant professionals and the public at large with a blizzard of laws. The Queensland Law Society recently identified 18 different state or federal laws on substitute decision-making or support for decision-making in that State.[92] This is compounded by variation between jurisdictions in the "pattern" of relevant laws, such as where and how health care decision-making powers are dealt with, as well as variations in the substantive provisions.[93]

And as yet there is no offsetting example of two or more stakeholders taking different approaches to supported decision making so their efficacy and merits can be compared in federalism's "natural laboratory", as was possible soon after 1980s guardianship reforms.[94]

3.2. HASTENING SLOWLY?

Australian progress towards implementation of supported decision-making has been slow; certainly much slower than the CRPD Committee believes appropriate. However international progress has also been glacial[95] and even guardianship reform has been gradual.[96] Why is this so?

One little canvassed explanation is that writing legislation and designing programs which genuinely honour supported decision-making sentiments is more difficult than assumed, carrying risks of miscarriage if poorly framed.

---

[91]   S.-N. THEN et al, "Supporting Decision-making of Adults with Cognitive Disabilities: The Role of Law Reform Agencies – Recommendations, Rationales and Influence" (2018) 61 *International Journal of Law & Psychiatry* 64.

[92]   L. MURPHY, President Qld Law Society September 2020 <https://www.qls.com.au/getattachment/c24ca30a-5e0c-4011-873f-ba052b635f09/2020-4169-qls-submission-on-multiplicity-of-decision-makers-in-guardianship-matters.pdf> accessed 22.03.2023.

[93]   B. WHITE, L. WILLMOTT and S.-N. THEN (n. 81).

[94]   T. CARNEY and D. TAIT, *The Adult Guardianship Experiment: Tribunals and Popular Justice*, Federation Press, Sydney 1997.

[95]   T. CARNEY, "Prioritising Supported Decision-Making: Running on Empty or a Basis for Glacial-to-Steady Progress?" (2017) 6 *Laws* 1.

[96]   S.-N. THEN et al (n. 91).

An obvious illustration of this is the previous discussion of Victoria's poor choice of language about what to call supporters.[97] Other risks are less obvious and more contestable.

Nina Kohn for instance is critical of the few US supported decision-making laws, characterising them as empowering and insulating families from accountability without conferring any real rights for the person supported:[98]

> In short, in the majority of states, supported decision-making statutes provide individuals with disabilities no substantial rights beyond those that they would have in the absence of such statutes, and remove certain rights (e.g., to revoke the agreement, to a fiduciary level of care, to privacy) that the individual might otherwise have.

Kohn attributes this to unfortunate copying of the least suitable of the available Canadian provincial models, the representation agreements legislation in British Columbia. This neoliberal model, the argument goes, empowers private actors (at the expense of some rights of the person supported) while failing to fund either the safeguards against abuse required by Article 12(4) of the CRPD, or invest in capacity-building to cultivate provision of support.

The evidentiary base for choosing optimal legislation or programs for support for decision-making capacity has improved since Kohn cautioned against uncritical acceptance in the early 2010s.[99] But the benefits remain largely speculated more than demonstrated, and soft spots such as lack of accountability and transparency need more attention. Australia has however made a disproportionate contribution to that slim international evidence base. The pilots between 2010–2015 did not have optimally robust evaluation designs but still demonstrated successes (if patchy for some sub-groups) and shed light on economic and organisational challenges.[100] This remains a major advance on the recent three South American pilots, only one of which was evaluated and with even less adequate methodology.[101]

---

[97] T. CARNEY, "Supporting People with Cognitive Disability with Decision-making: Any Australian Law Reform Contributions?" (2015) 2 *Research and Practice in Intellectual and Developmental Disabilities* 2.

[98] N. A. KOHN, "Legislating Supported Decision-Making" (2021) 58 *Harvard Journal on Legislation* 313, 333.

[99] N. A. KOHN and J. A. BLUMENTHAL, "A Critical Assessment of Supported Decision-Making for Persons Aging with Intellectual Disabilities" (2014) 7 *Disability and Health Journal* 40; N. A. KOHN, J. A. BLUMENTHAL and A. T. CAMPBELL, "Supported Decision-Making: A Viable Alternative to Guardianship?" (2013) 117 *Penn State Law Review* 1111.

[100] C. BIGBY et al (n. 38).

[101] A. V. ENCALADA, K. BIALIK and K. STOBER (n. 40).

Australian reform blueprints locating support for decision-making in an Assisted Decision-Making Act that retains reformed, last resort "representation orders" remains fraught. However, more nuanced assessments of guardianship and supported decision-making see the two regimes not as polar extremes but as comparatively near neighbours on the spectrum of policy balances, with optimal supported decision-making edging out optimal modern guardianship as the first-choice measure.[102] Such front-end alternatives to last resort guardianship are anathema for the CRPD Committee but it is not new,[103] having long been advocated.[104]

A recent study of guardianship and the potential for supported decision-making for people with dementia in Victoria, NSW and Western Australia found some substance to that claim. Although decision-making capacity assessment remained prominent, guardianship was *not* ordered when decision-making capacity was lost unless it was *necessary* to do so for lack of informal or other alternatives to realise will and preferences.[105] Even without legislated supported decision-making options, the analysis found "a degree of supported decision-making does go on informally, particularly prior to the formal appointment of a guardian".[106]

However, these are but baby steps forward. CRPD compliance surely requires *at least* the full suite of measures recommended by the NSW Law Reform Commission (2018).

3.3. EDUCATIVE IMPACTS TOWARDS CULTURAL CHANGE?

While adoption of Article 12 CRPD "will, preferences and rights" as the lodestar principle should not be under-estimated as a major educative source of cultural change towards recognising the agency of the person represented, its direct substantive force is harder to determine. This is because paternalism is not completely ousted by the new language – prioritising a person's long-term "will" when it is at odds with their "preferences" is a dangerously close proxy for

---

[102] C. J. STAVERT, "Supported Decision-Making and Paradigm Shifts: Word Play or Real Change?" (2020) 11 *Frontiers in Psychiatry* 11, 1559.

[103] M. PARKER, "Getting the Balance Right: Conceptual Considerations Concerning Legal Capacity and Supported Decision-Making" (2016) 13 *Journal of Bioethical Inquiry* 381; B. ALSTON (n. 28); P. BARTLETT, "At the Interface Between Paradigms: English Mental Capacity Law and the CRPD" (2020) 11 *Frontiers in Psychiatry* 1; T. CARNEY, "Australian Guardianship Tribunals: An Adequate Response to CRPD Disability Rights Recognition and Protection of the Vulnerable over the Lifecourse?" (2017) 10 *Journal of Ethics in Mental Health* 1.

[104] D. TAIT and T. CARNEY, "Too Much Access? The Case for Intermediate Options to Guardianship" (1995) 30 *Australian Journal of Social Issues* 445.

[105] M. BLAKE et al (n. 3), p. 418.

[106] Ibid.

ascertaining their "best interests".[107] Nor in practice does it prove easy to know whether decisions are actually less paternalistic than previously.[108]

The educative impact of the new formulation and associated principles certainly may yet prove to be a powerful agent of cultural change, but assessing the reality of such impacts is both understudied and challenging.[109] Australia's reform blueprints reflect the strengths and limitations of a law reform lens (strong translation of CRPD norms but more limited understanding of socio-legal constraints and unintended effects). Necessarily, they were constructed from first principles given lack of knowledge of what support works, in what circumstances, and to what extent or duration.

However, the scope of coverage of the Australian proposals in ranging across the spectrum of different spheres of life impacted by current capacity-based or substitute decision-making laws, and their engagement with first principles, makes for a most important contribution to international scholarship and practice about how best to implement Article 12 of the CRPD.

4. CONCLUSION

An enduring question in law reform and social policy evaluation more generally is settling on the goal. There is always a choice. One common choice is to select the literal statement of the end to be achieved, a test of face validity. A second approach contextualises the goal in light of past experience with a similar endeavour to predict what might help or hinder implementation, including any unintended consequences. Least common of all is to ask what actually "works" (an evidence-based test).

Australia demonstrably is making discernible if slow progress in rolling out modest legislative and program initiatives in some parts of the country, with strong face validity. Policy debates demonstrate some willingness to incorporate lessons learned from cognate policy areas in shaping workable proposals, and more concrete evidence specific to supported decision-making is emerging. Australian research applying the *La Trobe training for supporters*[110] found meaningful development of skills by many – but not by any means all – parents

---

[107] T. CARNEY, "Australia" (n. 7).

[108] T. CARNEY et al, "Paternalism to Empowerment: All in the Eye of the Beholder?" (2023) 38(3) *Disability and Society* 503.

[109] S. ROY, "Theory of Social Proof and Legal Compliance: A Socio-Cognitive Explanation for Regulatory (Non) Compliance" (2021) 22 *German Law Journal* 238.

[110] J. DOUGLAS and C. BIGBY, "Development of an Evidence-Based Practice Framework to Guide Decision Making Support for People with Cognitive Impairment" (2020) 40 *Disability and Rehabilitation* 434.

of people with an intellectual disability in realising their will and preferences,[111] as also found overseas.[112] Similar outcomes are reported for people with an acquired brain injury, though take-up of programs is lower.[113] Positive responses have also been reported for supporter training materials for people with dementia.[114] Support for people with mental health conditions and psychosocial disability is less studied in Australia, but again appears receptive.[115]

It is unsurprising that there is no "one-size-fits-all" legal reform or program to cultivate good practice support for decision-making which appeals to all those potentially covered by Article 12 support; likewise that such a major paradigm and cultural shift away from paternalistic policies of imposing substitute decision-making is slow and costly given that they originated in the common law world in the 13th century.[116] Passing laws to effect fundamental cultural changes is only a small and perhaps symbolic component of what is required for real implementation of Article 12.[117]

As observed of the legal and program vacuum now existing in Colombia, Peru and Argentina, it is one thing to abandon substitute decision-making but another and more costly exercise to roll out programs, provide accountability safeguards, and crucially to foster the needed cultural change on the part of informal supporters. An overnight swing from substitute to supported decision-making risks the old adage about jumping from the frying pan to the fire. Australia's less than optimal pace of gradualist reform at least avoids that charge.

---

[111]   C. BIGBY et al, "'I Used to Call Him a Non-Decision-Maker: I Never Do That Anymore': Parental Reflections about Training to Support Decision Making of Adult Offspring with Intellectual Disabilities" (2023) 44 *Disability and Rehabilitation* 6356; C. BIGBY et al, "Parental Strategies That Support Adults with Intellectual Disabilities to Explore Decision Preferences, Constraints and Consequences" (2022) 47 *Journal of Intellectual and Developmental Disability* 165.

[112]   S. WERNER and R. CHABANY, "Guardianship Law Versus Supported Decision-Making Policies: Perceptions of Persons with Intellectual or Psychiatric Disabilities and Parents" (2016) 86 *American Journal of Orthopsychiatry* 486.

[113]   J. DOUGLAS, C. BIGBY and E. SMITH, *Building Capacity to Support Client Decision Making*, TAC Project No. T005, Melbourne 2020.

[114]   C. SINCLAIR et al, "'A Real Bucket of Worms': Views of People Living with Dementia and Family Members on Supported Decision-Making" (2019) 16 *Journal of Bioethical Inquiry* 587; C. SINCLAIR et al, "Professionals' Views and Experiences in Supporting Decision-Making Involvement for People Living with Dementia" (2021) 20 *Dementia* 84.

[115]   R. KOKANOVIC et al, "Supported Decision-Making from the Perspectives of Mental Health Service Users, Family Members Supporting Them and Mental Health Practitioners" (2018) 52 *Australian and New Zealand Journal of Psychiatry* 826.

[116]   T. CARNEY, "Civil and Social Guardianship for Intellectually Handicapped People" (1982) 8 *Monash University Law Review* 199.

[117]   G. QUINN, "Legal Culture and the CRPD" in E. KAKOULLIS and K. JOHNSON (eds), *Recognising Human Rights in Different Cultural Contexts*, Palgrave Macmillan, Singapore 2020.

As one of us has previously written "[I]t is from such small steps that sufficient incremental knowledge ultimately accrues and that apparently worthy social policies are refined over time. Wicked problems just have to be chipped away at."[118] As this chapter was being finalised, the Royal Commission into Violence, Abuse, Neglect and Exploitation of People with Disability[119] commissioned from an expanded Bigby-led La Trobe team, a 12-month study to inform the development and implementation of frameworks for supported decision-making and make recommendations to give effect to Australia's obligations under Article 12 of the CRPD. The report from that study is due to be provided in August 2022, while the Royal Commission is due to report by 29 September 2023.

The proof or otherwise of Australia's strategy of gradual chipping away at implementation of Article 12 will, however, not be known for some time.

---

[118] T. CARNEY, "Supported Decision-Making in Australia: Meeting the Challenge of Moving from Capacity to Capacity-Building?" (n. 20).

[119] Royal Commission into Violence, Abuse, Neglect and Exploitation of People with Disability, *Webpage*, 2021 <https://disability.royalcommission.gov.au> accessed 13.11.2022.

MENTAL CAPACITY IN HONG KONG

Inconsistencies, Uncertainties, and the Need for Reform

Urania CHIU* and Pok Yin S. CHOW**

1. Introduction 277
2. The Development of Mental Capacity Law in Hong Kong 278
3. The Definitions of Mental (In)Capacity in Hong Kong Law 281
4. Consent to Medical Treatment (Other than for Mental Disorder) 285
5. Guardianship and Management of Property by the Court 288
    5.1. Guardianship 288
    5.2. Management of Property and Affairs by the Court or a
        Committee.. 292
6. Decision-Making in Cases of Future Incapacity...................... 293
7. Conclusion.. 297

1. INTRODUCTION

In the area of mental health and capacity law, Hong Kong lags far behind many jurisdictions in terms of its compliance with international human rights standards. To this day, the Hong Kong Government's approach to issues around mental capacity continues to be heavily based upon the medical model of mental illness and disability, which equates functional impairment with the loss of legal capacity and stresses the need for psychiatric intervention and rehabilitation. This is despite resulting inconsistencies with norms set out in the various international human rights treaties applicable to Hong Kong, including the International Covenant on Civil Political Rights (ICCPR) and the International Covenant on Economic, Social and Cultural Rights (ICESCR), which had been ratified by the United Kingdom (and whose applicability was extended to the territory) prior to Hong Kong's handover to the People's Republic of China

---

*   DPhil Candidate, Centre for Socio-Legal Studies, Faculty of Law, University of Oxford, UK. Email: urania.chiu@law.ox.ac.uk.

**   Senior Lecturer, Newcastle Law School, New South Wales, Australia. Email: stephenson. chow@newcastle.edu.au.

(PRC). Both treaties are now entrenched in the Hong Kong Basic Law, with the ICCPR further domesticated through the Hong Kong Bill of Rights Ordinance (HKBORO). In August 2008, the PRC ratified the Convention on the Rights of Persons with Disabilities (CRPD), whose applicability was again extended to Hong Kong.[1] However, the provisions of the CRPD have not been incorporated into domestic law and are, as such, not directly litigable in local courts.[2]

This chapter looks at various legal provisions regulating mental capacity in Hong Kong and evaluates them against requirements set out by Article 12 of the CRPD, highlighting areas which demonstrate inconsistencies, uncertainties, and a need for reform in light of current international human rights norms and standards. The next section provides an overview of the development of Hong Kong law in the area, highlighting changes in its approach to mental health and capacity through the past decades. Section 3 examines how mental (in)capacity is defined in Hong Kong law while sections 4 to 6 closely examine the regulation of (civil) capacity in three significant areas: medical treatment of those without capacity to consent, substitute decision-making in the forms of guardianship and management of property by the Court, and advance decision-making. Finally, section 7 concludes with broader reflections on the compliance of Hong Kong mental capacity/health law with the norms and values set out under the CRPD and other international human rights treaties.

2. THE DEVELOPMENT OF MENTAL CAPACITY LAW IN HONG KONG

The origins of current laws in relation to mental capacity in Hong Kong date back to the colonial era. Hong Kong became a British colony in 1841 and, apart from a brief period under Japanese occupation from 1941 to 1945, remained so until its sovereignty was transferred to the PRC in July 1997. At the very beginning of colonial rule, English laws were received into Hong Kong by the enactment of several constitutional documents, including the 1843 Hong Kong Letters Patent and the 1843 Royal Instructions.[3] In 1844, the Supreme Court Ordinance was passed to establish the court system in Hong Kong and to formally introduce a wholesale incorporation of English laws, specifically providing that the common law and the laws as enacted in the UK shall apply in Hong Kong, except where they were "inapplicable to the local circumstances

---

[1]   C.J. PETERSEN, "China's Ratification of the Convention on the Rights of Persons with Disabilities: The Implications for Hong Kong" (2008) 38 *Hong Kong Law Journal* 611, 624–25.

[2]   Hong Kong takes a dualist approach in its international obligations. See M. RAMSDEN, "Dualism in the Basic Law: The First 20 Years" (2019) 49 *Hong Kong Law Journal* 239.

[3]   See P. WESLEY-SMITH, "The Reception of English Law in Hong Kong" (1988) 18 *Hong Kong Law Journal* 183.

of [Hong Kong] or of its inhabitants".[4] Even as Hong Kong acquired its own legislature as early as in 1843, it is generally undisputed that, at least up until the handover, laws and policies in Hong Kong were heavily influenced by those adopted in the UK.[5] It has been observed that the health care laws and policies set in place by the colonial government "combin[e] a British colonial history [with] a Chinese cultural context".[6]

In the early days of British Hong Kong, mental health legislation primarily addressed individuals suffering from some form of mental disorder. The first piece of mental health legislation enacted in Hong Kong separately from English law was the 1906 Asylums Ordinance, which replaced the English Lunacy Regulations Act 1853 as the applicable law for the compulsory detention and care of "persons of unsound mind". For the purposes of the Asylums Ordinance,

> every person shall be deemed to be of unsound mind who is so far deranged in mind as to render it either *necessary or expedient* that such person, either for his own sake or in the public interests, should be placed and kept under control (emphasis added).[7]

Section 5 of the Ordinance further provides that:

> Any medical practitioner, officer of police or any private person, *having reason to believe* that a person is of unsound mind may on the written order of any magistrate or justice of the peace cause such person to be conveyed, using such force as may be necessary, to an asylum (emphasis added).[8]

The Asylums Ordinance underwent a series of amendments until it was replaced by the Mental Hospitals Ordinance in 1950,[9] though little changed in relation to the definition of persons of "unsound mind" and the low threshold upon which a person might be compulsorily detained. The primary effect of the 1950 Mental Hospitals Ordinance was to put in place more stringent requirements in the regulation of the mental institutions, following the general change in mental health policy that individuals with mental illness ought to be medically attended and not simply locked away in the name of public safety/interest.[10]

---

4   Supreme Court Ordinance, 1873.
5   See *China Field Ltd v. Appeal Tribunal (Buildings) (No 2)* (2009) 12 HKCFAR 342, 351–52: "[Historically], Hong Kong courts had to develop what amounted to a common law of Hong Kong even though it was for the most part identical to English law."
6   V. SCHOEB, "Healthcare Service in Hong Kong and Its Challenges: The Role of Health Professionals within a Social Model of Health" [2016] *China Perspectives* 51.
7   Asylums Ordinance, s. 3.
8   Asylums Ordinance, s. 5.
9   The Asylums Ordinance was amended in 1927 and 1935. See D. CHEUNG, "Mental Health Law in Hong Kong: The Civil Context" (2018) 48 *Hong Kong Law Journal* 461.
10   For example, the Mental Hospitals Ordinance provided for voluntary admissions and included not only "custody and care" but also "treatment" of patients.

In the late 1950s and early 1960s, following the Guillebaud Report (1956),[11] the UK's approach to mental health began to shift towards de-institutionalisation.[12] Hong Kong soon followed: the first iteration of the Mental Health Ordinance (MHO) was enacted in 1960 (taking effect in 1962), through which the Government sought to make provisions for all aspects of care and treatment of individuals who, as a result of mental illness or intellectual disabilities, were unable to manage affairs in relation to their person or property, i.e., individuals who were "mentally incapacitated". In essence, the MHO empowers the Court to exercise *parens patriae* jurisdiction on the state's behalf, allowing treatment orders to be made and committees to be appointed to manage the financial and personal affairs of mentally incapacitated persons.[13] The MHO has since undergone several phases of amendment, establishing, in its Amendment Ordinance in 1988, the Mental Health Review Tribunal,[14] a quasi-judicial body responsible for the review of applications made by persons subjected to the compulsory regime, including those liable to be detained in a hospital and those in the community.[15] Another significant change took place in the 1996/7 reform, which was the introduction of a full-fledged guardianship regime with its own Guardianship Board,[16] another quasi-judicial body, empowered to make, review, and vary guardianship orders[17] with the aims of "support[ing], protect[ing] and advocat[ing] the best interests of mentally incapacitated adults" and "facilitat[ing] the resolution of disputes with relatives and service providers".[18] Under the current iteration of the MHO, where the Guardianship Board is, inter alia, of the view that an individual's ability to make "reasonable decisions in respect of all or a substantial proportion of the matters which relate to his personal circumstances" is limited by mental disorder or handicap and "no other less restrictive or intrusive means are available in the circumstances" to meet the individual's particular needs,[19] it may appoint a private guardian, such as a friend or a relative, or designate the Director of Social Welfare as a public guardian to make decisions on behalf of the individual.[20]

---

[11] See, for an overview of the Report, T.E. CHESTER, "The Guillebaud Report" (1956) 34 *Public Administration* 199.

[12] See, P. NOLAN, "The History of Community Mental Health Nursing" in B. HANNIGAN and M. COFFEY (eds), *The Handbook of Community Mental Health Nursing*, Routledge, London 2003, pp. 7–18.

[13] R. LEE, "The Adult Guardianship Dilemma in Hong Kong" (2019) 25 *Trusts & Trustees* 1073, 1074; MHO, pts. IVB, II. See Sections 4 and 5 below.

[14] MHO, pt. IVA.

[15] MHO, s. 59B.

[16] MHO, pt. IVB.

[17] MHO, s. 59K(1).

[18] GUARDIANSHIP BOARD (HONG KONG), "Vision, Mission and Values of the Guardianship Board" <http://www.adultguardianship.org.hk/content.aspx?id=home&lang=en> accessed 14.07.2022.

[19] MHO, s. 59O.

[20] MHO, s. 59S.

Today, the concept of mental incapacity is associated with a wider range of conditions which may impair a person's cognitive capacities than "unsound mind", such as dementia, stroke, schizophrenia, other forms of psychiatric or cognitive disorders, intellectual disabilities, or brain damage caused by injury, illness or substance abuse. The sections below discuss how mental (in)capacity is defined under different headings in Hong Kong mental health law and its practical implications.

3. THE DEFINITIONS OF MENTAL (IN)CAPACITY IN HONG KONG LAW

The law on mental (in)capacity in Hong Kong is made up of a complex matrix of judge-made and statutory principles. Given the jurisdiction's continued use of the common law legal system to this day, the starting point for assessing mental capacity in Hong Kong is found in English common law. The law is, however, complicated by the MHO, which provides not one but multiple definitions of capacity to be applied in different contexts. As will be demonstrated, these different tests are predicated upon different understandings of mental capacity and may yield results that are at odds with one another.

In common law, the overarching principle in relation to mental capacity is that every adult is presumed to have capacity to make decisions for themselves – including on medical treatment, care, or other non-medical matters – although this presumption may be rebutted with respect to each specific instance of decision-making.[21] A person may be said to lack capacity if "some impairment or disturbance of mental functioning" renders him/her unable to make a decision,[22] with this ability assessed through a three-stage test: (i) whether the person is capable of taking in and retaining the relevant information; (ii) whether they believe it; and (iii) whether they are capable of weighing that information, balancing risks and needs (the *Re C* test).[23] If someone is deemed capable of making a decision, their choice must be respected, even in life-threatening situations:

> [T]he principle of self-determination requires that respect must be given to the wishes of the patient, so that, if an adult patient of sound mind refuses, however unreasonably, to consent to treatment or care by which his life would or might be prolonged, the doctors responsible must give effect to his wishes, even though they do not consider it to be in his best interests to do so.[24]

---

21   *Re T (Adult: Refusal of Treatment)* [1992] 4 All ER 649 (CA) (Lord Donaldson).
22   *Re MB* [1997] EWCA Civ 3093 [4].
23   *Re C (Adult: Refusal of Treatment)* [1994] 1 All ER 819 (QBD).
24   *Re C (Adult: Refusal of Treatment)* [1994] 1 All ER 819 (QBD). See also *Airedale NHS Trust v. Bland* [1993] 1 All ER 821, at 860.

Intersentia

Other key principles in relation to the assessment of capacity may also be discerned from the case law:

- The capacity required for a specific decision in question is commensurate with its gravity.[25]
- A person is not deemed to lack capacity merely because their decision appears to be unreasonable or irrational.[26]
- It is not necessary for a person to "use and weigh every detail", but only the "salient factors", of the options available in order to demonstrate capacity.[27]
- Even though a person may be unable to use and weigh some of the relevant information, they may nevertheless be able to use and weigh other elements sufficiently enough to be able to make a capacitous decision.[28]
- Where capacity is found to be lacking, having considered the above, the decision must be made in the person's best interests.[29]

In England and Wales, these principles were consolidated into statutory law in 2005 through the Mental Capacity Act (MCA), as it was thought at the time that the uncertainty surrounding the common law framework had left professionals vulnerable to legal actions and delayed access to treatment for patients.[30] Under the MCA, section 1 first reaffirms the presumption of capacity and other key principles. The next sections then lay down the two parts in the capacity assessment: section 2 sets out the "diagnostic" threshold, requiring any inability to make a decision to be a result of "an impairment of, or a disturbance in the functioning of, the mind or brain" while section 3 sets out the "functional" threshold, i.e., what it means to be "unable" to make a decision. The section 3 test is similar to the three-stage test found in common law (the *Re C* test):[31] a person is unable to make a decision for themselves if they are unable to understand, retain, use, or weigh information relevant to the decision in the decision-making process *or* if they are unable to communicate that decision. Additionally, it is emphasised that a lack of capacity cannot be established merely by reference to the person's age, appearance, or other "unjustified assumptions" associated with their condition.[32]

In Hong Kong's case, however, the Government has not followed England's footsteps in putting these common law principles into legislation. Instead, in parallel to the common law test, a separate statutory framework for mental capacity

---

[25] *Re T (Adult: Refusal of Treatment)* [1992] 4 All ER 649 (CA) (Lord Donaldson).
[26] *Re T (Adult: Refusal of Treatment)* [1992] 4 All ER 649 (CA) (Lord Donaldson).
[27] *CC v. KK and STCC* [2012] EWHC 2136 (COP) [69].
[28] *Re SB (A Patient; Capacity to Consent to Termination)* [2013] EWHC 1417 (COP) [44]; *WBC (Local Authority) v. Z, X, Y* [2016] EWCOP 4 [12].
[29] *Re F (Mental Patient: Sterilisation)* [1990] 2 AC 1, at 55.
[30] E. JACKSON, *Medical Law: Text, Cases, and Materials*, 4th ed., OUP, Oxford 2016, p. 243.
[31] *Re C (Adult: Refusal of Treatment)* [1994] 1 All ER 819 (QBD).
[32] MCA 2005, s. 2(3).

Mental Capacity in Hong Kong

has been developed. Under section 2 of the MHO, the general interpretation provision, "mental incapacity" means "(a) mental disorder; or (b) mental handicap", which are in turn defined as follows:

"mental disorder" means—

(a) mental illness;
(b) a state of arrested or incomplete development of mind which amounts to a significant impairment of intelligence and social functioning which is associated with abnormally aggressive or seriously irresponsible conduct on the part of the person concerned;
(c) psychopathic disorder; or
(d) any other disorder or disability of mind which does not amount to mental handicap,

and "mentally disordered" shall be construed accordingly;

"mental handicap" means sub-average general intellectual functioning with deficiencies in adaptive behaviour, and "mentally handicapped" shall be construed accordingly.

There is a separate definition for "mentally incapacitated person":

"mentally incapacitated person" means—

(a) for the purposes of Part II ["Management of property and affairs of mentally incapacitated persons"], a person who is incapable, by reason of mental incapacity, of managing and administering his property and affairs; or
(b) for all other purposes, a patient or a mentally handicapped person, as the case may be.

In the same subsection, a "patient" is defined as "a person suffering or appearing to be suffering from mental disorder". This definition of "mentally incapacitated person" is thus wider than simply someone with "mental incapacity" as defined above, as "patient" includes not only those diagnosed with a mental disorder but also those who *appear* to be suffering from a mental disorder.

It should be noted that a finding of "mental incapacity" or that someone is a "mentally incapacitated person" under section 2 does not mean that the person is deemed by the law to lack capacity to make a particular decision; rather, it operates similarly to the diagnostic threshold of the common law test (the requirement of the presence of "some impairment or disturbance of mental functioning"),[33] which delineates the broad category of individuals who may be subject to the second part of the capacity test involving the functional threshold. The function thresholds vary with specific areas of regulation in

---

[33]   *Re MB* [1997] EWCA Civ 3093 [4].

Intersentia

283

relation to "mentally incapacitated persons" and are provided for under different Parts of the Ordinance. For example, section 7 under Part II of the Ordinance ("Management of property and affairs of mentally incapacitated persons") obliges the Court to order an inquiry into whether someone is "incapable, by reason of mental incapacity, of managing or administering his property and affairs" so as to determine whether a committee should be established to manage the individual's property on his/her behalf. In short, having established that the individual in question is "mentally *incapacitated*", the Court will have to determine whether they are also thereby *incapable* of making certain decisions.

Similarly, a different functional threshold may be found in section 59ZB under Part IVC ("Medical and dental treatment") which provides for the treatment (other than for mental disorder) of "a mentally incapacitated person who has attained the age of 18 years and is incapable of giving consent" to said treatment. Consent here refers to the person's ability to "understand" "the general nature and effect of the treatment".[34] This test for capacity in relation to medical treatments appears to be more akin to the general common law test compared to the test for the management of property. Nevertheless, it presents a more simplistic threshold compared to the *Re C* test, which requires the person to be able to retain, believe, *and* weigh information relevant to the decision.

The result of the above is that, while the *Re C* common law test has general applicability to decisions in relation to all matters, if the situation of a "mentally incapacitated person" (as defined by section 2 of the MHO) falls under any of the specific areas detailed under the MHO, the test prescribed under the relevant section will apply. This (unnecessary) complexity surrounding the definition of "mentally incapacitated persons" is partly attributable to the government's desire to adopt a single "generic name" in the legislation to refer to both those with mental illness and those with mental handicap in drafting the 1997 amendments to the MHO, supposedly for the sake of convenience.[35] In practice, the co-existence of these different definitions of capacity in common and statutory law has produced a legal framework that is rather too complex for both private individuals and medical and legal professionals to navigate.

The complication in the framework governing mental capacity is further evidenced by the fact that the Hong Kong Hospital Authority has separately issued guidelines on the subject for medical practitioners. For example, in relation to in-hospital resuscitation decisions, the Hospital Authority has set out the following test for capacity:

> A competent adult is defined as one with decision-making capacity, which consists of the elements of (i) the ability to understand the medical information presented;

---

[34]   MHO, s. 59ZB.

[35]   D. CHEUNG (2018) (n. 9), p. 480.

(ii) the ability to reason and consider this information in relation to his own personal values and goals; and (iii) the ability to communicate meaningfully.[36]

More recently, the Hospital Authority issued the *Guidelines on Life-Sustaining Treatment in the Terminally Ill*, which explicitly adopts the British Medical Association's guidance on capacity and includes understanding the treatment's "purpose and nature" and "mak[ing] a free choice".[37] Both of these tests are evidently distinct from the section 59ZB MHO test of "understanding the general nature and effect of treatment". Not only does this myriad of very dissimilar guidelines demonstrate a gap between what the law says and what is done in actual practice, the fact that the Hospital Authority feels the need to issue additional guidance in this area is perhaps a telling sign that the current law is inadequate in providing clarity and certainty to practitioners.

This patchwork of legal and non-legal regulations has consequences for both practical efficacy and conceptual coherence: apart from the difficulty in working out how to interpret and apply the law (and other relevant rules) when there is doubt about an individual's decision-making capacity, the way "mental incapacity" is structured and assessed under the current legal framework is also conceptually problematic in a number of ways, especially in light of Article 12 of the CRPD, which reaffirms persons with disabilities' right to equal recognition before the law. These challenges will be explored in turn in the following sections, focusing on two broadly defined areas in civil mental health law.

4. CONSENT TO MEDICAL TREATMENT (OTHER THAN FOR MENTAL DISORDER)

As noted above, in determining whether an individual has the requisite mental capacity to consent to medical treatment (other than for mental disorder),[38] there are two relevant tests: (i) the common law test and (ii) the test under section 59ZB(2) of the MHO. The general rule is that the common law test applies, unless the person is a "mentally incapacitated person" under section 2

---

[36]   As quoted in LAW REFORM COMMISSION OF HONG KONG, *Substitute Decision-Making and Advance Directives in Relation to Medical Treatment* (2006), p. 52 <https://www.hkreform. gov.hk/en/docs/rdecision-e.pdf> accessed 14.07.2022.

[37]   HOSPITAL AUTHORITY (HONG KONG), *HA Guidelines on Life-Sustaining Treatment in the Terminally Ill* (2020), para. 5 <https://www.ha.org.hk/haho/ho/psrm/LSTEng.pdf> accessed 14.07.2022.

[38]   The compulsory detention and treatment of individuals for their mental disorder is provided for by Part III of the MHO. As very different considerations are at stake here to those involved in mental capacity assessments – compulsory measures are justified not based on mental incapacity but on treatment/public safety-related considerations – they will not be discussed in this chapter.

of the MHO. The section 59ZB(2) and common law tests are not necessarily consistent with each other and, depending on whether a person is deemed to be a "mentally incapacitated person" under the MHO, vastly different answers to the question of whether someone has legal capacity to make a particular decision may result. While the section 59ZB(2) test, by requiring the individual to "understand" "the general nature and effect of the treatment", appears to be a threshold that is easier to meet than the common law test, "understanding" remains to be interpreted and may presumably take the *Re C* common law definition of *taking in, retaining, believing,* and *weighing* information relevant to the decision.[39] Of more concern is the fact that none of the key common law principles regarding the application of the capacity test, such as the principle that a person is not to be treated as lacking capacity simply because she makes an "unwise" decision, are included in the MHO.[40] Meanwhile, section 2 of the MHO labels all those with mental disabilities as "*mentally* incapacitated", which, of course, is in itself incredibly stigmatising and discriminatory.

Under the current legal framework in Hong Kong, the "best interests" test is used to determine whether treatment should be carried out in relation to a person deemed to lack capacity, according to both the MHO and common law tests. Section 59ZB(3) requires the Court to ensure the proposed treatment is "carried out in the best interests" of the individual, while common law allows the Court, in its inherent jurisdiction, to make the declaration that a proposed treatment is in a patient's best interests and therefore lawful for the doctor to administer in their professional duty.[41] Under section 59ZA, "in the best interests" may mean in the best interests of that person in order to

(a) save the life of the mentally incapacitated person;
(b) prevent the damage or deterioration to the physical or mental health and well-being of that person; or
(c) bring about an improvement in the physical or mental health and well-being of that person[.]

Best interests under the MHO, then, is very much oriented towards the individual's *medical* best interests. In contrast, the common law framework includes not only what an individual's physical and mental wellbeing may require but also other factors, including their wishes, feelings, and values.[42] Still, although the latter encompasses a much broader range of considerations, both regimes amount to *substitute* decision-making on the individual's behalf.

---

[39] *Re C (Adult: Refusal of Treatment)* [1994] 1 All ER 819 (QBD).
[40] C.f. MCA 2005, ss. 2–3.
[41] *Re F (Mental Patient: Sterilisation)* [1990] 2 AC 1, at 77 (Lord Goff).
[42] In English law, these principles are now consolidated under MCA 2005, s. 4.

In terms of compliance with CRPD standards and values, the first and most glaring problem in both the common law and MHO regimes is that, by using the presence of "some impairment or disturbance of mental functioning",[43] mental disorder, or "mental handicap" as the diagnostic threshold in capacity assessments, the concept of "mental incapacity" applies to persons with, or who appear to have, mental disabilities in a manner that is clearly discriminatory. This provision runs directly against the principle of equal recognition before the law under Article 12 of the CRPD: the Committee on the Rights of Persons with Disabilities (CtteeRPD) has affirmed time and again that "a person's status as a person with a disability or the existence of an impairment (including a physical or sensory impairment) must never be grounds for denying legal capacity or any of the rights provided for in Article 12".[44]

Nevertheless, even if the diagnostic threshold were removed and only the functional test remained, the approaches in common law and the MHO would still fall short of what is required by Article 12 of the CRPD. According to the CtteeRPD, Article 12 recognises that everyone has the right to legal capacity.[45] Functional tests disproportionately deny persons with disabilities their legal capacity, as they impose too heavy a burden on the individual to meet the requisite threshold without considering the needs of the person or providing any assistance or support for them to exercise their decision-making skills.[46] The CtteeRPD maintains that, in cases where a capacity assessment must be carried out, such as in the context of medical decisions where informed consent is required, states have an obligation to provide the necessary support and reasonable accommodation to facilitate the individual in question in the exercise of their legal capacity, for example by legally recognising the role of supporters.[47]

To conclude, the consequence of failing the functional tests for capacity in Hong Kong is that the decision in question will be made *for* the person in their best interests. The "best interests" principle operates to substitute the person's judgment with medical or judicial opinion on what is in their best interests, in violation of Article 12 of the CPRD.[48] It is contended that the law should accommodate an approach based on the will and preference of the individual. Even where it is impracticable to *determine* such will and preferences, such as in the case of a person in a persistent vegetative state, an approach that could provide a best *interpretation* of his/her will and preferences should be adopted. In any event, alternative planning tools such as advance directives ought to be

---

[43]   *Re MB* [1997] EWCA Civ 3093 [4].

[44]   UN CtteeRPD, "General Comment No. 1 on Article 12: Equal Recognition before the Law" (2014) UN Doc CRPD/C/GC/1, para. 9.

[45]   Ibid., para. 9.

[46]   Ibid., para. 15.

[47]   Ibid., para. 15.

[48]   Ibid., para. 21.

available so as to enable individuals to indicate their preferences in advance in the event of loss of capacity.[49]

In the next section, the thorny questions of substitute decision-making and best interests will be further explored in relation to the guardianship system and the Court's power in managing a mentally incapacitated person's property and affairs.

5. GUARDIANSHIP AND MANAGEMENT OF PROPERTY BY THE COURT

As noted above, the MHO establishes a guardianship regime for "mentally incapacitated persons" who are 18 or above under Part IVB.[50] A guardian is a person appointed to assist the mentally incapacitated adult in "facilitat[ing] the management of their finances" and "ensur[ing] that their needs for services and medical treatment are met".[51] It should be noted that guardians can only give consent to treatment on behalf of the mentally incapacitated person to the extent that he/she is "incapable of understanding the general nature and effect of any such treatment".[52] A mentally incapacitated adult's property and other financial affairs, such as their bank accounts, stocks, and other investments may also be managed by the Court or a committee established under Part II of the MHO. Often, when a person is found to be mentally incapacitated (for example, due to old age and accompanying deterioration in their mental health), the concurrent appointment of both a guardian and a committee may be deemed necessary under the MHO. Both mechanisms constitute forms of substitute decision-making under international human rights law.

5.1. GUARDIANSHIP

Section 59M of the MHO sets out the criteria for a mentally incapacitated person to be eligible for reception into guardianship: an application may be made in respect of them if (a) they are suffering from mental disorder or has a mental handicap "of a nature or degree which warrants" such reception *and* (b) it is

---

[49]   The legal status of advance directives in Hong Kong is addressed in Section 6 below.

[50]   The guardianship of minors is addressed separately in other legislation, including the Guardianship of Minors Ordinance and the Protection of Children and Juveniles Ordinance.

[51]   GUARDIANSHIP BOARD (HONG KONG), "Vision, Mission and Values of the Guardianship Board" (n. 18). This should not be confused with the Court's power to appoint a committee for the management of property and affairs for mentally incapacitated persons, which is provided for separately under Part II of the MHO and which will be discussed below in Section 5.2.

[52]   MHO, s. 59R(3)(d).

288

"necessary in the interests of the welfare of the mentally incapacitated person or for the protection of other persons" to do so. In considering the merits of an application, in addition to being satisfied that the above criteria are met,[53] the Guardianship Board must also ensure the mental disorder or handicap in question "*limits* the mentally incapacitated person in making *reasonable* decisions in respect of *all or a substantial proportion of the matters which relate to his personal circumstances*" (emphasis added) and that "the particular needs of the mentally incapacitated person may only be met or attended to by his being received into guardianship", with "no other less restrictive or intrusive" alternative available.[54]

The first requirement here appears to present a rather low and uncertain threshold at odds with both the common law and section 59ZB(2) tests for capacity, as the individual is only required to be *limited* in their decision-making ability. Although this must be in relation to "all or a substantial proportion" of their personal matters, it is unclear if there is a threshold for the degree of "limitation" which is required and what that might be.[55] Moreover, the emphasis on making "reasonable" decisions is not only strange, as this term does not appear in any other capacity tests under the MHO, but also plainly inconsistent with the now widely accepted principle that individuals cannot be deemed to lack capacity merely because their choices seem "unwise" or "unreasonable".[56] The latter requirement of less restrictive alternatives is presumably to offer greater protection for the autonomy of those eligible to be received into guardianship, but such alternatives are currently lacking in the legislative framework. Nevertheless, it may encourage informal arrangements between the mentally incapacitated person in question and their family and/or carers be attempted first, before a guardianship order is made.[57]

The powers conferred upon a guardian are very broad and touch upon a wide range of matters in relation to the individual's personal care, including the power to require them to reside at or attend specified places and the power to hold, receive, or pay money on behalf of the individual for their maintenance or benefit.[58] The main criticism often lodged against the guardianship system is that, once the individual is deemed eligible for guardianship *at the point of the initial assessment* and an order made, the individual will completely lose the ability to make decisions in many domains of their personal life. In other

---

53 MHO, s. 59O(3)(a)(d).
54 MHO, s. 59O(3)(b)(c).
55 D. CHEUNG (2018) (n. 9), p. 482.
56 See *Re T (Adult: Refusal of Treatment)* [1992] 4 All ER 649 (CA) and the MCA 2005, s. 1(4).
57 H.W.M. KWOK and P. SCULLY, "Guardianship for People with Learning Disabilities: The Current Perspective in Hong Kong" (2005) 33 *British Journal of Learning Disabilities* 145, 146.
58 MHO, s. 59R(3).

words, mental (in)capacity becomes an all-or-nothing concept, contrary to the now prevalent idea at common law that capacity is time-specific and dependent upon the nature and gravity of each decision that has to be made.[59] Furthermore, once a person has been received into the largely paternalistic guardianship regime, there is no room for them to exercise their residual autonomy, there being no formal provisions for their participation in the decision-making process or support for doing so.[60]

Throughout Part IVB of the MHO, a clear tension thus emerges between the two key principles underpinning the guardianship system: the best interests principle and the protection of autonomy. Sections 59K(2) and 59S(1) require the Board and the guardian, respectively, to observe and apply the following in the exercise of their powers: that "the interests of the mentally incapacitated person ... are promoted, *including overriding the views and wishes of that person where [the Board or the proposed guardian] considers such action is in the interests of that person*" (emphasis added) and that despite this, "the views and wishes of the mentally incapacitated person are, in so far as they may be ascertained, respected". Recall the CtteeRPD's strong interpretation of the CRPD, which requires the adoption of a "universal legal capacity" approach and under which any form of substitute decision-making, including one based on a best interests assessment, is prohibited.[61] It is explicit in the wording in sections 59K(2) and 59S(1) that, while the views and wishes of the mentally incapacitated person are to be respected where ascertainable, it is only to the extent that they cohere with what is in their best interests, according to the Board or the guardian; if there is any inconsistency between the two, the latter prevails. Hence, even though the best interests test may have "a strong element of 'substituted judgment'"[62] or, in the CtteeRPD's language, an element of the "best interpretation" of wills and preferences approach,[63] it does not in fact guarantee the individual the opportunity to participate in the decision-making process. Their wishes are, ultimately, only considered as part of a paternalistic assessment of best interests and could be overridden by professional views. This is shown in some of the cases referred to the Guardianship Board, where the individual's wishes and feelings, whilst taken into consideration in the proceedings and determinative

---

59   D. Cheung (2018) (n. 9), p. 482.
60   R. Lee (n. 13), pp. 1075–77.
61   UN CtteeRPD (2014) (n. 44), para. 25.
62   The difference between the best interests and substituted judgment tests is encapsulated in the English case of *Aintree University Hospitals NHS Foundation Trust v. James* [2013] UKSC 67, [24]: "the best interests test should also contain 'a strong element of "substituted judgment"', taking into account both the past and present wishes and feelings of patient as an individual, and also the factors which he would consider if able to do ... This is ... still a 'best interests' rather than a 'substituted judgment' test, but one which accepts that the preferences of the person concerned are an important component in deciding where his best interests lie."
63   UN CtteeRPD (2014) (n. 44), para. 21.

Mental Capacity in Hong Kong

of the outcome in some cases,[64] may also be discounted in others for being "unrealistic"[65] or "grossly disoriented".[66]

Overall, the current guardianship system in Hong Kong represents what is commonly referred to as "plenary guardianship",[67] whereby the individual under guardianship loses virtually all their legal capacity to manage their personal and/or financial affairs. Despite the requirement of guardianship being the least restrictive means of meeting the person's needs,[68] there is currently no legal provision for supported decision-making (or even a formal recognition of the principle) for people who are lacking or limited in decision-making capacity. The CtteeRPD has expressed concerns in its Concluding Observations on China that there is a "complete absence of a system of supported decision-making measures which recognize the rights of persons with disabilities to make their own decisions and to have their autonomy, will and preferences respected" and recommended the implementation of a system of supported decision-making in place of existing guardianship laws and policies.[69]

Besides these deficiencies in protecting the autonomy of the mentally incapacitated person, the current guardianship system also runs the danger of placing the person with disability at risk of physical and psychological neglect and abuse, given the far-reaching powers granted to the guardian. When instances of mistreatment do occur, an application to the Board to review the guardianship order can only be made if they are discovered by others.[70] Given the fact that those subject to the guardianship regime are left in an extremely vulnerable position by virtue of both their mental state and the lack of safeguards offered by the law, this raises concerns about potential violations of the rights to physical

---

64   See, e.g., *Ref No GB/P/4/10*: "In the instant case, visits by the subject's eldest son would be in the best interests of the subject, who also wishes to be so visited."; *Ref No GB/P/6/16*: "Since the subject valued son more than daughters, [the potential guardian] was thinking of restoring the subject to his care and as such it would respect the subject's wish and feelings."

65   *Ref No GB/P/1/18*: "As the subject still harbours the unrealistic wish to return to Dongguan for an independent living, it is obvious that a guardian should be appointed to decide on his long-term care plan".

66   *Ref No GB/P/2/15*: "The Board observes that the subject is grossly disoriented and has marked cognitive deficits including extremely poor memory. Hence, the subject's will and wishes, expressed verbally at the hearing, would carry little weight in the assessment of future welfare plan."

67   L. Series and A. Nilsson, "Article 12 CRPD Equal Recognition before the Law" in L. Bentekas, M.A. Stein, and D. Anastasiou (eds), *The UN Convention on the Rights of Persons with Disabilities: A Commentary*, OUP, Oxford 2018, p. 377.

68   MHO, s. 59O(3)(c).

69   UN CtteeRPD, "Concluding Observations on the Initial Report of China" (2012) UN Doc CRPD/C/CHN/CO/1, paras. 21–22.

70   Section 59U of the MHO allows the mentally incapacitated person in question, the guardian of that person, the Director of Social Welfare, and any other person who "has a genuine interest in the welfare of the mentally incapacitated person", such as a relative, to submit requests to the Guardian Board for the review of guardianship orders.

Intersentia

and mental integrity and freedom from exploitation, violence and abuse under Articles 16 and 17 of the CRPD.

5.2. MANAGEMENT OF PROPERTY AND AFFAIRS BY THE COURT OR A COMMITTEE

The MHO provides another mechanism for substitute decision-making under Part II ("Management of Property and Affairs of Mentally Incapacitated Persons"), which runs independently from, but often operates concurrently, with the guardianship regime. Here, the Court may, on application, order an inquiry into whether an individual is "incapable, by reason of mental incapacity, of managing and administering his property and affairs".[71] Most commonly, a relative or next-of-kin will be the applicant, but where no such application has been made by the relative, an application may also be made by the Director of Social Welfare, the Official Solicitor, or any guardian of the person. This latter course is especially common in cases of financial abuse.[72] Two medical reports of the concerned person by registered medical practitioners are required in the application.[73]

Generally speaking, having decided the person is "incapable" of managing and administering their property and affairs, the Court may, under section 10A, "do or secure the doing of all such things as appear necessary or expedient" for the maintenance or other benefit of that person or members of their family, having regard "as a paramount consideration, to the requirements of the mentally incapacitated person". Section 10B further specifies the extensive powers the Court may exercise, including the control, transfer, sale, acquisition of property, dissolution of partnership, carrying out of contract, and conduct of legal proceedings. Moreover, it may "appoint a committee of the estate", which shall "do all such things in relation to the property and affairs of the mentally incapacitated person" as the Court orders or authorises it to do, in exercise of the powers mentioned above. The Hong Kong Judiciary has additionally published a Guidance Note, spelling out clearly, for the reference of those appointed to a committee, what their duties are. The first of these is to "act in the best interest of the [mentally incapacitated person] at all times" and to "make sure that the [mentally incapacitated person's] money is being used to give him/her the best quality of life".[74]

---

[71] MHO, s. 7(1).
[72] S.G. CHAN, *A Practical Guide to Mental Health Law in Hong Kong*, Hong Kong University Press, Hong Kong 2019, p. 39.
[73] MHO, s. 7(5).
[74] HONG KONG JUDICIARY, "Guidance Note to Persons Appointed as Committee of Estate of a Mentally Incapacitated Person" <https://www.judiciary.hk/en/court_services_facilities/guidance_note.html> accessed 14.07.2022.

As with guardians, once the Court or a committee is charged with responsibility for a person found to lack capacity under Part II, their duty is to act in the best interests of the individual concerned – the individual's will and preferences are only taken into account as part of a best interests assessment. And, as with guardianship, the determination of mental capacity here consists of a one-off assessment covering a potentially unlimited realm of decisions relating to one's property and financial affairs. As such, the wide-ranging powers for the Court and appointed committees under Part II are likely to be inconsistent with Article 12.5 of the CRPD, which requires states to "take all appropriate and effective measures to ensure the equal right of persons with disabilities to own or inherit property" and "control their own financial affairs". As with our observations above in relation to medical decisions, the right to legal capacity requires a corresponding duty on governments to provide support in relation to decision-making, recognising that legal capacity should rest with the individual in question regardless of their decision-making skills, and to formally acknowledge the role of supporters.

6. DECISION-MAKING IN CASES OF FUTURE INCAPACITY

Sometimes, a person may wish to make provisions for the future possibility that they might "lose" their mental and legal capacity to make certain decisions. For example, instead of waiting for provisions under Parts IVB and II of the MHO to kick in when they become mentally incapacitated, they may want to choose someone beforehand to (continue to) act on their behalf with respect to their property and financial affairs in the case that it happens. The Enduring Powers of Attorney Ordinance (EPAO) provides for the creation of *enduring* powers of attorney (EPAs), which can continue after the individual in question (the "donor") becomes "mentally incapable".[75] "Mentally incapable" here takes its meaning from the Powers of Attorney Ordinance,[76] which provides that a person is "mentally incapable or suffering from mental incapacity" if:

(a) he is suffering from mental disorder or mental handicap and—
  (i) is unable to understand the effect of the power of attorney; or
  (ii) is unable by reason of his mental disorder or mental handicap to make a decision to grant a power of attorney; or
(b) he is unable to communicate to any other person who has made a reasonable effort to understand him, any intention or wish to grant a power of attorney.[77]

---

[75] EPAO, s. 4(1).
[76] EPAO, s. 2.
[77] Powers of Attorney Ordinance, s. 1A(1).

To create an EPA, the donor has to have the requisite mental capacity as defined above, i.e., they have to be able to understand the effect of the power of attorney and able to communicate an intention or wish to grant such a power.[78] The instrument creating the EPA must be signed before a registered medical practitioner and a solicitor: the former must certify that they were *satisfied* the donor was mentally capable and the latter must certify that the donor *appeared* to be mentally capable.[79] Once executed (which could be either before or after the donor becomes "mentally incapable"), the attorney is under fiduciary duty towards the donor, which means that, inter alia, they have to exercise their powers "honestly and with due diligence".[80] They may have authority only over particular matters, property, or financial affairs as specified by the donor.[81] An enduring power may be revoked by the donor, when they have capacity or after they have recovered their capacity, or by a Court on the appointment of a committee under Part II of the MHO to manage the donor's affairs.[82]

Theoretically, the EPA regime in Hong Kong can be a useful way for individuals to extend their autonomous choice in matters related to their property and financial affairs, allowing them to begin communicating their wishes with a *chosen* representative before becoming incapacitated and minimising the legal hassle needed to appoint a guardian after the fact.[83] Practically, however, it has been argued that the complicated procedural requirements in the creation of an EPA, given the formality requirements and the requirement for the donor to list every particular matter or property they would like to grant the attorney power over, discourage the community which need it the most – the elderly – from making use of the mechanism, whilst there is a lack of formal legal safeguards once the donor becomes incapacitated.[84]

As noted above, section 8(1)(a) of the EPAO stipulates that an EPA "must not confer on the attorney any authority other than authority to act in relation to the property of the donor and his financial affairs". EPAs therefore cannot be used to authorise an attorney to make medical treatment or other care decisions for donors in the case of mental incapacity, even though these decisions hold, arguably, more significance than property and finances to many elderly donors.[85]

There is currently no legislative provision for the making of advance decisions in the context of medical care and treatment in Hong Kong. Under the common

---

[78]   EPAO, s. 5(1).
[79]   EPAO, s. 5(2)(a)(d)(e).
[80]   EPAO, s. 12.
[81]   EPAO, s. 8(1).
[82]   EPAO, s.13(1)(a)(e).
[83]   L. Ho, "Financial Planning for Mental Incapacity: Antiquated Law in a Modern Financial Centre" (2014) 44 *Hong Kong Law Journal*, 795, 796.
[84]   Ibid., p. 799. See also LAW REFORM COMMISSION OF HONG KONG, *Report on Enduring Powers of Attorney: Personal Care* (2011) <https://www.hkreform.gov.hk/en/docs/repa2_e.pdf> accessed 14.07.2022.
[85]   L. Ho (n. 83), p. 804.

law, however, it is possible for an individual with the requisite decision-making capacity to give advance refusal to life-sustaining treatment for when they no longer have such capacity, as the Law Reform Commission (LRC) comments:

> An individual's right of self-determination is embodied in his capacity to give advance instructions as to his medical treatment, including a refusal of such treatment. This is interwoven with the fundamental principle of consent[.][86]

The English authority confirms this:

> A medical practitioner must comply with clear instructions given by an adult of sound mind as to the treatment to be given or not given in certain circumstances, whether those instructions are rational or irrational .... This principle applies even if, by the time the specified circumstances obtain, the patient is unconscious or no longer of sound mind.[87]

In 2006, the LRC put forward recommendations to promote the use of advance directives (ADs) – (usually written) instructions about a person's future medical care, made by that person when they have the relevant capacity, which only enter into effect when they lose the ability to make the relevant decision(s).[88] At this point in time, the LRC considered various approaches, including extending or changing the scope of EPAs, expanding the functions of the Guardianship Board, and legislating for ADs, but ultimately favoured retaining the existing law and promoting ADs through non-legislative means. Its reasoning was that the common law approach had the advantage of flexibility, and that the community was not familiar enough with the concept of ADs for legislative measures to be introduced. The ultimate goal was to achieve wider use of advance directives through public awareness campaigns and non-statutory guidelines and thereby enhance patient autonomy and provide greater certainty for medical professionals.[89] One such document is the Hospital Authority's guidance for clinicians on advance directives for adults, first published in 2010 and last updated in 2020, which reiterates the common law position that an adult may make an advance refusal of life-sustaining treatment and sets out a model form for making an AD, as put forward by the LRC, so that patients may give directions with more ease and certainty.[90]

---

[86] LAW REFORM COMMISSION OF HONG KONG (2006) (n. 36), para. 4.41.
[87] *Airedale NHS Trust v. Bland* [1993] 1 All ER 821, at 835–36 (Sir Bingham MR).
[88] See, e.g., MCA 2005, s. 24.
[89] LAW REFORM COMMISSION OF HONG KONG (2006) (n. 36), ch. 8.
[90] HOSPITAL AUTHORITY (HONG KONG), *Guidance for HA Clinicians on Advance Directives in Adults* (2020) <https://www.ha.org.hk/haho/ho/psrm/ADguidelineEng.pdf> accessed 14.07.2022.

In 2019, the Hong Kong Government put forward *legislative* proposals for end-of-life care and ADs for public consultation, noting a rise in awareness about ADs amongst professionals and the public over the years and acknowledging that the lack of legislation for ADs posed concerns about legal uncertainties around the validity of ADs, especially in interaction with other mental capacity/health-related legislation, which made it difficult for patients and professionals to make use of the mechanism.[91] Amongst the proposals were plans to promote advance care planning (ACP), "a process of communication among a patient, his/her healthcare providers, family members or caregivers regarding the kind of care that will be considered appropriate when he/she can no longer make a decision".[92] Whilst ADs are supposedly grounded in the principle of informed consent, there is generally a lack of attention to the process of deliberation/communication and how the patient's autonomy is realised through that process. Through the broader process of ACP, patients and family members may hopefully become better prepared for future health crises, when emotional, in-the-moment treatment decisions will have to be made.[93] The final legislative proposals provide that:

> any mentally competent person who is aged 18 or above [could] make an [AD] to refuse life-sustaining treatment (including artificial nutrition and hydration) under pre-specified conditions.[94]

These pre-specified conditions include terminal illness, persistent vegetative state or state of irreversible coma, and other end-stage irreversible life-limiting condition.[95] Two witnesses with no interest in the estate of the person making the AD, one of whom should be a medical practitioner, are required in the creation or modification of an AD. Moreover, the medical practitioner should be satisfied that the person "has capability to make an [AD] and has been informed of the nature and effect of the [AD] and the consequences of refusing the treatments specified".[96] The "capability" to make an AD here is not further

---

[91] FOOD AND HEALTH BUREAU (HONG KONG) (NOW HEALTH BUREAU), *End-of-Life Care: Legislative Proposals on Advance Directives and Dying in Place – Consultation Document* (2019) <https://www.healthbureau.gov.hk/download/press_and_publications/consultation/190900_eolcare/e_EOL_care_legisiative_proposals.pdf> accessed 14.07.2022.

[92] Ibid., para. 2.2.

[93] H.S. PERKINS, "Controlling Death: The False Promise of Advance Directives" (2007) 147 *Annals of Internal Medicine* 51; R.L. SUDORE and T.R. FRIED, "Redefining the 'Planning' in Advance Care Planning: Preparing for End-of-Life Decision Making" (2010) 153 *Annals of Internal Medicine* 256. See also HOSPITAL AUTHORITY (HONG KONG) (2019) (n. 37).

[94] FOOD AND HEALTH BUREAU (HONG KONG) (NOW HEALTH BUREAU), *End-of-Life Care: Moving Forward: Legislative Proposals on Advance Directives and Dying in Place – Consultation Report* (2020) para. 4.2 <https://www.healthbureau.gov.hk/download/press_and_publications/consultation/190900_eolcare/e_EOL_consultation_report.pdf> accessed 14.07.2022.

[95] Ibid., para. 4.3.

[96] Ibid., para. 4.7.

elaborated upon, and it is notable that the requirement is only for the person to have been *informed* about the relevant matters but not to *understand* (as in the MHO test for medical treatment) or further deliberate (as additionally required the common law test) them.[97] It is unclear whether this will remain the case when the proposal is eventually introduced in the legislature. It has also been suggested during the consultation exercise that there should be an all-encompassing legislation for mental incapacity, which would cover issues including ADs, health care decision-making by attorneys, and guardianship, but the Government has explicitly rejected this, as they see the subject as too controversial at this time.[98] As Daisy Cheung has argued, for a new statutory AD regime to be effective in creating legal certainty and encouraging individuals to plan their end-of-life care in advance, it might indeed be necessary to first reform the current law on mental (in)capacity to clear up existing uncertainties and inconsistencies.[99]

7. CONCLUSION

To conclude, Hong Kong's laws in relation to mental capacity continue to severely lag behind international human rights standards. Many provisions and concepts within the MHO – last amended substantially two decades ago – are outdated[100] and inconsistent with both Article 12 of the CRPD and the spirit of the treaty as a whole. These include, first of all, the lack of a coherent, uniform test for mental capacity in statutory law and the troubling conflation of mental disorder and mental incapacity. Where an individual is found to lack capacity, substitute decision-making based on welfare or best interests, whether by courts or by a party appointed to care for the individual, is always employed. In other words, once an individual is deemed to have impaired decision-making skills, they may lose their legal capacity entirely, with no room or support to participate in the decision-making process, contrary to the principle of universal legal capacity and states' obligation to take appropriate measures to provide support for the exercise of legal capacity under the CRPD.

---

[97] Ibid., para. 5.8.

[98] Ibid., para. 5.8.

[99] D. CHEUNG, "The Importance of Supporting Legislation: Mental Capacity Law in Hong Kong" at *Living Will, Living Well? Advance Directives Across Asia Workshop*, Centre for Medical Ethics and Law, University of Hong Kong, Hong Kong 2020.

[100] The terminology of "mental handicap", for example, is no longer used in the scholarship and legislation in many jurisdictions to describe intellectual disabilities. See, e.g., A. TER HAAR, "Attitudes and Words Referring to Mental Handicap" (1993) 16 *International Journal of Rehabilitation Research* 77; P.J. DEVLIEGER, "From Handicap to Disability: Language Use and Cultural Meaning in the United States" (1999) 21 *Disability and Rehabilitation* 346; P. FOREMAN, "Language and Disability" (2005) 30 *Journal of Intellectual and Developmental Disability* 57.

These mechanisms for substitute decision-making fail to recognise the right of persons with disabilities to equal treatment and recognition before the law, amounting to an "imposition of dependence" which "negates human aspiration, respect, and choice".[101]

As many have rightly observed, reforms in mental health/capacity law in Hong Kong have been long overdue, especially in light of the enactment of the Hong Kong Bill of Rights Ordinance in 1992 and the Disability Discrimination Ordinance in 1997, the incorporation of the ICCPR into Hong Kong constitutional law in the form of the Basic Law, and the ratification of the CRPD by China in 2008.[102] The need for reform is especially striking given the myriad of practical and conceptual problems presented by the current law in terms of both the care of persons deemed to be mentally incapacitated and the compulsory psychiatric regime.[103] However, given the continued stigmatisation of mental illness and discrimination against persons with disabilities, there is little political momentum for the Government to initiate any such proposals. As the population in Hong Kong continues to age, it is further estimated that individuals suffering from different forms of cognitive impairment will grow rapidly.[104] Reforms are therefore not only necessary but pressing, which may begin with rethinking and consolidating the current piecemeal and incongruent tests for mental capacity in various contexts into a uniform approach that does not strip individuals of their legal capacity based on their decision-making skills or replace their views and preferences with what is considered by others as their best interests. At the same time, a system of supported decision-making should be implemented to empower individuals in the exercise their legal capacity.

---

[101] A. Dhanda, "Legal Capacity in the Disability Rights Convention: Stranglehold of the Past or Lodestar for the Future?" (2007) 34 *Syracuse Journal of International Law and Commerce* 429, 446.

[102] C.J. Petersen, "Unfinished Business: Reforming Hong Kong's Mental Health Ordinance to Comply with International Norms" at *Compulsory Mental Health Treatment in Hong Kong: Which Way Forward? Conference*, Centre for Medical Ethics and Law, University of Hong Kong, Hong Kong 2017 <https://www.cmel.hku.hk/upload/files/CMentalHealth-Day-1-Presentation-3-Professor-Carole-Petersen-ppt.pdf> accessed 14.07.2022.

[103] D. Cheung et. al., "Articulating Future Directions of Law Reform for Compulsory Mental Health Admission and Treatment in Hong Kong" (2020) 68 *International Journal of Law and Psychiatry* 101513 <https://doi.org/10.1016/j.ijlp.2019.101513> accessed 14.07.2022.

[104] R. Yu et. al., "Trends in Prevalence and Mortality of Dementia in Elderly Hong Kong Population: Projections, Disease Burden, and Implications for Long-Term Care" [2012] *International Journal of Alzheimer's Disease* 406852 <https://doi.org/10.1155/2012/406852> accessed 14.07.2022; Guardianship Board (Hong Kong), *Enigma of Guardianship: An exploration into the challenges of aging population through the lens of mental incapacity* (Chinese only) (2019) <http://www.adultguardianship.org.hk/ebook/Enigma-of-Guardianship.pdf> accessed 14.07.2022.

PART III

LEGAL QUESTIONS, PERSISTENT CHALLENGES

INFORMED CONSENT AND SUPPORT FOR DECISION-MAKING

A Critical Review of Legal Reforms in Latin America

Pablo MARSHALL*

1. Introduction 301
2. Capacity in Informed Consent 304
3. Supports for Informed Consent 307
   3.1. Supports and Functional Assessment 307
   3.2. Autonomy and Well-Being 308
   3.3. Legal Operation and Functional Model 310
4. Informed Consent and Reforms to Legal Capacity in Latin America..... 312
   4.1. Reforms in Latin America................................... 312
   4.2. Legislating Support for Informed Consent................... 315
5. Conclusions 317

1. INTRODUCTION

Persons with intellectual and cognitive disabilities (hereinafter PICDs) face significant barriers when accessing health treatment and satisfying their right to enjoy the highest possible standard of health. This is worrying to the extent that these persons also experience a greater need for such treatments and have higher mortality and morbidity rates than the rest of the population.[1] These difficulties impact access to health promotion policies and curative health

---

*   Doctor of Law from the University of Glasgow. Professor at the Institute of Public Law of the Austral University of Chile. Co-Director Millennium Nucleus Studies on Disability and Citizenship (DISCA), Chile; and Associate Researcher Millennium Institute for Care Research (MICARE), Santiago, Chile. This work is supported by the National Research and Development Agency of Chile (ANID), through the Fondecyt 1190434 project. The author thanks Renata Bregaglio, Renato Constantino, Constanza de la Fuente, Loreto Godoy, Carla Iuspa, Eduardo Marchant, Violeta Purán, and Susan Turner for their comments.

[1]   L.A. ALLERTON, V. WELCH and E. EMERSON, "Health Inequalities Experienced by Children and Young People with Intellectual Disabilities: A Review of Literature from the United Kingdom" (2011) 15 *Journal of Intellectual Disabilities* 4, pp. 269–278; E. EMERSON, S. BAINES,

treatments, and include, for example, inadequate time allocation by health care workers, discrimination, lack of reasonable adjustments or poor accessibility to premises and health systems.[2] These barriers also affect the ability to select health care treatment and to control how it is provided. The latter affects PICDs in a particularly acute way due to a diversity of factors, which include, on the one hand, barriers associated with their impairments, such as those that affect communication, perception or memory, and, on the other hand, barriers socially constructed in their environment, which include, among others, paternalistic attitudes, lack of support from their caregivers and lack of expertise and training of health care workers, which often leads to discrimination and mistreatment.[3]

To the extent that historically, PICDs have been subjected to regimes of legal incapacity where they are appointed a representative to make decisions for them on property and personal matters – as is the case with interdiction and guardianship in Latin America –, health legislation has relied on these institutions to determine who should make decisions regarding their health treatment. With the emergence of the debate on the need to provide informed consent (hereinafter IC) in the second half of the 20th century, which reconstructs the doctor-patient relationship in terms of individual autonomy, the question has arisen about how PICDs can authorise health treatment.[4] The default legal response, to the extent that IC appears as a personal legal act, is that if the person is under a regime of legal incapacity, the person who must provide IC as a substitute is their legal representative. Departing from this answer, bioethics has offered a slightly different one by establishing the capacity to consent – *competence* – as a prerequisite to providing the IC. This parallel development has confirmed the substitution of decision-making by the legal representatives and, in their absence, by the health care personnel, as an adequate response for those cases in which the patient is not considered capable. At the same time, it has disassociated capacity to consent from the PICDs' legal status, requiring

---

S. ALLERTON et al., *Health Inequalities and People with Learning Disabilities in the UK: 2012*, Improving Health and Lives Learning Disability Observatory, Durham 2012.

[2] A. ALI, K. SCIOR, V. RATTI et al., "Discrimination and Other Barriers to Accessing Health Care: Perspectives of Patients with Mild and Moderate Intellectual Disability and Their Carers" 8 *PLoS ONE*, 8, e70855; G.L. KRAHN, D.K. WALKER and R. CORREA-DE-ARAUJO, "Persons with Disabilities as an Unrecognized Health Disparity Population" (2015) 105 *American Journal of Public Health*, S198–S206; H.J. WILLIAMSON, G.M. CONTRERAS, E.S. RODRIGUES et al., "Health Care Access for Adults With Intellectual and Developmental Disabilities: A Scoping Review" (2017) 37 *OTJR: Occupation, Participation and Health* 4, pp. 227–236.

[3] Y. LUNSKY, P. FEDOROFF, K. KLASSEN et al., "Medical Rights for People with Intellectual Disabilities", in F. OWEN and D.M. GRIFFITHS (eds), *Challenges to the human rights of people with intellectual disabilities*, Jessica Kingsley Publishers, London 2009; A. ALI, K. SCIOR, V. RATTI et al., (n. 2); P. NAVAS, S. LLORENTE, L. GARCIA et al., "Improving Healthcare Access for Older Adults with Intellectual Disability: What Are the Needs?" (2009) 32 *Journal of Applied Research in Intellectual Disabilities* 6, pp. 1453–1464.

[4] R.R. FADEN, T.L. BEAUCHAMP and N.M. KING, *A History and Theory of Informed Consent*, Oxford University Press, Oxford 1986.

that it must be assessed on a case-by-case basis. Although IC regulation has often tried to bridge the gap between legal and bioethical regimes – for example, making explicit that the opportunity to provide IC is dependent on the PICDs' legal status – related regulation allows the idea that the capacity to consent to health treatment is something that must be assessed case by case in the medical context. This does not mean to suggest that bioethics has established a more favourable regime for PICDs to exercise their autonomy – in both cases, it has been considered convenient to resort to a third party to make decisions for them –, but rather that the decoupling between a general rule of legal capacity and a specific capacity regime for IC has allowed the configuration of a different legal capacity regime in the health sphere. Simply put: while legal capacity in patrimonial and personal matters has been, until recent years, tied to a status model – that is, dependent on an impairment diagnosis – its practice in the medical field has moved in a more or less interrupted way towards a functional model of specific capacity assessment.

So far in the 21st century, decision-making by a third party – or the substituted decision-making model – has been increasingly questioned. Its replacement by a decision-making support (DMS) model has been proposed in accordance with which a person of trust collaborates with the PICDs, supporting them in making their own decisions, thus allowing them to retain autonomy in important decisions, including those concerning medical treatments. DMSs have the potential to improve decisions concerning PICDs, both from the point of view of the quality of decisions and the prevention of abuses, as well as from the respect for their autonomy.[5] The CRPD has motivated the defence of DMSs as a way to guarantee a universal right to legal capacity.[6] From this perspective, legal capacity is decoupled from decision-making capacity: while legal capacity is a universal characteristic held by every human being, a person's decision-making capacity, essentially varying between human beings and dependent on internal and external factors, is not a condition for the exercise of rights, but, at most, a circumstance for the activation and use of DMSs. This understanding has opened a series of questions and a debate on how to proceed in complex cases, primarily due to the radical call to avoid mental capacity assessment. As its main virtue, this understanding has the vindication of DMSs as a tool, not to replace but to improve or enable decision-making capacity. The emergence of DMSs raises the question of the extent to which they can enable IC and thus

---

[5] D.V. JESTE, G.M.L. EGLIT, B.W. PALMER et al., "Supported Decision Making in Serious Mental Illness" (2018) 81 *Psychiatry* 1, pp. 28–40.

[6] Committee on the Rights of Persons with Disabilities (CRPD Committee), General Recommendation No. 1, 2014; A. ARSTEIN-KERSLAKE, *Restoring Voice to People with Cognitive Disabilities*, Cambridge University Press, Cambridge 2017; E. FLYNN and A. ARSTEIN-KERSLAKE, "Legislating Personhood: Realising the Right to Support in Exercising Legal Capacity" (2014) 10 *International Journal of Law in Context* 1, pp. 81–104.

avoid the need to substitute the PICDs' will in the medical context. Although the vindication of the DMS model, crystallised in the CRPD, is directed more decidedly against the existence of general substituted decision-making regimes, such as interdiction and guardianships, the CRPD Committee has extended the criticism of substitution even to functional models where the capacity is assessed on a case-by-case basis and in which the assessment is relative only to a specific decision-making situation.

This chapter evaluates the idea that IC would be a particular type of the exercise of legal capacity. This means considering whether there should be particular sensitivity to the decisions for which IC is usually required, and also the tensions in normative regimes of law and bioethics, where interests of distinctive actors – crucially medical personnel – must be considered.

This analysis can be carried out at various levels. It engages important empirical questions that, however, are beyond the scope of this work. Are DMSs really effective? What is their nature, and what are their hallmarks in the medical sphere? Along these lines, it has been pointed out that the application of DMSs in IC is an issue that requires further reflection, development of practices and applied research.[7] It also involves normative issues on which this work will focus. At the theoretical level, DMSs challenge an understanding entrenched in IC bioethical discourse, in which capacity assessment plays a constitutive role. To what extent can DMSs help to avoid the use of capacity assessments? Are DMSs exclusive or compatible with the functional model developed by bioethics? Sections 2 and 3 of this chapter offer a theoretical discussion on the particularities of IC for a DMS implementation, including legal and bioethical aspects. At the regulation level, it must be determined how the support model for the exercise of legal capacity, enshrined in Article 12 of the CRPD, can affect or has managed to affect – the IC legal regulation. Section 4 focuses on examining the impact that legal capacity reforms, inspired by the CRPD and carried out in Latin America during the last decade in implementing the DMS model as a general regime for the exercise of legal capacity for PICDs, have had on IC regulation. It shows how IC regulation has not been modified, generating doubts regarding DMSs' overall validity, and suggests that this presents an opportunity for its future regulation to consider the particularities of IC.

2. CAPACITY IN INFORMED CONSENT

The widespread consensus is that patients have the right to make decisions about their health and be informed of all available information about those decisions.

---

[7] D. ADAMS, C. CARR, D. MARSDEN, et al., "An Update on Informed Consent and the Effect on the Clinical Practice of Those Working with People with a Learning Disability" (2018) 21 *Learning Disability Practice* 4, pp. 36–40.

IC, therefore, refers to the act of authorising a medical intervention or participation in research carried out by a person in the exercise of their individual autonomy.[8] The bioethical literature shows that the role of IC is to guarantee the principle of patient autonomy, resting on three elements: disclosure, voluntariness and capacity. Through *disclosure*, the doctor provides general information to the patient about the treatment in question, the risks involved, the foreseeable consequences and the available options. *Voluntariness* refers to the fact that the patient must express their decision to undergo the health treatment and that the will must be free from undue influences, such as force, coercion or manipulation. As for capacity, it concerns the same principle of autonomy that demands a special solution for those cases in which the patient does not show signs of being able to express an autonomous will. Therefore, the capacity to consent is conceived as a preliminary concept, a *gatekeeper*, for implementing the IC.[9] From this perspective, capacity is an articulating element of the antecedent and consequential aspects of the principle of autonomy, which seeks to ensure that only autonomous persons can exercise the regulatory powers recognised for this class of individuals. Since its function is to control the entry to the group of people in a position to provide IC, the central question is the identification of those situations in which someone lacks the capacity to consent. To this end, bioethics has rejected the determination of disability by status associated with permanent belonging to a category of persons and has embraced the idea that the capacity to consent must be functionally assessed. This has to do with the fact that variation in decision-making capacity is highly affected by different impairments, contexts and moments in people's lives. How to perform such an assessment is a matter of ethical, legal and scientific debate.[10] However, over the last few decades, a four-item psycho-legal test has been gaining prominence: evidence must be shown (i) of a decision; (ii) of understanding the problem; (iii) of being able to appreciate the specific situation; and (iv) of rationally manipulating the information provided.[11] The treating physician can do this assessment, but formalised capacity assessment tools can also be used, such as the MacCAT-T – MacArthur Competence Assessment Tool for Treatment – typically managed by experts. The non-appearance of any of these functionalities will affect the lack of capacity to consent and the need for substituted IC.

---

[8] T.L. Beauchamp and J.F. Childredss, *Principles of Biomedical Ethics*, Oxford University Press, Oxford 2001, p. 78.

[9] R.R. Faden, T.L. Beauchamp and N.M. King (n. 4); A. Maclean *Autonomy, Informed Consent and Medical Law: A Relational Challenge*, Cambridge University Press, Cambridge 2009; M. Donnelly, *Healthcare Decision-Making and the Law: Autonomy, Capacity and the Limits of Liberalism*, Cambridge University Press, Cambridge 2014.

[10] C.D. Cea and C.B. Fisher, "Health Care Decision-Making by Adults with Mental Retardation" (2003) 41 *Mental Retardation* 2, pp. 78–87.

[11] T. Grisso and P.S. Appelbaum, *Assessing Competence to Consent to Treatment: A Guide for Physicians and Other Health Professionals*, Oxford University Press, Oxford 1998.

It is important to point out that this kind of test has expanded from bioethical literature and practice to other spheres, revolutionising the legal regulation of legal capacity in the common law. The paradigmatic case is that of the Mental Capacity Act of 2005 (MCA), in England, where a person is considered to lack the capacity to make decisions or to lack mental capacity if they cannot: "(a) understand the relevant information for decision, (b) retain that information, (c) use or weigh that information as part of the decision-making process, or (d) communicate their decision (whether by speaking, in sign language, or by any other means)."[12] It should be noted that this capacity test is based on a presumption of capacity;[13] it is performed only when there is a diagnosis of a functional impairment – for example, a PICD diagnosis –[14] and all steps taken to help the person make their own decision have been unsuccessful,[15] which is consistent with the functional capacity assessment approach in the bioethics literature.[16] The medical team is in charge of informally administering the functional test, and optionally a more formal assessment can occur. This assessment can be questioned before a specialised Court of Protection.[17]

As can be inferred from the following quote, the bioethical concept of *capacity*, included in the legislation on mental capacity, is at the centre of the criticism formulated by the CRPD Committee of what it calls *the functional criterion for denial of legal capacity*:

> The functional approach attempts to assess mental capacity and deny legal capacity accordingly. It is often based on whether a person can understand the nature and consequences of a decision and/or whether he or she can use or weigh the relevant information. This approach is flawed for two key reasons: (a) it is discriminatorily applied to people with disabilities; and (b) it presumes to be able to accurately assess the inner-workings of the human mind and, when the person does not pass the assessment, it then denies him or her a core human right – the right to equal recognition before the law.[18]

Concerning the discriminatory effect that applying the assessment would have on PICDs, in the case of the MCA, the effect is shaped by incorporating the diagnostic element of an impairment as a functional evaluation requirement, an

---

[12] MCA, s. 3(1).

[13] Ibid., s. 1(1).

[14] Ibid., s. 2(2).

[15] Ibid., s. 1(3).

[16] E. ETCHELLS, G. SHARPE, C. ELLIOT, et al., "Bioethics for Clinicians: 3. Capacity" (1996) 155 *CMAJ: Canadian Medical Association Journal* 6, pp. 657–661.

[17] G.R. ASHTON, M. MARIN, C. VAN OBERDJIK, et al. (eds), *Mental Capacity: Law and Practice*, 2nd ed., Jordans, London 2012.

[18] CRPD Committee, (n. 6), para. 15.

issue that other jurisdictions have tended to eliminate, as in Northern Ireland's 2016 Mental Capacity Act.[19] The Committee's doubts about the scientific validity of the functional capacity assessment are much more challenging to answer. It is not possible to carry out that task here. However, it can be argued that the Committee's demand for the application of a universal regime of legal capacity, independent of a person's decision-making capacity, has been linked to its reliance on DMSs to remove any impediment to knowing the will and preferences of PICDs. This is perhaps the key aspect that separates, at least conceptually, a functional model of legal capacity from a universal one. While the universal model considers the existence of a will as a universal human element, lowering the demanding standards of rationality imposed to act legally, the functional model defends the existence of these standards, gives them a more precise meaning and seeks a concrete assessment.[20]

3. SUPPORTS FOR INFORMED CONSENT

3.1. SUPPORTS AND FUNCTIONAL ASSESSMENT

In general terms, the DMS model supposes that a third person provides support – explaining issues, exploring options, helping to express preferences, executing decisions – to another person who requires it to exercise their legal capacity.[21] It can be understood, first, as an alternative to institutions of incapacitation for persons with disabilities that see capacity as an all-or-nothing issue, but also as a mechanism that allows PICDs to make decisions. Secondly, the DMS model questions not only the binary approach to capacity but also the traditional understanding that autonomy must be exercised independently.[22] DMSs seek to address the deficits in the decision-making capacity of PICDs. Its defenders make a case for rejecting capability assessment and replacing it with decisions

---

[19] W. Martin, S. Michalowski and J. Stavert, "Three Jurisdictions Report: Towards Compliance with CRPD Art. 12 in Capacity/Incapacity Legislation across the UK" (2016) Autonomy Project, University of Essex, p. 19.

[20] A. Arstein-Kerslake (n. 6), p. 38 et seq.; M. Scholten, J. Gather and J. Vollmann "Equality in the Informed Consent Process: Competence to Consent, Substitute Decision-Making, and Discrimination of Persons with Mental Disorders" (2021) 46 *The Journal of Medicine and Philosophy: A Forum for Bioethics and Philosophy of Medicine* 1, pp. 108–136.

[21] M. Bach and L. Kerzner, *A New Paradigm for Protecting Autonomy and the Right to Legal Capacity*, Law Commission of Ontario, Toronto 2010.

[22] G. Quinn and A. Arstein-Kerslake, "Restoring the 'Human' in 'Human Rights': Personhood and Doctrinal Innovation in the UN Disability Convention", in C. Gearty and C. Douzinas (eds), *The Cambridge Companion to Human Rights Law*, Cambridge University Press, Cambridge 2012.

on support needs and assessing the success of support processes.[23] In the case of people with more severe difficulties, whose determination would finally correspond to the application of a certain kind of functional assessment, the supports may involve the interpretation of will and preferences, ascribing agency to the person's actions or jointly constructing preferences.[24] In such cases, DMSs can be understood as substitute decision-making that puts the person's will and preferences at the centre of the decision.

Applying DMSs to these cases shows the commitment to the idea of legal capacity as a universal attribute that must be separated from mental decision-making capacity, essentially dependent on contextual elements, variable in time and space, and, therefore, capable of being supported. This approach to DMSs generates tension with the functional capacity model to the extent that the expectation of demonstrating certain functionalities is replaced by the more modest expectation of determining the will and preferences held by – or at least attributable to – every human being.

Despite this difficulty, the implementation of DMSs is generally compatible with the functional model. As suggested above, both the bioethical and legal versions of the functional model allow the idea of DMSs to be incorporated into the elements prior to the capacity assessment. Declaring a person incapable of making decisions requires prior support measures to know their will and preferences, which, added to the presumption of capacity, means that the evaluation of capacity is shifted to exceptional cases. It is not clear that the standards used to satisfy this requirement in the practical application of the functional model, which for example, refers to *practicable* measures – *practicable steps* – coincide with the wide range of resources to which the DMS literature refers. However, as a principle, DMSs are compatible with the functional model.

Despite the significant general disagreements surrounding the universal application of DMSs, certain aspects are specifically relative to IC. Although the information to evaluate the use of DMSs in the context of IC is limited, two relevant aspects can be discussed in the abstract.

3.2. AUTONOMY AND WELL-BEING

A first challenge for applying DMSs in the field of IC is to accommodate the obligation to respect PICDs as autonomous beings with the need to avoid

---

[23]   M. BROWNING, C. BIGBY and J. DOUGLAS, "Supported Decision Making: Understanding How Its Conceptual Link to Legal Capacity Is Influencing the Development of Practice" (2014) 1 *Research and Practice in Intellectual and Developmental Disabilities* 1, pp. 34–45.

[24]   L. SERIES, "Relationships, Autonomy and Legal Capacity: Mental Capacity and Support Paradigms" (2015) 40 *International Journal of Law and Psychiatry*, pp. 80–91; and E. FLYNN and A. ARSTEIN-KERSLAKE (n. 6).

decisions that may put their health and well-being at serious risk.[25] This challenge can be seen from different prisms. Although the favourite prism of bioethics is the balance between *autonomy and beneficence*,[26] a prism claimed by the disability movement is that of the *dignity of risk*.[27] From this perspective, the decrease in opportunities to take risks experienced by PICDs can be seen as eroding the dignity associated with autonomy.[28] On the other hand, however – and this is a much less popular stance – the emphasis on the idea of autonomy can lead to the neglect of health care necessary for the well-being of PICDs.[29] Faced with this dilemma, DMSs can be seen as a way of accommodating autonomy and well-being, a characteristic that it shares with other relational decision-making perspectives, such as intersubjective risk negotiation or patient-centred planning.[30]

At least two ideas suggest that DMSs do not ensure the conditions required for an IC. The first is related to the significant impact that certain medical decisions have on the personal integrity of patients and the complexity of the information to be transmitted to them. The DMS may help to know the PICD's will and preferences but this does not ensure an understanding of the risks, consequences and alternatives of the treatments to which they must consent. Variable thresholds of capacity to consent could be proposed that depend on elements such as the risk involved in the procedure, the benefit that the patient will experience from the procedure, the complexity of the diagnosis and the procedure itself, or the therapeutic alternatives. Certain risks would require that even PICDs receiving support be subject to an examination that would allow the doctor to ensure that the risk is being assumed knowingly and voluntarily. Respect for autonomy cannot depend on a judgment about the permissibility of the result of the decision made by a third party.[31] The idea of variable capacity thresholds appears to be nothing more than a covert way of applying *output-based capacity models*, so common in the field of mental health. Notwithstanding that concern, the idea that patients or those serving as DMS could be empowered to

---

[25] C.D. CEA and C.B. FISHER (n. 10); C.B. FISHER, "Goodness-of-Fit Ethic for Informed Consent to Research Involving Adults with Mental Retardation and Developmental Disabilities" (2003) 9 *Mental Retardation and Developmental Disabilities Research Reviews* 1, pp. 27–31.

[26] T. L. BEAUCHAMP and J.F. CHILDRESS (n. 8), p. 176 et seq.

[27] R. PERSKE, "The Dignity of Risk and the MR" (1972) 10 *Mental Retardation* 1, pp. 24–27.

[28] P. MARCH and L. KELLY, "Dignity of Risk in the Community: A Review of and Reflections on the Literature" (2018) 20 *Health, Risk & Society*, 5–6, pp. 297–311.

[29] R. FYSON and J. CROMBY, "Human Rights and Intellectual Disabilities in an Era of 'Choice'" 57 *Journal of Intellectual Disability Research* 12, pp. 1164–1172; A. ROULTONE and H. MORGAN, "Neo-Liberal Individualism or Self-Directed Support: Are We All Speaking the Same Language on Modernizing Adult Social Care?" (2009) 8 *Social Policy and Society* 3, pp. 333–345.

[30] N.A. KOHN, "Legislating Supported Decision-Making" (2021) 58 *Harvard Journal on Legislation*, pp. 313–356.

[31] CRPD Committee (n. 6), para. 15.

make decisions about options that do not exist or about risks they do not know is deeply disturbing.

The second idea does not refer exclusively to IC but can reinforce the previous argument. The use of DMSs also implies taking seriously some of the criticisms directed at the purely enabling emphasis on relational autonomy as a structuring element in the exercise of legal capacity with DMSs. DMSs are often provided by those who have the PICDs under their care, with the natural emergence of conflicts of interest. Not paying attention to the complexity of the relationships through which DMSs work could blur the possibility of detecting situations of abuse, manipulation and coercion in these relationships.[32] Adopting a relational framework could mean a shift in the evaluation of decision-making capacity, from an evaluation focused on the intellectual and cognitive deficits of the person to an evaluation focused on environmental and relational elements, enabling and inhibiting the ability to make autonomous decisions. Particular attention should be paid to how the modification of these elements can generate an IC process that responds to and protects the autonomy and well-being of PICDs,[33] especially considering that decision-making capability can fluctuate over time and with context, type of decision, motivation, and emotion.

Both elements mentioned may constitute arguments for a defence of capacity assessment. However, both promote the use of such assessment that differs from the conventional bioethical literature. On the one hand, capacity assessment is understood as a check on factors in the support relationship that inhibit autonomy. On the other, it ensures that the patient, by themselves or through the DMSs, assumes serious or irreversible risks to their health in an informed manner. Together, these configure the evaluation of the capability to make decisions autonomously, not as a form of substituted decision-making, but as a particularly strict safeguard in situations where intensive supports are provided[34] or in contexts of high risk or apparent conflicts of interest.

3.3. LEGAL OPERATION AND FUNCTIONAL MODEL

The application of DMSs in the context of an IC regulation focused on the authorisation for a medical intervention that would be prohibited in other

---

[32] C. Kong, *Mental Capacity in Relationship: Decision-Making, Dialogue, and Autonomy*, Cambridge University Press, Cambridge 2017.

[33] C.B. Fisher (n. 25); L. Ferguson and G.H. Murphy, "The Effects of Training on the Ability of Adults with an Intellectual Disability to Give Informed Consent to Medication" (2014) 58 *Journal of Intellectual Disability Research* 9, pp. 864–873; and S. Wark, C. Macphail, K. McKay, et al., "Informed Consent in a Vulnerable Population Group: Supporting Individuals Aging with Intellectual Disability to Participate in Developing Their Own Health and Support Programs" (2017) 41 *Australian Health Review* 4, pp. 436–442.

[34] M. Bach and L. Kerzner (n. 21), pp. 129–130.

scenarios and whose effect is, at least partially, the limitation of liability for damages of the health care personnel, is also a challenge to consider. Specifically, IC normative requirements have been developed in a broader discussion of medical malpractice. IC is seen as a way of defending the physician against accusations of malpractice or negligence.[35] In this regard, it is important to consider the possible outreach of DMSs in legal consequences attributable to IC. The use of DMSs is especially problematic, as mentioned earlier, in cases where patients have expressed their will and preferences through support but their consent cannot be verified as being based on an understanding and acceptance of the information they have been given.

Regarding this problem, it is important to clarify that it is usually assumed that low-risk medical decisions do not require an IC, a simple consent being sufficient. Simple consent requires a general understanding of the health care procedure, although discussing how much information is sufficient continues to generate discrepancies. Only invasive procedures or procedures involving a risk to the patient's health or life require informed consent, in which case a written record is customarily kept.[36] The information provided in the IC context is considerably more detailed and includes alternatives, risks, foreseeable consequences and a clinical opinion. The distinction between simple consent and IC may correlate with the type of offence the doctor would commit in the absence of consent. While a therapeutic intervention without consent or with vitiated consent could constitute a criminal offence, it has been understood that the breach of the duty to provide sufficient information when issuing an IC could only constitute a hypothesis of negligence and give rise to liability for damages. In this scenario, there is pressure for the doctor to make sure that the PICD effectively has the capacity to consent; otherwise, if it were clear that the PICD does not have the capacity to understand general information, then, hypothetically, the doctor would not have obtained consent, which is a crime.

However, the lack of understanding of the detailed information required by the IC is not always linked to a lack of capacity; otherwise, any person who fails to understand the alternatives, risks and foreseeable consequences of medical intervention would have to be considered incapable of consent.[37] In this regard, it is important to determine the correlation, if any, between the information provided and the understanding required. If the standard of understanding is set too high, we find that most people do not understand what they consent to; if it is set too low, the consent loses its defining character. We must remember

---

[35]   R.R. FADEN, T.L. BEAUCHAMP and N.M. KING (n. 4), p. 114–143.

[36]   In the case of risky procedures, the therapeutic alternatives constitute another variable to consider. If only one therapeutic alternative exists, according to established scientific evidence, the patient can only consent to or reject the intervention. On the contrary, in the case of multiple therapeutic alternatives, the patient may also be involved in the choice between the alternatives.

[37]   E. CAVE, "Valid Consent to Medical Treatment", forthcoming in *Journal of Medical Ethics*.

that IC differs from other expressions of will by its permissive nature; that is, it allows doing something that would be prohibited without consent. If the patient did not know or understand what they are consenting to, the authorisation for a bodily intervention would have been invalid. That is why it is reasonable to understand that IC requires an intermediate understanding; it does not require an understanding of all the details of the procedure, but it does require at least three things: understanding that one is looking at a request for consent; knowing how consent can be given or refused; and being able to identify the intervention for which the consent is requested.[38] If DMSs effectively allow PICDs to reach that threshold of understanding, apprehensions about the legal consequences of DMSs should be dismissed. When, on the contrary, they do not allow this threshold to be crossed, the willingness to be subjected to a procedure, as expressed by the PICD or by the person providing support, would not comply with the requirement for which the IC was introduced in the legislation.

The use of DMSs should not be idealised. They should be qualified in specific contexts, as is the case for the IC. It is also reasonable for an IC DMS design to seek to articulate the interests of all the relevant actors. On the one hand, allow PICDs to actively participate in their health decisions and do so, ideally, in a way that DMSs promote an informed decision. On the other hand, however, the medical profession is interested in generating regulations that allow minimising associated risks, standardising information thresholds required for IC and limiting medical liability.

4. INFORMED CONSENT AND REFORMS TO LEGAL CAPACITY IN LATIN AMERICA

4.1. REFORMS IN LATIN AMERICA

Latin America has been a pioneer in implementing Article 12 of the United Nations Convention on the Rights of Persons with Disabilities (CRPD). This is because the reforms to legal capacity in this region of the world have opted for a regulation that seeks to apply, in the most profound way seen so far, a system of legal capacity supports. The ambition of the reforms is to recognise in the legislation the universal exercise of legal capacity, following the guidelines offered by the CRPD Committee in its General Comment No. 1.

To fulfil the promise of applying Article 12 of the CRPD, the reforms should have carried out a systematic modification of legal capacity in all sectors of the legal system. In the context of health care, this should have translated

---

[38]   J. MILLUM and D. BROMWICH, "Informed Consent: What Must Be Disclosed and What Must Be Understood?" forthcoming in *The American Journal of Bioethics*.

Informed Consent and Support for Decision-Making

into applying reasonable adjustments and DMSs for IC and reforming forced practices in psychiatry and mental health. However, it is symptomatic that the reforms carried out in Costa Rica (2016), Peru (2018) and Colombia (2019) have not carried out reform of this type and have left health regulation aside in its various aspects.[39] Only the Argentine legislative reform, as we will see, addressed IC.[40]

Costa Rica, Peru and Colombia radically modified the PICDs situation by eliminating the interdiction and the appointment of a guardian for individuals declared incapacitated. To this end, they designed a system of support and safeguards for the exercise of legal capacity. They modified the general legal capacity system contained in their respective civil codes. When regulating the material scope of the support measures, however, the three jurisdictions used general formulas. None of the three reforms openly addressed the use of support for IC.[41] While the Colombian reform is explicit in mentioning the extension of advance directives in the health sphere,[42] none of the reforms modified the legislation that generally regulates IC.[43] Therefore, the reforms left in force the IC rules which provide for the substituted decision-making of disabled persons, without establishing specific rules for PICDs or expressly establishing supports or safeguards.

What is worrisome about this situation is that it is unclear in which cases the supports would apply or how they would operate.[44] It may be the case that specific judicial interpretations link the general regulation of supports and

---

[39] A general analysis of these three reforms can be consulted in A. Vásquez, F. Isaza and A. Parra, "Legal Capacity Regime Reforms in Costa Rica, Peru and Colombia: A Comparative and Critical Analysis" in this volume.

[40] National Civil and Commercial Code 2015.

[41] See in Costa Rica, Law 9234, which promotes "the personal autonomy of people with disabilities" (2016), art. 11; in Peru, Legislative Decree 1384, which recognises and regulates the legal capacity of persons with disabilities under equal conditions (2018), which modified the Civil Code, especially art. 42.

[42] The Colombian case is different from the aforesaid; although Law 1996, by means of which the regime for the exercise of the legal capacity of persons with disabilities of legal age (2019) is established, does not expressly mention IC among the areas covered by the supports agreements, it does consider that advance directives can deal with health, financial or personal matters, among other acts aimed at having legal effects (art. 21) and at enabling the judge to establish supports for "financial management, health and other relevant aspects" in the review of the interdiction process (art. 56). The application of conventional or judicial supports, in the health sphere and ultimately to IC, appears to stem from this.

[43] The general regulation of consent in health matters in Costa Rica is regulated by Law 5395, General Health (1973), arts. 11 and 27. In Peru, in Law 26,842, General Health (1997), arts. 4 and 15; and also in Law 30,947, on Mental Health (2019), art. 9. In Colombia, in Law 23, on Medical Ethics (1981); Law 1733, on palliative care (2014); and Law 1751, on the fundamental right to health (2015), art. 10.

[44] R. Bregaglio and R. Constantino, "The Informed Medical Consent of People with Intellectual and Psychosocial Disabilities in Peru" in *A convenção sobre os direitos da pessoa com deficiência em aplicação na america latina e seus impactos no direito civil*, Focus, São Paulo, Brazil 2021.

Intersentia

313

safeguards to the IC regulation. Such a task, which may involve harmonisation techniques, tacit derogations, and human rights compliant interpretation among other considerations, is complex, risky and unlikely when a legislated right explicitly covers the IC hypotheses. The reforms clearly did not explicitly consider the application of supports to the IC sphere, which only casts doubt on the regulation the PICDs are subject to concerning their IC. As seen in this chapter, the application of DMSs to IC is not self-evident. It would be desirable to rely on explicit and specific regulations for such an important issue. Although it is perhaps too early to judge the Colombian case – as its regulations are still being implemented –, the centrality of IC in the struggle for the autonomy of persons with disabilities, expressed in several Constitutional Court rulings on the matter,[45] raises the question of why the application of supports to IC was not expressly regulated.

Unlike the other reforms in the region, the new Argentine Civil and Commercial Code (2015) was clear, both in regulating IC in the case of PICDs and in making DMSs applicable to this area.[46] The regulation does not embrace, as the other reforms do, the idea of universal legal capacity, retaining instances in which PICDs can be subjected to interdiction and guardianship. Not only does the Code explicitly regulate the application of DMSs to IC, but it does so in a harmonic and non-contradictory manner with other relevant legislation that generally regulates IC.[47]

Several hypotheses can be put forward to try to explain the lack of DMSs regulation for IC. Some are simple, such as the fact that the centrality of transforming the general incapacitation regime led to losing sight of the regulation of supports in various areas where a specific harmonisation is required, which is also the case, for example, in criminal and public law. It could also be argued that there was a conviction that a reform in the health field requires a systematic treatment that the general reforms to legal capacity were not in a position to provide, except for the Argentine reform, which had recently legislated a Law of Mental Health with the same standards used by the subsequent legal capacity reform. These hypotheses only speculate in search of a reasonable explanation for the omission.

If we move from the explanations to the opportunities that are opened by such an omission, the Latin American jurisdictions could carry out a future reform to

---

[45]   N. Avevedo, "Relational Autonomy, Legal Capacity Reform, and Decision-Making in Health in Colombia" in *A convenção sobre os direitos da pessoa com deficiência em aplicação na america latina e seus impactos no direito civil*, Focus, São Paulo, Brazil 2021. The author cites the following rulings: Judgment T-653-08; Judgment T-216-08; Judgment T-1019-06; Judgment T-1021-03; Judgment T-597-01; Judgment T-850-02; Judgment SU-337-99.

[46]   Art. 59 Civil and Commercial Code 2015.

[47]   Law 26,657 on Mental Health (2010) and Law 26,529 on Patient Rights (2009). In said laws, however, the person who performs the support is not considered as authorised to grant the CI for the PICD and the reform to the Code did not create harmonisation by including the support.

their IC regulation in order to incorporate DMSs in a way that responds to the specific demands of this sphere of legal capacity. This is also an opportunity for jurisdictions planning to reform their legislation and adapt it to the standards set by the CRPD.

4.2. LEGISLATING SUPPORT FOR INFORMED CONSENT

If the purpose of legal capacity reform in health care is to enhance the autonomy of PICDs, this reform must be carried out carefully and consider all the elements that may be relevant to its design. To that end, three orders of concerns should be considered: first, IC particularities; second, regulatory problems; and third, other socio-legal aspects.

Concerning IC particularities as a qualified form of expression of will and exercise of legal capacity, we can try to synthesise some conclusions of the analysis carried out in section 3 of this chapter. First, it must be assumed that reform involves intervening in an area where the idea of functional assessment of capacity is an established practice, at least in theory. Of course, this will depend on the regulation of each jurisdiction and on what happens in medical practice. This means seriously considering whether it is necessary to move away from the functional model for implementing DMSs. On the one hand, there is an intense doctrinal debate on the compatibility of the functional model with the CRPD, so it would not be surprising if this debate were repeated. In any case, as we have seen, DMSs are compatible with both a universal and functional model. The preservation or incorporation of a functional model in the IC sphere should not, therefore, be an obstacle to developing a DMS system.

The second issue observed concerns administering the *dignity of the risk* for PICDs. Using this conceptual matrix predisposes the application of supports and the restriction of arguments based on vulnerability and need for protection. However, the significant risks to health and life involved in certain medical decisions, on the one hand, and the potential inhibitor of autonomy inherent in some support relationships, on the other hand, require safeguards to avoid unnecessary harm based on neglect or abuse. The central question here is whether some form of capacity assessment can safeguard the rights while constraining the preferences of a PICD involved in a support relationship.

The third conclusion reached is that, for the IC to be effective from a legal point of view, there must be a certain understanding of the information delivered on behalf of the PICD. Without a certain minimum understanding of it, it cannot be said that we are dealing with an IC. This brings with it a challenge from the point of view of the functionality that the IC plays in the legal system: a tool that allows conduct that could otherwise result in criminal and civil liabilities. With these three elements in mind, it is possible to suggest that perhaps the universal legal capacity system that Latin American jurisdictions have applied as a general rule needs to be qualified in the case of IC. Along with the DMSs, therefore, legislative reform in terms of IC should incorporate a functional evaluation specially designed to account for the needs identified.

In relation to the problems of regulation, a coherent and systematic regulation must have a general system of support, specified or qualified in the specific areas in which the general regulation could be inadequate. In this regard, the proliferation of parallel regimes should be avoided. This has the virtue of presenting a supplementary regime to which to turn when special regulation is insufficient. With this objective, it is necessary to carefully calibrate the relationships between the general regulation of supports for legal capacity and the general regulation of IC. Moreover, it requires, as we have already seen, considering the particularities of PICDs' IC and the special cases of IC, such as donation of organs, tissues, cells and blood, both living and *post-mortem*; contraception and fertility, particularly concerning surgical sterilisation; abortion; palliative care; or related to scientific research.

By socio-legal aspects, reference is made to the fact that, although regulation can be understood as a system of rules that govern human behaviour in a specific area of social life, regulation interacts with a reality made up of entrenched practices. Although reform of this type may have the potential to empower PICDs to exercise their autonomy, the success of this objective is not guaranteed. To the extent that regulation considers in more specificity the reality that it seeks to regulate and the behaviour it seeks to channel, the chances of success increase. The first aspect relates to the actors involved. Although the main actors promoting the general reform of legal capacity have been actors related to the world of human rights and, in particular, to the movement of persons with disabilities, it is important to consider that IC regulation should incorporate the interests and perspectives of health professionals. This is critical as these professionals, particularly doctors, will be the primary recipients of this regulation – and probably the most important appliers of its provisions. We must remember that the medical profession has a professional culture that resists external intervention and that the normativity of the bioethical discourse that adopts capacity as an instrument for managing autonomy is central to this culture.[48] A second socio-legal aspect refers to ensuring that what is established in the law is applied in practice. As comparative experience shows,[49] legal change does not bring a change in the practices of previously regulated fields. Implementing a regulation as avant-garde as the one described must combine tools to implement supports with tools to evaluate their performance. It could

---

[48] J. Miola, *Medical Ethics and Medical Law: A Symbiotic Relationship*, Hart, London 2007.

[49] C. Davies, F. Fattori, D. O'Donnell, et al., "What Are the Mechanisms That Support Healthcare Professionals to Adopt Assisted Decision-Making Practice? A Rapid Realist Review" (2019) *BMC Health Services Research* 1, p. 960.

include pilots, monitoring and evaluation, such as training, protocols and codes of good practice. Finally, a third aspect is the work that must be carried out with PICDs, with a view to empower them in using DMSs. The preponderant role of care relationships in their lives and the need for protection, which mark how PICDs have been treated under interdiction and guardianship regimes – prevalent in the region – must give way to treatment that is more respectful of their will and preferences. This involves extending the culture of rights in the medical field towards a group hitherto excluded from its exercise.

5. CONCLUSIONS

In the context of a generally adverse experience for PICDs in accessing health treatments and an understanding of IC aimed at guaranteeing patient autonomy and limiting the responsibility of health care personnel, the emergence of DMSs for IC represents a revolutionary innovation. These DMSs can potentially serve as a way to develop the autonomy of PICDs giving a rational and balanced vehicle to realise the principle of dignity of risk. However, IC requires that the DMSs must be adequate, maintaining certain qualified forms of capacity assessment or understanding of the information, which can be considered safeguard mechanisms.

Substituted decision-making in the health sphere has been one of the primary sources of inspiration for the CRPD and the CRPD Committee to conceive their support model. However, in Latin America, where the reforms inspired by Article 12 of the CRPD have gone further in applying this model, the regulatory exclusion of IC seems to be the general rule. This omission represents an opportunity to regulate DMSs in IC, with full consideration of needed requirements analysed in this chapter. In particular, there is a need for future research along the following lines and topics: (i) the empirical study of the elements that account for the development and application of DMSs in the field of health is desirable; (ii) it is necessary to attend to the different IC categories when designing DMSs and safeguards, to the extent that clinical IC, and IC in biomedical research, imply a considerably different relationship between doctor/researcher and patient/volunteer; (iii) further study is needed on the *extension* of reforms to legal capacity in the region to different spheres – for example, electoral, psychiatric, civil, matrimonial, reproductive and criminal, among others – which can contribute their own particularities to the regulation of legal capacity.

CONTRACTUAL CAPACITY OF PERSONS WITH A DISABILITY IN THE SPANISH CIVIL CODE

Maria Paz Garcia Rubio[*]

1. Contractual Capacity in the Spanish Civil Code 319
2. Contractual Capacity of Persons with Disability under the "LAPD" 322
   2.1. General Rule of Capacity and Absence of Consent. 322
   2.2. Lack of Support for Decision-Making. 323
      2.2.1. There is No Support for Decision-Making 324
      2.2.2. Support for Decision-Making is Rejected, and Contractual Risk is Assumed. 324
      2.2.3. Formerly Available Support for Decision-Making is not Used, but its Rejection is not Proven Either 326
3. The Annulment Action 330
4. Limitations to the Power to Annul and Restitution. 330

1. CONTRACTUAL CAPACITY IN THE SPANISH CIVIL CODE

In its original version, the Spanish Civil Code (CC) of 1889 considered "insane" or "demented" persons who were unable to govern themselves and manage their property as persons susceptible to be legally incapacitated. Incapacitation was contemplated as an instrument to protect the personal and property interests of the incapacitated person declaring their contractual irresponsibility (Article 1301,[1] which supposed that the guardian was empowered to act in place of their ward[2]).

---

[*] Professor of Civil Law, Universidad de Santiago de Compostela. Permanent Member of the First Section of the General Coding Commission of Spain.

[1] F. De Castro y Bravo, *Derecho Civil de España*, Civitas, Madrid, Reprint. Facsimile 1984, from the 1952 edition, pp. 297–299, estimated that the system in the Code, in contrast with the precedent to the 1851 Project, was to subject the *idiot* or *imbecile* to full guardianship aimed at protecting their person and property.

[2] L. Diez-Picazo y Ponce de León reminds that contracting capacity matches substantially the general capacity to act, in *Fundamentos de Derecho civil patrimonial, I. Introducción. Teoría del Contrato*, 6th ed., Thomson-Civitas. Cizur Menor, 2007, p. 170.

Maria Paz Garcia Rubio

Leaving aside the contractual capacity of minors, I will indicate that the second item of Article 1263 CC, in its original version, stated that the following could not grant consent "2°. The insane and demented persons and the deaf and dumb who cannot write". It was understood that when a person lacked the capacity to understand and express a will,[3] the action or business they entered into could not be valid and effective. From the possible solutions – nullity of all actions, validity of the actions, unless "insanity" or voidability were shown – the law historically opted for the latter considering it to be the most favourable to the interests of the incapacitated, and also applied, for their benefit, the various protective provisions outlined for guardians of minors.[4]

In the original version of Article 1263.2, the Code did not make a distinction between those who were judicially incapacitated or not.[5] From this precept, F. de Castro held that it is incapacitation that vitiates the contract entered into by the incapacitated and that, if being done for the benefit of the protected person, capable persons who contracted with the incapacitated person could not allege incapacity (Article 1302 CC). Castro adds that an easy and rapid defence was thus provided for the incapacitated person, which does not preclude the possibility of requesting a declaration of nullity for lack of consent (Article 1261 CC). In this case it is necessary to prove that the person acted without the necessary reason at the time of contracting.[6] According to the doctrine of the time, the contract executed by the incapacitated person within the framework of incapacitation was voidable, whereas in the case of contracts entered into by non-incapacitated persons, who lacked of awareness and will, the basis for invalidity did not rest in the absence of capacity but in the lack of contractual consent, which is why the act or contract would be legally void.[7]

The important amendment to the Civil Code introduced by the law passed on 24 October 1983, limited the causes of incapacitation to "Persistent physical or mental illnesses or deficiencies which prevent a person from governing himself" (Article 200 CC, in force at the time of writing). This norm, although based on the medical model of disability, represented a major advance in relation to the previous regime.[8] A system of gradation of incapacity was admitted, at

---

[3] F. De Castro y Bravo, *El negocio jurídico*, Civitas, Madrid, Reprint. Facsimile, 1985, from the 1971 edition, Reprint 2002, p. 57, explains that will is motivated by *vis cognoscitiva* and by *vis appetitiva.*.

[4] F. De Castro y Bravo (n. 1), p. 311.

[5] "2nd Insane or demented persons and the deaf and dumb who cannot write cannot grant consent." This does not prevent, in the opinion of L. Diez-Picazo y Ponce de León (n. 2), p. 171, this from being a piece of information of special relevance that should always be considered.

[6] F. De Castro y Bravo (n. 1), p. 312.

[7] F. De Castro y Bravo, ibid.

[8] According to L. Diez-Picazo y Ponce de León, "New perspectives on the Rights of persons", in *Presentations and Conclusions of the Congress on Guardianship and Incapacity,*

least in theory, which allowed for different levels of incapacity depending on the circumstances of each person. Regardless of the purpose of the model, when the incapacitation was total or the judicial decision did not recognise it as partial, the criterion of annulment was maintained at the request of the representative of the incapacitated person or at his or her own request, once he or she had been reinstated in his or her capacity (Articles 1301 and 1302 CC). This annullability is similar in effect to contracts entered into by a minor and subsequently annulled or confirmed (Articles 1304 and 1314 CC).

Surprisingly, the 1983 reform left Article 1263.2 CC intact. It was amended many years later by the LO 1/1996 of 15 January, by replacing the reference to "insane or demented persons and the deaf and dumb who cannot write" simply with "the incapacitated". This precept was amended again by Law 20/2015 of 28 July, declaring in Article 1263 CC that those persons who cannot give consent include "Incapacitated persons, under the terms indicated in the judicial decision". This norm was valid until 2 June 2021, when Law 8/2021 – which amends civil and procedural legislation to support persons with disabilities in the exercise of their juridical capacity (hereinafter LAPD) – came into effect.

A scheme like the one previously established in Article 1263 of the CC was quite clear; incapacitation was designed for the safety of legal acts,[9] but the costs were very high for the rights of persons with this type of disability. The costs consisted of preventing these persons from exercising legal acts independently or, at least, making their participation in contracts very difficult. As one of the most important specialists on the subject said expressly about the system repealed by the LAPD,[10] restrictions on the capacity of the minor or incapacitated persons to act, did not exclude them from entering into contracts and being bound by them, but the protection afforded (cf. Articles 1300, 1301, 1302, 1304 and 1314 CC) was an important deterrent to contracting with them.[11]

Incapacitation of some adult persons due to their cognitive or intellectual disability is incompatible with the United Nations Convention on the Rights of Persons with Disabilities (UNCRPD), which, since 2008, has been part of

---

Barcelona, 1999; cited in *Political Essays*, t. 1, Cizur Menor, Civitas Thomson-Reuters, 2011, pp. 980–992, spec. p. 981, that in 1983 an attempt was made to eliminate the most significant rigidities of the prior Law; also, diversification of guardianship systems was sought so that, if possible, there would be a tailoring to individual needs. However, the author considers that incapacitation still constitutes a violation against persons.

[9]   F. DE CASTRO Y BRAVO affirmed (n. 1), p. 288, notes that with the judicial resolution of incapacitation, greater stability is provided to the status of the person and higher security for third parties is also achieved.

[10]   Published in the BOE (Boletín Oficial del Estado) 3 June 2021. The new regulation has been in force since 3 September 2021.

[11]   A. M. MORALES MORENO, "Comment on article 1263 CC", *Comments to the Civil Code*, II, Ministry of Justice, Madrid, 1991, p. 456.

domestic law in Spain. Recognition that disabled persons may enter into legal relations with others on an equal basis is an essential corollary for recognising juridical personality and the total juridical capacity (in its dual dimension as holder of the right and of the power to exercise it), stipulated in paragraphs 1 and 2 of Article 12 CRPD.[12]

2. CONTRACTUAL CAPACITY OF PERSONS WITH DISABILITY UNDER THE "LAPD"

In the following section, I will try to demonstrate how the legal requirements set forth in Article 12 of the UNCRPD have been included in the LAPD with respect to the contractual capacity of persons with disability.[13]

Several precepts were amended in this legal reform, with a substantial impact on civil law and other state laws.[14] Having said this, I will focus only on the general rules that refer directly to the contractual capacity of persons with disabilities and highlight only some of the most notable changes.

2.1. GENERAL RULE OF CAPACITY AND ABSENCE OF CONSENT

The first subject of analysis is Article 1263 of the CC. The current wording of this article means that persons with disabilities, including those with mental or

---

[12] In a similar sense, E. VARNEY, "Redefining contractual capacity? The UN Convention of the Rights of Persons with Disabilities and the incapacity defence in English contract law", *Legal Studies*, Vol. 37, Nº 3, 2017, pp. 493–519, spec., p. 493.

[13] E. VARNEY, 2017, ibid. and p. 499, alludes to the difficulties of implementation of Article 12 CRPD, due to the "strange silence" in the separation between juridical capacity, mental capacity and contractual capacity; it does not establish any guidelines either that might serve as support on the contractual issue, although it stresses that from its ethos it follows that any examination of the possibility of using the incapacity exception in contracts must go, not only through consideration of economic factors, such as transaction security, but also through social factors, including protection of human dignity.

[14] For a general view of the reform in the draft project phase, see M. P. GARCÍA RUBIO, "The necessary and urgent adaptation of the Spanish Civil Code to article 12 of the Nueva York Convention on the rights of persons with disabilities", *Anales de la Academia Matritense del Notariado*, course 2017/2018, pp. 143–191; before presenting the Bill of Law, M. P. GARCÍA RUBIO, "Notes on the purpose and meaning of the Draft project of the Law wherein civil and procedural legislation is reformed to support persons with disabilities in the exercise of their juridical capacity", in *Jornadas sobre el nuevo modelo de discapacidad*, M. C. GETE-ALONSO and CALERA, (coord.), Barcelona, Marcial Pons, 2020, pp. 39–61; in the phase of parliamentary processing M. P. GARCÍA RUBIO, "Reform of incapacity in the civil Code. Its incidence in senior adults", *AFDUAM*, 25, (2021a), pp. 79–107; with the already published LAPD, M. P. GARCÍA RUBIO, "Contents and general meaning of the civil and procedural reform on the subject of disability", *Sepin, Cuaderno Jurídico de Familia y Sucesiones, n.º 136*, 221 (2021b), pp. 45–62.

psychosocial conditions that might impact *a priori* on their decision-making abilities and in the formation and expression of their will to act and conduct legal transactions, have the same capacity to contract as everyone else. In addition, they have the right to do so with the support they require, as is clearly recognised in Article 12.3 CRPD.

This approach suggests that in some instances valid contractual consent could be absent in the sense of Article 1261.1 CC. If this is the case, the contract is burdened by a fundamental structural defect that impedes its fully valid and effective consideration: i.e., the lack of consent. Nevertheless, it is important to observe that, in the interpretation presented above, the defect lies in the lack of consent and not in the disability, absence of support, or inadequate support. In reality such situations are very common,[15] and can be integrated into a broader group, such as those wherein contracts are made with a lack of conscience and will for any reason (for example, when under the influence of psychotropic substances[16]).

In this group of cases, the question is related to the type of disability affecting the execution of the contract. As seen in the foregoing analysis, the response switches between two options. On the one hand, some authors consider that the law provides for the voiding of a contract due to the absence of consent of the contracting parties (Article 1261.1 CC), which allows any interested party to demand that the contract be nullified. On the other hand, there are those who consider that voidability is dependent on the request of the person whose consent has not really been granted, in a similar way to what happens in the cases of vitiated consent. Undoubtedly, voidability has the advantage of leaving it in the hands of the person whose consent was dispensed with, to challenge the transaction.

2.2. LACK OF SUPPORT FOR DECISION-MAKING

I consider now the situation of contracts executed by persons with cognitive or intellectual disabilities without the support they are entitled to. It is helpful to distinguish between several possible situations. Specifically, I consider, as different situations, the following: (i) a person with a disability who has not had support available to enter into the contract but who does have sufficient awareness and will to express a valid contractual consent; (ii) a person with a

---

[15]   J. DELGADO ECHEVERRÍA, *Elementos de Derecho civil. I. Parte General. Vol. 2ª. Personas,* Madrid, Dykinson, 1998, p. 146, called attention over 20 years ago to the fact that the actions of those who had not been incapacitated, when indeed they were, were not treated as marginal or juridical cases without interest, but as customary situations that should be responded to according to constitutional principles.

[16]   F. DE CASTRO Y BRAVO (n. 3), p. 95, included, within the cases of non-existence of the will for lack of reasoning, the condition of madness, intoxication or hypnosis.

disability who has waived the support voluntarily they have the right to, and assumes the risks of contracting; (iii) a person with a disability who does not use the support available, although it is not rejected either and, nevertheless, executes the contract.

2.2.1. *There is No Support for Decision-Making*

In the first scenario, the person with a disability enters into a contract without the support they had the right to. Despite this, their awareness and will is sufficient to understand that there is contractual consent; the person with a disability has natural capacity or capacity for that specific legal act. Nonetheless, something is missing in the process of formation of the contract because, as stated above, the person with a disability has not had the option to use the support that was available. I wonder, however, about the legal response to such a situation since it is not anticipated in the law.

Of course, the contract cannot be void because, hypothetically, all its essential elements are present. I do not believe either, in contrast with what happens with a total absence of consent or other limitations in the process of will formation, that lacking support which has not been sought allows for the nullifying of the legal act at the request of the person with a disability. This is because nullifying the contract would leave the other party's interest in the contract unprotected and the other party had no responsibility for such lack of support.[17] From this starting point, my position is that in this situation the contract can only be voided by the person with a disability, if and only if, the other contracting party knew of the lack of support and took advantage of it to obtain an unfair advantage.

2.2.2. *Support for Decision-Making is Rejected, and Contractual Risk is Assumed*

The second scenario is that of the contract entered into by a person with a disability who has or can access support measures to exercise their contractual capacity; nevertheless, the support is not used because the person voluntarily rejects or waives its use.

I reference this second hypothesis because I understand that the new disability regime allows for the rejecting of and acting without support. Regrettably, the LAPD does not refer directly to the right to reject support, an issue on which the UNCRPD also fails to say anything expressly – even if support is understood here as a right that the person with a disability may demand from the State, not as one that they have a duty to use. The first Concluding Observations of the UN Committee on the Rights of Persons with Disability

---

[17] As F. DE CASTRO Y BRAVO (n. 3), p. 507, indicates regulation of voidability began from the roles attributed to each contracting party: one is considered deserving of protection and juridical refuge, the other's behaviour is deemed deserving of a penalty.

(CRPD Committee) repeatedly affirms that the person with a disability has a right to reject the support both, *ex-ante* and *ex-post*.[18]

In my view, there are good arguments to make it possible and legitimate for the person with a disability to reject the support offered or to which they are entitled. The first is the undisputed principle guiding the whole reform, which is that in any reference to support and the exercise of capacity, the will of the person must prevail. This principle has as its corollary the right to reject any support.[19] I also believe that some rules in the LAPD, particularly concerning contracting, support the idea of the right to reject support. Undoubtedly, there is a possibility of contracting without the support and of not voiding the contract within the next four years following its execution (Article 1301.4 CC), and even to confirm it within an earlier term. Both things can happen, even against the will of the person responsible for providing the support, as indicated in the third paragraph of Article 1302 CC. Voidability of the contract at the request of the latter "will only be in order when the other contracting party knew of the existence of support measures at the time of contracting or if it had taken advantage in any way from the disability condition, obtaining unfair advantage therefrom." As will be explained below, it is this circumstance of taking unfair advantage, and not the fact that the disabled person has contracted without the support they had available, that legitimises the request to nullify the contract.

However, I recognise there are also reasons to sustain the opposite view of the new legal text. As I have indicated elsewhere,[20] the main reason is the procedural configuration of the support provision system, which will be of voluntary jurisdiction except if "there is opposition," which could become a contentious proceeding. Nothing seems to prevent this opposition coming from the same interested party. In my opinion, this possibility reconciles poorly with the principle of respecting the will of the person with a disability heralded by the UNCRPD, which is also considered to be the basis of the new LAPD. However, this has been precisely the argument used by the Supreme Court of Spain (*Tribunal Supremo de España*) dated 8 September 2021,[21] the first wherein the high court applied the LAPD. The decision considers very significant that the "opposition from the person with a disability to any type of support," in addition to bringing forth termination of the voluntary jurisdiction file,

---

[18]   CRPD Committee, *General Comment No. 1 – Article 12: Equal recognition before the law (Adopted 11 April 2014) – Plain English version*, CRPD/C/GC/1 Plain English version, 19 May 2014. Also, the new §1814. 2 BGB, after the law of 4 May 2021, *Gesetz zur Reform des Vormundschafts und Betreuungsrechts*, expressly recognises that it is not possible to appoint an assistant against the free will of the person. Cf., C. Riveros Ferrada, "The new regulation of juridical assistance for adults due to illness or disability in German law", *La Ley. Derecho de familia n° 31, julio-septiembre, La reforma civil y procesal de la discapacidad. Un tsunami en el ordenamiento jurídico*, (M. P. García Rubio, coord.) n° 31, 1 July 2021.

[19]   M. P. García Rubio (n. 14), 2020, p. 52.

[20]   M. P. García Rubio (n. 14), 2021b, p. 50.

[21]   Tribunal Supremo de España, Sala de lo Civil, ECLI:ES:TS:2021:3276.

"does not prevent measures from being requested through a contradictory judgment, which supposes that said judgment may conclude the adoption of the measures, even against the will of the interested party." I reiterate that, in my opinion, this position is not coherent with UNCRPD, and, of course, it openly contradicts the opinion of the CRPD Committee.

In fact, it is possible to think about the case of a person with cognitive or intellectual disabilities who has sufficient natural capacity to contract and has been able to confirm this before a notary. That same person could have rejected – voluntarily and without undue pressure or influence – the support to enter into a specific contract, thus assuming the risks of contracting voluntarily.[22] If we admit this power of rejection, as I think should be done, logic requires that the same subject cannot later demand the voidability of the contract. Doing so would be a contradictory act (*venire contra factum propium*) that would provide the other contracting party a defence against nullifying the contract. In this sense, the contract would be valid, except if there was another cause for voidability, such as lack of valid consent due to deceit, violence, or intimidation (Articles 1265 and 1270 CC), as would apply in cases with any other person. Any such reasons would be irrespective of the fact that the person with a disability voluntarily rejected the support measures.

2.2.3. Formerly Available Support for Decision-Making is not Used, but its Rejection is not Proven Either

The third and certainly most complex hypothesis is when the person with a disability has concluded the transaction without the proper support, but there is no evidence that they had waived the support or done so voluntarily. We must distinguish two scenarios.

On the one hand, a person might have contracted while they were susceptible to a flaw in their will, because they were a victim of error, deceit, violence or intimidation, or because they lacked the needed support to which they were entitled. In such a situation, the contract would be voidable by the interested party themselves (with the corresponding supporter, if required), not because the person acted without support, but because their contractual will lacked integrity, as would be the case with any other victim of a flawed consent.

On the other hand, there are those cases where there is no certainty or evidence that the person with a disability has voluntarily waived support measures, and there is no indication that there was any flawed consent. On a first reading, this is the case contemplated in the new Article 1302.3 CC, when

---

[22] In a similar sense, see J. RIBOT IGUALADA, "The new conservatorship: differences with the former system and perspectives of performance", in *Claves para la adaptación del ordenamiento juridico privado a la convencion de las Naciones Unidas en materia de discapacidad*, Valencia, Tirant lo Blanch, 2019, p. 221.

alluding to "Contracts entered into by persons with disability who have support measures for the exercise of their contractual capacity dispensing with said measures when they needed to ...". In this case, Article 1301 CC, authorises nullification of the contract. Such power may be exercised, as the first paragraph in Article 1302.3 CC provides, by the person with a disability (with the support they may require), as well as by their heirs, if the person dies before the term of the contract. In addition, the second paragraph of the same Article 1302.3 CC, authorises the person responsible for providing support to annul the contract.

Consequently, the 2021 legislation opted for voidability of the contract and not for its rescission.[23] My preference for voidability[24] is because this is a much more flexible mechanism that can be activated in court and out-of-court. In contrast to rescission,[25] it does not have a subsidiary character and if a judgment of annulment is issued, it brings forth full restitution which is not the case with rescission.[26]

In order to annul the contract at the request of the contracting party with a disability (or of their heirs), omission of the support is not enough.[27] If it were the case that such lack of support is sufficient to nullify the transaction, we would incur a situation of direct discrimination of persons with disabilities, in that they could be under an additional requirement to use support measures to contract. To avoid this inequity, I understand Article 1302.3 CC to mean that in order to annul the contracts executed in the circumstances described, something more is required besides the contract having been made without support. This is not mentioned expressly in the first section of Article 1302.3 CC but is reflected in the second paragraph of Article 1302.3 CC, which provides that the support provider has the power to annul the contract. Specifically, according to this provision, the annulment will only be resolved when "the other contracting party

---

[23]   Preferred rescission for the contracts of persons with disability, E. López Barba, *Capacidad jurídica. El artículo 12 de la Convención sobre los Derechos de las Personas con Discapacidad y las medidas no discriminatorias de defensa de su patrimonio*, Madrid, Dykinson, 2020, pp. 110 et seq; for the contracts wherein unfair advantage is produced, if it is legally recognised by rescission, R. Barceló Compte, *Ventaja injusta y protección de la parte débil del contrato*, Madrid, Marcial Pons, 2019, p. 181.

[24]   It is also the option for situations of unfair advantage for E. Gómez Calle, *Desequilibrio contractual y tutela del contratante débil*, Cizur Menor, Thomson Reuters-Aranzadi, 2018, p. 187.

[25]   Cf. Article 1294 CC.

[26]   Cf. Article 1295 CC, for the rescission for lesion, where, in the words of F. De Castro y Bravo (n. 3), p. 527, only what he calls a mandatory retroactive effect is recognised, but not the real one because, in contrast to what occurs with the voidance of the business, the rescinded business does not lose its primitive condition of validity because of this.

[27]   With another interpretation, F. Mariño Pardo, "Notes about the reforms to the civil Code by the Law 8/2021 of June 2, to support persons with disabilities" (on issues I have commented, or I should have commented), *Blog Iuris Prudente, June 21 2021*, at http://www.iurisprudente. com/2021/06/notes-on-the-civil-code-reform-by-html, accessed 04.04.2023, says that "The cause for challenging seems to be dispensing with the support measures provided".

knew of the existence of support measures at the time of contract execution or otherwise took advantage of the disability situation in other ways, obtaining unfair advantage." In my opinion this circumstance must be understood to apply not only to the case where the person who would have provided support seeks to annul the contract, but also to cases where the person with a disability seeks to do so in the situation just described.

It may be challenged that the literal text of the second paragraph in Article 1302.3 CC, "in this case ... only ...", means that it applies exclusively to the case of the person who would have been responsible for providing support challenges the contract, a conclusion reinforced by the division of the third item in two separate sub-items. However, such literal interpretation must be rejected in favour of giving the reformed statute a more coherent understanding, and in accordance with the spirit and the letter of the UNCRPD.

On this issue, it would be very helpful to describe the tortuous parliamentary process that concluded with the approval of the LAPD, as well as the various changes and replacements produced around Article 1302 CC. These lie at the origin of certain perplexities arising from the literal text which the interpreter must resolve; regretfully I cannot elaborate on such procedural explanations here, a task for which I refer to other works.[28] It should suffice here to indicate that the ultimate purpose of Article 1302 CC was to allow for the annulment of the contract executed by the person with a disability who dispensed with the support measures, where, as a result, the other contracting party gained an unfair advantage. This reasoning was very present throughout the parliamentary process, despite the fact that the final text of Article 1302.3 CC can lead to an understanding that such cause for challenging a contract is reserved only for the case contemplated in its second paragraph (annulment at the request of the support provider) and not in the first one (annulment requested by the person with a disability or their heirs). However, such an interpretation would establish a difference in the treatment of the person with a disability and the support person, which has no apparent justification.

The interpretation I propose here supposes a teleological interpretation of Article 1302 CC that tries to reconcile the promotion of autonomy and independence of the person with a disability, with their right to have the support they may require. However, this interpretation does not see the use of such support as a necessary condition for the exercise of legal capacity. Nor does it rely on an illogical differentiation between those authorised to challenge a contract (i.e., the supporter but not the person with a disability), where the other

---

[28] M. P. García Rubio, "Contracting capacity of persons with disability", in A. M. Morales Moreno (dir), E. Blanco Martínez (Coord.), *Estudios de Derecho de Contratos*, vol. I, BOE, Madrid, 2022, pp. 333–357. M. P. García Rubio and I. Varela Castro, "Comments to art. 1302 CC" in M. P. García Rubio and M. J. Moro Almaraz (dirs), *Comentario articulado a la reforma civil y procesal en materia de discapacidad*, Thomson-Reuters, Civitas, 2022, pp. 645–668.

contracting party gained an unfair advantage on the basis that the person with a disability did not use the support measures.[29]

Let us consider further the specific situation wherein it is the person responsible for providing support to the person with a disability who requests the annulment of the contract. As indicated above, their inclusion as a legitimate subject was added during the parliamentary phase,[30] probably with the intention that they could not undo the contract against the will of the person with a disability. The person responsible for providing support in that specific contract, whose participation was dispensed with, may not challenge the contract exclusively on the basis that they did not provide the authorised support measure, nor on the fact of disability of the contracting party whom they were to assist. These circumstances will not be sufficient reason to invalidate the transaction. This can only be done when (i) the other contracting party knew of the existence of the support measures at the time of contracting; and (ii) the other party obtained an unfair advantage as a result. Again, the literal text of the provision is not entirely accurate, even if the circumstances described are distinct. The first paragraph of Article 1302.3 CC, where the person with a disability is authorised to challenge the contract seems redundant as the terms for exercising a challenge are articulated in the second paragraph: where a contracting party takes advantage of "in [any] other way" the disability situation of the other contracting party, obtaining an unfair advantage.

It must be clarified that the person responsible for providing the support, whose support measure was dispensed with by the person with a disability, cannot annul the contract against the will of the person with a disability, not even in the specific case where the other party obtains an unfair advantage. Both the UNCRPD and the LAPD prohibit substitution of the will of the person with a disability, and this is not the purpose of the rule contained in this second paragraph of Article 1302.3 CC.[31]

In summary, my proposed interpretation of Article 1302.3 CC – after the LAPD has entered into force – is that the contract entered into by a person with

---

[29]   From another perspective that prioritises the safety of traffic and the protection of the trust from third parties, A. CARRASCO PERERA, "A compass to navigate the new contracting with persons with disability, their guardians and conservators", *CESCO*, 30 June 2021, pp. 1–16, spec. pp. 7–9. (http://centrodeestudiosdeconsumo.com/images/Brujula_para_navegar_la_nueva_contrataci%C3%B3n_con_personas_con_discapacidad.pdf, accessed 04.04.2023).

[30]   F. PANTALEÓN PRIETO "Consumation again? Perseverare diabolicum (I)", *Almacén de Derecho*, 7 April 2021, (available at https://almacendederecho.org/otra-vez-la-consumacion-perseverare-diabolicum-i, accessed 04.04.2023), criticised that in the Bill of Law this legitimation included in the Draft project was eliminated, may be because it was understood that the person with disability "stopped being the owner" of the decision about annulment of the contract, which, as the author rightly indicated, would be a hypothesis that would be rejected by a "sensible interpretation".

[31]   Although I admit there are boundary cases wherein a substitution action of the representative is possible, as I explain in M. P. GARCÍA RUBIO (n. 14), 2020, p. 53.

a disability, who has not used a support measure to contract, may be annulled by the person with, without or through the person who could provide them that support. The annulment will be possible, both in the general case of suffering a vitiated contractual consent and in the specific case that the other contracting party, taking advantage of the situation of disability, obtained an unfair advantage.

3. THE ANNULMENT ACTION

Concerning the start of the term for the annulment action, the repealed paragraph read: "When the action refers to the contracts entered into by minors or disabled persons after they were released from guardianship." After the reform, there are two paragraphs: the third, which alludes to "When the action refers to the contracts entered into by minors after they were released from guardianship, legal or not", and the fourth, which refers to "When the action refers to the contracts entered into by persons with a disability doing away with the support measures provided when these were necessary, from the execution of the contract". Consistent with the whole reform and in opposition to the prior status, the provision now distinguishes as different the situations for minors, and persons with disabilities who have the right to support to contract.

Under the new legal regime, the person with a disability can exercise the annulment action despite having a support measure in place and, in addition, they may initiate the request with or without the support measure. The existence of the support measure cannot, in any case, impose an additional requirement with the effect of barring the person from appearing before a court of justice, on an equal basis with others as recognised in Article 13 UNCRPD.

A four-year only term makes sense insofar as it provides that the period of possibility for voiding a contract is not extended unnecessarily. In this case, the term will start running the day on which the contract is executed, which has the benefit of juridical security in the situation.[32]

4. LIMITATIONS TO THE POWER TO ANNUL AND RESTITUTION

Articles 1304 and 1314 of the CC have also been amended by the LAPD, which is the logical consequence of proscribing previous references to incapacity. In the

---

[32] Criteria adopted also in Article 226-5 of the Catalonia Civil Code, after the amendment by Executive Order Law 19/2021, of August 31 where by the Catalonia Civil Code adapts to the reform in the judicial amendment procedure for capacity.

version prior to LAPD, Article 1304 CC indicated that when nullity stems from the incapacity of one of the contracting parties, the incapacitated person was not obliged to provide restitution, except where they were enriched by the benefit received. Doctrine and courts understood "incapacity" to include minors and the condition of disability, even if the person were not incapacitated.[33] The rule contemplated the case of a contract entered into by a minor or incapacitated person that was annulled for this reason[34] and wherein that contracting party (the minor/incapacitated person) did not keep in their power the consideration received (i.e., they spent the money, or lost or extinguished the goods received). In those cases it was established that the said subject would have to make restitution only to the extent that the use of the lost resources had been made at the necessary expenses of the incapacitated person him- or herself. Expenses that, in any case, would have been made with the use of their own resources.[35] This rule treated minors and persons with disabilities the same,[36] a legal solution historically rooted in Spanish law,[37] but inconsistent with Article 12 of the UNCRPD.

Distribution in the assignment of rights made by Article 1304 CC was reproduced in Article 1314 of the CC.[38] Before the LAPD, the first paragraph indicated that the action of nullity of contracts was extinguished when the thing/object of the contract, would have been lost through deceit or blame of the person who could exercise it. However, the second paragraph included an exception to this rule according to which "If the reason for the action was a disability of any of the contracting parties, loss of the thing/object will not be an obstacle for the action to prevail unless it would have happened out of deceit or blame of the claimant after having acquired the capacity". Again, it was mainly considered that the exception included minors and disabled persons, whether incapacitated or not.

After the reform brought by the LAPD, Articles 1304 and 1314 CC continue to mention persons with disability and the support measures.[39] Personally,

---

[33]   J. Delgado Echeverría, "Comment on article 1304" (n. 15), p. 554 and A. Carrasco Perera (n. 29), p. 715.

[34]   J. Delgado Echeverría insists that limitation to restitution provided in this article is not derived, simply, because the person bound to return is disabled, but that the cause of disability presented is, precisely the disability, J. Delgado Echeverría (n. 15), pp. 553–554.

[35]   A. Carrasco Perera (n. 29), pp. 715–716, who also states that if the disabled person keeps the thing or the money, it must be returned fully, and if they do not have the thing or the price, they will then assign to the other party the actions to collect one or the other.

[36]   J. Delgado Echeverría (n. 15), p. 553, the purpose of the precept was to arbitrate adequate protection for disabled persons, especially minors, who might sell their property and waste the proceeds of the sale.

[37]   F. De Castro y Bravo (n. 1), p. 311.

[38]   J. Delgado Echeverría (n. 15), p. 553 and p. 571.

[39]   Article 1304: "When nullity stems from underage, the contracting minor will not be bound to return but to the extent they profited from the consideration received. This rule will be applicable when nullity stems from dispensing with the support measures established and

I would have preferred that all mention of disability was erased from both norms and that the privilege they embrace would have been reserved exclusively for minors. There are two reasons for this. On the one hand, because the equalisation of minors and adults with disabilities for the purpose of reducing or even eliminating their obligation to restitute the other party after the invalidation of the contract, supposes a discriminatory treatment that directly violates the mandate of the UNCRPD. On the other hand, the reduction of responsibility that implies a reduced restitution obligation, far from being a privilege, supposes one more barrier that keeps people with disabilities from their full integration in the market for goods and services, and in legal transactions in general. It becomes more likely, as happened with the system prior to the LAPD, that other parties become more reticent to enter legal relationships with persons with disabilities who, later, not only can void them (even if they have lost the thing received), but be responsible only for returning the extent of their enrichment.

For all the above, I think that the new paragraphs in Articles 1304 and 1314 CC must be read in the light of Article 1302 CC, with an understanding that the provisions for restitution apply only when the nullity of the contract was due to the other contracting party obtaining an unfair benefit for having taken advantage of a situation of disability.

Overall, I believe that the new text of Articles 1304 and 1314 CC are inconsistent with the assumptions and norms of the UNCRPD and the philosophy of the LAPD. These norms retain rules whose structure, logic and foundations offer a privileged regime of restitution based on the circumstance of the person ("disability"). Furthermore, whereas Article 12.5 of the UNCRPD recognises the right of persons with disability "to control their own financial affairs", Articles 1304 and 1314 CC are structured precisely on the idea that these persons do not know how to control their financial matters and are going to "lose" the consideration received.

---

considered necessary, so long as the contracting party with the right to restitution knew of the existence of the support measure at the time of contracting or would have profited otherwise from the disability situation obtaining unfair advantage therefrom". Article 1314: "Contract nullity action will also extinguish when the thing, subject of these, would have been lost by deceit or blame of whom might exercise it. If the cause of the action was that any of the contracting parties were minor, the loss of the thing will not be an obstacle for the action to prevail, unless it had occurred due to deceit or blame of the claimant after having reached majority age. If the cause of the action was that the contracting person with disability had dispensed with the support measures established when necessary, the loss of the thing will not be an obstacle for the action to prevail, so long as the other contracting party knew of the existence of the support measures at the time of contracting or if they would have taken advantage somehow of the situation of disability obtaining unfair advantage therefrom."

SAFEGUARDS FOR THE EXERCISE OF LEGAL CAPACITY BY PERSONS WITH DISABILITIES

A Form of Justified Paternalism

Renato Antonio Constantino Caycho* and
Renata Anahí Bregaglio Lazarte**

1. Introduction 334
2. Starting Point: Disability as a Vulnerability 335
   2.1. Internal Vulnerability and its Relationship with Functionality as
        a Criterion for Determining the Validity of Will................. 337
   2.2. Relational Vulnerability and its Relationship to Undue Influence,
        Conflict of Interest and Abuse 340
3. Safeguards in Conjunction with the Vulnerability of a Person with
   a Disability.. 341
   3.1. Purposes of Safeguards 342
        3.1.1. Respecting Rights, Will and Preferences 342
        3.1.2. Avoiding Conflicts of Interest 343
        3.1.3. Avoiding Undue Influence............................. 344
   3.2. Scope of Safeguards 346
   3.3. Main Characteristics of Safeguards 349
4. Conclusion: Safeguards, a Form of Justified Paternalism 351

---

* Full-Time Professor at the Law Academic Department of the Pontifical Catholic University of Peru (PUCP). Member of the Interdisciplinary Research Group on Disability of the PUCP (GRIDIS)

** Associate Professor of the Law Academic Department of the PUCP. GRIDIS Coordinator.

1. INTRODUCTION

Article 12 of the Convention on the Rights of Persons with Disabilities (UNCRPD) revolutionised the understanding of the capability of persons with disabilities, particularly persons with intellectual and psychosocial disabilities,[1] to engage in juridical acts.[2] They are no longer seen as incapable, but rather enjoy legal capacity on equal terms with others. The literature on the subject has focused on equal legal capacity and the role of supports for the exercise of legal capacity. However, few studies analyse the scope of Article 12.4 of the UNCRPD.

For a long time, one of the primary arguments to deny legal capacity to persons with disabilities was that they did not have the capacity to make relevant decisions and, therefore, should not bear the negative consequences of their actions. As such, it was better for someone else to make decisions on their behalf. In this regard, one of the clearest demands during negotiation of the UNCRPD was the freedom to make mistakes and take risks in decision-making, on the understanding that this was intrinsically related to human dignity.[3]

For persons with disabilities to be able to make their own decisions obviously implies accepting that there will be times when they will make decisions that may appear to go against their interests, be risky or even dangerous. However, this "freedom to make one's own decisions"[4] can also be an invitation to take advantage of a situation of vulnerability. Any such outcome would undermine respect for the "inherent dignity" of the person with a disability.[5] Article 12.4 of the UNCRPD confronts this tension by establishing safeguards, intended to prevent protections for the exercise of freedom from becoming a condition for others to abuse a person and do damage to their dignity.

The fact that the safeguards envisioned by Article 12.4 of the UNCRPD have been relatively undeveloped by the Committee on the Rights of Persons with Disabilities (CRPD Committee) may be due to the difficulty of constructing an argument that articulates the notion of autonomy with the need for protective

---

[1]   By *persons with intellectual disabilities* we refer to those in a situation of disability originating from a temporary or permanent condition resulting in significant limitations in intellectual functioning or adaptive behaviour, such as a person with Down syndrome. By *people with psychosocial disabilities* we mean those who have a temporary or permanent condition impairing the way they think, relate or interact, such as a person with schizophrenia, bipolar disorder or Asperger's syndrome. The term "impairment" can be stigmatising, although it is the term used by the CRPD.

[2]   We use *juridical act* to refer to a declaration of will aimed at the formation modification or termination of legal relationships. Even if *legal transaction* may be a better translation for the German term of *Rechtsgeschäft*, in most Latin American countries, *juridical act* is the correct term. See L. León, *El sentido de la codificación civil. Estudios sobre la influencia de los modelos jurídicos y su influencia en el Código Civil Peruano*, Palestra Editores, Lima 2004.

[3]   P. Gooding, "Supported Decision-Making: A Rights-Based Disability Concept and its Implications for Mental Health Law" (2013) 20 *Psychiatry, Psychology and Law* 3, pp. 431–451.

[4]   CRPD, Article 3.a.

[5]   Ibid.

measures in situations of vulnerability. Recognising this challenge, this chapter analyses the safeguards and their configuration.

2. STARTING POINT: DISABILITY AS A VULNERABILITY

The UNCRPD establishes that disability is not an intrinsic condition of the person but rather arises from the interaction of a physical, mental, intellectual, or sensory impairment with a social barrier. However, in a society where disability is a reason for discrimination, persons with disabilities are in a disadvantaged position in various areas of social life. The UNCRPD recognises that these disadvantages, however, cannot lead to the absolute denial of rights or entirely limit the freedom to conclude contracts.

In general, laws have established some protections against material inequalities. Thus, labour law understands that the employer and the worker are not on equal terms and establishes limitations on contractual freedom, such as the minimum wage. Similarly, concepts such as the "supervened excessive onerous burden, [the] abuse of rights or the sanctioning of abusive clauses have been established in civil law."[6] According to León, the basis of similar concepts has to do with a general principle of private contracting that rejects the abuse of a vulnerable situation in the will of others and prohibits taking advantage of real inequality between the contracting parties.[7]

Based on the foregoing, disability should be perceived as a form of vulnerability in the face of any juridical act and that, moreover, it will be a form of real inequality in any exercise of bilateral or multilateral contractual freedom. This does not imply imposing absolute restrictions on exercising this freedom. However, it does justify the safeguard measures outlined in Article 12.4 of the UNCRPD to avoid unwanted harm for a person with a disability.

In our opinion, the vulnerability of a person with a disability has two types of consequences: internal and relational. The first has to do with the difficulties in understanding the juridical act and is strongly linked to the model of functional restriction of legal capacity. In its General Comment No. 1, the CRPD Committee pointed out that there are three models in comparative law for restricting the legal capacity of persons with disabilities: status, outcome and functionality. Restriction by status occurs when it is based on a diagnosis of

---

[6] R. MOMBERG, *Contra la igualdad en el derecho de contratos*, in F. MUÑOZ (ed), *Igualdad, inclusión y derecho: lo político, lo social y lo jurídico en clave igualitaria*, LOM Ediciones, Santiago 2013.

[7] See L. LEON, *Derecho privado. Parte general. Negocios, actos y hechos jurídicos*, Fondo Editorial de la Pontificia Universidad Católica del Perú, Lima 2019, p. 109.

disability. Restriction by outcome restricts legal capacity based on the decision made by the person in a specific situation, considering that it is not in their best interests. In both cases, the CRPD Committee concluded these approaches to restricting legal capacity were incompatible with Article 12 of the UNCRPD.[8]

Finally, the third model, restriction based on functional ability, seeks to determine if the person with a disability understands the implications and effects of the juridical act to be carried out. In the draft of General Comment No. 1, the CRPD Committee did not completely reject this model. It only rejected functional or outcome-based approaches if they were discriminatory or "if they disproportionately affect the right of persons with disabilities to equality before the law."[9] However, in its final version, the functional model was also found to be incompatible with Article 12, which "does not permit such discriminatory denial of legal capacity."[10]

Despite the foregoing, it is not so easy to disregard the functional approach as a criterion to determine who can and who cannot engage in juridical acts. Contrary to what is stated by the CRPD Committee, we believe that while the functional model is not applicable for determining who has legal capacity in general, it does provide an approach to determining who can express a valid will regarding a specific legal transaction. This difficulty in expressing a valid will, and the risks that could arise from validating a decision made without an adequate understanding of the consequences,[11] is precisely what the safeguard measures seek to protect.

The second consequence of vulnerability, which we call *relational*, is linked to the possibility of persons with disabilities being manipulated within the framework of the support relationship. In these cases, it is not relevant whether the person understands the legal act. What is relevant is whether the statement they make responds to their true will or if it is vitiated by the undue influence of a person exercising support or by the other party in a juridical act. We acknowledge that the differentiation between the internal and relational dimensions of vulnerability is primarily theoretical and that, in real life, both dimensions most likely occur side by side.

It is also important to recognise that the analysis of vulnerability in decision-making, which we examine in this chapter in relation to disability, has also been considered in other scenarios. Thus, in situations of labour or sexual exploitation, it is essential to analyse the situation of vulnerability of the consenting person.

---

[8]   See CRPD Committee, General Comment No. 1, Article 12: equal recognition as a person before the law, CRPD/C/GC/1, 2014, para. 15.

[9]   CRPD Committee (n. 8), para. 21.

[10]   CRPD Committee (n. 8), para. 15.

[11]   According to Catalina Devandas, one of the functions of supports is "to evaluate the possible alternatives to a decision and its consequences" – C. DEVANDAS, Informe de la Relatora Especial sobre los Derechos de las Personas con Discapacidad, A/HRC/37/56, 2017, para. 41.

We could also ask whether conditions such as illiteracy would put a person in a situation of vulnerability in legal transactions requiring functional abilities to read or write. In this sense, functional inabilities can constrain a person's exercise of their will in situations other than disability. This raises the prospect of, and debate about, whether these other situations also require complementary safeguards like those indicated in Article 12.4 of the UNCRPD.

2.1. INTERNAL VULNERABILITY AND ITS RELATIONSHIP WITH FUNCTIONALITY AS A CRITERION FOR DETERMINING THE VALIDITY OF WILL

In the debates about the functional approach to legal capacity, some authors defend this approach, claiming that it results in assessments which are neutral and allow for an adequate determination of whether the person can make a specific decision.[12] On this basis, they argue that a functional approach complies with the guidelines of the CRPD Committee.[13] As Series argues, while these evaluations can be used in a discriminatory way, they are not "*inevitably* discriminatory or disproportionate in *all* circumstances" (emphasis added).[14]

Another view questions this positive assessment of the functional approach, on the basis that it is not neutral.[15] Accordingly, Minkowitz[16] and Devandas[17] claim that it is not possible to restrict legal capacity based on functional disability. However, the problem with this position is that what is meant by "based on disability" is not clear, nor do they offer a truly disability-neutral model. Although efforts have been made to build these models,[18] it seems inevitable that, at the end of the day, the recipients of such restrictive measures are mainly – or are also – persons with disabilities.

---

[12] See L. SERIES and A. NILSSON, "Article 12 CRPD. Equal recognition before the law" in I. BANTEKAS, M. A. STEIN and D. ANASTASIOU (eds), *The UN Convention on the Rights of Persons with Disabilities, a commentary*, Oxford University Press, Oxford 2018, p. 353.

[13] W. MARTIN, S. MICHALOWSKI, T. JUTTEN, et al., *Achieving CRPD Compliance: Is the Mental Capacity Act of England and Wales compatible with the UN Convention on the Rights of Persons with Disabilities? If not, what next?*, Essex Autonomy Project, University of Essex 2014.

[14] L. SERIES, *Comments on Draft General Comment on Article 12 – the right to equal recognition before the law*, 2014.

[15] L. SERIES, "Relationships, autonomy and legal capacity: Mental Capacity and Support Paradigms" (2015) 40 *International Journal of Law and Psychiatry*.

[16] T. MINKOWITZ, "CRPD Article 12 and the Alternative to Functional Capacity: Preliminary Thoughts Towards Transformation" (2013) *SSRN Electronic Journal*.

[17] See C. DEVANDAS (n. 11), para. 26.

[18] See E. FLYNN and A. ARSTEIN-KERSLAKE, "State intervention in the lives of people with disabilities: the case for a disability-neutral framework" (2017) 13 *International Journal of Law in Context*, pp. 39–57; and M. BACH and L. KERZNER, *A new paradigm for protecting autonomy and the right to legal capacity*, The Law Commission of Ontario, Toronto 2010, p. 133.

However, this does not necessarily constitute discrimination based on disability. For example, denying a blind person a driver's licence is not an act of discrimination. It is true that if all blind persons applied for a driver's licence the denial rate would significantly impact this population group. To prevent a restriction from constituting systemic discrimination on a prohibited ground such as disability, the reasons for restricting the exercise of a right must be submitted to an analysis of *reasonableness*.[19] In the above example, it seems quite reasonable that a blind person could not drive a vehicle since they would not be able to know which route to take. The fact that a measure has a more significant impact on a group in a vulnerable situation, although discriminatory on its face, may be justified differential treatment.

However, there is something else at stake here. The analysis to determine the reasonableness of a licence denial is based on a *bona fide* requirement of visual functionality or proficiency. It must be proven that the person sees with such sufficiency that they can not only drive along a road but also notice the possible dangers that could arise. This is to protect both the person behind the wheel and third parties. Therefore, we must accept that, in other areas recognising rights beyond that of legal capacity, it is accepted that a functional approach can be used to reasonably restrict persons with disabilities from enjoying and exercising a right without being considered discriminatory *per se*.

Applying this analysis to the field of legal capacity, it seems appropriate to postulate that, to express a valid will in law, a minimum understanding is required; that is, the scope and consequences of a juridical act must be understood. However, we consider that this functional requirement cannot be applied in a general way to restrict legal capacity. As the CRPD Committee itself points out, a person's capacity to make decisions, "naturally vary from one person to another and may be different for a given person depending on many factors, including environmental and social factors."[20] To this statement, we would add that this capacity not only varies from person to person but can also vary from juridical act to juridical act. For this reason, as Dawson suggests, it seems necessary to recognise in the law itself a certain level of functionality to carry out legal transactions or corroborate the existence of a will. Concepts such as malice or wilful intent in criminal law or informed consent in health care and bioethics fulfil this function.[21] In addition, as we pointed out above, functional capacity could be altered not only by an impairment but also by other types of situations: illiteracy, stress, insurmountable fear or extreme pain.

---

[19] On the differences in the conceptions of discrimination of the United Nations bodies, See S. Gurbai, "Beyond the Pragmatic Definition? The Right to Non-discrimination of Persons with Disabilities in the Context of Coercive Interventions" (2020) 22 *Health and Human Rights Journal*, pp. 279–292.

[20] CRPD Committee (n. 8), para. 13.

[21] See J. Dawson, "A realistic approach to assessing mental health laws' compliance with the UNCRPD" (2015) 40 *International Journal of Law and Psychiatry*, pp. 70–79.

However, if we delve into the field of disability, it would seem reasonable that the complexity of a juridical act and the possible limits to understanding – which cannot be ameliorated by provision of accessible communication measures in the circumstances – could justify limiting the capacity to carry out a particular juridical act. Such determinations depend on the decisional requirements in a specific decisional situation. Thus, buying a television is not the same as donating a human organ. It may be, for example, that a person with an intellectual disability could exercise their right to vote with or without supports, or could decide to sell property with or without support, but may not be in a position to acquire shares and trade them on the stock market or be able to understand the scope of a clinical trial and the risks of submitting to it – even if they use support.[22] For this reason, in these last two cases, from a functional point of view, it would be valid to restrict their capacity to act: they are not able to express a will based on an adequate understanding of the act they would take.

Every transaction's positive and negative consequences are different, and a person may simply be unable to understand or appreciate them. In such cases, it is not a matter of supporting a person and waiting for them to arrive at the necessary level of reasoning process to make a decision. Doing so would effectively amount to restricting their capacity based on the outcome approach. A person must be able to understand the possible consequences and assess them freely based on their preferences, life experiences, emotions and feelings. Let us take, for example, the case of an older adult with Alzheimer's who might want to sell a house. When approaching a notary, the person might be confused, not remembering wanting to sell the house, and feeling attacked or scammed. A functional assessment would adequately determine the person's true will in such situations. The debate over which manifestation should be taken as their true will is particularly complex and has been the subject of analysis in the field of advanced directives.[23]

The assessment of functional capacity, in our opinion, would also depend on the functionality of a person's supports in the decision-making process. According to the former United Nations Rapporteur for the rights of persons with disabilities, Catalina Devandas, supports must help the person with a disability to "obtain and understand information."[24]

We do not consider that limiting a person's ability to decide on a particular juridical act implies denying their legal capacity. Rather, it will imply a valid,

---

[22]   See R. Bregaglio and R. Constantino, "Consentimiento médico informado de las personas con discapacidad intelectual y psicosocial en el Perú" (2020) 26 *Revista Brasileira de Direito Civil*, pp. 155–180.

[23]   See G. Owen, T. Gergel, L. A. Stephenson, et al., "Advance decision-making in mental health – Suggestions for legal reform in England and Wales" (2019) 64 *International Journal of Law and Psychiatry*, pp. 162–177.

[24]   C. Devandas (n. 11), para. 41.

concrete and proportional restriction which is justified given that the person is facing a specific act whose implications they cannot understand. *Understand* is a complex verb. Building on legislation that uses the notion of mental capacity,[25] comprehension has to do with understanding the relevant information, retaining it, and weighing it in a decision-making process. This does not mean, of course, that the information to be comprehended has to be exhaustive. However, it must include the minimum information necessary given the scope of the legal transaction and its consequences for the person.

With this in mind, we consider that the functional model is not in itself discriminatory towards persons with disabilities. Instead, we believe that civil law should stop considering legal capacity in binary terms – capable/incapable – and instead recognise a broad spectrum of capacities and competencies. Capacities should not be determined based on disability in a generic sense, but rather by the person's competence or specific functionality in relation to a specific act.

Based on this approach to legal capacity, not every manifestation can be considered an authentic will intended to create, modify or extinguish legal relationships. Therefore, it is appropriate for the law to establish mechanisms to guarantee that what is expressed is truly the will of the person.

## 2.2.	RELATIONAL VULNERABILITY AND ITS RELATIONSHIP TO UNDUE INFLUENCE, CONFLICT OF INTEREST AND ABUSE

The person's vulnerability also means that abuse can arise in interactions with others, including those with support duties. This kind of vulnerability can be configured in various ways. The coercive or threatening actions of third parties, or their undue influence on a person, or their conflicts of interest may supress that person's true will. For example, it would be relational exploitation of the vulnerability of the person with disabilities if their supporter – with whom a relationship of trust may undeniably be established but which is also one of dependency – constantly urges them to sell their property to the in-laws of the supporter. In such case, a conflict of interest combines with undue influence. The same would happen, for example, if the supporter repeatedly requested the disabled person to donate an organ for the supporter or the supporter's family.

In these cases, the unequal relations between the supporter and the person with a disability gives rise to situations not desired by the person with a disability and which harm their rights and interests. That is why safeguards are needed.

---

[25]	The UK Mental Capacity Act (MCA) defines mental capacity as "(a) understanding decision-relevant information, (b) retaining that information, (c) using or weighing that information as part of the decision-making process, or (d) communicating one's decision (whether by speaking, in sign language, or by any other means)."

While there are well established legal protections to prevent abuses in certain legal relations – for example, sanctions against fraud – decision-making supports are a relatively new configuration in law. Therefore, it is entirely appropriate to consider how best to prevent abuses in their application, which gives rise to the need to establish safeguards.

Because it may be difficult to determine in a particular situation whether a supporter's influence was "undue," and in any case seeking to prove it could undermine a trusting relationship between a supporter and the person they support, it is helpful to generally identify the risks of the improper exercise of support and, based on them, to identify those acts of supporters which should be prohibited.

For a start, as a general rule, supporters – and their direct relatives – should not benefit unduly from the decisions made by the person with a disability. This rule, of course, may have exceptions since, in some cases, it will be inevitable that the supporter has a conflict of interest – i.e., where they directly benefit from decisions of the person with a disability. Safeguards should anticipate such situations and identify how to resolve them.

3.   SAFEGUARDS IN CONJUNCTION WITH THE VULNERABILITY OF A PERSON WITH A DISABILITY

In some readings of a universalist understanding of legal capacity,[26] safeguards would not be necessary, and the functioning of the supports would suffice for the person with a disability to exercise their legal capacity under equal conditions. However, Article 12 of the UNCRPD cannot be understood to recognise universal legal capacity in the sense that every person may conduct legal transactions under any circumstance. This recognition must be accompanied by a support system and also – despite its scant theoretical development – by safeguards, as prescribed in Article 12.4 of the same international treaty.

The safeguards recognised in Article 12.4 respond to a concern of the States at the time of the treaty negotiation on measures that prevent abuses and the possible assumption of hazardous risks by persons with disabilities.[27] The wording of paragraph 12.4. of the UNCRPD seek a middle position between the universalist position and others that sought to maintain the possibility of restricting legal capacity in specific circumstances.[28] To understand Article 12.4 of the UNCRPD, we propose a three-part analysis: its purposes, its scope and its characteristics.

---

[26]   See L. SERIES and A. NILSSON (n. 12), p. 365.
[27]   See Ibid., p. 346.
[28]   See Ibid., p. 368.

Intersentia

341

3.1. PURPOSES OF SAFEGUARDS

For Martin and others, safeguards can be divided into three categories: (i) those related to the rights, will and preferences of the person; (ii) those related to undue influence; and (iii) those that concern conflicts of interest.[29]

3.1.1. Respecting Rights, Will and Preferences

Article 12.4 of the UNCRPD establishes that "the safeguards will ensure that the measures related to the exercise of legal capacity respect the person's rights, will and preferences." The first point of this sentence is that a legal decision could be motivated by the person's will or preferences, which are different categories.

At this point, following Szmukler, it is important to specify that *will* and *preferences* are different elements.[30] Will would be a reflection on values and what is best to do, while preferences are desires or inclinations.[31] Thus, will could be to acquire a property and the preference to live on a street without traffic. However, will and preference are not always be aligned. For example, a person's will may be to lose weight by dieting and exercising; but their preference, may lean towards consuming greasy food. However, the fact that a juridical act is based on a preference does not imply that it is null. People with and without disabilities constantly make decisions based on their preferences with different levels of legal relevance.

A second issue derived from Article 12.4 of the UNCRPD is that it is not just about respecting the will and preference of the person with disabilities – with the difficulties that this may generate – but also about respecting their rights. This is important because the CRPD Committee has, on occasions, avoided the reference to the expression "rights", stating only that the will and preferences of the person with a disability must be respected.[32] Just as will and preferences may be unaligned, respect for rights could also be in conflict with their will or preferences, or both, and it would be necessary to determine which should prevail.[33] With this in mind, Szmukler poses four relevant questions:

> How to determine or interpret the will and preferences of a person? How to deal with the fact that a person's will can vary profoundly? Could situations arise where

---

[29]   See W. MARTIN, S. MICHALOWSKI, J. STAVERT, et al., *Three jurisdictions report. Towards Compliance with CRPD Art. 12 in Capacity/Incapacity Legislation across the UK*, Essex Autonomy Project, University of Essex 2016, p. 38.

[30]   G. SZMUKLER, "The UN Convention on the Rights of Persons with Disabilities: 'Rights, will and preferences' in relation to mental health disabilities" (2017) 54 *International Journal of Law and Psychiatry*, pp. 90–97; and G. SZMUKLER, "'Capacity', 'best interests', 'will and preferences' and the UN Convention on the Rights of Persons with Disabilities" (2019) 18 *World Psychiatry*, pp. 34–41.

[31]   See G. SZMUKLER, "The UN Convention on the Rights" (n. 30), p. 93.

[32]   See CRPD Committee (n. 8), paras. 17, 21, 26 and 27.

[33]   See G. SZMUKLER, "The UN Convention on the Rights" (n. 30), p. 95.

preferences should prevail over the will, although said preferences are inconsistent with that will? Furthermore, what to do in situations where we cannot determine a person's will because they cannot express it or because circumstances prevent us from knowing it?[34]

According to civil law, will and its externalisation "must be concordant."[35] Savigny's will theory resides in the declarant's intent.[36] Therefore, if the declaration is inconsistent with the intention, it would not be binding for whatever reason. If the person signs a contract by force, there is no will. The same is true if they manifest will without real intention to engage in a juridical act.[37] Following the general theory of juridical act, will must not be vitiated by an error, deception, or preying on need. On the contrary, will must be sufficiently informed, serious, free of deception or other vicious influences, and reflect what the person truly wants.

With all this in mind, notaries, or those who verify the will of a person in a juridical act, assume a fundamental role since they need to assess whether all these elements are met adequately. To guarantee the consistency of will, notaries might require more than one session for the person to come and express their will and to verify that it is an authentic or serious-minded will.[38] Notaries also need to verify that the person comes to express their will without coercion or undue influence. To do this, they could hold one or more preliminary interviews with the person involved.

3.1.2. Avoiding Conflicts of Interest

A conflict of interest occurs when a person's interest may interfere with their duties.[39] Law practitioners are often tempted to resolve conflicts of interest by removing or disclosing them. However, to meet the standard set forth in Article 12.4 of the UNCRPD, sometimes the conflict with the support must be managed and not avoided.[40] Indeed, how can it be ascertained that the supports are "free of conflict of interest" when they are generally close to the person with a disability?

---

[34]   Ibid., p. 92.
[35]   L. Leon (n. 7), p. 53.
[36]   See J. P. Schmidt, "Juridical Act" in J. Basedow (ed), *The Max Planck encyclopedia of European private law*, Oxford University Press, Oxford 2012, p. 1017.
[37]   See L. Leon (n. 7), p. 61.
[38]   See R. Bregaglio and R. Constantino, "Un modelo para armar: la regulación de la capacidad jurídica de las personas con discapacidad en el Perú a partir del Decreto Legislativo 1384" (2020) 4 *Revista Latinoamericana en Discapacidad, Sociedad y Derechos Humanos*, p. 54.
[39]   See W. Martin, S. Michalowski and J. Stavert (n. 29), p. 49.
[40]   Ibid.

Consider the case of a person with a mild intellectual disability who appoints their mother as support for a wide range of juridical acts with no designated safeguards. This person has no siblings and has been fatherless for 15 years. One day, the person decides to open a bank account, and the bank offers the possibility of signing an insurance contract in favour of a third person. When the person asks what it means exactly, the bank explains that this will give money to an individual of their choice in the event of their death. Not fully understanding the figure, they decide to stop the process and find their mother for consultation. Could the mother support this decision in which she will likely become the beneficiary of said contract?

Because of this, one possibility could be to require the bank – or any third party – to act in any situation where a conflict of interest arises. However, this could lead to persons with disabilities rarely being able to contract since the supports are usually relatives or close friends with whom there will be frequent conflicts of interest. Another possibility could be to establish that a third person must avoid the legal act when it would bring the supporter of the person with a disability into a conflict of interest, and the decision would appear to create an unfair advantage for the support, seriously affecting the rights of the person with a disability. If this solution were followed, in the above example, the conflict of interest would be irrelevant since the insurance contract does not seriously affect the person's rights.

3.1.3. Avoiding Undue Influence

Undue influence is not a typical term in continental civil law but rather stems from *common law*. According to the latter, undue influence is the use of any act of persuasion to overcome another person's free will and judgment.[41]

Suppose a young woman with an intellectual disability has just turned 18. Her father abandoned her when she was three, and they had a very intermittent relationship: he seldom visited her, several birthdays went by without a present and some Christmases without phone calls. Her mother has told her that it would be convenient for her to initiate a maintenance proceeding for what she did not receive in her childhood. The young woman initiates the proceeding and obtains a resolution that orders a payment of six thousand dollars. However, after the judgment, the father calls her, asks for a meeting and, from then on, they begin a closer relationship. Two months later, the father's lawyer enters a document signed by the young woman forgiving one thousand dollars of the debt. Could the mother apply for the annulment of that forgiveness, arguing that the father exerted undue influence?

---

41 See J. LEHMAN and S. PHELPS (eds), *West's encyclopedia of American law*, 2nd ed., Thomson/ Gale, Detroit 2005.

There are several issues to deal with in this case. The first one concerns the scope of the safeguards: who is obliged not to exert undue influence? Is it a general obligation for those who interact with persons with disabilities? Or does it only concern those designated as supporters? As we will discuss later, we believe a broad interpretation should be sought.

Secondly, it is necessary to identify which situations would constitute undue influence and when these would be grounds for annulment or nullity of the legal act. In this regard, Californian law establishes four elements that must be considered in a finding of undue influence: (i) vulnerability of the victim, (ii) apparent authority of the perpetrator, (iii) actions or tactics used by the perpetrator, and (iv) equity of the result.[42]

From this, we consider that, for annulment based on undue influence to proceed, two elements must be present: there has to be undue influence, and such undue influence must seriously damage the person's rights.[43] Regarding the first element, it is appropriate to use what George Szmukler called the "treatment pressure spectrum."[44] Although originally designed for medical treatment, it is quite helpful for these situations. The spectrum includes five types of action: persuasion, interpersonal influence, inducement, threats, and coercion. Coercion and threats would justify the annulment of the legal act alone, so it is unnecessary to address them. However, the remaining three concepts must be carefully analysed.

Persuasion goes beyond information and tries to "appeal to reason (and, to a certain extent, to emotions)."[45] Nevertheless, it is also part of ordinary human relationships. Usually, we want to convince others that what we believe is correct, and that they should follow our advice. Interpersonal influence means using a relationship as a source of pressure.[46] Comments such as "if you do not do this, I will be very sad" and actions with similar intentions would amount to interpersonal influence. Lastly, the incentives – offers in exchange for an action – would mean that the act performed does not reflect the true will of *the* person. However, this does not immediately translate into undue influence: people without disabilities also change their opinions all the time, and incentives are part of everyday life – commercial offers, for instance.

In all three cases, we could say that *prima facie*, by themselves and at a given time, they do not amount to undue influence. However, if conceived as part of a strategy designed to break the will of the person with a disability, in bad faith, constantly and consistently seeking an undue advantage or taking advantage of

---

[42] See California Welfare and Institutions Code, s. 15610.70.
[43] Idea emerged in conversation between Renato Constantino and Robert Dinerstein.
[44] G. Szmukler, *Men in white coats: treatment under coercion*, Oxford University Press, Oxford 2018, p. 151.
[45] Ibid., p. 154.
[46] Ibid., p. 155.

positions of power, they would be situations of undue influence. Each case will need to be assessed to identify the key elements at stake in a specific instance. Verifying a situation of undue influence and severe damage to the rights of the person with disabilities would have the effect of annulling the juridical act in question. In continental civil law, the basis would have to do with the existence of a vitiated will.

3.2. SCOPE OF SAFEGUARDS

A relevant aspect of safeguarding has to do with who it binds. Article 12.4 of the UNCRPD indicates that safeguards must be applied in "all measures related to the exercise of legal capacity." This would seem to indicate that instances where decision-making supports are used fall within its scope. Therefore, when supports are established, safeguards should also be indicated. Nonetheless, given that the safeguards seek to avoid abuses of persons with disabilities in their legal transactions, we consider that its scope of demand goes beyond support.

To date, Peru[47] and Colombia[48] have advanced in some of the most ambitious reforms on legal capacity. However, both reforms fail to establish or regulate – sufficiently – safeguards. In the Colombian case, for its part, the norm only states the purposes of the safeguards without establishing any specific regulation.[49]

In the Peruvian case, Articles 659-G of the Civil Code and 21 of the Reform Regulations[50] regulate three types of safeguards: (i) revision of supports, under the responsibility of the judicial authority; (ii) those that the person with a disability can designate – and which could include accountability, presentation of documents proving the administration of assets, audits, unexpected periodic supervision, unexpected home visits, conducting interviews with the person designated as supporter and people close to the person with a disability, or the request for information from public or private institutions; and (iii) others that the judge determines, only in the case of exceptional support.[51]

The Peruvian standards have several problems. First, both the periodic judicial control measure and the measures that the person with a disability could request are subsequent control measures that would not prevent conflicts of interest in a timely manner,[52] nor would they ensure that the will and preferences

---

[47] In Peru, the Civil Code was reformed through Legislative Decree 1384, published in the Official Gazette on 4 September 2018.
[48] In Colombia, Law 1996 of 2019 was published on 26 August 2019.
[49] Article 5 of Law 1996 of 2019, and Articles 396 and 586 of the General Code of Procedure.
[50] Supreme Decree 016-2019, published in the Official Gazette El Peruano on 25 August 2019.
[51] Regulated in Article 659-E of the Civil Code.
[52] See A. MARTÍNEZ-PUJALTE, "Legal Capacity and Supported Decision-Making: Lessons from Some Recent Legal Reforms" (2019) 8 *Laws* 4, p. 18.

Safeguards for the Exercise of Legal Capacity by Persons with Disabilities

of the person have been respected. If a person with a disability donates the property where they reside to their supporter, we would be facing a clear case of conflict of interest that should have been identified in the legal designation of supports. Restricting the possibility of such a legal transaction occurring – or establishing that it could only be undertaken with certain guarantees would be justified Secondly, the judge can only appoint safeguards *ex officio* in the cases of exceptional support which come before them. In the other cases, the person with a disability bears the difficult, heavy and sometimes impossible burdens of anticipating potential instances of undue influence, abuse of rights or conflict of interest, and of designing measures that guarantee their wishes will always be respected. To our knowledge, this has never happened in Peru.[53] Thirdly, the obligation to adopt safeguards only operates in the designations made by a judicial authority. If the designation were made in a notary's office, only the safeguards requested by the person with a disability would be activated.

The Peruvian and Colombian reforms propose similar models concerning the exercise of legal capacity and the designation of supports. Thus, if the person can express their will, there are two possibilities: acting alone or with supports.[54] For an action with supports, these can be chosen by the person who expresses their will, or they can be imposed on a person who does not express will.

If the person with a disability acts independently, the appropriate safeguard would require verification of the person's volition. That is to say, it must be corroborated that he or she has the necessary competence to carry out the juridical act and that the declaration coincides with his or her will. Thus, for example, a doctor should verify that the person with an intellectual disability really understands the risks of not having chemotherapy. A notary public would have the duty to verify that the declaration of the person with Alzheimer's to sell their house is their true will.

In this scenario, then, the scope of the safeguard goes beyond the support and imposes obligations on third parties to determine if there is a basis for nullifying a transaction. Thus, the notary must verify that the person with a disability understands at least minimally the juridical act that they are going to enter and that they really want to go ahead with it. This obligation would be extended to

---

[53]   R. BREGAGLIO and R. CONSTANTINO, "La capacidad jurídica en la jurisprudencia peruana. Análisis cualitativo de las decisiones judiciales de restitución de capacidad jurídica y designaciones de apoyo en aplicación del Decreto Legislativo 1384" (2022) 44 *Revista de Decreto Legislativo*, pp. 15–47.

[54]   Article 45 of the Peruvian Civil Code: "Any person with a disability who requires reasonable adjustments or support for the exercise of their legal capacity may request or designate them in keeping with their free choice." Article 9 of Law 1996 of 2019 of Colombia: "Mechanisms to establish supports for the performance of legal acts. All persons with disabilities, of legal age, have the right to carry out legal acts independently and to have support for carrying them out."

other people who verify the will in juridical acts, such as public officials who celebrate marriages or health professionals who have a responsibility to obtain informed consent.

If the person acts with supporters in expressing their will, there are two contexts for applying the safeguard. First, those appointing supporters – in Colombia and Peru, whether through the courts or via a notary – must consider possible conflicts of interest and design preventive and supervisory measures. Secondly, notaries, health professionals, and officials in charge of entering into juridical acts must verify whether, at the time of helping the person to form their will, the supporter exerted undue influence or obtained personal gain from a decision in which their personal interests conflicted with those of the person with a disability.

Where the person does not express their will in ways that others can understand, provision can be made for judicial appointment of exceptional or intense support[55] to avoid preventing the person from exercising their rights. In this scenario, the role of safeguards would be to guarantee three things. The judicial authority that designates the supporter must ensure that in practice they will act according to the will and preferences of the person with disabilities. For this, it is essential, in the process of assigning supports, to ascertain whether the person has previously expressed a will or preferences concerning the legal acts for which the support is going to be assigned. If this is the case, such reference to their will and preferences must be explicit in the authorisation.

In addition, the judicial authority must limit the possible cases of conflict of interest, especially if there is no clear expression of will that serves as a basis for determining how to proceed in a specific scenario. In these cases, the authorities should consider the person's rights or a presumed will. For example: if a woman with a severe intellectual disability is raped and cannot express any will, it would be appropriate to presume that her will would be not to maintain the pregnancy and, therefore – in those jurisdictions where abortion is appropriate for rape – authorise the intervention. Finally, notaries, health professionals and officials

---

[55]   Article 659-E of the Peruvian Civil Code: "The judge can determine, exceptionally, the necessary supports for persons with disabilities who cannot express their will and for those with restricted capacity to exercise, in accordance with numeral 9 of article 44. This measure is justified, after having made real, considerable and pertinent efforts to obtain a manifestation of the person's will, and having provided accessibility measures and reasonable adjustments, and when the appointment of supports is necessary for the exercise and protection of their rights."
Article 32 of Law 1996 of 2019 of Colombia: "Judicial adjudication of support for conducting legal acts. It is the judicial process through which formal supports are designated to a person with disabilities, of legal age, for the exercise of their legal capacity in the face of one or several specific legal acts. ... As an exception, the judicial adjudication of supports will be conducted through a verbal summary process when it is promoted by a person other than the holder of the legal act, in accordance with the requirements indicated in article 38 of this law."

in charge of conducting juridical acts must verify that the supporter is acting according to the will and preferences of the person as documented in the judicial authorisation appointment. In Figure 1, we illustrate the set of safeguarding provisions described above.

Figure 1. Safeguarding the Exercise of Legal Capacity

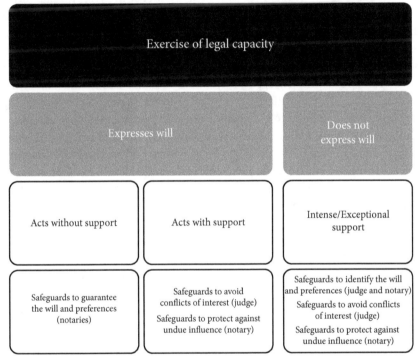

Source: Produced by the authors.

3.3. MAIN CHARACTERISTICS OF SAFEGUARDS

According to Martin et al., Article 12.4 of the UNCRPD (safeguards): (i) are intended to prevent abuse; (ii) must have the shortest term possible; (iii) must be reviewed periodically; and (iv) be proportional; (v) effective; and (vi) plural.[56] Analysis of these features enable us to better visualise how safeguards should be understood.

Preventing abuse can be one of the most complex features of safeguards. Since it is not necessarily responding to an inevitable fact but to a possibility – future and uncertain –, the judge should be cautious in adopting related

---

[56] See W. MARTIN, S. MICHALOWSKI, J. STAVERT et al. (n. 29), p. 38.

measures. Considering the need to carry out a proportionality test to determine the validity of a safeguard, we consider it critical to determine whether or not the imposed measure serves to prevent abuse. To do this, we will analyse one of the safeguards established by the Peruvian Civil Code, although the Code does not name it as such.

Article 659-E of the Peruvian Civil Code establishes that "individuals convicted of family violence or sexual violence cannot be designated as supports." Does this safeguard fulfil the purpose of avoiding abuse in the framework of the exercise of legal capacity? In principle, it seems that there should be no relationship between the commission of these crimes and the possibility of providing support in the patrimonial field. Although the people convicted of these acts have usually engaged in dynamics of abuse and manipulation, the need to assume a precautionary role and prevent these people from being supports should respond to the analysis of each specific case – for example, it could include the limitation that a person convicted of fraud may be a support for patrimonial decisions. Although the purpose of avoiding abuses requires that the safeguard measures be precisely suitable for the fulfilment of the goal, the principles of proportionality and precaution cannot ignore the fact that frequently the family member with a criminal record is the only one who can be a support for the person with a disability.

Another element is the temporality of the measures. Article 12.4 of the UNCRPD states that the measures related to the exercise of legal capacity must include the shortest term possible. This should be understood as an obligation for legal officials to verify the real need for support. Thus, the person with a disability is not permanently linked to support that, if unnecessary, could become an unwanted interference in their private life.

The third characteristic is the periodic review. This appears to be a principle of safeguards and a safeguard in itself. The periodic review of the functioning of the supports allows for their improvement in safeguarding the person's rights, will and preferences. Additionally, a review is a safeguard that can prevent abuse.

Fourthly, proportionality is one of the most interesting features. According to Martin and others, it means that autonomy may not always be the prevailing value or right.[57] It is the duty of the judge to adequately weigh the rights, will and preferences of a person in cases where they do not concur. Although the person's will must prevail in almost all cases, we identify three assumptions for the judge to intervene in this area. First, in cases of concurrent wills, such as when a person with a disability wants to be cured of an illness but does not wish to undergo the only operation that can achieve this purpose. Secondly, when the will is based on a falsehood for example, refusing to sign a medical consent because the person believes that a tumour will heal itself. Thirdly, in the absence of a previously

---

[57]   Ibid., p. 39.

expressed will and when it is no longer possible to obtain it – the case of abortion due to rape that we pointed out earlier. In these cases, the functional approach proposed in the first section of this chapter becomes relevant.

Finally, safeguards must be effective and plural. Safeguards must work. So, for example, there is no point in establishing a system for reviewing the performance of supports if there has already been an irreversible act, such as medical consent for a procedure previously conducted. Furthermore, they must be plural: it is not possible that a person with a disability who requires supports to exercise legal capacity can be protected with only one safeguard.

4. CONCLUSION: SAFEGUARDS, A FORM OF JUSTIFIED PATERNALISM

States must take (unspecified) measures to prevent abuses and ensure that "the rights, will and preferences of the person" are respected. Faced with the possibility that supporters may act inappropriately, States must set limits. Whether these restrictions can go against the person's wishes is relevant in this context. In light of inevitable risks, what exactly is the role of the State in balancing paternalism and autonomy? If it is appropriate to intervene, what criteria should be considered?

Paternalism is understood as the intervention in the freedom of a person, without their consent, on the premise that the act – or its omission – will promote the welfare or the values of the person.[58] Dworkin distinguishes various types of paternalism. Regarding support systems, the distinction between weak and strong paternalism is useful. *Weak paternalism* is understood as legitimate interventions to restrict an agent's means when their chosen means would be counterproductive to their chosen ends. *Strong paternalism*, on the other hand, is understood as legitimate interventions to prevent an agent from achieving their chosen ends, when those ends would be considered wrong or irrational by whoever applied the measure. In the author's words, "we may interfere with mistakes about the facts but not mistakes about values. So, if a person tries to jump out of a window believing he will float gently to the ground we may restrain him. If he jumps because he believes that it is important to be spontaneous we may not."[59]

In this regard, the safeguards discussed here would be a form of weak paternalism insofar as they interfere with what the disabled person decides or would like to decide, to prevent mistakes or lack of understanding from

---

[58] See G. Dworkin, "Paternalism" in E. N. Zalta (ed), *The Stanford Encyclopedia of Philosophy*, Metaphysics Research Lab, Stanford University 2019.

[59] Ibid.

becoming something that: (i) contravenes their will or previously manifested preferences or (ii) is counterproductive for the person when there is no expressed will.

Thus, properly limited, safeguards must prevent a decision in which there is a conflict of interest, reverse a contract in which there has been an undue influence or render a decision in the face of conflicting or vitiated wills or decisions based on false information. All such safeguards protect autonomy by valuing a person's authentic will. However, it is important to keep in mind that it will not always be possible to discern the authentic will, and other elements will have to be taken into account, such as rights or preferences or even presumptions in favour of specific values.

Since the entry into force of the UNCRPD, many voices have been critical of restriction on the exercise of contracting, arguing that this would imply denying legal capacity. In our view, these restrictions are necessary. Safeguards would be void of content if they meant nothing beyond endorsing everything the person with a disability communicates. However, their imposition requires recognition of the person's will and of any situation of vulnerability which can make them an object of abuse. Safeguards, therefore, are the defence of a will that, although silent, hidden or subjugated, is nevertheless real.

LEGAL CAPACITY IN CANADA

An Equality Rights Analysis in Light of the Canadian Charter of Rights and Freedoms and the Convention on the Rights of Persons with Disabilities

Lana KERZNER[*]

1. Introduction 354
2. The Prevailing Test of Capacity in Canada's Laws: The Cognitive
   "Understand and Appreciate" Test 356
3. An Inclusive Approach to Legal Capacity: Decision-Making
   Capability 357
4. Implementation of Article 12 in Canada: Relevance of the Canadian
   Charter of Rights and Freedoms 358
5. An Examination of the Cognitive Test of Capacity against the Equality
   Right in the Canadian Charter of Rights and Freedoms 359
   5.1. The Equality Rights Provision of the Charter 359
   5.2. Application of the Supreme Court's s. 15(1) Framework to the
        Cognitive Test of Capacity 362
        5.2.1. On its Face or in its Impact, does the Cognitive Test of
               Capacity Create a Distinction Based on Disability? 362
        5.2.2. Does the Cognitive Test of Capacity Impose Burdens or
               Deny a Benefit in a Manner that has the Effect of
               Reinforcing, Perpetuating, or Exacerbating
               Disadvantage? 365
6. The CRPD's Approach to Equality in the Exercise of Legal Capacity:
   Putting the s. 15 Analysis in Perspective 366

---

[*] Barrister and Solicitor specialising in disability law, Toronto, Canada.
I express my sincerest appreciation to Michael Bach, Managing Director, IRIS (Institute for Research and Development on Inclusion and Society), for his contribution to the analysis and edit of this chapter; and to Miriam Kerzner, of blessed memory, my life-long teacher on inclusion and equality.

7. Limitation of Rights: Can Discriminatory Legal Capacity Tests be Saved
   as a Justifiable Violation of Charter Rights under s. 1 of the Charter? 368
   7.1. The Issue and Sources in Canada and United Nations Human
        Rights Law. 368
   7.2. Section 1 of the Charter: Can the Cognitive Test of Capacity
        be Justified? 369
8. Conclusion. 372

1. INTRODUCTION

Article 12 of the Convention on the Rights of Persons with Disabilities (CRPD) has fuelled disability advocacy, law reform and community organising efforts in countries world-wide with the goal of ensuring that laws, policies and practices live up to the vision of equality in the exercise of legal capacity for people with disabilities. Article 12, paragraph 2, requires that States Parties recognise "that persons with disabilities enjoy legal capacity on an equal basis with others in all aspects of life". This paragraph is frequently cited by disability advocates to substantiate their claim to a right to control their own lives and to resist any attempt at interference with their decision-making, through legal avenues such as guardianship and other forms of substitute decision-making. Because of the exclusion that many people with disabilities face and the historical restrictions on their autonomy resulting in an affront to their dignity, their claim has been hard fought for, but largely unrealised in jurisdictions internationally.[1]

Understanding what is required to achieve Article 12's ideals demands an in-depth exploration of what is meant by the enjoyment of legal capacity *on an equal basis*. While equality, and the related concept of discrimination, are well understood in other contexts, such as physical accessibility, it is less clear what they mean in the context of legal capacity. What characterises a legal capacity law as discriminatory? In order to effect change, we must first be able to identify the problem with sufficient precision to guide action. This chapter explores legal

---

[1] The Committee on the Rights of Persons with Disabilities has recommended "... systematically in its concluding observations to States parties" that a shift be made from substitute decision-making paradigms to ones based on supported decision-making. THERESIA DEGENER, COMMITTEE ON THE RIGHTS OF PERSONS WITH DISABILITIES, "Towards inclusive equality: 10 years Committee on the Rights of Persons with Disabilities", 09.2018, at p. 54 <https://tbinternet.ohchr.org/Treaties/CRPD/Shared%20Documents/1_Global/INT_CRPD_INF_21_28325_E.pdf> accessed 02.09.2022. This is so even though Lucy Series and Anna Nilsson observed that, "... article 12 has influenced domestic and regional law-making bodies." L. SERIES and A. NILSSON, "Article 12 CRPD: Equal Recognition before the Law" in I. BANTEKAS, M. A. STEIN, D. ANASTASIOU, (eds), *The UN Convention on the Rights of Persons with Disabilities: A Commentary*, Oxford University Press, Oxford (UK) 2018, p. 9.

capacity through an equality lens, based on the equality right in the Canadian Charter of Rights and Freedoms (Charter)[2] and the CRPD.

The experience in Canadian law is examined to demonstrate one method of undertaking an equality rights analysis. Canada is an apt jurisdiction for this case study as Canada was the lead State Party at the United Nations in the development of Article 12.[3] As described by Julian Walker, and citing a joint paper by the Council of Canadians with Disabilities and the Canadian Association for Community Living, "Canada's strong contribution to the CRPD allowed certain Canadian values to be enshrined in international human rights law."[4] Quoting from that paper, Walker states: "… article 12 (equal recognition before the law) was 'facilitated by the Canadian delegation and secures a progressive approach to legal capacity and, for the first time in international law, recognizes a right to use support to exercise one's legal capacity – a made-in-Canada solution …'"[5]

This chapter describes the way in which equality and discrimination are interpreted in Canada's Constitution, and compares it to the treatment of those concepts in the CRPD. It also explores legitimate limits that may be placed on the right to equality, in both Canadian law and international human rights sources, based on an assessment of balancing of individual rights and societal interests.

The cognitive/functional test of capacity found in Canadian laws is used to demonstrate the equality analysis by concrete illustration. This test of capacity was chosen for examination because it is found in many of Canada's statutes that regulate legal capacity and has a profound impact on the lives of people with disabilities. These laws have the effect of determining when a person can make their own decisions, because the law considers them to be "capable", and when someone else will be required to make decisions for them, because the law considers them "incapable". The blunt reality is that, by virtue of these laws, a person will either maintain their autonomy and inclusion in society or will be excluded and made to feel like a non-person.

---

2   Canadian Charter of Rights and Freedoms, Part I of the Constitution Act 1982, being Schedule B to the Canada Act 1982 (U.K.), 1982, c. 11 (Charter).

3   D. McCallum, Expert Opinion for the Coalition on Alternatives to Guardianship, submitted to the Law Commission of Ontario in response to the Law Commission of Ontario Interim Report, "Legal Capacity, Decision-Making and Guardianship", 04.03.2016, p. 14.

4   J. Walker, "The United Nations Convention on the Rights of Persons with Disabilities: An Overview" Library of Parliament, Background Paper, Publication No. 2013-09-E, 27.02.2013, p. 5 <https://lop.parl.ca/staticfiles/PublicWebsite/Home/ResearchPublications/BackgroundPapers/PDF/2013-09-e.pdf> accessed 02.09.2022, citing Council of Canadians with Disabilities (CCD) and the Canadian Association for Community Living (CACL) (2011), "UN Convention on the Rights of Persons with Disabilities: Making Domestic Implementation Real and Meaningful", CCD-CACL Working Paper, 02.2011.

5   Ibid.

2. THE PREVAILING TEST OF CAPACITY IN CANADA'S LAWS: THE COGNITIVE "UNDERSTAND AND APPRECIATE" TEST

The majority of substitute decision-making laws in Canada, and even those that recognise supported decision-making, require that a person be "capable" to make legally valid decisions. They rest on a test of what it means to be capable. This is typically a cognitive test: capacity is commonly, but not always, defined by an ability to understand information relevant to making a decision and an ability to appreciate the reasonably foreseeable consequences of a decision or lack of decision.[6] This is sometimes referred to as the "understand and appreciate" test of capacity.[7] It is consistent with the cognitive/functional approach described by the United Nations Committee on the Rights of Persons with Disabilities, whereby cognitive requisites are considered necessary for exercising one's legal capacity, and having it respected by others.[8]

Some legislative provisions which enable people to create a supported decision-making agreement appointing a person to support them to make decisions also employ a cognitive test. Paradoxically, people whose disabilities affect their cognition to the extent that they do not meet the test, are also prevented from appointing a supporter to assist them to make decisions.[9]

There are variations of the test which, although requiring a requisite level of cognitive ability, allow for a broader range of people to meet the test. These fall into two categories. The first variation of the capacity test is an "understand and appreciate" test which gives explicit recognition to the role played by support or assistance to meet the test.[10] These are rare in Canada's legal capacity laws. However, human rights laws have been interpreted to require that third parties,

---

[6] Even tests of capacity that are not formulated precisely in this manner often contain similar requirements. However, some legislative provisions in Canada define capacity, not on the basis of cognitive ability, but based on diagnosis or the existence of a condition. See e.g., s. 17(1) of the Mentally Disabled Persons' Estates Act, R.S.N.L. 1990, c. M-10 (MDPE) of Newfoundland and Labrador.

[7] This chapter uses the short form, "test of capacity", to denote the legal criteria or factors employed in laws to determine whether someone is capable in law to make their own decisions. Whaley and Sultan use the term "tests" and note that they are, more accurately, "... the relevant factors in ascertaining capacity ...", K. A. WHALEY and A. SULTAN, "Capacity and the Estate Lawyer: Comparing the Various Standards of Decisional Capacity", (2013) 32(3) *Estates and Trusts Pensions Journal*, pp. 215–257, p. 216.

[8] General Comment No. 1 (2014) – Article 12 – Equal Recognition Before the Law, Committee on the Rights of Persons with Disabilities, (General Comment No. 1 (2014) – Equal Recognition Before the Law), para. 15 <https://tbinternet.ohchr.org/_layouts/15/treatybodyexternal/Download.aspx?symbolno=CRPD/C/GC/1&Lang=en> accessed 02.09.2022.

[9] E.g. The Adult Protection and Decision Making Act being Schedule A to the Decision-Making Support and Protection to Adults Act, S.Y. 2003, c. 21, s. 6.

[10] E.g. Adult Capacity and Decision-making Act, S.N.S. 2017, c. 4, s. 3(d); Guardianship and Trusteeship Act, S.N.W.T. 1994, c. 29, s. 12(1).

as an accommodation of disability, respect the roles played by support and assistance to assist a person to meet the test of capacity.[11] The second variation of the capacity test does not focus exclusively on cognitive abilities. Some have described it as a non-cognitive test.[12] It is a "test of incapability" found in British Columbia's Representation Agreement Act.[13] A person must meet this test to create a representation agreement to appoint a supporter (referred to as a representative) to help them make decisions.[14] This test casts the net widest. Some people with cognitive disabilities who cannot meet the cognitive tests of capacity can meet this test as it involves consideration of factors in addition to the cognitive criterion of whether the person is aware of the implications of the agreement. These factors include whether the relationship with the representative is characterised by trust and whether the person demonstrates choices and preferences. However, the ambiguous drafting leaves it open to interpretation of what is actually required to prove incapability.

Thus, a review of the formulations of the cognitive tests of capacity in Canada demonstrate that many people with significant cognitive disabilities, including people with intellectual disabilities, mental health disabilities and dementia, are not able to meet the test, either throughout their lives or at some points in their lives. While those tests that recognise assistance and supports will exclude fewer people, a significant number will never be able to demonstrate the level of cognition required, even with such assistance, and will be denied the exercise of legal capacity and forced into substitute decision-making. Unlike the rest of society, they may be denied the right to make fundamental personal choices, such as those about their health care, how to spend their money, and where to live.

3. AN INCLUSIVE APPROACH TO LEGAL CAPACITY: DECISION-MAKING CAPABILITY

What has been termed the "decision-making capability" approach has been proposed as an alternative approach to exercising legal capacity which responds

---

[11] Regarding the duty to accommodate for assessments of capacity in Ontario see ONTARIO HUMAN RIGHTS COMMISSION, "Policy on preventing discrimination based on mental health disabilities and addictions", Chapter 16, *Consent and Capacity* <http://www.ohrc.on.ca/en/policy-preventing-discrimination-based-mental-health-disabilities-and-addictions> accessed 02.09.2022.

[12] LAW COMMISSION OF ONTARIO, "Legal Capacity, Decision-making and Guardianship", *Final Report*, Toronto, 03.2017, p. 99 <http://www.lco-cdo.org/wp-content/uploads/2017/03/CG-Final-Report-EN-online.pdf> accessed 02.09.2022.

[13] Representation Agreement Act, R.S.B.C. 1996, c. 405, s. 8(2) (RAA). A similar test is found in Newfoundland and Labrador's Enduring Powers of Attorney Act, R.S.N.L. 1990, c. E-11, s. 15(2).

[14] Ibid., RAA, s. 7(1).

to the shortcomings of the approaches described above.[15] This approach is posited as one which is consistent with Canada's Constitutional right to equality, described below. It builds on the increasing recognition of supports and accommodations in Canadian laws.[16]

Rather than cognitive ability being required as the basis for decision-making, a person is recognised to direct their decisions based on their true intentions, will and preferences, which are not necessarily cognitive functions, but which form a valid alternate basis for decision-making. A person may exercise legal capacity through their supporters. The supporters do possess the cognitive requirements and it is their role to translate their best interpretation of the person's true intentions, will and preferences into actual decisions. Like the cognitive approach, the decision-making capability approach requires "understanding" and "appreciation" to constitute a legally valid decision. But with the latter approach the cognitive abilities required can be possessed by a person on their own or jointly with or by decision-making supporters.

It is a more inclusive approach than the cognitive approach as people who have significant cognitive disabilities can exercise legal capacity even if they do not possess a requisite level of cognition. Like laws based on the cognitive approach, this alternate approach can address harm prevention and abuse, and include mechanisms to respond to emergency situations and to appeal decisions.[17]

4. IMPLEMENTATION OF ARTICLE 12 IN CANADA: RELEVANCE OF THE CANADIAN CHARTER OF RIGHTS AND FREEDOMS

The CRPD does not prescribe precisely how it should be implemented. Rather, it employs a broad and flexible approach to implementation allowing States Parties to use "all appropriate legislative, administrative and other measures."[18] Thus, Canada is at liberty to tailor its implementation approach to Canada's

---

[15] Michael Bach and Lana Kerzner articulated the "decision-making capability" approach to legal capacity in a study for the Law Commission of Ontario. See M. BACH and L. KERZNER, *A New Paradigm for Protecting Autonomy and the Right to Legal Capacity*, prepared for the Law Commission of Ontario, p. 67, <https://www.lco-cdo.org/wp-content/uploads/2010/11/disabilities-commissioned-paper-bach-kerzner.pdf>, accessed 02.09.2022.

[16] M. BACH and L. KERZNER, "Supported Decision Making: A Roadmap for Reform in Newfoundland and Labrador", *Final Report, Legal Basis for the Decision-Making Capability Approach*, Appendix C. <https://irisinstitute.ca/wp-content/uploads/sites/2/2021/01/Final-NL-Legal-Capacity-Report-Nov-2020.pdf> accessed 02.09.2022.

[17] Ibid.

[18] Convention on the Rights of Persons with Disabilities, G.A. Res. 61/106, 76th plen. Mtg., U.N. Doc A/Res/61/106 [adopted by consensus at the UN on 13.12.2006], (CRPD) Art. 4(1)(a).

legal and political landscape.[19] Of particular importance to implementation in the Canadian context is the role played by the Canadian Charter of Rights and Freedoms. As part of Canada's Constitution Act,[20] the Charter delimits the scope for implementation of the CRPD. Implementation within Canada must be consistent with the Charter as all laws must conform to its provisions.[21]

The interplay between the Charter and CRPD goes in both directions. While the CRPD must be implemented consistent with the Charter, interpretation of the Charter must take into account United Nations treaties to which Canada is a party, including the CRPD. The Supreme Court of Canada has been clear in its opinion that the obligations found in international human rights treaties to which Canada is a party are "… a relevant and persuasive factor in *Charter* interpretation."[22] In this regard the Supreme Court said:

> the *Charter*, as a living document, grows with society and speaks to the current situations and needs of Canadians. Thus Canada's *current* international law commitments and the current state of international thought on human rights provide a persuasive source for interpreting the scope of the Charter.[23]

5. AN EXAMINATION OF THE COGNITIVE TEST OF CAPACITY AGAINST THE EQUALITY RIGHT IN THE CANADIAN CHARTER OF RIGHTS AND FREEDOMS

5.1. THE EQUALITY RIGHTS PROVISION OF THE CHARTER

This section explores the meaning of equality, and discrimination, pursuant to the Charter, and its applicability to the cognitive test of capacity in Canada's decision-making laws. The equality rights provision is found in s. 15, which

---

19 L. KERZNER, "Paving the way to Full Realization of the CRPD's Rights to Legal Capacity and Supported Decision-Making: A Canadian Perspective", University of British Columbia, p. 19, <https://citizenship.sites.olt.ubc.ca/files/2014/07/In_From_The_Margins_Paper-Lana_Kerzner-FINAL-April_22_2011__2_.pdf>, accessed 02.09.2022.

20 Constitution Act 1982, being Schedule B to the Canada Act 1982 (U.K.), 1982, c. 11.

21 Ibid., s. 52(1). The Constitution of Canada, of which the Charter is part, is the supreme law and all laws must conform to its provisions. See N. McCORMACK and M. R. BUECKERT, *Introduction to the Law and Legal System of Canada*, Carswell, Toronto 2013, p. 80.

22 *Reference Re Public Service Employee Relations Act (Alberta)*, [1987] 1 S.C.R. 313, [1987] S.C.J. No. 10, paras. 59–60, Dickson, C.J.C. dissenting. With respect to the applicability of this passage, Corbett and Sadoway state the following: "Although originally written in a dissenting judgment, the following passage by Brian Dickson C.J.C. has been cited often enough to permit its being regarded as a statement of the Supreme Court's approach to the relation between international human rights agreements and the *Charter*." S. M. CORBETT and G. SADOWAY, *Canadian Human Rights Law & Commentary*, 3rd ed., LexisNexis, Toronto 2016, p. 75.

23 *Health Services and Support – Facilities Subsector Bargaining Assn. v. British Columbia*, [2007] 2 S.C.R. 391, 2007 SCC 27, para. 78.

prohibits discrimination on a number of grounds, including "mental or physical disability".[24] Despite s. 15, Canada's legal capacity laws do not make an explicit connection between the exercise legal capacity and equality. Indeed, as described above, it is clear that Canada's legal capacity laws entirely exclude some people with disabilities from exercising legal capacity. Can this kind of exclusion be characterised as discrimination in law?

Section 15(1) of the Charter provides:

> Every individual is equal before and under the law and has the right to the equal protection and equal benefit of the law without discrimination and, in particular, without discrimination based on race, national or ethnic origin, colour, religion, sex, age or mental or physical disability.[25]

The Fram Report, which was delivered to the Ontario government over 30 years ago by the Advisory Committee on Substitute Decision-Making for Mentally Incapable Persons, while in the nascent days of s. 15, highlighted the relevance that s. 15 must have to any consideration of reform to decision-making laws, and moreover, emphasised that, consistent with the values which underpin s. 15, the role of supports must be recognised as a requirement for achieving equality.[26]

The root of s. 15, as described by Abella J. in *Quebec (Attorney General) v. A*, "... is our awareness that certain groups have been historically discriminated against, and that the perpetuation of such discrimination should be curtailed."[27] There has always been agreement that s.15 guarantees substantive equality.[28] The focus is on the effects of the law, rather than its purpose or appearance of neutrality.[29] The Supreme Court has rejected the idea that equality means treating likes alike. Thus, the Supreme Court in *R. v. Kapp* referenced McIntyre

---

[24] This chapter uses the term "mental disability" because "mental disability" is the term used in s.15(1) of the Canadian Charter of Rights and Freedoms, Part I of the Constitution Act 1982, being Schedule B to the Canada Act 1982 (U.K.), 1982. "Mental disability" includes a broad range of people who experience their disabilities in different and unique ways. It may include people with intellectual or developmental disabilities, people who have learning disabilities or people who experience mental health issues. Regarding people in the latter category, there has been long-standing debate and no consensus on appropriate terminology. Other terms in use include: "consumer/survivor", "psychiatric survivor", "psychiatric disability", "people with mental illness" or "mental illness", "people with psychosocial disabilities" or "mad-identified people".

[25] Canadian Charter of Rights and Freedoms, Part I of the Constitution Act 1982, being Schedule B to the Canada Act 1982 (U.K.), 1982, c. 11, s. 15.

[26] S. FRAM, *Final Report of the Advisory Committee on Substitute Decision-Making for Mentally Incapable Persons*, Advisory Committee on Substitute Decision-Making for Mentally Incapable Persons, Toronto 1987, pp. 41–43.

[27] *Quebec (Attorney General) v. A*, [2013] S.C.R. 61, 2013 SCC 5, para. 332.

[28] *Quebec (Attorney General) v. Alliance du personnel professionnel et technique de la sante et des services sociaux*, [2018] S.C.R. 464, 2018 SCC 17, para. 25.

[29] *Fraser v. Canada (Attorney General)*, 2020 SCC 28, para. 41 (*Fraser*).

J's statement in *Andrews v. Law Society of British Columbia*[30] wherein he pointed out "… that the concept of equality does not necessarily mean identical treatment and that the formal 'like treatment' model of discrimination may in fact produce inequality".[31]

Achieving substantive equality is particularly important for ensuring inclusion of people with disabilities in all areas of life, including decision-making. Disability law professor, Arlene Kanter, has applied a disability analysis to models of equality.[32] She describes the substantive equality model as "equality of results or outcomes".[33] She argues that the right to substantive equality is particularly relevant to achieving equality for people with disabilities. It allows for different treatment for those who may be differently situated, including notably people with disabilities.[34] In this model, a variety of means may be employed to achieve equality of outcome, including accommodations and affirmative action.

Even though it is relatively easy to describe the concept of substantive equality, knowing when substantive equality is achieved has challenged Canadian courts throughout s.15's history. The analytic approach to s.15 has evolved considerably over time and a lack of consensus persists.[35] This is not surprising given the challenges posed by s. 15. Sharpe and Roach describe these challenges, and articulate the values which they believe underpin s. 15, as follows:

> The equality rights jurisprudence under the Charter is complex, and it defies any attempt at a quick and accurate summary. This is hardly surprising. Equality is a fundamental value in a democratic society, and yet its precise meaning is elusive in political and legal discourse. As a legal concept, it includes the notion that every individual is entitled to dignity and respect and that the law should apply to all in an even-handed manner.[36]

Despite this, on its face, the cognitive test of capacity is inconsistent with substantive equality. The test excludes people with significant cognitive disabilities. Abella J. describes substantive equality as a "… remedy for exclusion

---

30   *Andrews v. Law Society of British Columbia*, [1989] 1 S.C.R. 143.

31   *R v. Kapp*, [2008] 2 S.C.R. 483, 2008 SCC 41, para. 15.

32   A. S. KANTER, "A Comparative View of Equality under the UN Convention on the Rights of Persons with Disabilities and the Disability Laws of the United States and Canada" (2015) 32 *Windsor Y B Access Just*, pp. 67–73.

33   Ibid., p. 71.

34   A. S. KANTER, "A Comparative View of Equality under the UN Convention on the Rights of Persons with Disabilities and the Disability Laws of the United States and Canada" (2015) 32 *Windsor Y B Access Just*, pp. 71–73.

35   J. W. HAMILTON, "Cautious Optimism: Fraser v Canada (Attorney General)", (2021) 30(2) *Constitutional Forum constitutionnel*, pp. 3 and 10–11. A. PUCHTA, "Quebec v A and Taypotat: Unpacking the Supreme Court's Latest Decisions on Section 15 of the Charter", (2019) 55(3) *Osgoode Hall Law Journal*, pp. 665–712, pp. 666–667.

36   R. J. SHARPE and K. ROACH, *The Charter of Rights and Freedoms*, 6th ed., Irwin Law, Toronto 2017, p. 354.

and a recipe for inclusion"[37] Thus, to achieve substantive equality requires remedying the exclusion caused by the cognitive test of capacity and replacing it with an appropriate "recipe for inclusion". A "recipe for inclusion" is the "decision-making capability approach" to legal capacity.

The next section of this chapter describes the Supreme Court's s. 15 analytical framework for achieving substantive equality and proposes how that framework might apply to a legal capacity test which is based on cognitive criteria. Even though, on its face, the cognitive test is inconsistent with substantive equality, assessing compliance with s. 15 requires a rigorous analysis following a test articulated by the Supreme Court.

5.2. APPLICATION OF THE SUPREME COURT'S S. 15(1) FRAMEWORK TO THE COGNITIVE TEST OF CAPACITY

The Supreme Court's current articulation of whether a law violates s. 15(1) is found in *Fraser v. Canada (Attorney General)* wherein Abella J. described the test as follows:

> To prove a *prima facie* violation of s. 15(1), a claimant must demonstrate that the impugned law or state action:
>
> - on its face or in its impact, creates a distinction based on enumerated or analogous grounds; and
> - imposes burdens or denies a benefit in a manner that has the effect of reinforcing, perpetuating, or exacerbating disadvantage.[38]

The section that follows examines the cognitive test of capacity against each of these components.

5.2.1. On its Face or in its Impact, does the Cognitive Test of Capacity Create a Distinction Based on Disability?

A law can create a distinction even though it does not explicitly treat people with disabilities differently. Laws can impose or exacerbate disadvantage indirectly. That is, laws which on their face apply equally to all can, in practice, disproportionately burden certain groups based on protected grounds, "mental disability" being one of the enumerated grounds in s. 15. The Supreme Court has recognised that such discrimination is one of the forms that discrimination can

---

[37] *Fraser v. Canada (Attorney General)*, 2020 SCC 28, para. 41.
[38] Ibid., at para. 27.

take.[39] This type of discrimination is referred to as "adverse impact" or "indirect" discrimination. International human rights practice also recognises "indirect discrimination".[40] In the context of the CRPD, "indirect discrimination" is defined to mean "… that laws, policies or practices appear neutral at face value, but have a disproportionate negative impact on a person with a disability."[41]

The cognitive test of capacity found in laws throughout Canada, while, on its face, applies to all Canadians equally, in practice, has a disproportionate impact on people with mental disabilities.[42] Two truisms ground the analysis. First, the cognitive test typically applies to everyone. It is usually contained in statutes governing guardianship, health care consent and other forms of substitute decision-making; these laws do not have selective application to people with disabilities or other subsets of the population. Anyone can be found incapable and be prevented from making their own decisions. Second, the cognitive test creates a distinction between people who meet the test and people who do not meet it. There is no arbitrariness surrounding who does not meet the test. On the contrary, most people who do not meet the test are members of an enumerated class of Canadians that the equality provision of the Charter protects: people with "mental disabilities".[43] More particularly, those who fail to meet the test are disproportionately those who have a disability that limits their cognitive or communication abilities. Most people who do not have these types of disabilities will meet the test. As such, the test has a disproportionate impact on this subset of people who have mental disabilities. People who do not meet the test are precluded from entering into legal relationships, whereas people who meet the test are entitled to engage in legal affairs without comparable restrictions imposed upon them. Used in this way the test has a disproportionate negative impact on many people who have mental disabilities.

Furthermore, the "absence of accommodation for members of protected groups" may represent an adverse impact on a protected group, such as people

---

[39] *Fraser v. Canada (Attorney General)*, 2020 SCC 28, paras. 43, 46 and 47; *Quebec (Commission des droits de la personne et des droits de la Jeunesse) v. Bombardier Inc. (Bombardier Aerospace Training Center)*, [2015] 2 S.C.R. 789, 2015 SCC 39, para. 32.

[40] COMMITTEE ON THE RIGHTS OF PERSONS WITH DISABILITIES, "General Comment No. 6 (2018) on equality and non-discrimination", UN Doc. CRPD/C/GC/6 (26.04.2018), ("General Comment No. 6 (2018) on equality and non-discrimination"), para. 18.

[41] General Comment No. 6 (2018) on equality and non-discrimination, ibid., para. 18(b).

[42] Similarly, it has been argued that the Mental Capacity Act of England and Wales denies legal capacity in a manner which has a disproportionate impact on people with disabilities. ESSEX AUTONOMY PROJECT, *Achieving CRPD Compliance: Is the Mental Capacity Act of England and Wales Compatible with the UN Convention on the Rights of Persons with Disabilities? If not, What Next?*, Report Submitted to the UK Ministry of Justice (2014), p. 16.

[43] Section 15(1) of the Canadian Charter of Rights and Freedoms, Part I of the Constitution Act 1982, being Schedule B to the Canada Act 1982 (U.K.), 1982, identifies "mental or physical disability" as an enumerated ground.

with disabilities.[44] In *Nova Scotia (Workers' Compensation Board) v. Martin; Nova Scotia (Workers' Compensation Board) v. Laseur* the Supreme Court emphasised the importance of reasonable accommodation as a measure in responding to the particular needs and circumstances of people with disabilities.[45] The Court stated that the rationale underlying the prohibition of discrimination on the basis of disability "… is to allow for the recognition of the special needs and actual capacities of persons affected by a broad variety of different disabilities in many different social contexts. In accordance with this rationale, s. 15(1) requires a considerable degree of reasonable accommodation and adaptation of state action to the circumstances of particular individuals with disabilities."[46]

Importantly, the CRPD includes "denial of reasonable accommodation" as a form of discrimination.[47] This is in recognition of the "dilemma of difference" which takes into account differences among human beings to achieve substantive equality, and "… requires both ignoring and acknowledging differences among human beings in order to achieve equality."[48] Non-discrimination includes the right to reasonable accommodation in the exercise of legal capacity.[49] Put another way, denial of reasonable accommodation constitutes discrimination.[50] On a plain reading of the cognitive test, with its constituent components being a requirement to have both the ability to understand information and appreciate reasonably foreseeable consequences, meeting these requirements requires possessing a particular set of cognitive skills. As such, it does not allow for the flexibility required to account for people's special needs or actual capabilities in the context of decision-making. It does not allow people with cognitive disabilities any alternative to their exercise of legal capacity in a way that is tailored to their special needs and actual capacities.

That the test creates a distinction on the basis of mental disability does not mean that everyone who has a mental disability will be equally disadvantaged by the cognitive test. In reality, there are many people who have mental disabilities who can meet the test. Canadian courts have established that this fact does not bar a claim of discrimination. Not everyone within the claimant group needs to be equally disadvantaged by the impact of the measure.[51]

---

44   *Fraser v. Canada (Attorney General)*, 2020 SCC 28, para. 54.
45   *Nova Scotia (Workers' Compensation Board) v. Martin; Nova Scotia (Workers' Compensation Board) v. Laseur*, 2003 SCC 54, para. 81 *(Martin; Laseur)*.
46   Ibid., at para. 93.
47   Convention on the Rights of Persons with Disabilities, G.A. Res. 61/106, 76th plen. Mtg., UN Doc A/Res/61/106 [adopted by consensus at the UN on 13.12.2006], Art. 2.
48   General Comment No. 6 (2018) on equality and non-discrimination, para. 10.
49   General Comment No. 1 (2014) – Equal Recognition Before the Law, para. 34.
50   General Comment No. 6 (2018) on equality and non-discrimination, paras. 10, 11 and 17.
51   *Nova Scotia (Workers' Compensation Board) v. Martin; Nova Scotia (Workers' Compensation Board) v. Laseur*, [2003] 2 S.C.R. 504, 2003 SCC 54, at para. 76.

5.2.2. Does the Cognitive Test of Capacity Impose Burdens or Deny a Benefit in a Manner that has the Effect of Reinforcing, Perpetuating, or Exacerbating Disadvantage?

This second stage of the inquiry asks whether the distinction is discriminatory.[52] To establish a violation of s. 15(1) the differential treatment must amount to discrimination in a substantive sense. The Supreme Court described the goal at this stage as being the examination of "... the impact of the harm caused to the affected group."[53] The focus is on "... the protection of groups that have experienced exclusionary disadvantage based on group characteristics ..."[54]

The Supreme Court in *Withler v. Canada (Attorney General)* explained that "Perpetuation of disadvantage typically occurs when the law treats a historically disadvantaged group in a way that exacerbates the situation of the group."[55] That people with disabilities have faced historic disadvantage is acknowledged in Canadian society. As described by the Supreme Court in *Ontario (Attorney General) v. G*,[56] "In our society, persons with disabilities regrettably 'face recurring coercion, marginalization, and social exclusion'". As this Court has recognised, "[t]his historical disadvantage has to a great extent been shaped and perpetuated by the notion that disability is an abnormality or flaw"[57]

The cognitive test reinforces and exacerbates the historic disadvantage people with cognitive disabilities face because it strips them of the exercise of legal capacity on an equal basis. With respect to guardianship laws, which typically employ a cognitive test of capacity to determine whether a guardian should be appointed, Fiala-Butora and Stein describe the role these laws play in perpetuating societal prejudice as follows: "By treating persons with intellectual disabilities as objects of protection, and at the same time denying their agency, the law strengthens outdated stereotypes that lead to exclusionary practices."[58] For people who are under substitute decision-making (whether by guardianship or another form) their disadvantage is further perpetuated because they lose the

---

[52] Department of Justice, Government of Canada, Charterpedia, Section 15 – Equality Rights available <https://www.justice.gc.ca/eng/csj-sjc/rfc-dlc/ccrf-ccdl/check/art15.html> accessed 02.09.2022.

[53] *Fraser v. Canada (Attorney General)*, 2020 SCC 28, para. 76.

[54] Ibid., para. 77.

[55] *Withler v. Canada (Attorney General)*, [2011] 1 S.C.R. 396, 2011 SCC 12, at para. 35 (*Withler*).

[56] *Ontario (Attorney General) v. G*, 2020 SCC 38 (*Ontario (Attorney General) v. G*).

[57] Ibid., para. 61.

[58] J. Fiala-Butora and M. A. Stein, "The Law as a source of stigma or empowerment: legal capacity and persons with intellectual disabilities" in K. Scior and S. Werner (eds), *Intellectual Disability and Stigma: Stepping Out from the Margins*, Palgrave Macmillan, London (UK) 2016, p. 199.

opportunity to develop the skills, and acquire the supports, as may be necessary, to meet the cognitive test.[59]

In creating a distinction based on mental disability, the cognitive test denies people the benefit of exercising autonomy over their decisions. They are restricted in enjoying something that most of society takes for granted: the ability to exercise power over the direction of their lives. Moreover, the distinction imposes a burden on this group because it requires that individuals who do not meet the test be placed under the authority of a substitute decision-maker. The ultimate effect is to undermine the equal status and equal respect for their value and dignity as human beings and members of society.

While the Supreme Court has moved away from defining discrimination in terms of the law's impact on human dignity as a component of the s. 15 analysis,[60] at least in the context of people with disabilities, consideration of human dignity still carries significance to the s. 15 analysis, although it is not a defining feature. For example, in *Ontario (Attorney General) v. G*, the Supreme Court stated that "[s]ection 15's promise of respect for 'the equal worth and human dignity of all persons' (Eldridge, at para. 54) requires that those with disabilities be considered and treated as worthy and afforded dignity in their plurality."[61] For those people with disabilities who are affected by the cognitive test, the core of the claim for inclusion and the right to make their own decisions stems from the affront on their dignity and autonomy that results from being deprived of a right to direct their decisions and live their lives as they wish. In summary, the above equality rights analysis demonstrates that the cognitive test of capacity discriminates against people with mental disabilities, contrary to s. 15 of the Charter. The ultimate impact of the test is to widen the gap between people with mental disabilities and society by undermining the equal status and respect for their value and dignity as human beings in Canadian society.

6. THE CRPD'S APPROACH TO EQUALITY IN THE EXERCISE OF LEGAL CAPACITY: PUTTING THE S. 15 ANALYSIS IN PERSPECTIVE

That the cognitive test of capacity is discriminatory is reinforced by the CRPD, and the manner in which it has been interpreted. Discrimination is defined in

---

[59] J. Fiala-Butora and M. A. Stein, ibid., p. 198.
[60] *R. v. Kapp*, [2008] 2 S.C.R. 483, 2008 SCC 41, paras. 21 and 22.
[61] *Ontario (Attorney General) v. G*, 2020 SCC 38, para. 61.

Article 2, and the obligations relating to non-discrimination, though permeating the entire Convention, are reinforced in Articles 3, 4 and 5.[62]

The Committee on the Rights of Persons with Disabilities sets the bar high in terms of evaluating Canada's legal capacity laws in the context of the CRPD. Regarding both the cognitive approach, also referred to as the functional approach, and the status approach, where capacity is removed on the basis of a diagnosis of an impairment, the Committee has made a strong statement that when "… a person's disability and/or decision-making skills are taken as legitimate grounds for denying his or her legal capacity and lowering his or her status as a person before the law, Article 12 does not permit such discriminatory denial of legal capacity, but, rather, requires that support be provided in the exercise of legal capacity."[63] Thus, the cognitive test of capacity in Canada's capacity laws are discriminatory contrary to Article 12.[64] This does not mean that legal capacity can never be denied. Rather, denial of legal capacity must be on the same basis for everyone.[65]

The Committee on the Rights of Persons with Disabilities stated in its General Comment on Article 12 that achieving enjoyment of legal capacity on an equal basis and without discrimination, as is required by Article 12, should come with the restoration of autonomy and respect for human dignity.[66] So too is Article 12 to be interpreted consistent with, and foster, the goals of equality of opportunity, and accessibility.[67] It is these same values which underlie s. 15 of the Charter.

In summary, there are similarities between the discrimination analysis under the Charter and CRPD. They each focus on values of autonomy, dignity and inclusion. They each recognise that discrimination can take different forms and is often in the nature of "indirect discrimination". They each emphasise that reasonable accommodation is critical to avoiding discrimination. While differences in the two approaches exist, regardless of which path of analysis

---

[62] Article 3 articulates non-discrimination, respect for inherent dignity and inclusion in society as principles of the Convention; Article 4 obliges States Parties "[t]o take all appropriate measures, including legislation, to modify or abolish existing laws, regulations, customs and practices that constitute discrimination against persons with disabilities"; Article 5 is directed exclusively to "equality and non-discrimination": Convention on the Rights of Persons with Disabilities, G.A. Res. 61/106, 76th plen. Mtg., U.N. Doc A/Res/61/106 [adopted by consensus at the UN on 13.12.2006].

[63] General Comment No. 1 (2014) – Equal Recognition Before the Law, para. 15.

[64] General Comment No. 6 (2018) on equality and non-discrimination, para. 47.

[65] For example, legal capacity can be restricted in circumstances such as criminal conviction. While it is restricted it does so not on the basis of disability and is thus not discriminatory. General Comment No. 1 (2014) – Equal Recognition Before the Law, para. 32.

[66] Ibid., para. 33.

[67] General Comment No. 1 (2014) – Equal Recognition Before the Law, para. 4.

is taken, the position that the cognitive test of capacity is discriminatory is supportable – either under s 15 of the Charter or the CRPD.

7. LIMITATION OF RIGHTS: CAN DISCRIMINATORY LEGAL CAPACITY TESTS BE SAVED AS A JUSTIFIABLE VIOLATION OF CHARTER RIGHTS UNDER S. 1 OF THE CHARTER?

7.1. THE ISSUE AND SOURCES IN CANADA AND UNITED NATIONS HUMAN RIGHTS LAW

Legal capacity law reform has been perennially plagued by concerns about whether guardianship is ever appropriate, what safeguards are needed, whether supporters should be recognised in law, and processes for appeal and review, to name a few. But the nub of the problem is the need to balance competing rights and societal values. It is usually understood that society should not leave people who are vulnerable in harm's way to the point of placing their health, life or sustenance at risk. It is also usually understood that everyone should have a right to autonomy and equality, and to live their lives without state interference. Both Canada's laws, and United Nations human rights law, require the balancing of these values and rights to be addressed head on. There is an important balance to be made in a democratic society between individual rights and societal interests as a whole.

In the United Nations context, discrimination analysis evidences a balancing through what has been termed the "pragmatic definition of discrimination". Sandor Gurbai describes this approach as follows: "... differential treatment does not constitute discrimination if the purpose or effect of the differential treatment is to achieve a legitimate aim and if the differential treatment can be objectively and reasonably justified."[68]

The analogous balancing in the Canadian context is conducted under s. 1 of the Charter, which provides:

> The Canadian *Charter* of Rights and Freedoms guarantees the rights and freedoms set out in it subject only to such reasonable limits prescribed by law as can be demonstrably justified in a free and democratic society.

---

[68]   S. GURBAI, "Beyond the Pragmatic Definition? The Right to Non-discrimination of Persons with Disabilities in the Context of Coercive Interventions", (2020) 22(1) *Health and Human Rights Journal*, p. 289. Gurbai's research, however, questions whether the pragmatic definition of discrimination applies to the CRPD. He concluded that there is a lack of certainty, both based on an analysis of the text of the CRPD itself, and the work of the CRPD Committee: Gurbai, ibid., p. 290.

7.2. SECTION 1 OF THE CHARTER: CAN THE COGNITIVE TEST OF CAPACITY BE JUSTIFIED?

The Supreme Court of Canada's decision in *R v. Oakes* (*Oakes*)[69] provides the framework for a s. 1 analysis which is employed to determine whether a law which limits a Charter right can be justified. This assessment requires a balancing of societal interests against individual rights. This is achieved by "... focussing on the legitimacy of the government's objective and the 'proportionality' between the means chosen to achieve that objective and the burden on the rights claimant."[70] Sharpe and Roach summarise the factors to be considered as follows:

(1) The objective of the measure must be important enough to warrant overriding a Charter right.
(2) There must be a rational connection between the limit on the Charter right and the legislative objective.
(3) The limit should impair the Charter right as little as possible.
(4) There should be an overall balance or proportionality between the benefits of the limit and its deleterious effects.[71]

The first criterion under *Oakes* is that the objective of the legislation be "of sufficient importance to warrant overriding a constitutionally protected right or freedom."[72] In order to meet this test, "[i]t is necessary, at a minimum, that an objective relate to concerns which are pressing *and* substantial in a free and democratic society before it can be characterized as sufficiently important".[73]

The objective of legal capacity laws, and the test of capacity upon which they rely, originated in the need to act for the protection of people who are perceived to be vulnerable, unable to care for themselves, and as such, at risk of harm. More recently, the promotion of autonomy has been recognised as a competing value that must be taken into account in the regulation of legal capacity. For example, the Ontario Superior Court, in *Park and Park*,[74] described the purpose of Ontario's *Substitute Decisions Act* (which employs the cognitive test in its regulation of guardianship and adult protection-type measures) as protection of the vulnerable, and highlighted that the Act reflects "... the principle that the dignity and privacy of a person must be assiduously respected."[75] The court went on to say that it "... is therefore placed in a position where it must weigh the

---

[69] *R. v. Oakes*, [1986] 1 S.C.R. 103, [1986] S.C.J. No. 7 (*Oakes*).
[70] R. J. SHARP and K. ROACH, *The Charter of Rights and Freedoms*, 6th ed., Irwin Law, Toronto 2017, p. 70.
[71] Ibid.
[72] *R. v. Big M Drug Mart Ltd.*, [1985] 1 S.C.R. 295, para. 139.
[73] *R. v. Oakes*, [1986] 1 S.C.R. 103, [1986] S.C.J. No. 7, para. 69.
[74] *Park and Park*, 2010 ONSC 2627 (S.C.J.) (*Park*).
[75] Ibid., para. 47.

fundamental rights of each citizen against the danger that that vulnerable person may be taken advantage of due to his/her incapacity to protect or care for her/himself or his/her assets and property."[76]

These objectives are articulated time and again and it is fair to say that, in the Canadian context, they are considered of sufficient importance to warrant overriding a constitutionally protected right or freedom. Even the CRPD, which has as a main focus the promotion of individual autonomy, both in relation to the exercise of legal capacity, and all matters covered by the CRPD,[77] recognises the importance of addressing situations of harm. For example, Article 12(4) demands safeguards relating to the exercise of legal capacity, Article 16 recognises the importance of measures relating to "freedom from exploitation, violence and abuse," and Article 15 recognises the importance of measures to address "freedom from torture or cruel, inhuman or degrading treatment or punishment."

The second criterion requires that the measures adopted must be rationally connected to the objective. That is, they must not be arbitrary or unfair. Will the means adopted help to bring about the objective? Some would argue that the test of capacity that results in the imposition of a substitute decision-maker on someone who does not have the cognitive ability to understand decisions that need to be made, is the most effective way to ensure that the person's interests are protected. Decisions are made so the person is not neglected and their affairs are managed. At the same time, the substitute who is making the decisions is a person who does possess the requisite cognitive ability to make those decisions. Against this, an argument can be made that there is no sufficient rational connection. It has been argued that people who are under guardianship or other forms of substitute decision-making are not necessarily protected from harm, contrary to the objective of the legislation. Harms and/or neglect caused by the guardianship vehicle itself[78] have been a concern that must be considered in assessing whether the objective is in fact rationally connected to the statutory instruments aimed to achieve those objectives. Fiala-Butora and Stein emphatically make this point: "Ironically and tragically, while guardianship is supposed to protect persons with disabilities from abuse, it makes abuse by guardians not only possible but also commonplace."[79]

---

[76] *Park and Park*, 2010 ONSC 2627, para. 48 (S.C.J.).

[77] Convention on the Rights of Persons with Disabilities, G.A. Res. 61/106, 76th plen. Mtg., U.N. Doc A/Res/61/106 [adopted by consensus at the UN on 13.12.2006], Art. 3.

[78] NATIONAL COUNCIL ON DISABILITY, *Beyond Guardianship: Toward Alternatives That Promote Greater Self-Determination for People with Disabilities*, Washington, 2018, pp. 101–110; K. JOFFE and E.-A. MONTIGNY, *Decisions, Decisions: Promoting and Protecting the Rights of Persons with Disabilities Who Are Subject to Guardianship*, Law Commission of Ontario, Toronto 2014.

[79] J. FIALA-BUTORA and M. A. STEIN, "The Law as a source of stigma or empowerment: legal capacity and persons with intellectual disabilities", in K. SCIOR and S. WERNER (eds), *Intellectual Disability and Stigma: Stepping Out from the Margins*, Palgrave Macmillan, London (UK) 2016, p. 198.

The third criterion requires the means to impair as little as possible the right or freedom in question. It is at this stage that it is difficult to argue that the cognitive test of capacity can be saved by s. 1. Indeed, the decision-making capability approach, described above, is a minimally impairing alternative to the cognitive test of capacity. It can achieve the same objective and does not discriminate against people with mental disabilities. In contrast to the cognitive test of capacity, the decision-making capability approach is more inclusive of people with a range of disabilities.[80] It grounds legal recognition of decisions on the basis of a person's will and preferences, and legally recognises supports and accommodations to exercise legal capacity, and does so while keeping intact the understanding and appreciation requirements for legally valid decisions. Embedding this approach in law can be achieved in a manner that addresses harm and at the same time respects, rather than removes, people's autonomy and power over their lives.

The fourth criterion requires that an assessment be undertaken of the proportionality between the effects of the measures which are responsible for limiting the Charter right or freedom and the objective which has been identified as of "sufficient importance." Courts are required to use a "contextual approach."[81] Both the objective and effectiveness at achieving the objective are relevant considerations at this stage.[82] It is at this branch that full account is taken of the "severity of the deleterious effects of a measure on individuals or groups."[83]

The impact of being found incapable by virtue of the cognitive test is profound and far-reaching. The person loses their right to be part of community, whether it be an inability to open a bank account, purchase clothes, travel or consent to a risky medical treatment that might improve their quality of life. At every step and every turn, the messaging they receive is that their wishes and preferences are not valued. They feel unheard and devalued as their autonomy is stripped away. While there are guidelines in the Canadian context for making substitute decisions which require the person's wishes to be followed and for including support people,[84] removal of one's right to decide leaves the person at the periphery, rather than the centre of making decisions about them.

---

[80]   The decision-making capability approach to legal capacity has been elaborated and applied by Michael Bach and Lana Kerzner in various studies. Most recently, see M. BACH and L. KERZNER, "Legal Basis for the Decision Making Capability Approach" in M. BACH and L. KERZNER, *Supported Decision Making: A Roadmap for Reform in Newfoundland and Labrador*, Institute for Research and Development on Inclusion and Society, Oshawa 2020, pp. 85–100 <https://irisinstitute.ca/resource/supported-decision-making-a-roadmap-for-reform-in-newfoundland-labrador-final-report/> accessed 02.09.2022.

[81]   *Edmonton Journal v. Alberta (Attorney General)*, [1989] 2 S.C.R. 1326, [1989] S.C.J. No. 124.

[82]   *Alberta v. Hutterian Brethren of Wilson Colony*, [2009] 2 S.C.R. 567, 2009 SCC 37, para. 76.

[83]   Ibid., para. 76.

[84]   See e.g., Substitute Decisions Act 1992, S.O. 1992, c. 30, s. 32(4) and (5); s. 66(3), (6) and (7).

To argue that the benefits of the cognitive test, including substitute decision-making arrangements which result, outweigh their discriminatory impact, and assault on dignity and autonomy, would require substantial and uncontroverted evidence that the cognitive tests in Canada's substitute decision-making regimes are not only aimed at preventing harm but that they actually do so. This is a challenging claim given evidence of harms resulting from guardianship.[85] Moreover, the more inclusive decision-making capability approach to legal capacity proposes a robust approach to addressing the various harms that may come about to people who are vulnerable, including abuse and neglect. In sum, while substitute decision-making based on the cognitive test may have salutary effects in terms of harm prevention in some cases, there are other ways to prevent harm more effectively and at the same time minimise intrusion in people's lives.

While the above analysis asserts that the cognitive test of capacity is discriminatory and cannot be saved by s. 1, it is acknowledged that it is not necessarily a commonly held view that the test violates the Charter. Indeed, the view has been expressed that the cognitive test is not discriminatory. [86] This is not surprising. The Charter analysis above demonstrated how malleable the test for determining whether a law violates the equality provision is. Moreover, neither the equality analysis nor the balancing of interests required of s. 1 lend themselves to a definitive, unambiguous conclusion.

8. CONCLUSION

The right to equality in the exercise of legal capacity is the cornerstone of Article 12 of the CRPD. Moreover, as stated by the Committee on the Rights of Persons with Disabilities "Equality and non-discrimination are at the heart of the Convention and evoked consistently throughout its substantive articles with the repeated use of the wording 'on an equal basis with others', which links all substantive rights of the Convention to the non-discrimination principle."[87] In order to implement Article 12, it is essential to be able to recognise what elements of laws must exist to ensure equality in the exercise of legal capacity, and as a corollary, what elements would be indicative of discrimination. The relationship

---

[85] M. BACH, *The Decision Making Capability Approach to Legal Capacity: A Disability Rights Analysis*, IRIS – Institute for Research and Development on Inclusion and Society, Oshawa 2021.

[86] See the Court of Appeal for Ontario decision in *Thompson v. Ontario (Attorney General)*, 2016 ONCA 676, paras. 66 and 67, wherein Sharpe J.A. stated that the test of capacity to make treatment decisions in Ontario's Health Care Consent Act, that is, the understand and appreciate test, is not discriminatory and does not violate s. 15 because the test requires an individualised assessment.

[87] General Comment No. 6 (2018) on equality and non-discrimination, para. 7.

between the right to equality in the CRPD and the equality right in Canada's Charter can be seen as a symbiotic one, in that they can each be used to bolster and deepen the other to create a more precise and comprehensive understanding of what equality in the exercise of legal capacity means. The advantage of doing so is not solely of academic benefit, but to provide guidance for Article 12 implementation by States Parties, with the ultimate goal of promoting inclusion in decision-making for all people with disabilities.

The cognitive test of capacity exists in many of Canada's legal capacity laws, and its application results in determinations about who is entitled to make decisions for themselves and whose decisions are instead made by a substitute decision-maker. The test results in an adverse impact and disproportionate burden on people with cognitive disabilities in a way that entrenches their historic disadvantage, substantiating a conclusion that it violates the right to equality in s. 15 of the Charter.

Nonetheless, violations of Charter rights, including s. 15, can be upheld if they are "reasonable limits" in a free and democratic society. This type of justification requires a balancing of individual rights against societal interests. Thus, equality and autonomy must be balanced against protection from harm. A defensible argument can be made that the laws which incorporate the cognitive test of capacity cannot be upheld. The harms caused by these laws cannot be justified, especially since the cognitive test of capacity is not the only option for regulating decision-making. Replacing it with one of decision-making capability would promote equality and prevent discrimination, consistent with both the Charter and the CRPD. Thus, we must ask ourselves why the cognitive test is so pervasive in laws in Canada and in other jurisdictions. What underlies the resistance to viewing the test as discriminatory? Perhaps rejecting the view that the test discriminates is simply a guise for fear that any alternative will result in rampant abuse, neglect and harm to those most vulnerable in our society. But it is this same resistance that puts people's autonomy, dignity and inclusion at stake.

INDEX

A

Accommodation, *see* Reasonable
accommodation/adjustments
Africa Region
African Disability Protocol   178
African Charter on Human and Peoples
Rights, legal capacity   182
African Charter on the Rights of Women
in Africa, legal capacity   182–183
legal capacity reforms, and critique
185–197
ratification of UNCRPD by African
countries   177–179
Argentina
legal capacity provisions   115–118, 124
right to family and parental rights   124
sexual and reproductive rights and legal
capacity   121–123
supports for informed consent   330
Australia
compliance with UN Convention on the
Rights of Persons with Disabilities
257–263
gradualist reform approach   274–275
legal capacity law reform   263–270
evolution of supported decision-
making   263–270
regimes in states of Victoria, Tasmania,
and New South Wales   264–268
Autonomy
cognitive requirements for respect of   69
planning theory of   70–74
principle of respect for, and legal
capacity   66–70
see also Relational autonomy

B

Best interests principle
critique of   53, 180, 219, 256, 286–287,
290, 293
reforms to respect autonomy, will and
preferences (and need for)   166, 243,
265, 273–274, 298
Best interpretation of will and preferences,
principle of   79–81, 83, 87, 97, 136–137,
141, 147, 204, 262, 287, 290, 358
distinct from best interests principle   80,
261
Bulgaria
draft Natural Persons and Support Measures
Bill   44–45, 202–203

guardianship provisions and limitations on
legal capacity   200–201
law reform on legal capacity   210–215
Persons with Disabilities Act and legal capacity
support measures   212–214
reform process, strategies and lessons
learned   46–47, 215–220
supported decision-making pilot projects –
"The Next Step Program"   203–207

C

Canada
Canadian *Charter of Rights and Freedoms*,
equality and cognitive capacity
359–362
cognitive capacity test and
discrimination   356–357
CRPD approach and its relevance to
Section 15 of the Charter   366–368
legal capacity regime   354–355
Capacity assessment   261, 273, 282–285, 287
as consistent with decision-making
supports and legal capacity   310
in CRPD   36
functional approach to   67–68, 289, 306
guidelines for conducting   67, 282
Capacity to act
as *capax* in Roman law   25–30
as capacity to transact   37–38
distinct from capacity to have/hold
rights   29, 201
disability/need for support not a reason
to restrict   147, 180
presumption of   133–134
restrictions on   240, 242, 339
China Mainland
legal capacity and guardianship laws
239–244
legal capacity and mental health law
247–249
restrictions associated with loss of legal
capacity   244–246
Colombia
Constitutional Court affirms reforms   111,
115–116
legal capacity reforms   145–149
Conflicts of interest, *see* Safeguards
Contracts and capacity
contractual capacity and restrictions   30,
36–37, 40, 47–48, 114, 133, 138, 142, 224,
260, 292, 335, 343–344, 352

Intersentia

375

Index

contractual political theory 93–94
immunity from liability 161
voidability 133, 326
see also Spain
Costa Rica
Constitutional Court rules against substitute
decision making 111
legal capacity reforms 132–137

D

Decision-making capability approach 66,
74–82, 90–92, 95–96, 303, 357–358
Decision-making supports, *see* Supports for
exercising capacity
Deprivation of liberty and legal capacity
120–121, 184–185, 201–204, 241–243
Discrimination, *see* Equality rights analysis
and legal capacity

E

Equality rights analysis and legal capacity
and cognitive test of legal capacity 359–366
and contract law 335–336
and need for support 115
and women 63–64
as recognised in the CRPD 105, 366–368
cognitive test and equality rights 359–366
feminist perspectives 69
in natural law 20
jurisprudence 111–118, 123–126, 128
legal equality, equal recognition and legal
capacity 134–137, 181–183, 202
structural inequality 129–130
see also Sexual and reproductive rights and
legal capacity

F

Family members
concerns about influence 84
de facto role as guardians 253–254
exercising power over decisions 58, 84–85,
272
in China context, 250–251, 253–254
need for supports 54–55
role in supporting legal capacity 250–251,
254, 274–275
Feminist approaches 50–53; *see also*
Intersectional approaches, Vulnerability
analysis
Functional assessment of legal capacity
argument for, as non-discriminatory
336–340
debates about 337–338
functional test 162

G

Guardianship/substitute decision making
and aging population 156
and the CRPD 180
and the will 46
Australia 257–259, 264–265

Bulgaria 200–2011
China 239–246, 250, 253
Colombia 145–148
Costa Rica 134–135
de facto, in families and community 183,
217
discriminatory impact 55
Germany 92
harms of 370–372
Hong Kong 280, 288–292
India 224–230
jurisprudential findings 55, 112–113, 125,
159, 171, 207
Peru 140–143
plenary and partial 92, 299
US 157–159
see also Interdiction

H

Hong Kong
consent to medical treatment 285–288
development of mental capacity laws
278–285
future planning and end of life
decisions 293–297
guardianship law 288–292
property, management of 292–293

I

Incapacitation 52
legal capacity 52
India
legal capacity jurisprudence 233–235
legal capacity law reform processes
225–232
legal capacity laws 222–225
limitations of reform processes 235–236
Informed consent
basis for legislating supports for 315–317
challenges in verifying 311
requirements for 285–288, 304–307
supports for 307–308
Interdiction 92, 97, 112–114, 121, 127,
133–148, 303–304, 313–317; *see also*
Guardianship/substitute decision making
Interpretive supports 47–48, 79–85, 112,
209, 219, 308
Intersectional approaches 54–55; *see also*
Vulnerability analysis
Involuntary treatment, internment/admission
Australia 266–268
China 237–238, 248–256
India 232
Peru 120–121
US 155
Zambia 189, 192–195

K

Kenya
jurisprudence and Article 12, CRPD 185–188
legal capacity reforms and critique 190–192

Index

L

Latin America
  informed consent reforms   312–315
  judicial precedents supporting reform
    110–114
  legal recognition of support mechanisms,
    safeguards, and reasonable
    adjustments   115–116
  reform challenges   149–152
  right to family and parental rights
    124–126, 129
  sexual and reproductive rights and legal
    capacity   56–57, 119, 121–123, 129

Legal capacity
  acting independently or interdependently
    with supports   67, 83–85, 167, 213, 239,
    244, 246, 307, 347–348
  advance directives/decision-making   73,
    148–149, 231, 287–288, 293–296
  ancient regimes of   25–32
  cognitive approach   356, 359–366
  discrimination in exercising   115, 154–155
  functional approach   67, 310–312,
    337–340
  health care decisions, *see* Informed
    consent
  juridical agency as legal capacity   35–38
  mainstream approaches and critique
    66–69, 97–98, 335
  outcome approach   67, 335–336, 339
  property decisions   30, 33, 52, 114, 184–185,
    190, 193, 196–197, 204, 213, 223–224, 264,
    278, 283–284, 288, 292–293, 319, 370
  right to family life and parental
    responsibility   55, 60, 124–126, 129, 190
  right to vote   112–113, 119–120, 137
  universal legal capacity   44, 82–83, 87, 135,
    178–179, 198, 223, 290, 297, 303, 307–308,
    312, 315–316, 341
  see also Contractual capacity, Decision-
    making capability, Guardianship,
    Interdiction, Informed consent

Legal capacity law reform, *see* under countries

M

Mental capacity/incapacity
  as "unsound mind"   183–184, 279, 281
  definition of   97–98, 281–285
  distinct from legal capacity   91–92, 128–129
  incapacity to transact, history   38–39
  in common law   281

Mental Health law, *see* Involuntary treatment/
  admissions

Mexico
  interdiction precedents   112

P

"Person"
  and Roman law   15–16
  as a space of freedom   23
  as capable subject of law   28–30

  in 15th–18th century law   16–22
  in theories of justice and social contract
    theory   92–94, 96–98
  status of, *naturalis* or *civilis*   22–23

Peru
  Constitutional Court affirms reforms   111
  legal reforms   137–143
  safeguards   350

R

Reasonable accommodation/adjustments   77,
  81–82, 85–86, 115–118, 140, 204, 211–212
Relational autonomy   70, 102–103
Roman law, *see* "Persons"

S

Safeguards and legal capacity
  abuse prevention   103–105, 340–346, 349–351
  as justified "paternalism"   351–352
  balancing risk   308–309
  disability rights and safeguard
    mechanisms   103–105
  legal recognition in Latin America   115–116
  purposes   342–346
  safeguards scope   103–104, 346–351
  undue influence and conflict of
    interest   340–346

Sexual and reproductive rights and legal
  capacity
  sterilisation without consent   58–60,
    121–123, 136
  see also Latin America region

South Africa
  legal capacity reforms, and critique
    195–197

Spain
  annulling contracts   330–332
  contractual capacity reforms   319–323
  supports to exercise contractual
    capacity   323–330

Supported decision-making
  concept of   158–159, 163, 205, 207
  jurisprudence and courts recognising   73,
    111, 159, 209
  lack of provision for   291
  legislated provisions for (including
    proposed)   44, 139–140, 143, 160–172,
    179, 191, 195, 197, 204, 210–214, 264–273,
    356
  personal planning for   87
  principles of   45–47, 260
  projects implementing   173–174, 203–207,
    262–263
  replacement for guardianship/
    interdiction   44, 83, 180, 214, 219,
    264–265, 291, 303
  supported decision-making
    agreements   160–172, 175
  training related to (and need for)   137, 143,
    149, 151, 161, 170, 172, 214, 219, 252, 263,
    274–275

Intersentia

377

Index

Supporters
  appointment of   348, 356–357
  liability and immunity   166–167
  roles, responsibilities, limitations
      164–167, 179–180, 206, 209, 213–214,
      219, 265, 267, 346, 348, 350
  see also Safeguards and legal capacity
Supports for exercising legal capacity   180, 207,
    213–214, 308, 310
  a new configuration in law   341
  as an alternative to mental capacity
      assessment   303
  as compatible with functional model
      307–308, 339
  as scaffolding   105
  in informed consent   323–330
  need for   244, 313–314
  recognition in law   358
  refusal of   325
  supports needs assessment   149, 214,
      307–312
  see also Supported decision-making

U
UN Committee on the Rights of Persons with
    Disabilities   66, 68, 89–92, 110–111,
    177–179
UN Convention on the Rights of Persons
    with Disabilities   31–48, 66–69, 89–92,
    110, 112, 114, 118, 120, 123–125, 127, 130,
    177–179, 221–222, 238–239, 258–260, 287,
    322, 335, 358–359
Undue influence, *see* Safeguards
United States
  antipathy to human rights conventions
      154–156
  critiques of supported decision-making
      laws   170–172
  emergence of supported decision-making
      reforms   158–160
  initial reforms to guardianship law   157–158
  supported decision-making agreements
      laws   160–170
  Supported Decision-Making New York –
      practice model   173–174

V
Vulnerability analysis and legal capacity
  disability as a form of   335–336
  gender identity, sexual and reproductive
      rights   56–60
  institutionalisation   60–61
  intersectional analysis of   49–52, 97–101

  violence and discrimination   52–56
  vulnerability and relational autonomy   97–100

W
Will and preferences
  ancient history of   32–35
  and legal power   77–78
  as expressed through supporters   81–82, 97,
      115, 261
  as juridical agency   35–36
  as *voluntas*   32, 35, 39, 42, 44
  conflict between respecting will and
      respecting rights   342–343
  conflicts of interest in interpreting   348
  contractual will   343
  "flawed" will and "vices" of the will   41–43,
      305, 326, 344–345
  in modern civil law   35–39
  in the CRPD   31, 63, 66, 104, 273, 342
  legal examination/validation of   211–212,
      343, 348–349
  legal recognition and respect for   27,
      31–48, 114–117, 135–136, 147–148,
      208, 210, 229, 235, 266
  not linked to mental capacity   113
  planning theory of   71–73
  preferences distinct from will   342
  principle of respect for   78, 135, 180, 203,
      206, 213, 260, 265, 342–343
  relationship to legal capacity   44–48
  substitution of   113, 243, 261, 302–304,
      313, 317, 329
  supports for   140–141, 166, 307–308, 310,
      348–349
  "true," "valid," or "authentic" will   78–79, 81,
      104, 336, 338–340, 345, 347, 358
  unable to be expressed   112, 115, 123,
      138–139, 201, 287, 305, 320, 323, 339,
      345, 348
  violations/negations of   58, 61, 223, 235,
      254, 293
  vulnerability in relation to   102
  will ascription   40, 47
  will attestation   40–42, 47
  "wishes" as alternative to   44–48, 206
  see also Best interpretation of will and
      preferences, Interpretive supports,
      Safeguards

Z
Zambia
  jurisprudence and Article 12, CRPD   188–189
  legal capacity reforms and critique   192–195

ABOUT THE EDITORS

MICHAEL BACH is Managing Director of the Institute for Research and Development on Inclusion and Society (IRIS), Adjunct Professor at the School of Disability Studies, Toronto Metropolitan University and was a Fellow at the Open Society Foundations, during which he conducted research on key concepts on which this collection is based, and convened with many of the authors. He has a PhD in Sociology and Equity Studies from the University of Toronto and has undertaken legal and policy research on disability rights, as well as published numerous professional papers, articles and books in this area.

NICOLÁS ESPEJO-YAKSIC is Researcher at the Centre for Constitutional Studies (CEC) of the Supreme Court Justice of Mexico, Visiting Fellow at Exeter College, University of Oxford, Guest Lecturer in Law at the University of Leiden, Adjunct Professor at the School of Law, University College Cork and Corresponding Member of the Cambridge Family Law Centre at the University of Cambridge. He is also Chair of the International Network on Constitutional Family Law (INCFL) and has served as advisor for the United Nations. He has researched and published in the fields of children's rights in theory and practice, international human rights, family law, disability and comparative constitutional law.

Printed in the USA
CPSIA information can be obtained
at www.ICGtesting.com
LVHW070013020324
773010LV00007B/4